FOR I WAS HUNGRY AND YOU GAVE ME FOOD

For I Was Hungry and
You Gave Me Food

Pragmatics of Food Access in the Gospel of Matthew

Carol Bakker Wilson

Foreword by
Warren Carter

◆PICKWICK *Publications* • Eugene, Oregon

FOR I WAS HUNGRY AND YOU GAVE ME FOOD
Pragmatics of Food Access in the Gospel of Matthew

Copyright © 2014 Carol Bakker Wilson. All rights reserved. Except for brief quotations in critical publications or reviews, no part of this book may be reproduced in any manner without prior written permission from the publisher. Write: Permissions, Wipf and Stock Publishers, 199 W. 8th Ave., Suite 3, Eugene, OR 97401.

Pickwick Publications
An Imprint of Wipf and Stock Publishers
199 W. 8th Ave., Suite 3
Eugene, OR 97401

www.wipfandstock.com

ISBN 13: 978-1-62564-046-8

Scripture quotations contained herein (unless otherwise noted) are from the New Revised Standard Version of the Bible, copyright ©1989 by the National Council of Churches of Christ in the USA. Used by permission. All rights reserved.

Cataloging-in-Publication data:

Wilson, Carol Bakker.

For I was hungry and you gave me food : pragmatics of food access in the gospel of Matthew / Carol Bakker Wilson with a foreword by Warren Carter.

xiv + 298 pp. ; 23 cm. Includes bibliographical references.

ISBN 13: 978-1-62564-046-8

1. Bible. Matthew—Criticism, interpretation, etc. 2. Food in the Bible. 3. Food supply—Social aspects. I. Title.

BS2575.2 W45 2014

Manufactured in the U.S.A.

Contents

Figures | vi

Tables | vi

Foreword by Warren Carter | vii

Acknowledgments | ix

Abbreviations | xi

1. Introduction and Overview | 1
2. Contextualized Interpretation | 25
3. How Did People Get Access to Food? | 57
4. Most People Could Eke Out a Living | 81
5. The Gospel Reflects the Trauma of Experienced Food Shortages | 133
6. Not Enough Food and the Dominant Entitlement System | 163
7. Not Enough Food and Social Safety Networks | 211
8. It Is Important That No One Goes Hungry | 229
9. Concluding Remarks | 268

Bibliography | 273

Figures

1. Full model | 64
2. Model levels 1 and 2 | 65
3. Model level 3 | 66
4. Model level 4 | 68
5. Model level 5 | 71
6. Grinding room in commercial baking establishment at Ostia | 74
7. Baking room in commercial baking establishment at Ostia | 74
8. Effect of military occupation presence | 78
9. Uses of stored grain | 106
10. Inner room of a *horrea* in Ostia | 107
11. Outside view of *horrea* in Ostia | 107
12. Reciprocal relations | 112
13. Coins depicting emperors and *alimenta* | 217

Tables

1. Expanded Friesen Poverty Scale | 6
2. Matthean passages associated with phases of the Goody Framework | 12
3. Goody Framework for food processes | 58
4. Poverty Scale | 91
5. Scheidel and Friesen: Table 8 | 93
6. Poverty Scale to subsistence needs | 94
7. Poverty Scale with survival mechanisms | 127
8. Food access in visions for two realms found in narrative block two | 245
9. Food access in visions for two realms found in narrative block three | 253

Foreword

MATTHEAN SCHOLARSHIP HAS NOT often attended to the pragmatics of anything. Despite the Gospel's attention to "doing" (7:24; 12:50), our scholarly attention has often been elsewhere, on cognitive matters and theological concepts and themes. Copious discussions of the law and/or righteousness, for example, have managed to focus on so-called "religious" issues like Sabbath and purity but not so much on supplying food, drink, and clothing to those who lack. Somehow, despite its own important interpretive tradition and contribution, Matt 25:31–46 has not been much integrated into discussions of law or righteousness or interpretations of the Gospel as a whole.

Carol Wilson takes the practice of supplying food seriously in her reading of Matthew. Attentive to the implications of the presence of the empire of God, she places a concern with food supply in the context of and as an expression of the sort of society the Gospel of Matthew is interested in shaping. She asks an insightful question with regard to the issue of food insecurity pervasive in the ancient Roman imperial world: What practices should followers of Jesus and readers of this Gospel carry out to address food insecurity? Undergirding this question is an affirmation that the Gospel advocates for a just society in which all people have access to sufficient food.

This concern with practices to alleviate food insecurity has been a neglected topic in Matthean studies. Generally scholarship on Matthew has focused its attention elsewhere on matters such as Christology and ecclesiology or on the Gospel's engagement with first century Judaisms. There has been a little attention paid to food matters in the Gospel—notably the eschatological and meal scenes—but attention to the alleviating practices vis-à-vis food that the Gospel affirms has been lacking.

So this study takes up a largely unexplored topic in Matthean studies. While previous work has frequently quoted the line from Matthew 25, "For I was hungry and you gave me food," it has paid little attention to elaborating the pragmatics—the actual practices and structures—of food access in the first-century imperial world marked by significant societal inequality and addressed by Matthew's Gospel. Even classical studies of food access such as Peter Garnsey's pioneering work have not pressed the question as to how particularly non-elites (some 50 percent of the empire's population were "food insecure") secured sufficient food to maintain at least subsistence existence.

In this well-researched and sophisticated study, Wilson pulls together both social-science work on food access and data on historical practices concerning food access in a narrative reading of the Gospel. Her goal is to identify survival strategies of both elites and non-elites to prevent lower socio-economic people from slipping completely into and below subsistence existence. Such a collection of data on strategies of food access is a significant contribution to current biblical scholarship. Moreover, not only does she identify and collect data from a range of sources, she is able to bring the various components into a coherent structure by creating a model of food access. The model she produces in chapter 3 is worth the price of admission alone. She then uses the model to engage various parts of the Gospel.

In pursuing her detailed and careful research, Wilson's work has significant implications for the reading of Matthew's Gospel. She underscores that material and societal matters, particularly food matters, have often been neglected in previous scholarship's preference for doctrinal or "spiritualized" readings. She demonstrates that the experiences of food insecurity are integral to the Gospel narrative and to the circumstances of the people addressed by the Gospel. She shows how the Gospel's vision of life is shaped by God's reign among communities of disciples that engage practices of food access. She fleshes out imperial-critical approaches with the help of social-science investigation by engaging food access in a framework of power and by showing what the Gospel's vision of societal justice and mercy look like in securing food access. She identifies survival strategies and communal practices of food-access for which the Gospel advocates. These are important developments in Matthean studies and continue a move toward material and imperial-critical readings of the Gospel.

This study makes significant contributions in terms of both the understanding of Matthew's Gospel, and in terms of understanding food access issues in the first-century world. This is important work.

Warren Carter

Acknowledgments

WARREN CARTER DESERVES GRATEFUL commendations for many hours spent on reviews of earlier versions of this study. His critical readings and suggestions raised my academic standards and writing skills needed for a career in the humanities. Moreover, he was an unflagging source of encouragement in this long and arduous process of piecing together the disparate sources and disciplines to sustain the arguments of my hypothesis in a cogent manner.

Sharon H. Ringe has been a friend and mentor since my master's studies at Wesley Theogolgical Seminary. She encouraged me to present papers at our regional SBL meetings when I was her student. Without her gentle, but persistent, encouragement to pursue doctoral studies, I would not have embarked upon this endeavor. In addition to encouraging my scholarly pursuits, she offered me opportunities to remain grounded by utilizing me as her teaching assistant for several semesters.

David Balch introduced me to the intriguing world of first-century writers. Further, his course on *Baptism and Eucharist* was the genesis of this topic. A close reading of the Gospel of Matthew led me to the conclusion that it was concerned about people having enough to eat. *The Didache* having a Eucharist based on the feeding stories allowed me to move away from Eucharist as a banquet to Eucharist as God providing food for people on the verge of starvation. Further examination of the Gospel led to the hypothesis argued in this study that not only did God provide food, but that the realm of the heavens expounded in the Gospel is to be a place where people have sufficient food when disciples both trust God and share what resources they have.

Finally, I could not have completed this project without the constant love of my husband, Donald. He supported and encouraged me despite the requirement for us to live separately while I was in class work and then later when I returned to Brite Divinity School to concentrate on dissertation writing. He kept the home fires burning. Donald exhibited only kindness, patience, love, and support for me throughout this long effort. In many ways great and small, he provided needed saneness and stability, including cutting out and sending me the daily *Washington Post* crossword puzzles every week to provide continuity of my breakfast routine. Words cannot express the depth of my love for him. Thank you, Donald.

Abbreviations

AJA	American Journal of Archaeology
ABRL	Anchor Bible Reference Library
ANET	Ancient Near Eastern Texts Relating to the Old Testament. Edited by J. B. Pritchard. Princeton, 1954
AThR	Anglican Theological Review
AUSS	Andrews University Seminary Studies
AJT	Asia Journal of Theology
BBMS	Baker Biblical Monograph Series
BEB	Baker Encyclopedia of the Bible
BDAG	Bauer, W., F. W. Danker, W. F. Arndt, and F. W. Gingrich. *Greek-English Lexicon of the New Testament and Other Early Christian Literature*. 3rd ed. Chicago, 1999
BRev	Bible Review
BT	The Bible Translator
Bib	*Biblica*
BA	Biblical Archaeologist
BAR	Biblical Archaeology Review
BibInt	Biblical Interpretation
BR	Biblical Research
BTB	Biblical Theology Bulletin
BSac	*Bibliotheca sacra*
BJRL	Bulletin of the John Rylands University Library of Manchester
CBQ	Catholic Biblical Quarterly
CH	Church History
CJ	Classical Journal

CP	Classical Philology	
CV	Communio Viatorum	
Cont	Continuum	
CIG	*Corpus inscriptionum graecarum.* Edited by A. Boeckh. 4 vols. Berlin, 1828–1877	
CPJ	*Corpus papyrorium judaicorum.* Edited by V. Tcherikover. 3 vols. Cambridge, 1957–1964	
CIJ	*Corpus inscriptionum judaicarum*	
CIL	*Corpus inscriptionum latinarum*	
CTR	Criswell Theological Review	
CurTM	Currents in Theology and Mission	
DSD	Dead Seas Discoveries	
Enc	Encounter	
EEC	*Encyclopedia of Early Christianity.* Edited by F. Ferguson. 2nd ed. New York, 1990	
ETL	Ephemerides theologicae lovanienses	
ExAud	Ex auditu	
ExpTim	Expository Times	
GRBS	Greek, Roman, and Byzantine Studies	
HBD	*HarperCollins Bible Dictionary.* Edited P. J. Achtemeier et al. 2nd ed. San Francisco, 1996	
HTR	Harvard Theological Review	
HTS	Harvard Theological Studies	
Hesperia	Hesperia: Journal of the American School of Classical Studies at Athens	
HeyJ	Heythrop Journal	
HR	History of Religions	
IDB	*Interpreter's Dictionary of the Bible.* Edited by G. A. Buttrick. 4 vols. Nashville, 1962	
IG	*Inscriptiones graecae.* Editio minor. Berlin, 1924–	
IESS	*International Encyclopedia of the Social Sciences.* Edited by D. L. Sills. New York, 1968–	
Int	Interpretation	
IEJ	Israel Exploration Journal	
JAC	Jahrbuch für Antike und Christentum	

JSJ	Journal for the Study of Judaism in the Persian, Hellenistic and Roman Period
JSNT	Journal for the Study of the New Testament
JSNTSup	Journal for the Study of the New Testament: Supplement Series
JSOT	Journal for the Study of the Old Testament
JBL	Journal of Biblical Literature
JECS	Journal of Early Christian Studies
JES	Journal of Ecumenical Studies
JJS	Journal of Jewish Studies
JR	Journal of Religion
JRS	Journal of Roman Studies
JSS	Journal of Semitic Studies
JAAR	Journal of the American Academy of Religion
JESHO	Journal of the Economic and Social History of the Orient
JTS	Journal of Theological Studies
Judaism	*Judaism*
KD	*Kerygma und Dogma*
LCL	Loeb Classical Library
OrSyr	*L'orient syrien*
LSJ	Liddell, H. G., R. Scott, H. S. Jones, *A Greek-English Lexicon*. 9th ed. with revised supplement. Oxford, 1996
NewDocs	New Documents Illustrating Early Christianity. Edited by G. H. Horsley and S. Llewelyn. North Ryde, New South Wales, 1981–
NTS	*New Testament Studies*
NovT	*Novum Testamentum*
Numen	*Numen: International Review for the History of Religions*
PEQ	Palestine Exploration Journal
PRSt	*Perspectives in Religious Studies*
RevExp	*Review & Expositor*
RB	*Revue biblique*
RevQ	*Revue de Qumran*
Semeia	*Semeia*
SBLDS	Society of Biblical Studies Dissertation Series
SBLSP	*Society of Biblical Literature Seminar Papers*
SwJT	*Southwestern Journal of Theology*

BT		The Bible Translator
BW		The Biblical World: AQ Dictionary of Biblical Archaeology. Edited by C. F. Pfeiffer. Grand Rapids, 1966.
HTR		The Harvard Theological Review
NEAWHL		The New Encyclopedia of Archaeological Excavations in the Holy Land. Edited E. Stern. 4 vols. Jerusalem, 1993
TZ		*Theologische Zeitschrift*
ThTo		*Theology Today*
TDNT		*Theological Dictionary of the New Testament*. Edited by G. Kittel and G. Fredrich. Translated by G. W. Bromiley. 10 vols. Grand Rapids, 1964–1976
TynBul		*Tyndale Bulletin*
USQR		*Union Seminary Quarterly Review*
VT		*Vetus Testamentum*
VC		*Vigiliae christianae*
ZAW		*Zeitschrift für die alttestamentliche Wissenschaft*
ZTK		*Zeitschrift für Theologie und Kirche*

1

Introduction and Overview

Statement of Argument

ACCESS TO FOOD IS always about power:[1] about who controls the production, distribution, and the laws and customs validating the system of privilege.[2] Gerhard Lenski argues that the pattern of food distribution parallels the distribution of privilege, which is a function of power.[3] He further states that power determines the distribution of most of the surplus goods, including food, of a society. In agrarian societies, control of distribution by a few people produces marked social inequity.[4] His observations fit the first-century Roman East, in which taxes and rents could take more crops from a peasant[5] household than it had produced as surplus and transferred

---

1. McGowan, *Ascetic Eucharists: Food and Drink in Early Christian Ritual Meals*, 1.

2. Friesen, "Injustice or God's Will," 241; Kautsky, *Aristocratic Empires*, 115: "Rights and duties are simply aspects of the exploitative relationship that have become established by custom and accepted by both sides."

3. Lenski, *Power and Privilege*, 2, 44–45; Mann, *The Sources of Social Power*, 24. Early in his book, Mann has a thorough discussion of the issues surrounding power in societies. He writes, "Those able to monopolize control over production, distribution, exchange, and consumption, that is, a dominant class, can obtain general and distributive power in societies" (ibid., 24).

4. "Without exception, one finds pronounced difficulties in power, privilege, and honor associated with mature agrarian economies" (Lenski, *Power and Privilege*, 45, esp. 210).

5. Defining *peasant* for a first-century Roman East setting is not simple. There is no one term for peasant in Latin (for example, *rusticus*, *agricola*, *colonus*). Following Kolendo, my definition includes people who owned the land they worked as well as

the crops to the more powerful aristocracy.⁶ This situation created endemic food shortages among large segments of the population.⁷

My argument is that the Gospel of Matthew advocates for a society in which all people would have access to sufficient food. I argue that the Gospel critiques first-century practices of both aristocrats and peasants that helped or hindered that goal. The Matthean narrative presents Jesus as teaching and performing positive practices that provided the Matthean community with a model to emulate living in the new realm of the heavens. Matthew understands the realm of the heavens as being from heaven, with heavenly traits, and different from the realms of the earth (for example, the Roman empire).⁸ In the face of endemic food shortages, punctuated by episodic

---

the large number of people who worked, and perhaps lived on, land owned by others. These people are to be distinguished from landless day laborers whose association with the land was less stable, and often seasonal. Some peasants hired themselves out as day laborers to supplement their incomes. Slave labor is also not included. Peasants had limited participation in the market economy of the villages and cities. Thus far, this description could include larger landowners (PS 4 and PS 5), but I limit the term *peasant* to PS 6 and PS 7 levels (see table 1 below for PS descriptions). This definition does not include people living in cities in the lower socio-economic segments of the population. Kolendo, "The Peasant," 199–200.

6. I use the term *aristocracy* instead of *elite*. Elite is a relative term but one can better define aristocracy. Kautsky defines aristocracy as "a ruling class in an agrarian economy that does not engage in productive labor but lives wholly or primarily off the labor of peasants." One can add adjectives such as priestly, municipal, native, senatorial, and Roman to further delineate about whom within this general type one is speaking. But all variations share Kautsky's definition. Kautsky, *Aristocratic Empires*, 24.

7. For a concise discussion of the changes in economics leading to this situation in first-century Galilee, see Crossley, *Why Christianity Happened*, chap. 2, especially 43–49.

8. Pennington, *Heaven and Earth in the Gospel of Matthew*, 126, chaps. 5 and 6, especially 131–50 and 293–96; Pennington, "The Kingdom of Heaven in the Gospel of Matthew," 44–46; Overman, *Matthew's Gospel and Formative Judaism*, 322. Pennington asserts that *kingdom* is the central message of the Matthean Jesus and appears at crucial points in the narrative. Pennington examines the distinct manner in which Matthew uses the singular and plural forms of οὐρανός, as well as heaven and earth pairs. He discusses various interpretations of the genitive construction "of the heavens." As a subjective genitive, the meaning connotes "god rules." As a genitive of origin, heaven is the source or origin of the kingdom Jesus is proclaiming. As an attributive genitive, the kingdom is heavenly in the sense of a kingdom whose characteristics relate to the divine, heavenly realm that stands in contrast to the earth. Instead of picking one meaning, Pennington suggests that the meanings overlap and one should take in each meaning simultaneously. I will use the phrase *realm of the heavens* as the visible, earthly kingdom inaugurated by Jesus that is to be a reflection, even if flawed, of God's realm in heaven. In this realm, God reigns as Immanuel. The realm has been inaugurated but has not come eschatologically to fullness. I choose *realm* over *reign* to reinforce its tangible nature. Overman suggests that the Matthean community understood itself as a reflection of God's realm in heaven. I understand the realm of the heavens as encompassing

extreme food shortages, the narrative addresses the questions: Who has the power and desire to provide sufficient food for the people? Is the Emperor or God the true *paterfamilias*?[9] Given its answer would have been God (Matt 6:10–11, 31–33; 7:7–11; 19:13–15), the companion issue for the Matthean community is "What does God expect of us to be members of God's family?" The Matthean Jesus says they are to do "the will of my father in the heavens" (Matt 12:50). I will argue that the Gospel identified what practices constituted doing God's will when it came to people having enough to eat.

To sustain this argument, I will argue the six claims summarized below. The claims progress from general context to the Matthean community context, to the Gospel critique of society practices, to the importance of everyone having sufficient food.

1. Access to food was a complex web of interrelationships that affected the ability of various groups of people to gain access to food (chapters 1 and 3).

2. While 25 percent of the population lived below subsistence level, most households were able to eke out at least a living, although many of these households (30 percent) were at risk of slipping below subsistence (chapter 4).

3. People in the lower socio-economic segments of the population in the first-century Roman East used survival mechanisms to keep from slipping below subsistence level. If already below the threshold, mechanisms helped them to stave off starvation by relying on the cooperation of neighbors and strangers (chapter 4).

4. The Matthean community experienced food shortages during the period in which the community developed its identity and solidified its foundational story. The trauma of these shortages affected the way the Matthean community remembered the teaching and actions of Jesus relative to food shortages, which are found in the Gospel (chapter 5).

5. People in various segments of the population in the first-century Roman East made decisions and took actions condoned by the dominant entitlement system that undermined the critical survival mechanisms (discussed in claim 3). Occasionally, people in various segments of the population took actions that alleviated or mitigated the effects of food shortages. The Gospel of Matthew offers critiques of the wider societal practices concerning food provision positively (for example,

---

more than the Matthean community does.

9. Carter, "Contested Claims: Roman Imperial Theology and Matthew's Gospel," 58–59.

an aristocrat providing food to the poor in Matt 14:13–21; 15:29–38) and some negatively (for example, stockpiling grain in Matt 6:19–21). Other practices are re-inscribed to include people usually excluded from receiving food distributions (for example, the destitute at a public meal in Matt 15:32–39) (chapters 6 and 7).

6. The narrative of the Gospel alludes to food-access practices throughout the Gospel. Using a narrative analysis process, I argue that the Gospel uses food access as a sub-theme to demonstrate its view of Immanuel's new realm of the heavens with its call back to covenant with God and neighbors, as well as its message countering the dominant entitlement system that was causing people to go hungry (chapter 8).

I am not arguing that the vision and provision of adequate food is a principal theme of the Gospel, but only that the issue of sufficient food is a significant embodiment of what the realm of the heavens means. Nor am I arguing that the Gospel of Matthew is the only gospel to address this theme. Given the pervasiveness of food shortages in the first-century Roman East, one would expect the other gospels also to exhibit an interest in food-access issues. For example, the Gospel of Luke does have a similar strong sub-text complete with additional passages unique to it (Luke 15:11–32; 16:1–13; 17:7–10), but in the Gospel of Mark the sub-text is weak. For reasons of space, my argument concerns only the Gospel of Matthew.

In the following sections of this chapter, I locate my argument in relation to three contexts that justify its investigation, and I give an overview of the remaining chapters and their arguments.

An Important But Overlooked Topic

In this section, I argue that attention to this topic is overdue. I identify three contexts that point to the importance of examining the Matthean advocacy of a society in which all have access to sufficient food. First, I argue that access to sufficient food was a problem for many people in the first century. Second, I argue that the Gospel of Matthew presents Jesus both teaching and performing acts related to the full gamut of food-related activities, with special emphasis on how food was distributed to people. Third, I show that despite the first two points, Matthean scholars have not addressed this topic.

Access to Sufficient Food was a Serious Problem in the First Century

As I noted in the introductory remarks, Lenski describes the Roman Empire as an advanced agrarian society in which a relatively few aristocratic families controlled the distribution of food. This social control scheme led to pervasive endemic food shortages for a substantial number of peoples who had virtually no power and little control over access to sufficient food, with many starving to death. In this section, I address the question of the seriousness of the problem of sufficient food from two perspectives. First, I use economic modeling work by Steven Friesen to argue that the commonly held view of the aristocratic 3 percent enjoying abundance while the other 97 percent of the population were starving to death is overstated.[10] I return to this topic in chapter 4 with a more detailed and nuanced argument. Second, I argue that aristocratic actions and practices added to the precarious situation for peasants related to their growing sufficient food due to the fickleness of the Mediterranean climate. In this section, I argue in general terms, but I address the topic in detail in chapter 4. The specific practices identified in those latter chapters provide the setting to understand the rhetoric of the Gospel related to a realm of the heavens in which God through God's people provides sufficient food. At this juncture in the argument, it is sufficient to make the point without specific details.

Economic Analysis of the Pervasiveness of Food Shortages

In 2004, Friesen addressed the problem of a lack of specificity in describing the abilities of the 97 percent to acquire sufficient food by defining a Poverty Scale.[11] Friesen placed various occupational groups in categories based on their access to resources, as shown in table 1. He acknowledged varying levels of income for some occupational groups and put them in multiple categories.[12]

---

10. Scholars apply Lenski's work on advanced agrarian societies with its social stratification scheme to the Roman Empire. For examples of scholars who expand insights from Lenski to further their own arguments and models, see Saldarini, *Pharisees, Scribes, and Sadducees in Palestinian Society: A Sociological Approach*, 35–49; Finger, *Of Widows and Meals: Communal Meals in the Book of Acts*, multiple places and arguments; Hanson and Oakman, *Palestine in the Time of Jesus*, 101; Wire, "Gender Roles in a Scribal Community," multiple places and arguments.

11. Friesen, "Poverty in Pauline Studies," 341.

12. Ibid., 337–47.

Table 1: Expanded Friesen Poverty Scale

Scale	Description	Includes	Percent of population	Income to subsistence
PS 7	Below subsistence level[1]	some farm families, unattached widows, orphans, beggars, disabled, unskilled day laborers	25% (25%)	.5—1
PS 6	At subsistence level (and often below minimum level to sustain life)	small farm families, laborers (skilled and unskilled), artisans (esp. those employed by others), wage earners, most merchants and traders, small shop/tavern owners	30% (55%)	1—1.5
PS 5	Stable near subsistence level (with reasonable hope of remaining above the minimum level to sustain life.)	many merchants and traders, regular wage earners, artisans, large shop owners, freedpersons, some farm families	25% (80%)	1.5—7
PS 4	Moderate surplus[2]	some merchants, some traders, some freedpersons, some artisans (especially those who employ others), and military veterans	17% (97%)	7—13
PS 3	Municipal elites[3]	most *decurial* families, wealthy men and women who do not hold office, some freedpersons, some retainers, some veterans, some merchants	2% (99%)	substantial

1. Morley, "The Poor in the City of Rome," 29. Morley makes the obvious point that PS 7 cannot be considered a social group but "only a collection of individuals in temporary distress, most of whom would either quickly recover or perish."

2. Friesen, "Poverty in Pauline Studies," 346; Barclay, "Poverty in Pauline Studies: A Response to Steven Friesen," 365. Friesen notes that it is impossible to measure this group, especially since we know little about the number of people in PS 5. Barclay notes the irony that the more we realize the need to know more about the different economic classes, the more we know we do not know.

3. Friesen, "Poverty in Pauline Studies," 337–47; Whittaker, "The Poor," 278. The top three categories comprise three percent of the population, and their incomes could be astronomical compared to lower four categories. For example, Whitaker says the day laborer might earn three sesterces per day compared to Cato's property alone yielding 550–650 sesterces per day.

Scale	Description	Includes	Percent of population	Income to subsistence
PS 2	Regional or provincial elites	equestrian families, provincial officials, some retainers, some *decurial* families, some freedpersons, some retired military officers	1%	large
PS 1	Imperial elites	imperial dynasty, Roman senatorial families, a few retainers, local royalty, a few freedpersons	.04%	huge

In defining his Poverty Scale, Friesen did not use wealth exclusively but defined subsistence level as "the resources needed to procure enough calories in food to maintain the human body."[13] Friesen's definition has to do with access to food and he recognized that access was much more complex than social level or wealth, although both of these factors were important. He recognized that some households could grow much of their food, and others did not have direct access to land. Nonetheless, his economic bias would follow his primary interest in the urban environment. In 2010, Bruce Longenecker refined the percentages in each category of the scale to reflect the general population, not just urban populations.[14] In 2009, Friesen joined with Walter Scheidel to refine estimates of percentages of people at various income levels.[15] I use their combined analyses in scaling the Roman economy to estimate the severity of food shortages in the first century as depicted in table 1.

Friesen's descriptions of the categories are in the first three columns. The fourth column, labeled *Percent of population*, lists the percentages estimated by Longenecker for the general population. The number in parentheses is the cumulative percentage. The numbers in the last column indicate how close to subsistence level people were living.[16] For example, the income

13. Friesen, "Poverty in Pauline Studies," 343.

14. Longenecker, *Remember the Poor*, 44–59. Longenecker rejects the nomenclature used by Friesen of *poverty scale* and instead moves to *economy scale*. While in agreement with him that putting imperial elites into a poverty category seems counter intuitive, a large portion of this study is concerned with people who were indeed in poverty, and using the term *poverty scale* would keep this point to the forefront.

15. Scheidel and Friesen, "The Size of the Economy and the Distribution of Income in the Roman Empire," 75–90.

16. Ibid., 83. Table 7. Non-elite income scale. I derived the last column, labeled *Income/subsistence*, from the Scheidel-Friesen work and the first four columns of table 1. In chapter 4, I present a detailed discussion of column 5.

for the PS 7 level ranged from a person having only half of what was required to live at subsistence level to barely having enough in any given year. PS 7 comprises the people in structural poverty[17] (that is, people born into a situation of mere subsistence who remain there). If a problem occurs that keeps them from acquiring food, they will eventually starve.[18] The income for the PS 6 level ranged from barely having enough to having a slight surplus, which they might store against a bad period. These are the people in conjunctural poverty[19] (that is, if they fall below subsistence level, they will recover quickly). No other categories contain *poor* people.

The percentage of people slowly starving to death (PS 7) is twenty-five. The combined percentage for the first two categories (PS 7 and PS 6)—those most at risk during food shortages—is 55 percent. These people, including many peasant households, lived precariously, but did survive. Freisen and Scheidel acknowledge that their calculations exclude access to the supplemental food sources of peasants, such as wild game and birds, as well as berries and nuts, that provided food for periods in which cultivated crop food sources were scarce. Although scholars have not estimated how much food comes from these sources, I suggest that access to supplemental food sources would move a substantial number of rural small farm households from PS 7 to PS 6.[20] On the other hand, the entitlement system enabled the aristocracy to undermine the principal survival mechanisms for peasants: planting a variety of crops, storing surplus for a bad year, and relying on kin and neighbors when the other mechanisms did not suffice.[21]

---

17. Morley, "The Poor in the City of Rome," 28–29.

18. Gapp, "The Universal Famine under Claudius," 261. Gapp writes that famine was always class famine. During a more severe food shortage, everyone experienced economic hardship, but only the poor actually went hungry and starved to death.

19. Morley, "The Poor in the City of Rome," 28–29.

20. I use the PS nomenclature or the phrase "lower socio-economic segments of the population." There is no compatibility between models of *classes* in contemporary industrialized societies and the Roman empire. I rarely distinguish between men and women, except when archeological data confirms differences (for example, more malnutrition for women than for men). As Tolbert argues, gender is a major structural factor in the construction of all societies. Unfortunately, little data is available for this topic at the specificity required for this study. Further, feminist critiques of primary written sources have noted the ritualized or symbolized portrayal of women, which makes their use suspect. My analysis remains cognizant of this bias. Jobling writes an insightful essay on the analyses of female roles in scripture, including roles in production. Tolbert, "Social, Sociological, and Anthropological Methods," 268, 264–65; Jobling, "Feminism and 'Mode of Production' in Ancient Israel," 241–45.

21. Garnsey, *Famine and Food Supply*, 43, 55–63; Horden and Purcell, *The Corrupting Sea*, chap. 4. I address the topic of survival mechanisms in chapter 4.

Disruptive Aristocratic Practices

Thus far, I have used economic models to sustain the argument that access to sufficient food was a problem for a sizeable portion of the people. However, a more significant argument involves practices that contributed to, and helped alleviate, the problem, especially for peasants. I now argue that in the first-century Roman East, aristocrats took actions that wreaked havoc with the ability of many peasants to produce and to retain sufficient food needed to live a full life.[22] I argue by way of a scenario reflecting such a situation in the first century.

A major survival technique for peasants was the planting of many different types of crops on small, distributed plots of land. This technique ensured that failure of a few plots would not be catastrophic (that is, undernourishment to starvation). In the imperial period, some aristocrats entered into the lucrative grain trade business, which changed their view with respect to controlling crop selection. Grain stored well making it a good cash crop, which the wealthy owners could hold back until they could sell it at a higher price to people in an area experiencing a severe food shortage.[23] To increase the amount of grain available for speculation, the large landowners moved to monoculture grain production.[24] The risk to a subsistence-level, or barely above subsistence-level, peasant household working the large owner's land increased.[25] Peter Garnsey estimates crop failures to be as high as one year in three for some types of wheat.[26] When in response to landowner pressures a

---

22. A full life encompasses more than having sufficient food and includes, for example, social obligations, and honor and status requirements be discharged.

23. Reed, *Archaeology and the Galilean Jesus*, 89; Applebaum, "Economic Life in Palestine," 660. See Acts 12:20.

24. Reed, *Archaeology and the Galilean Jesus*, 87; Kloppenborg, *The Tenants in the Vineyard*, 297n275. Kloppenborg asserts that the writings of the agriculturalists around the first-century period clearly indicate polycultural management of estates did still exist.

25. Safrai, *The Economy of Roman Palestine*, 85; Oakman, *Jesus and the Economic Questions*; Herzog, *Jesus, Justice, and the Reign of God*, 96; Josephus, *Ant.* 17.289. A formerly independent small farm landowner could have his land given to a city or a political ally of the Roman ruler. At best, he would have to pay rent that put an additional demand on his crop production. At worse, he had rent to pay and lost control of crop selection. For example, Safrai writes that Herod gave the village of Arus to Ptolemy of Rhodes.

26. Garnsey, *Famine and Food Supply*, chap. 1; Horden and Purcell, *The Corrupting Sea*, 152. Garnsey bases his arguments on literary and epigraphic data from Athens covering 600–322 BCE and Rome from 509 BCE through 250 CE, as well as comparable modern statistics on agricultural yields and climate. Horden and Purcell note that the production of wine and oil was also variable and could affect the price of grain and thus its availability.

peasant household was predominantly growing wheat, starvation was a real possibility in a year that the crop failed[27] since all, or most, of its plots would fail simultaneously. The failure would push the household into debt, which would take more food off its table in succeeding years as the household struggled to repay its loan.[28] Taxes and financial obligations weighed the peasant down leading to debt and loss of land. Those who benefited as the receiver of defaulted land established the laws. Peasants had little recourse or power to change their situation. Consequently, these systems favored aristocrats in terms of property ownership and control of land.[29]

Richard Saller argues that local officials enforced laws with no pretense at impartiality and, in fact, were supposed to use their positions to benefit family and friends.[30] This overarching structure and ideology of aristocratic entitlements shifted dynamics away from most people getting what they needed to some people in power getting what they wanted.[31] Crops, particularly grain, became the means for the aristocracy to get what it wanted at the expense of enough food to eat for the poor. By acquiring more land and ownership of more food held in storage, the large landowning aristocrats affected the lives of peasants they would never see.[32]

As actions by the aristocrats put increasing pressures on the rural society, the rural social safety network,[33] through which households received

---

27. Goodman, "The First Jewish Revolt: Social Conflict and the Problem of Debt," 419; Horden and Purcell, *The Corrupting Sea*, 205–9, 260–63.

28. Oakman, *Jesus and the Economic Questions*, 72–75; Horsley, "Jesus Movements and the Renewal of Israel," 35; Hanson and Oakman, *Palestine in the Time of Jesus*, 153; Finger, *Of Widows and Meals: Communal Meals in the Book of Acts*, 104. Hanson and Oakman and Finger argue that this cycle eventually leads to loss of land by a peasant.

29. Garnsey and Scheidel, *Cities, Peasants, and Food*, 98–99; Friesen, "Injustice or God's Will," 241; MacMullen, *Roman Social Relations*, 10–12.

30. Saller, *Personal Patronage under the Early Empire*, 31.

31. Horden and Purcell, *The Corrupting Sea*, 268.

32. Kautsky, *Aristocratic Empires*, 105; Lenski, *Power and Privilege*, 100; Columella, *On Agriculture* 1.1.20, 11.21.16. An oft-used word to describe this situation is *exploitation*. Kautsky argues that no matter how cruel and greedy one might think a landowner to be, exploitation was limited. Lenski argues that landowners, in practice, could not deprive peasants and tenants of all their products and surpluses because landowners needed peasant and tenant labor and their good to survive. Moreover, it took too much effort and peasants and tenants would have devised ways to hold on to some of their surplus. Columella, a first-century agriculturalist, says that on estates that are far from the owners, the workers will become corrupted and, once corrupted, they will be more interested in pillage than in farming. If the honest bailiff does not pay attention to the workers, they will trifle away their time.

33. On pages 96–103, I describe the social safety net in terms of reciprocal relations ascribed to rural societies by economic sociologists.

temporary aid from their kin and neighbors, broke down.³⁴ I will argue in chapters 6 through 8 that the Gospel of Matthew critiqued both problems. Surprisingly perhaps, I will argue that the Gospel directs more criticism toward the breakdown of the peasant system than the practices of aristocrats.

In summary, I have argued in this section that many gradations of wealth existed. Yet, 25 percent of people (PS 7) were in structural poverty, and slowly starving to death. Another 30 percent of the population (PS 6) lived precariously near the edge of subsistence level. For this 55 percent, consistent access to sufficient food was a problem. The next 25 percent of the population (PS 5) were relatively stable with respect to access to food. However, if a more powerful person decided to acquire their land, a PS 5 household could easily fall into a lower scale position. I have used the example of shifts in aristocratic use of land for cash crops to argue that actions by aristocrats led to more restrictions on access to food for the lower socio-economic segments of the population. The lessening availability of any surplus food caused a breakdown in the rural safety network since there was not food to share. I have made these arguments in abbreviated form here, but I will argue in detail in subsequent chapters. It is sufficient at this point to have argued in broad-brush strokes that food shortages were a problem for many people in the lower socio-economic segments of the population.

Food Practices Are a Frequent Topic in the Gospel of Matthew

A second context points to the importance of Matthew's advocacy of a society in which all have access to sufficient food. As I will show, the Gospel references various food-access practices throughout most of the text. In order to understand what constitutes *food access*, I employ the work of Jack Goody. Goody developed a generic framework in which he laid out five phases in the full life cycle of food use: production, distribution, preparation, consumption, and clean up.³⁵ Especially relevant for this study are the first two phases of the framework, production and distribution. These phases are the ones most directly connected with food access. The production phase encompasses preparation, including acquisition of labor; planting or breeding; cultivating or herding; harvesting or slaughtering; and conservation of resources needed to continue the following year, for example seed for

---

34. Garnsey and Saller, *The Roman Empire*, 76. Note that I am referring to a breakdown of functioning of the peasant entitlement system. I am not proposing the collapse of the independent peasantry. Garnsey and Saller argue against the collapse of the peasantry.

35. Goody, *Cooking, Cuisine, and Class*.

planting.³⁶ The distribution phase indicates specific sets of relations within a society.³⁷ Processes include allocation within the producing unit, reciprocal and market exchanges, and obligatory transfers such as taxes and rents. Included in this phase are issues of the equality of the distribution, nature of the transfers, and the uses of storage. When examining the different phases, the focus of attention changes. For this study, the focus for production is land use, and for distribution is using, storing, and selling crops needed for food,³⁸ but used for other purposes.

Table 2 supplies a tabulation of references in the Gospel to the phases of the Goody Framework, notably food production, distribution, preparation, consumption, and clean-up. The table shows that the Gospel indeed has many references to practices concerned with the food life cycle,³⁹ and the distribution phase, which is central to access to sufficient food, has the largest number of the references. The Matthean text refers to food-related activities in approximately 30 percent of its passages.⁴⁰ Moreover, the references span Matthean chapters three through twenty-six. These chapters contain most of the teachings and actions of Jesus related to the general population. In chapters 5 and 6, I discuss a number of these references in detail as part of the Gospel's rhetoric concerned with the material vision of the new realm of the heavens. It is sufficient at this point to note the Gospel's pervasive concern with the issue of food access.

Table 2. Matthean passages associated with phases of the Goody Framework

Phases	Matthean passages
1. Production	3:8–10; 4:18–22; 5:45; 6:26; 7:16–20; 9:37–38; 11:28–30; 12:1–8, 31–32, 33; 13:1–9, 24–30, 31–32, 47–50; 15:13; 18:12–13; 19:12–15; 20:1–16; 21:18–19, 28–32, 33–39

36. Ibid., 44.
37. Ibid., 45.
38. Ibid., 37.

39. Stambaugh and Balch, *The New Testament in Its Social Environment*, 68. They note that the Synoptic gospels in general deal rather extensively with the processes of "planting seed, harvesting fruit, grinding grain, and eating bread." They also point out that the New Testament is different than most Greco-Roman literature in that it depicts the realities of life as often being a harsh, subsistence living.

40. Another 20 percent of the passages shows Jesus performing healings. Sickness was a companion to malnutrition. Hence, I would suggest these passages also point to the Matthean text being concerned with people having sufficient food to eat.

Phases	Matthean passages
2. Distribution (includes taxes, rent, debt, and tithes)	3:12; 5:25–26, 31–32, 40–41, 42; 6:1–4, 11, 12 , 19–21, 25–26, 31–33; 7:2, 7–11; 9:9; 10:10, 42; 12:1–8, 29; 14:13–21; 15:1–16, 12–13, 32–39; 17:24–27; 18:23–35; 19:1–12, 13–15; 16–30; 21:10–16, 33–41; 22:1–14, 17–22; 23:23; 24:45–51; 25:14–30, 31–46; 26:6–13
3. Preparation	Not a key access issue 13:33; 26:17–19
4. Consumption	3:4; 4:3–4; 6:11, 16–18, 25–26, 31–33; 7:9–11; 8:11; 9:10–13, 14–15; 11:16–19; 12:1–8; 14:13–21; 15:1–11, 21–28, 37; 16:5–12; 22:1–14; 26:20–21
5. Clean-up	Not a key access issue 14:20; 15:27, 37

Food-Access Practices Are a Neglected Topic

Having established the widespread food scarcity in the first century and a pervasive concern with access to food in Matthew's gospel, I note a further reason for attending to the Matthean vision of sufficient food; namely, the scholarly neglect of discussions of food access practices in the Gospel. A substantial body of literature exists which analyzes and interprets the Gospel of Matthew from many perspectives. Significantly lacking is attention to food access. The popularity of the Gospel, especially the Sermon on the Mount,[41] goes back to Patristic writings[42] and its popularity continues to this day. Sean Kealy generated two volumes of abstracts primarily dealing with books on Matthew beginning with the Patristic Fathers and continuing through 1990.[43] None of the works he catalogued deals with food as its primary subject. The NT Abstracts database covers approximately two hundred books, essays, and articles per year on the Gospel of Matthew. In the past twenty-five years, twenty-eight of the approximately five thousand items have dealt with food issues, and only eight of those tangentially relate

---

41. McArthur, *Understanding the Sermon on the Mount*, 11. McArthur notes that the early Church fathers quoted the fifth chapter of Matthew more frequently than any other chapter in the Bible. Given that Matt 5 is a standard for Christian life, the fact that a cluster of food access images occur in the Sermon on the Mount further substantiates the importance of the topic in the Gospel.

42. Allison, *Studies in Matthew: Interpretation Past and Present*, chap. 6.

43. Kealy, *Matthew's Gospel and the History of Biblical Interpretation*.

to the argument of this study that the Gospel advocates for a society in which all people have access to sufficient food.

In this section, I argue that long-standing scholarly debates on Matthew do not engage food-access practices. Some scholars write about access to food in the Gospel, but their focus is not on practices. Not only is my topic neglected in Matthean studies, Synoptic studies neglect it as well. There is one work on the Gospel of Luke that addresses physical food exchanges that helped bring together rural and urban members of the Lukan community. The importance of the topic as I argued in the sub-sections above coupled with the general neglect of the topic as I argue below justify the focus of this study on Matthew's vision of adequate access to food for all people.

Matthean Scholarship Does Not Engage the Pragmatics of Food Access

Several authors have published reviews of Matthean research. Based on three such sources, I argue that Matthean scholarship does not engage the sub-topic in the Gospel related to the pragmatics of food access. First, Donald Senior, in the revised and expanded 1996 version of his book entitled *What Are They Saying About Matthew?*, indexes the work of various Matthean scholars on a number of topics. In his preface, Senior takes note of the recent development in Matthean scholarship with the application of "positive sciences"—cultural anthropology, sociology, and economics—to interpretation of the text.[44] These disciplines inform the arguments of this study. Yet, for example, in Senior's chapter 1 concerned with the setting of the Gospel, none of the eleven authors he reviews indicated endemic food shortages were a relevant setting of the Gospel.[45] In chapter 2, Senior suggests that perhaps the question of structure is posed incorrectly and moves the discussion toward the gospel as a story moving its audience along with devices and motifs. No acknowledgment is made of a prevalent motif of food processes. The rest of the chapters—salvation history, attitudes toward the Law, use of the OT, Christology, and Discipleship and Church—likewise show no interest in food access issues. In 2001, he returns to the topic and suggests future directions for Matthean studies. Even then, food access is not a topic.[46] While a number of these topics, especially with the advent of the positive sciences, could entertain a study of food-access processes, none has thus far.

---

44. Senior, *What Are They Saying About Matthew?*, 3.
45. Ibid., 4.
46. Senior, "Directions in Matthean Studies," 19–20.

In 1999, Donald Hagner wrote on trends in Matthean scholarship. He deals with the topics found in Senior's review, and adds the topics of anti-Semitism and integrity of the tradition in Matthew. In addition, he reviews Matthean literature with respect to the methods of deep structural analysis and reader-response. None of the authors in his review shows interest in food access. He says that setting and social history are a very active area of Matthean scholarship, but none of his overviews of the current areas in Matthean study indicates any studies informed by the Matthean vision of everyone having enough to eat.[47]

An example of the neglect occurs in the debate on the role of the Law,[48] which could have numerous opportunities to address food-access issues. The debate has posited variously that Matthew redacted passages dealing with the Law in order to overcome Gentile resistance to stringent adherence to the Law,[49] or made other redactions, such as Matt 5:17–19, as an apologetic statement for the benefit of the Jewish community.[50] Discussions of the relationship of the Law to the prominent Matthean motif concerned with doing the will of God,[51] the double-love commandment,[52] or the role of Law in the Gospel as *halakhah*, which is in contrast with Pharisaic ethics and practice,[53] have not embraced matters of food access.

To recap, the mainline Matthean debates have not embraced the issue of food access and the pragmatic ethical demand of the Gospel on its community. My work is a next step in the progression of Matthean studies. The early theological and Christological interpretations moved to include social context.[54] That context then needed the correction of social science criticism to bring it specifically to circum-Mediterranean culture.[55] Subsequently, Empire criticism discussed theology, soteriology, eschatology,

---

47. Hagner, "The Gospel of Matthew," 34.

48. I identified over 250 sources on this topic. I use a few scholars to frame the discussion. For a good overview of the debate, see Senior, *What Are They Saying About Matthew?*, chap. 5.

49. Meier, *Law and History in Matthew's Gospel: A Redactional Study of Mt. 5:17–48*, 71, 23.

50. Slee, *The Church in Antioch in the First Century CE: Communion and Conflict*, 136.

51. Barth, "Matthew's Understanding of the Law," 58.

52. Donaldson, "The Law That Hangs (Matthew 22:40)"; Brooks, "The Function of the Double Love Command in Matthew 22:34–40."

53. Bockmuehl, *Jewish Law in Gentile Churches: Halakhah and the Beginning of Christian Public Ethics*, 163.

54. Kingsbury, *Matthew as Story*.

55. Duling, "The Matthean Brotherhood and Marginal Scribal Leadership"; Malina, "Social Scientific Approaches and the Gospel of Matthew"; Duling, *A Marginal Scribe*.

ecclesiology, and Christology in negotiating Empire ideology to make more specific the context of a counter-vision.[56] The argument in this study moves from the current imperial-criticism emphasis on a counter-vision to include the pragmatics of practices that embody the Matthean counter-vision of the realm of the heavens. This study will provide an expanded understanding of the Matthean community by postulating possible practices in the community, based on the confluence of the received text and specific socio-rhetorical critical approaches applied to the text with a pragmatic lens. Gerd Theissen writes, "If we presuppose that a tradition is genuine, we may assume that those who handed it down shaped their lives in accordance with the tradition. If we assume that it originated within the Jesus movement in the period after Easter, we can presuppose that those who handed it down shaped the tradition in accordance with their life. In either case the result is the same: there is a correspondence between the social groups which handed down the tradition and the tradition itself."[57]

A Few Matthean Scholars Engage Food-Access Issues, But Not Practices

When food is the topic in Matthean scholarship, scholars discuss the topic often from the perspectives of boundary defining[58] or the type of meal[59] or eschatology.[60] When addressing meals as boundary defining, the work

56. Carter, "Contested Claims: Roman Imperial Theology and Matthew's Gospel"; Carter, *Matthew and the Margins*.

57. Theissen, *Sociology of Early Palestinian Christianity*, 3–4.

58. Douglas, "Deciphering a Meal," 61; Reinhartz, "Reflections on Table Fellowship and Community Identity"; Smith, "The Historical Jesus at Table." Most work on the boundary breaking aspect of meals in the Gospels begins with the work of Mary Douglas. She writes, "If food is treated as a code, the messages it encodes will be found in the pattern of social relations being expressed. The message is about different degrees of hierarchy, inclusion and exclusion, boundaries and transactions across the boundaries" (Douglas, "Deciphering a Meal," 61). Reinhartz critiques the work of several of authors on this topic. Smith writes about the social functions of meals in Roman societies. In his discussion, he identifies Jesus as the hero-at-the-table type.

59. Smith, *From Symposium to Eucharist*, 2, 6, 10, 272–75; Stringer, *Rethinking the Origins of the Eucharist*, chap. 5. Smith has written extensively on this topic in general. In chapter 8, "The Banquet in the Gospels," in *From Symposium to Eucharist*, Smith begins with the theme of table fellowship and moves to the type of banquets depicted being Greco-Roman in the symposium tradition (222). He has a short section on Matthew. His emphasis is on Mark. However, the passages he analyzes usually have parallels in Matthew. Although Stringer only spends a few pages in passing on Matthew, he devotes an entire chapter to Antioch and meal(s) portrayed in the Didache.

60. Smit, *Fellowship and Food in the Kingdom*, 2–12. Smit presents a focused literature review on this topic.

centers on who is in the *eating community*.⁶¹ My focus is on how the *eating community* gains access to food. Dennis Smith is tangentially relevant when he argues that bonding at community meals brings with it a sense of social obligation, but he does pursue the issue of practices.⁶² Studies concerned with what type of meal often concentrate on the depiction of what type of banquet.⁶³ Overlooked is the fact that Matthew negatively depicts banquets. There are five banquet settings: the parable of the wedding banquet (Matt 22:1–14); Herod's birthday celebration (Matt 14:1–12); dinner with Matthew, the tax collector (Matt 9:10–13); the anointing while dining at Simon the leper's home (Matt 26:6–13); and the Last Supper (Matt 26:26–35). In none of these occasions is the banquet presented in a positive light. The two banquets at which Jesus is not present are violent. Herod's birthday celebration involves the beheading of John, a prophet of God. Matthew's version of the parable of the wedding banquet is much more violent than its parallel in Luke with a number of people killed. The other three incidents occur when Jesus is at someone's house and he is reclining (ἀνάκαιμαι), which indicated a more formal affair. In the first two incidents, Jesus is dining with the wrong sorts of people: a tax collector and a leper. At the Lord's Supper, he is also dining with an improper sort—a traitor who had been a friend— and the banquet discussion is about violence that will befall Jesus. Banquets are not something the community would be encouraged to do according to the examples set for it. On the other hand, the Gospel does present scenes of public meals (Matt 14:13–21; 15:32–39) in a positive manner. These meals of abundant food re-inscribed societal custom to include poor people usually left out of typical public meals.⁶⁴ Finally, whereas some discussions have taken a spiritualized or eschatological approach to the Lord's Prayer, a few scholars have highlighted the pragmatic concerns reflected in the reading of the petition about "daily bread."⁶⁵

Of all the Matthean sources surveyed, three authors have recently dealt with Matthew and food-access issues: Peter-Ben Smit, James Grimshaw,

---

61. Smith, *From Symposium to Eucharist*, 232–47, 272. He argues that eating is a community-building function and identifies the following passages as boundary breaking including any passage that counters dietary rules: Matt 5:6, 13; 8:11–12; 9:10–13, 16–17; 15:1–9, 11; 16:6, 11; 18:17; 21:31; 22:2–13; and 23:25–26. He argues that Matthew portrays Jesus as hero at table and the table symbolized the reign of heaven.

62. Ibid., 9–10, 242–43. Smith refers to the work by Mary Douglas on boundary-definition symbolism associated with table fellowship.

63. Carmichael, "David Daube on the Eucharist and the Passover Seder."

64. van Nijf, *The Civic World of Professional Associations in the Roman East*, 157–64, 187.

65. Oakman, *Jesus and the Peasants*, 4, 199–242; Carter, *Matthew and the Margins*, 166–67.

and Warren Carter. Smit bridges the work on banquets and the vision of the realm of the heavens countering the vision of the Golden Age taken up by Augustus and continued through later emperors. In his view, the issue is what he terms *utopian abundance*. Smit argues rather cogently that the in-breaking of God's righteous rule may be envisioned in terms of copious provision of foodstuffs.[66] God ensures in the full establishment of God's purposes that everyone has sufficient food. Another of Smit's concerns is how the passages "express the hopes and expectations of the groups developing and transmitting them,"[67] which demonstrate the rhetorical impact on the Matthean community. His analysis normally remains at the symbolic and vision level and he does not engage questions concerning access to food in the present for the community.

Grimshaw examines food exchange in the Gospel of Matthew from the perspective of social and theological motivations for exchange. He argues that the text shows ever-widening circles of people exchanging food. His principal goal is to use this theme to show that the Matthean community is not sectarian.[68] He points out that Matt 4:1–11 flags major issues that inform his work. (1) Given the exchange of food is real and material, and serves biological needs, what are the implications of the exchange of food for social, theological, and political relationships? (2) Who provides the food? (3) What is the role of people in the acquisition of food? (4) How do people share food, and with whom? He devotes the bulk of his book to tracing the fourth issue with respect to ever enlarging spheres of exchange, beginning within the private household and eventually arriving at the larger world outside of the Matthean community. He makes an interesting observation that goes to the importance of access to food in the Gospel. "[T]he degree of conflict increases through the narrative yet food exchange continues to be present as a means of encouragement and divine help."[69] The arguments of this study significantly overlap with those of Grimshaw on issues three and four, but he does not engage them from the perspective of practices.

The closest effort to my research is work done over a number of years by Carter. In a series of forthcoming essays on the topic of "How Would Jesus Eat?", he touches on the pragmatic, although his emphasis is on competing symbol systems. He observes that if the gospel community does not perform similar works to those Jesus practiced, the gospel vision will be no better than Rome's propaganda claims. Carter supports my assumption

---

66. Smit, *Fellowship and Food in the Kingdom*, 210.
67. Ibid., 1.
68. Grimshaw, *Analysis of Matthew's Food Exchange*.
69. Ibid., 36–37.

that the Matthean community would not have questioned some underlying imperial structures related to food access, which one now might consider unfair or unjust. He argues further that the Matthean community would have embraced various practices since its members were naturally a part of the social milieu that was the Roman Empire.[70]

In summary, searches of databases that detail Matthean scholarship over many decades yield very little work on food issues. The few works identified usually address food-consumption issues. Only three sources deal with food-access issues and none of them deals at a pragmatic level with the practices that the Gospel critiques and advocates. This study will address this neglect.

Synoptic Studies Neglect Food Access As a Topic

A search of published works in the other synoptic gospels, written over the past ten years, yields over eight thousand entries. Fifty entries deal with some aspect of food, and only one article by Grimshaw relates closely to this study.

Against previous scholarship that used a broad categorization of material possessions, Grimshaw uses physical food exchange as a mechanism for examining the relationship between the urban and rural components of the Lukan community.[71] His study, like mine, concentrates on how the gospel depicts the production and distribution phases of the Goody framework. He argues that the exchange of food brought the urban and rural community members into contact. That contact bridged normal social differences. Peasants were more than just the recipients of handouts from wealthier urban residents. The result was an extended community composed of interrelated urban and rural components functioning as a market exchange district. His work is relevant to the present study, concerned with social safety networks, in that it examines the effects of material food-access processes and correlates them to gospel passages.

Summary

I have argued in this section the importance of this topic by showing that food shortages were a problem for many in the first century. Food shortages are important in the Gospel of Matthew that portrays Jesus responding to various aspects of food shortages. The Gospel narrative presents Jesus as a

---

70. Carter, "How Would Jesus Eat? Matthew."
71. Grimshaw, "Luke's Market Exchange District," 38–46.

model to be emulated by narrating his own actions that provided food to the hungry and by relating his teachings against practices that contributed to food shortages. Despite the fact that food shortages were prevalent in the society and in the narrative of the Gospel, Matthean scholarship has not engaged the topic, using a pragmatic lens, to examine the practices that the Gospel advocated for its community to live in the realm of the heavens, where no one goes hungry. Not only is the topic overlooked in Matthean studies, it is also neglected in Synoptic studies. Further, previous New Testament scholarship that deals with food shortages stops after providing an overview of the severity of the food-access issues without discussing the detailed context, or the function of specific texts that address the causes and practices to alleviate food shortages. My argument is that the Gospel of Matthew advocated for a society in which all people would have access to sufficient food. The argument addresses the previous neglect by examining how the Gospel critiqued first-century practices that helped or hindered the goal of sufficient food.

Chapter Outline and Descriptions

This study comprises nine chapters. In chapter 1, I have introduced my argument that the Gospel of Matthew envisions a heaven on earth in which all people have enough to eat. The Gospel critiques first-century practices that helped or hindered the embodiment of that vision. I have argued that the issue merits attention for three reasons. First, food shortages were a problem in the first century. Second, food-related images and processes permeate the Gospel narrative of the ministry of Jesus. Third, this topic is neglected in Matthean and Synoptic studies and could encourage scholars to examine the Gospel with a more pragmatic lens.

Chapter 2, "Contextualized Interpretation," discusses the methods I employ, namely modeling and socio-rhetorical interpretation. I argue that socio-rhetorical interpretation simultaneously addresses the rhetorical message of the text and the social context of the Matthean community. I note that the Matthean community lived under, and responded to, imperial practices. I argue that existing primary sources are not sufficient for defining the complex relationships surrounding people in the lower socio-economic segments of the population getting enough to eat. I argue that the form of the Gospel is patterned after ancient biographical narratives. Examination of such ancient narratives suggests that the Gospel portrays Jesus as the Greek ideal man who had the power to take the spirit and purpose of a god's law and become the incarnation of it. I then discuss the second method undergirding this study, modeling, which is a method commonly used in social scientific work when data is limited. I argue that modeling can facilitate the understanding of the complex network of societal factors that directly and tangentially relate to practices hindering and facilitating access to food. I argue that the models most commonly used for the first-century Roman East do not provide sufficient explanatory detail for the arguments of this study and a new model is needed.

Chapter 3, "How Did People Eat?" describes the complex web of relationships that affected the ability of various groups of people gaining access to food. The discussion uses a specially developed descriptive model of food access for the first-century Roman East. The model sustains the argument of this study by providing a paradigm to evaluate the effect of positive and negative practices on the availability of food for the lower socio-economic segments of the population. As an example of this evaluative approach, I use the model to demonstrate the uneven effects on food access that might have occurred for different rural and urban groups as a result of Roman military presence in Antioch.

Chapter 4, "Most People Could Eke Out a Living," substantiates the claim that the majority of the people in the first century were able to eke out a bare subsistence-level living, but only because they practiced survival mechanisms. The glaring exception of survival is the occurrence of severe shortage conditions caused by drought, locust, or war. I begin the chapter with a discussion of what constitutes subsistence-level living. I argue that the diets could be healthy theoretically, and the prevalence of malnutrition in the first century indicates the problem must lie in consuming enough foods and foods containing the needed proteins, carbohydrates, vitamins, and minerals. I engage the emerging work on categorization of the population with respect to resources for subsistence living and argue that the majority of the households lived close to subsistence level (that is, they could eke out sufficient food). My argument concerns practices that the Gospel critiques. I describe the survival practices and safety nets employed by both rural and urban households in the lower socio-economic segments of the population. I draw together the data related to categories of people who were at risk and the data about survival mechanisms. I demonstrate that the lower socio-economic segments of the population not only had fewer resources, they had limited survival mechanisms. Hence, the majority of the population was living precariously and, if their survival mechanisms failed, they would fall below subsistence-level living.

Chapter 5, "The Trauma of Experienced Food Shortages is Reflected in the Gospel," argues the third claim. Having argued that food shortages were a problem in general, I turn to the question of whether the Matthean community would have experienced food shortages and the effect such shortages might have had on the identity of the community. I posit that a specific Matthean community existed. I argue that the city of Antioch is a good candidate for the location and I date the finalization of the gospel to c. 80—c. 100 CE. I show that the Matthean community would have experienced situations in Antioch of both endemic and extreme food shortages. Assuming the Matthean community would reflect the general society of Antioch, its members would have experienced impaired access to food. This painful experience caused them to address the questions raised at the beginning of this chapter. "Who has the power and desire to provide sufficient food for the people?" "Is the Emperor or God the true *paterfamilias*?" "What does God expect of us to be members of God's family?" The answers to these questions are found in the Gospel narrative.

Chapter 6, "Not Enough Food and the Dominant Entitlement System," brings together practices in the first-century Roman East that were causing people to slip below subsistence level and the critique of Matthew's gospel of those practices. In this society, ownership of land and control of crop selection were the two most important pieces of production of the necessary amounts of food. The second most important factor in society relative to food access was distribution practices. Distribution is about power. I describe the two entitlement systems: dominant and local (peasant), under which practices are condoned and supported. I discuss these topics to lay the groundwork for the ensuing arguments. I use three scenarios from the first century to delineate practices and attitudes that affected two of the most important safety mechanisms for the lower socio-economic segments of the population. The scenarios are (1) polyculture (Matt 25:24–46), (2) grain storage taking food away from people (Matt 6:19—17:12), and (3) the release of stored grain in more severe food shortages (Matt 14:13–21; 15:29–38). I describe the effect the practices had on food access, and then examine the responses the Gospel makes to the situations depicted in the three scenarios.

Chapter 7, "Not Enough Food and Social Safety Networks (Matt 19:1—20:14)," is a continuation of chapter 6 with the focus shifting to the breakdown of reciprocal relationships between peasants, which had been the primary survival mechanism. I argue that the context of Matt 19 suggests a scenario of food shortages, perhaps due to increased taxes or rents, which was pressuring people to keep what few resources they have for themselves and not share with needier neighbors. I examine the Gospel and its message concerned with practices of disciples doing the will of a just God in this more acutely negative environment.

Chapter 8, "It is Important that No One Goes Hungry," explicates the final claim that access to sufficient food was a substantial embodiment of the realm of the heavens in the Gospel. The crux of my argument demonstrates the food-access passages in Matthew participate in its revelation of Jesus' realm of the heavens. I connect the references with the narrative flow of the Gospel to demonstrate how Matthew used the concept of access to sufficient food as one marker to distinguish the realm of the heavens from the dominant entitlement system. First, I briefly link the Savior-Immanuel commission in Matthew's gospel (Matt 1:21–23) to three questions that I propose the Gospel rhetoric will answer through the course of its narrative. Second, the majority of this chapter examines both the teachings and actions related to everyone having sufficient food that are portrayed in the Gospel. I examine the narrative and the role that passages addressing food-access issues play in the context of the narrative rhetoric and the realm of the heavens.[72] Lastly, I summarize the topic of food access in the narrative blocks.

Chapter 9, "Concluding Remarks" summarizes the major findings of this study's argument.

Concluding Remarks

The idea that the Gospel deals with the first-century reality that people were going hungry, and perhaps even starving to death, due to oppressive and exploitative practices is not new.[73] What sets my argument apart from current Matthean research is that it concentrates on the pragmatic practices concerned with all people having enough food to sustain life. Any previous analyses that dealt with practices rarely addressed those practices that helped provide access to food. The helpful practices are important in that they form part of the embodied vision that the Gospel declared in its counter-vision of the realm of the heavens.[74] The study provides a pragmatic lens and a model

---

72. Carter, "Challenging by Confirming, Renewing by Repeating: The Parables of 'the Reign of the Heavens' in Matthew 13 as Embedded Narratives," 399–400; Gowler, *What Are They Saying About the Parables?* Many of the passages related to food access are parables, and one needs to take special attention with respect to the studies on parables and on their context within the Gospel. See Carter and Gowler for preliminary discussions of positions and bibliography of this topic and Carter for a sample analysis of the parables in Matt 13. The emphasis on pragmatics of this study moves my parable interpretations away from allegorical, and to some extent, away from metaphorical unless metaphor is obvious.

73. One example is Carter, *The Roman Empire and the New Testament*, 46.

74. Carter, "Matthew's Gospel: An Anti-Imperial/Imperial Reading," 425–29. Carter

to use when analyzing passages concerned with the life-and-death issue of the first-century Matthean community, or any other Christian gospel community. Does a person have enough food to sustain physical life?

---

offers a synopsis of some of his previous works on this topic. He states his hypothesis at the beginning, "Matthew's plot is an act of imperial negotiation." He identifies general areas that affect access to food such as elite-entitlement structures (425) and banquets of the aristocracy excluding those whom God through Jesus feeds (428–29). "Land, the basis of life in an agrarian empire, will be returned to the powerless (5:5, citing Psalm 37)" (426). Carter speaks directly to the consequences of insufficient food and the expected reversal "when God's empire is fully established." (427) His analysis is an overview and identifies the themes within his six-part structure. He does not deal with specific practices.

2

Contextualized Interpretation

THE ARGUMENT, STATED IN chapter 1 concerning the Gospel of Matthew's advocacy for a society in which all have access to sufficient food, involves analyzing the critique the Gospel makes of practices that limit or enhance access to food. It is important to understand both the first-century imperial context of the Gospel, as well as the characteristics of the methods used to uncover and explain the Gospel's critique. Vernon Robbins developed a framework, which he calls socio-rhetorical interpretation (SRI) to bring together social context and rhetorical analysis. He contends that SRI "integrates the ways people use language with the ways they live in the world."[1] By focusing on values, convictions, and beliefs found both in texts and in the actual world, SRI provides strategies and tools for scholars to interpret the New Testament as a discourse within the first-century Mediterranean society. In this chapter, I narrow the focus to issues related to using SRI to interpret the Gospel of Matthew in light of practices that helped and hindered the ability of people in the lower socio-economic segments of the population (PS 5 and below) to have access consistently to sufficient food. This narrowing of the focus places on SRI more stringent requirements for understanding the first-century social context.

This chapter describes and discusses the two principal methodological aspects of my study: a descriptive model and SRI. I begin by describing what I understand when I assert that the Gospel is a rhetorical artifact. I briefly argue that the primary social context is the Roman empire. I then present an overview of SRI as it developed into a methodology capable of analyzing the critique across the full Gospel narrative. Finally, I discuss

1. Robbins, *Exploring the Texture*, 1.

whether a model such as the one presented in chapter 3 is an appropriate tool for biblical studies.

The Gospel of Matthew Is a Rhetorical Artifact

The Matthean community was trying to make sense of the Jesus event for itself, through what I consider its foundational story[2] based on the social memory of the life—practices, teaching, and character—of Jesus, the Christ[3] and his enemies.[4] Human beings need to find some sort of order in their world. They create a symbolic world[5] through a system of tales and traditions, called myths,[6] which reinforce that perceived and desired order.[7] The myths last as long as they are meaningful to the community.[8] Sociological studies using small group cultures, similar to what might have been found in the first-century Roman East, demonstrate that kinship myth stories function as a strategy of social control for the kinship group.[9] Elizabeth Stone writes, "families believe in their myths for reasons more compelling than respect for the versatility of metaphor. What the family tells us has a force and power that we never leave behind. What they tell us is our first syntax, our first grammar, the foundation onto which we

---

2. Dunn, "Jesus in Oral Memory," 306; Talbert, *What Is a Gospel?*, 105, 106; Talbert, *Matthew*, 9. While not referring to the gospels as foundational stories, Dunn's description indicates that they were foundational stories. He writes, "They were the lifeblood of the communities in which they were told and retold. What Jesus did was important to these communities for their own continuing identity" (Dunn, "Jesus in Oral Memory," 306). Talbert refers to the gospels as cult documents and myths of origin.

3. Carter, "Community Definition and Matthew's Gospel," 637.

4. Weber, "Plot and Matthew," 418.

5. Ausband, *Myth and Meaning, Myth and Order*, 6. Ausband says that most members of the community treated seriously their myths that they believe convey truly the understanding by the community of its history and the natural world.

6. Burke, "Colloquy," 64; Geertz, *The Interpretation of Cultures*, 5. Burke asserts that sometimes humans are a rational animal. All the time humans are a symbol-using animal. Geertz writes, "Man is an animal suspended in webs of significance he himself has spun."

7. Carpenter, *History as Rhetoric*, 6. Carpenter asserts that humans are by nature narrative beings and have an inherent awareness of whether the stories they hear are coherent with their life stories.

8. Stone, *Black Sheep and Kissing Cousins*, 5.

9. Ibid., 101; Langellier and Peterson, "Family Storytelling as Social Control," 50–56; McFeat, *Small-Group Cultures*, 9: "The major dimensions of interaction so far identified are frequency, duration, and direction. From these we expect certain effects in behavior in persons who have been grouping . . . With the repetition of events, persons who group should show evidence of attitude changes which tend to become positive toward one another and behavior changes should be similar among them."

later add our own perceptions and modifications. We are not entirely free to challenge the family's beliefs as we might challenge any other system of beliefs. And even when we do challenge, we half believe ourselves."[10] Instead of a list of rules to follow, the group constructs a narrative with an important individual to emulate. In developing its distinctive legacy, a community remembers, exaggerates, or forgets[11] stories to help its members understand its present conditions.[12] A community hands down stories because the stories matter. The stories disappear when they are no longer germane.[13] The truth of the stories is not as important as encouraging belief in a shared truth.[14] A narrative helps community members make sense out of their experience because the narrative portrays an experience similar to theirs in terms of people making decisions, taking actions and causing things to happen.[15] The narrative permits people to assign motives and responsibility, praise and blame, and arouse feelings.[16] The stories tell what acceptable behavior and roles are and how to relate to community members and to outsiders by giving significance and meaning to events that happened to the community.[17]

10. Stone, *Black Sheep and Kissing Cousins*, 101.

11. Zerubavel, *Social Mindscapes*, 84; Butler, *Memory: History, Culture, and the Mind*, 18. In speaking about invention and memory, Butler notes that features of a memory are filed generically, i.e., abstracted, and then under similar emotional conditions the memory is revived and "acts synecdochically, restoring the whole."

12. Halbwachs, *On Collective Memory*, 38; Burke, "History as Social Memory," 104. In discussing why some myths stick and others do not, Burke observes that the fit of the story with the auditor's situation leads to the story being circulated orally. During this phase, the normal functions of distortion—leveling and sharpening—take place.

13. Scott, *Arts of Resistance*, 160–61; In a similar vein to Scott's work, Hodgkin and Radstone "Introduction: Contested Pasts," 5, write, "The idea of memory as a tool with which to contest 'official' versions of the past, too, shifts from an opposition between the subordinate truth versus the dominant lie, to a concern with the ways in which particular versions of an event may be at various times and for various reasons promoted, reformulated, or silenced. This is not to deny that the dominant versions of the past are inextricably entangled with relations of power in society, but rather to refocus the question around the many ways in which conflict and contest emerge."

14. Stone, *Black Sheep and Kissing Cousins*, 5–7.

15. Carpenter, *History as Rhetoric*, 6; Cohen, *The Symbolic Construction of Community*, 17–21. Cohen argues that the meaning of observed behavior comes through interpretation and interpretations can vary among members of the group. He continues, "The triumph of community is to so contain this variety that its inherent discordance does not subvert the apparent coherence which is expressed by its boundaries" (ibid. 20).

16. Bormann, "Symbolic Convergence," 104.

17. "Attitudes and actions are molded by a matrix of message inputs, many of which are 'unorganized' and 'overlay' to form a complex communication 'mosaic' which

Arguing that the Gospel of Matthew is a rhetorical artifact implies that the author(s) intended to influence its community toward certain practices, attitudes, and values and away from others.[18] I suggest that the Gospel lets the community know what makes one a good community member and what processes to follow in situations of food shortages.[19] The gospel in its entirety, not just the teaching sections, is a rhetorical artifact. The gospel presents stories about the life and ministry of Jesus and stories about early disciples and followers and opposition groups as models of proper and improper behaviors. The Gospel's popularity then and now counters any notion that it had no effect on its auditors.

The Gospel conveyed to the community how it should negotiate the imperial world. Simultaneously, the Gospel described the new realm of the heavens with its particular values and practices related to people having access to food. The two worlds overlapped with the principal difference being that in the realm of the heavens everyone had sufficient food.

The Context for the Matthean Community is the Roman Empire

In chapter 5, I will argue that the Jesus portrayed in the Gospel of Matthew is a product of the Matthean community's understanding of and reaction to their societies'—Jewish and Roman—outlooks, values, and behaviors.[20]

---

consist of an immense number of fragments or bits of information on an immense number of topics. These are scattered over time and space in modes of communication. Each individual must grasp from this mosaic those bits which serve his needs, must group them into message sets which are relevant for him at any given time . . . and close the gap between them in order to arrive at a coherent picture of the world to which he can respond" (Carpenter, *History as Rhetoric*, 7).

18. Wuellner, "Where Is Rhetorical Criticism Taking Us?," 449; Kennedy, *Interpretation through Rhetorical Criticism*, 3. Kennedy asserts that all religious systems are rhetorical. By extension, one might say that all religious texts are rhetorical.

19. Beardslee, "Saving One's Life by Losing It," 58; Weber, "Plot and Matthew," 415–19. Beardslee argues that proverbs, paradoxes, and hyperbole helped point to ways the community members were to shape their lives. Weber argues repeatedly that the strong plot line in the gospel "makes its own readers characters in the narrative" whose *transformation* to live its demands will be judged from a teleogical perspective by Jesus who may be a hostile antagonist to their complacency.

20. Scholars do not dispute this assumption dealing with the gospel in its first-century context. See for example, Vermès, *Jesus the Jew*; Horsley, "Jesus Movements and the Renewal of Israel," 31; Rhoads, "The Political Jesus: Can There Be Any Other?"; Oakman, *Jesus and the Economic Questions*, 2: "Jesus' values and behavior were formulated, therefore, within a unique set of experiences and aimed to a certain extent at overcoming the socially destructive effects of maldistributed wealth and differential control over material goods that existed in early Roman Palestine."

Some of the material that refers to food-access issues is in the form of parables and is metaphorical.[21] Nevertheless, my argument assumes the scenarios presented in the parables bear some consonance with real-life structures and practices.[22] As I argue in chapter 4, inadequate access to sufficient food was too serious a reality for a sizeable portion of the population in the first century to soften this reality by relegating it to symbol alone. Parables and metaphors would not have been effective if they did not portray situations that auditors commonly encountered and understood. Approaching some texts pragmatically is difficult because the long reception history more often spiritualizes and dematerializes the stories and casts them in terms of an individual relationship with Jesus,[23] rather than understands them as a community's response to its current material issues. Against this position, I assert that the Matthean texts critique actual processes and practices that some of the early hearers of the stories would have painfully experienced.

The Roman Empire as a primary context, kept in the foreground, is essential to the argument of this study. I argue in chapters 6 and 7 that major economic[24] and power dynamics of imperial Roman times shaped the responses to food shortages seen in the Gospel.

Socio-Rhetorical Interpretation

Within his framework of multiple approaches, Robbins defines what he calls *textures*: *Inner, Inter, Social and Cultural, Ideological*, and *Sacred*. Each texture has an associated method and a lens to employ when analyzing the Gospel of Matthew. Robbins does not specify a particular ordering of textures for analysis, and in practice, the process is cyclic. He describes this process as "spiraling repetition." A preliminary close reading of the text (the Inner Texture) helps form the preliminary hypotheses being explored in the more general textures. When one returns to the close reading, the analysis may have nuances arising from new insights of the general textures, which may lead again to a need to modify the analysis of the more general

21. Fernandez, *Persuasions and Performances*, 58. Fernandez argues that the cross-referencing nature of metaphors assists in integration and a sense of wholeness in the group. The more the metaphors are shared, the higher the integration.

22. Oakman, *Jesus and the Economic Questions*, 2–4; Goulder, *Midrash and Lection in Matthew*, 57. Goulder would argue against this position as he sees the parables as being consistently allegorical.

23. Carter, "How Would Jesus Eat? Matthew." Source is a pre-publication version.

24. Oakman, *Jesus and the Economic Questions*, 2. Oakman examines many of the economic issues leading to food shortage situations.

texture.[25] Below I briefly outline the approach taken by Robbins to each of the textures.

The *Inner Texture* analysis examines "the ways a text employs language to communicate."[26] It involves a close reading of the text, paying attention to word patterns found in the text such as repetitions, progressions, and boundary markers,[27] as well as identifying whose voices are heard along with argumentation patterns.[28] For example, Jeffrey Reed argues knowledge of Koine Greek usage of various classes of connector words can help the interpreter discern shifts in the discourse.[29] Roland Meynet supports Robbins by arguing that New Testament scholars need to be aware of biblical rhetoric and its forms. He observes that exegetes have always done close readings, but usually not in a manner based on ancient forms.

The *Inter Texture* brings together the text with material known about the outside world.[30] Originally, Robbins formulated the goal as investigating how the text differs from, or conforms to, the outside world of conventional literary forms found in Jewish and Greco-Roman traditions. Since his initial formulation of the method, Robbins has advocated for using more than literary forms, particularly oral forms.[31] I agree with his argument to consider oral forms, but he argues unconvincingly that early Christians replaced the common rhetorical forms with their own.[32] I will remain with the original formulation of this texture.[33]

---

25. Robbins, "The Rhetorical Full-Turn in Biblical Interpretation," 58; Malina, "Intepretation: Reading, Abduction, Metaphor," 256–60.

26. Robbins, *The Invention of Christian Discourse*, 1, xiii.

27. Meynet, *Rhetorical Analysis*, 172–77, 309.

28. Robbins, *Exploring the Texture*, 21–23. Robbins describes a generic way to analyze arguments. As an alternative, I would suggest the rhetorical criticism technique developed by Stephen Toulmin and expanded by other scholars. It is much more complete while remaining straightforward. Toulmin, *The Uses of Argument*; Brockriede and Ehninger, "Toulmin on Argument"; Hitchcock, "Good Reasoning on the Toulmin Model"; Reed and Rowe, "Translating Toulmin Diagrams."

29. Reed, "Cohesiveness of Discourse," 32–37. The Inner Texture level of Robbins's SRI does not explicitly mention a need to know anything about first-century Greek to execute this analysis, but one would assume the scholar is working in the Greek.

30. Robbins, *Exploring the Texture*, 40.

31. Robbins, "The Rhetorical Full-Turn in Biblical Interpretation," 57; Robbins, *The Invention of Christian Discourse*, 1, xxiii, 9–13.

32. Robbins, *The Invention of Christian Discourse*, 1, 2, 14–17, 61–63.

33. Kennedy, *Classical Rhetoric & Its Christian & Secular Tradition from Ancient to Modern Times*; Kennedy, *Interpretation through Rhetorical Criticism*, chap. 2, chap. 4. Kennedy, a scholar of first-century rhetoric, has written about the rhetorical forms found in the New Testament. In particular, he has performed analyses of Matthean texts based on ancient forms. He concluded the Sermon on the Mount is deliberative

The Inter Texture is similar to the Inner Texture, but it involves analyzing larger sections of the text. Pulling together the analyses from Inner and Inter Textures, one would have a good sense of the structure and style of the passage. Duane Watson argues that using methods to reveal structure and style could have the side benefit of uncovering social and cultural presuppositions informing the structures and styles.[34] Using these textures, one can uncover subtleties of the original arguments, which analyzing the text from modern linguistic patterns would not produce.[35]

The *Social and Cultural Texture* addresses how the text characterizes the world (that is, what types of social and cultural worlds the text evoked).[36] The texture also deals with what the text says is specifically needed to live in the world, or to change the world. The Roman world in which the Matthean community lived affected what it wrote, as well as the examples and metaphors it used to describe a desired new world. Analysis using the model described in chapter 3 helps to show where the text is affirming, challenging, or re-inscribing the first-century practices depicted by and for the Matthean community.[37] One of the strengths of socio-rhetorical criticism, comes from its attention to phenomena outside of the text[38] that interacts or contextualizes the text.[39] The approach values the perceived original situation of the text and the responses the intended auditors might have made to the text.

---

rhetoric, and Matt 21:23—23:39 is judicial rhetoric.

34. Watson, "Why We Need Socio-Rhetorical Commentary and What It Might Look Like," 143.

35. Bednarz, "Humor-Neutics: Analyzing Humor and Humor Functions in the Synoptic Gospels." Bednarz developed a model of first-century humor and analyzed passages from the gospels. Being alert to the subtleties of Greco-Roman humor, she developed interpretations that differed from the traditional interpretations for passages previously overlooked as having humor elements in them.

36. Robbins, *Exploring the Texture*, 71.

37. Watson, "Why We Need Socio-Rhetorical Commentary and What It Might Look Like," 144.

38. The term *text* for post-modernists includes all artifacts in the society contributing to the discourse under discussion. In that sense, any external phenomena would automatically be included as part of the text. Indeed, that is entirely true but such a broad reach would obfuscate my research. In the rest of this document, the term text is used in its normal sense of referring to the received documents. For an example of the philosophical issues related to the term *text*, see Phillips, "History and Text: The Reader in Context in Matthew's Parables Discourse."

39. Robbins, *Exploring the Texture*, 36. Robbins draws from Malina, *New Testament World*.

The *Ideological Texture* opens up the dialog between the interpreter and her readers by foregrounding her background, opinions, and biases.[40] It also deals with the ideology of the passage. Previous scholars have dealt extensively with this texture. Itumeleng Mosala independently suggested a need for the ideological texture.[41] Watson writes that the meaning comes from "analyzing the social and cultural location of the implied author through social and cultural data built into the language of the text, analyzing the ideology of power in the text, and analyzing the ideology in the mode of intellectual discourse in the text."[42] I will address the effects of the ideology of power in the form of practices undergirded by the dominant entitlement system as the text comments on them.

The *Sacred Texture* examines how the text conveys information about the relationship of the holy to humankind.[43] The items of interest in this texture—the deity, spirits, holy persons, divine history, human redemption and human commitment, and ethics in the religious community[44]—are often embedded in the other textures. Given my emphasis on the pragmatic, one might think this texture is unimportant. However, Matthew depicts God frequently sanctioning practices and teachings through quotations of sacred scripture, through voices, or through entities from heaven. Hence, while my argument emphasizes the pragmatic, the sacred is still present and plays an important role by sanctioning practices related to people having enough to eat.

---

40. Robbins, *Exploring the Texture*, 95. It is no accident that this study deals with a pragmatic issue. I grew up in a tradition in which biblical study was to inform both who God and Jesus are and who I am to be in values, attitudes, and behaviors. During my formative lay Bible teaching period, a major emphasis was social gospel as exemplified in the Hebrew prophets whose message was that God demanded just practices as the key to a righteous relationship with God. My theology evolved into a covenant theology, which requires me to live my faith and beliefs pragmatically in response to what I perceive to be God's desires for God's world and my place in the bringing about that world. Exposure to strange customs described in the biblical text made plain to me that understanding the biblical text would require knowledge of the ancient cultures. Subsequent seminary training brought this point into clearer focus, and so began my interest in archeological, anthropological, and social scientific descriptions of the biblical periods. Lastly, my experience in the computer science field frequently involved the generation of models to explore and explain real-life activities. While the types of models used in biblical research are qualitatively different from computer-based modeling, I lean toward the use of models as explanatory devices.

41. Mosala, "Social Scientific Approaches to the Bible," 65.

42. Watson, "Why We Need Socio-Rhetorical Commentary and What It Might Look Like," 147.

43. Robbins, *Exploring the Texture*, chap. 5.

44. Watson, "Why We Need Socio-Rhetorical Commentary and What It Might Look Like," 149.

The goal of the multiple methods is to bring the insights afforded by one particular exegetical method into the analysis of another method that is applied to the same biblical text (for example, literary, social-scientific, rhetorical, postmodern, and theological criticisms[45]). Such synergism enables a more robust understanding of the topic under examination. Each exegetical method produces questions and insights that another method would not normally generate. Struggling to answer a question from one method with another method (that is, crossing its boundary), provides nuances to the answer and can afford fresh insights into the passage.

Despite its strengths, I do not find SRI, as initially formulated in 1996, to be robust enough on the rhetorical side. SRI deals with rhetoric, but more from the perspective of rhetorical forms employed by the biblical author than by looking at the way the author builds the argument across the narrative. Analyzing the Gospel rhetorically requires looking at the message of the Gospel, not just the forms of its arguments. My sentiments echo those of J. David Amador. He presents a very thought-provoking critique of rhetorical practices found in biblical studies through 1996, which still applies for the most part. He begins by lamenting that tunnel vision is the state of affairs within biblical studies despite the plethora of rhetorical criticism techniques available outside of biblical studies. He writes that there is a "monotonous/monolithic dominance of a particular constellation of methodological assumptions governing nearly the entire production of rhetorical-critical activity"[46] restricted to ancient rhetorical models within biblical studies. Rhetorical analysis has remained primarily an identification of form and not an analysis of the message to the auditors. Such work on forms is not sufficient, although an analysis of ancient rhetorical forms is a precursor to all other analyses[47] since techniques that were persuasive in the first-century Roman East are not necessarily in use today.[48] While Armador argues against work that deals pointedly with the otherness of the first century in its interpretation,[49] he would most probably agree with using a more broadly based rhetorical criticism to analyze a gospel that was, and is, aimed at evoking response of action in its auditors.[50]

45. Robbins, *Exploring the Texture*, 1–2.
46. Amador, *Academic Constraints in Rhetorical Criticism*, 25.
47. Meynet, *Rhetorical Analysis*, 309.
48. Hariman, "The Forum: Norms of Rhetorical Criticism," 332.
49. Referring to Vernon Robbins, Amador says, "he falls into the trap of every interpreter by assuming that it is this 'foreign-ness' that should become the object of interpretation and the foundation of further reception of the text" (Amador, *Academic Constraints in Rhetorical Criticism*, 201).
50. "[T]here is no good reason for excluding *a priori* any rhetorical theory as

Robbins has continued to develop his method since its initial formulation in 1996.⁵¹ In a publication in the same year, he advocated a move from the more form-based rhetorical criticism, such as the nature of the *chreia*, to engage the "complete situation" of the narrative.⁵² I will argue in chapter 5 that the Matthean community was trying to make sense of the Jesus event for itself based on its social memory of the life of Jesus, the Christ. The gospel was its foundational story and showed the community how Jesus would have expected the community members to respond to current events. To address the Matthean message concerning food access, I approach the Gospel as a complete narrative by arguing that the Matthean community understood the realm of the heavens to be a place where everyone had enough to eat, which was not the case in the Roman world. Examining the complete narrative in the sense of SRI is best accomplished by using rhetorical narrative analysis.

Several scholars have examined Matthew's Gospel from a narrative perspective.⁵³ Warren Carter and F. J. Matera based their examinations on Seymour Chatman's approach. Carter writes that Chatman's approach to plot with its emphasis on the arrangement of the scenes—episodes—is appropriate for analyzing a first-century biographical narrative.⁵⁴ Chatman's underlying premise is that plot is about declining or narrowing

---

potentially useful [a concept (pre?-) determined by the critic him/herself] for analysis of these ancient texts" (ibid., 44).

51. Robbins, *Exploring the Texture*; Robbins, "Narrative in Ancient Rhetoric and Rhetoric in Ancient Narrative," 373–82. In the latter reference, Robbins applied his expanded method to a narrative analysis to parts of Luke-Acts.

52. "A careful reading of the Gospels, in fact, makes clear that they are multicultural; they merge biblical patterns with Hellenistic patterns and conventions. This multicultural context is essential for understanding the words and actions of Jesus as portrayed in the Gospels and, therefore, for the study of the historical Jesus himself. The recognition of the chreia form, for example, has significant implications for the study of the New Testament in general and the Synoptic Gospels in particular" (Gowler, "The Chreia," 132). Work like Gowler's provides the infrastructure scholarship on which higher-level arguments rely.

53. "It is important at the outset of this section to address the nature of the relationship between plot and structure. Structure is not equivalent to plot. In literary diagnosis structure does not entail characters in any direct way nor does it elucidate conflict . . . Analyzing structure, then, is a step in delineating a plot but it is not equivalent to plot" (Branden, *Satanic Conflict and the Plot of Matthew*, 90). Branden argues that all other subplots can be argued under the general plot of Jesus in conflict with Satan.

54. Carter, "Structure of Matthew's Gospel," 466. I would add that while structure is not the same as plot, being mindful of the extensive analyses of Greek grammatical features that contribute to the structure of the Gospel is a good check on any proposed narrative structure.

possibilities, which limits choices. Events that drive this narrowing are more important than events that fill in details. He calls the important events *kernels* and the events that fill in details *satellites*.[55] Kernels push the plot along by raising and satisfying questions and serve as branching points. Kernels cannot be deleted without destroying the logic of the narrative since there are causality relationships between them.[56] Kernels are "the real properties of plots; they exist, may be isolated, and should be named."[57] Finally, the plot organizes kernels and satellites into *narrative blocks*.[58] The narrative critic identifies narrative blocks, kernels, and satellites intuitively as the critic reads and re-reads the narrative. The intuitive nature of the process may lead to non-consensus on the kernels and narrative blocks. For example, both Carter and Matera identify kernels and their narrative blocks, but their lists only have some overlap in their definitions.[59] I find Carter's selection to be more suited to the arguments of this study, although as will become evident in chapter 8, we differ on the questions we identify for the various kernels and their corresponding narrative blocks. Differences could be expected since I am concentrating on food-access issues.

Not all scholars who do narrative analysis follow the approach of Matera and Carter. David Howell references Chatman, but develops his plot based on temporal ordering. For example, he argues that prolepses advance the plot and intensify the drama. A prolepsis is a passage that narrates or evokes an event that takes place later in the story line.[60] Janice Anderson argues that Chatman's approach is somewhat lacking when the narrative plot is less linear and contains subplots, parallelism, anticipation and retrospection, redundancy, and chiastic structures.[61] Robert Longacre uses a non-Chatman approach

55. Chatman, *Story and Discourse*, 53.
56. Ibid., 44, 53.
57. Ibid., 94.
58. Carter, "Structure of Matthew's Gospel," 467.
59. Ibid., 472–80.
60. Howell, *Matthew's Inclusive Story*, 96–110. There are two aspects of the text: story and narrative. The story depicts characters acting, speaking, and relating to one another. The narrative supplies information that the characters are not privy to but the auditors, and implied readers, are told. Further, the ordering of the two aspects is different. For example, the passion predictions are propelses since in the story the actual passion events occur near the end. The narrative refers to a genealogy whose events are not in the story line at all.
61. Anderson, *Matthew's Narrative Web*. Anderson discusses plot in terms of temporal arrangement of the episodes, the motivation for the events being where they are in the story, and the pragmatic effects of the first two plot aspects on the reader. She

when analyzing gospel plots based on a narrative template. The template includes: (1) stage, (2) inciting incidence, (3) mounting tension, (4) climax, (5) denouement, and (6) closure, with the possible addition of (7) lessening tension and (8) final suspense.[62] His method addresses portions of a story that show increased detail, which he calls *action peaks*. He posits the companion *didactic peaks*.[63] The technique goes into more detail than is appropriate for the limited argument made in chapter 8. His technique has the potential to address recursiveness, chiasms, and multi-level sub-plots better than the Chatman approach. However, I will follow generally the Chatman approach, while remaining alert to summaries and to redundancies. I limit my analysis to plot and the role that access to food fits into the Gospel's development of its plot regarding Immanuel.

Charles Talbert identified the Gospel as having a number of traits of ancient biographical narratives that undergird an analysis based on an Immanuel theme (chapter 8 below). He places ancient narratives into categories depending on the perspectives of ancient rhetoricians based on five argumentation forms. (Type A) An epideictic biography presents a person's life as a pattern to copy. (Type B) One type of judicial biography counters false accusations about a person and provides the true model. (Type C) Another type of judicial biographical exposes and discredits a false person. (Type D) One type of deliberative biography uses the true tradition of the founder as a pattern to copy. (Type E) Another deliberative biography provides a hermeneutical key for the teacher's doctrine.[64] Talbert says all the gospels have a similarity with Type B, but he types Matthew more as a Type E,[65] a point of view that I find convincing although I see Type D also present in the Gospel.

The uses of ancient biographies offer insight into the rhetoric and possible specific purpose of Matthew's Gospel. Talbert writes that when both the life and teachings of a founder were brought together, it was usually to legitimate the founder's stance on an issue.[66] Particularly germane to the

---

argues that the plot moves forward with the interaction of Jesus with various characters or groups of characters. She argues that the "plotted, temporal arrangement of the story" affects anticipation and retrospection of the reader (143).

62. Longacre, "A Top-Down, Template-Driven Narrative Analysis," 141.

63. Ibid., 141–42.

64. Talbert, *What Is a Gospel?*, 92–109, 124–27; Robbins, "Narrative in Ancient Rhetoric and Rhetoric in Ancient Narrative," 368–69; Burridge, *What Are the Gospels? A Comparison with Graeco-Roman Biographies*; Carter, "Community Definition and Matthew's Gospel." As will be noted in the discussion in chapter 5, Burridge and Carter both see Matthew as biographical narrative.

65. Talbert, *What Is a Gospel?*, 92, 108.

66. Neyrey, *Honor and Shame in the Gospel of Matthew*, 78–83. Neyrey argues that

plot of Matthew is Talbert's observation that presenting only the words of a founder without presenting his actions would have been regarded as invalid or trustworthy.[67] Also germane to the argument in chapter 8 is Talbert's examination of Philo's work on the *Life of Moses* (Type E) with its juxtaposition of the life with the teaching (legislation). Talbert compares it to the Hellenistic concept of the ideal king. In this concept, an ideal man (that is, the topic of the biography) becomes the incarnation of both the spirit and purpose of the law. Hence, under this rubric, Jesus' life became the paradigm for the Law.[68] Jesus is the incarnation of the spirit and purpose for living in God's world as encapsulated in the Law. Jesus is Immanuel, whose life is the paradigm for the Law of the new realm of the heavens. The Law of the new realm of the heavens becomes an extension of the Hebrew Law given at Sinai (Matt 5:17).

To recap, SRI enables the correlation of different views supported by different methods, but not the robust integration as Robbins originally claimed. In a recent book from 2009, Robbins admits to the difficulty of integration but asserts that it is still a goal.[69] Gregory Bloomquist argues that correlation is the most that can happen.[70] He poses the question, "If socio-rhetorical analysis is to be more than a bringing together of a variety of existing models for a kind of ongoing dialogue among them and to become in itself 'an interpretive analytics', what is required?" He argues that employing SRI will not produce one meaning for a passage since each phase has its own view. Bloomquist cautions against privileging any texture. He writes:

> [F]or the picture of correlation of textures that I am left with is less one of linear ascent through starting with one privileged texture and moving on to the next and more one of juggling, whereby the balls in the air, while clearly and carefully ordered, cannot be said to be in relation to one another in only one, linear fashion or only occupying one space at one time. If we could somehow conceive of a juggler expanding his juggling with spirals, ever larger and wider, we would have a perfect image.[71]

Matthew, as a product of a honor-shame culture, would have been familiar with the *encomium*, which was a speech of praise used often on memorials and at public ceremonies. Consequently, the gospel glorifies Jesus in a similar manner to the *encomium*.

67. Talbert, *What Is a Gospel?*, 92–96, 109.
68. Ibid., 102–4.
69. Robbins, *The Invention of Christian Discourse*, 1, 6.
70. Bloomquist, "Possible Direction for Correlation in Socio-Rhetorical Analysis," 64–68.
71. Ibid., 62, 94.

Robbins would agree with Bloomquist when he argues that while an interpreter may not employ each of the textures, she should at least employ two textures since each texture by itself only brings limited insight into the text.[72]

I agree with Robbins that the social, cultural, and material world of the first century permeates the text of the Gospel of Matthew. All textures of SRI require knowledge of the first-century Roman East. Even the more text-oriented textures are prone to less robustness, if not outright misinterpretation, if the real-world context is not seriously considered. The Social and Cultural texture, in particular, concerns itself with describing how the constructed world of the text is not only informed by the external-world setting, but also might vary from it. I will argue that the Gospel narrated two worlds, namely, the Roman Empire in which the Matthean community lived and the world it believed Jesus proclaimed by word and deed. These worlds are not necessarily distinct from each other in all facets, but they do differ in at least one significant way. In one of the worlds, some people do not have enough to eat. In the other world, the members of the Matthean community are to work toward all people having enough to eat.

In summary, SRI facilitates the assessment of the Gospel critique of food access practices that were contributing to food shortages for many people. It permits the exploration of competing visions in the Gospel: realm of the heavens and the imperial realm of Rome. A basic tenant of SRI is the understanding of the social contexts of the Gospel and, particularly for this study, food access practices in the first-century Roman East. Food access processes, nevertheless, are quite complex and difficult to understand. Modeling permits the exegete to highlight salient features used in the Matthean argument.

Modeling for Clarity of Context

Attention to the Roman Empire and imperial practices is an important consideration for interpreting New Testament material. Several prominent scholars have described the imperial context and analyzed texts using that context across a rather broad spectrum of societal issues found in the gospels.[73] Matthew's gospel is firmly situated in its imperial setting and

---

72. Robbins, "Narrative in Ancient Rhetoric and Rhetoric in Ancient Narrative," 2.

73. The following references are examples of the breadth of work being done in this area of Biblical studies. Danker, *Benefactor*; Meeks, *The First Urban Christians: The Social World of the Apostle Paul*; Edwards, "Socio-Economic and Cultural Ethos of the Lower Galilee"; Freyne, "Herodian Economics in Galilee."; Carter, *Matthew and the Margins*; Cotter, "Greco-Roman Apotheosis Traditions and the Resurrection Appearances in Matthew"; Duling, "Theories, Methods, Models"; Herzog, *Jesus, Justice, and the*

portrays strategies with which to negotiate and interact with the Empire.[74] The Gospel critiques some of the wider societal practices concerning food provision positively (for example, an aristocrat provides food to the poor in Matt 19:16–30) and some negatively (for example, stockpiling grain in Matt 6:19–21). Other practices are re-inscribed to include people usually excluded from receiving food distributions (for example, the destitute at a public meal in Matt 15:32–39).

With respect to context, I make four claims: (1) the Roman Empire is the primary context, (2) primary data sources are scarce, (3) social-scientific modeling can fill the gaps caused by insufficient primary data, and (4) current models are not sufficient for the detail needed to understand food-access practices in the first-century.

Primary Data Sources Concerning Food Access Issues Are Scarce

The confluence of literary works, inscriptions,[75] and archaeological data,[76] including coins, provides a broad picture of the first-century Roman East from many perspectives. Unfortunately, a major challenge for uncovering practices that helped and hindered access to food for the Matthean community is the lack of primary sources dealing with this issue in the first century at Antioch.[77] For example, inscriptions detailing actions taken by aristocrats

---

Reign of God; Horsley, *Jesus and Empire*; Riches and Sim, *The Gospel of Matthew in Its Roman Imperial Context*; Carter, *The Roman Empire and the New Testament*.

74. Carter, "Matthew: Empire, Synagogues, and Horizontal Violence," 298–303. I argue this position in greater detail in chapters 6 and 7.

75. McLean, "Epigraphical Evidence in Caesarea Maritima," 57. McLean suggests strongly that inscriptions are valuable not only for historical events but as a window into daily life.

76. Reed, *Archaeology and the Galilean Jesus*, 214–16, uses a crossword puzzle analogy to discuss the relationship of literary sources to archaeological sources. He argues that each should be independent of the other, but together they can solve the puzzle. In particular, he argues against scholars only using archaeology to fill the lacunae of the text. Garnsey and Saller write, "Peasants do not leave monuments. Their farmsteads, built of perishable materials, have not survived" (*The Roman Empire*, 76).

77. I will argue on pp. 146–55 that Antioch is the probable location of the Matthean community.

in severe food shortages are common in Asia Minor,[78] but not for Antioch.[79] The available literary sources come from men who are writing secondhand descriptions of events,[80] from later periods,[81] or from other locations.[82] Exceptions are Josephus and the agriculturalists, particularly Columella.[83] Compounding the problem for making an argument about practices is that primary literary sources rarely deal with the lower socio-economic segments of the population.[84] Yet, one can assemble enough disparate data items to form a picture of some conditions and practices.

Extant sources are valuable because they convey some sense of the conditions of the first-century, even if imprecise.[85] For example, perhaps the number of people dying during a particular famine was not eight hundred thousand as Joshua, the Stylite,[86] described, but the reality would have been that many, many people died. The extant source is *valid* with respect to the devastation and seriousness with which people in the first century viewed famine, in this example.

The lack of primary sources for Antioch can be overcome by using sources from similar situations in the Roman East,[87] that comment on

78. Danker, *Benefactor*; Di Segni, "Dated Greek Inscriptions from Palestine"; Hands, *Charities and Social Aid in Greece and Rome*; Horsley, *New Documents*; Lehmann and Holum, *The Greek and Latin Inscriptions of Caesarea Maritima*; Lewis and Reinhold, *Roman Civilization*, 2; Llewelyn and Macquarie University, *New Documents Illustrating Early Christianity: A Review of Greek Inscriptions and Papyri Published in 1986–87*, 9; Reynolds, Beard, and Roueche, "Roman Inscriptions 1981–85"; Strubbe, "The Sitonia in the Cities of Asia Minor under the Principate."

79. Lassus, "Antioch on the Orontes," 63; Bockmuehl, *Jewish Law in Gentile Churches: Halakhah and the Beginning of Christian Public Ethics*, 51, notes that there are only two hundred inscriptions of the entire ancient history of Antioch and only one related to the Jewish community. He says the number of inscriptions is "an extraordinarily poor basis on which to assess a metropolis of Antioch's size."

80. Dio Cassius, *Hist.*; Cicero, *Off.*; Epictetus, *Discourses*; Petronius; Pliny, *Letters*; Plutarch, *Mor.*; Seneca, *Moral Essays*; Tacitus, *Ann.*

81. Libanius, *Or.*; Julianus; Eusebius, *Eccl. Hist.*; Lassus, "Antioch on the Orontes," 62, asserts that "few ancient cities are as well known from the texts as Antioch." Unfortunately, the writers are not from the first century.

82. Livy; Philo, *Spec. Leg.*; David Braund, *Augustus to Nero: A Sourcebook on Roman History, 31 BC-AD 68*. Braund catalogs papyri from Egypt.

83. Columella, *On Agriculture*; Hesiod, *Work and Days*; Theophrastus, *Enquiry into Plants*; Varro, *On Agriculture*.

84. Dio Chrysostom and Galen (second century CE) provide limited information.

85. Vaage, *Galilean Upstarts*, 3, discusses problems with social histories of the time and says they are useful for painting general pictures, but that they tend to exclude "all particular or peculiar phenomena."

86. Joshua, *The Chronicle of Joshua the Stylite*, chap. 38.

87. I limit citations to Asia Minor since sources from Gaul and Britain would

people and activities that occurred during food shortages. For example, Galilee paralleled Antioch in many features. Both were in fertile areas, on trade routes, and had strong Jewish connections. The principal differences are Antioch had a greater Roman military presence than Galilee, a greater Gentile population, and a sizeable urban center. Unlike work on Antioch, scholars have been active in analyzing the social and economic environment of Galilee. In the past thirty years, scholars have made many refinements to their descriptions of the conditions in Galilee that they derived from both literary sources and archaeological findings.[88]

To recap, while few sources are available for Antioch, many sources exist for Galilee, which had similarities to Antioch in the first century. While neither Antioch nor Galilee had many inscriptions before the second century, inscriptions do exist for other cities in Asia Minor. In the next section, I highlight sources for three areas important to a discussion of sufficient food: agricultural practices, food shortages, and diets.

Agricultural Practices

Cultivators followed particular agricultural practices that helped them to survive frequent crop failures and that provided the household with the varieties of food needed for a healthy diet. Extant sources by Hesiod, Theophrastus, Varro, and Columella provide detailed information on what

---

reflect different social and political arrangements that the Roman presence heavily influenced. The Romans ruled Gaul and Britain differently than the Levant. The Levant was already politically structured to support being ruled by an outside oppressor, and Rome delegated more power to local officials. Moreover, primary sources from the first century are preferable over earlier and later primary sources. The problem with relying on earlier and later sources is that some practices were changing that would have affected the ability of many people to have access to sufficient food. While cultivation practices did not show much variation, economic practices that affected access to food were changing.

88. Hopkins, "The City Region in Roman Palestine"; Goodman, *State and Society in Roman Galilee, A.D. 132–212*; Hamel, *Poverty and Charity in Roman Palestine*; Arav, "Bethsaida Excavations: Preliminary Report, 1994–1996"; Freyne, "Urban-Rural Relations in First-Century Galilee"; Strange, *Six Campaigns at Sepphoris: The University of South Florida Excavations, 1983–1989*; Edwards, "Socio-Economic and Cultural Ethos of the Lower Galilee"; Freyne, "Herodian Economics in Galilee"; Nagy, *Sepphoris in Galilee*; Hanson, "The Galilean Fishing Economy"; Di Segni, "Dated Greek Inscriptions from Palestine"; Freyne, *Galilee: From Alexander the Great to Hadrian*; Meyers, *Galilee through the Centuries: Confluence of Cultures*; Reed, *Archaeology and the Galilean Jesus*; Geyer, "Evidence of Flax Cultivation from the Temple-Granary Complex Et-Tell (Bethsaida/Julias)"; Chancey, *Greco-Roman Culture and the Galilee of Jesus*; Freyne, "Galilee and Judaea in the First Century," 40.

were considered best practices over several centuries.[89] These agriculturalists dealt with survival mechanisms, such as planting a diversity of crops in scattered plots, growing herbs for preserving food, storage techniques, and treatment of workers. These sources provide valuable information on practices mentioned in the Gospel. In addition, two secondary sources provide comprehensive information on practices in the circum-Mediterranean. First, Peter Garnsey provides material on agricultural production, which he derives from comparative analyses of studies of current production in similar climates.[90] Second, Peregrine Horden and Nicholas Purcell collated and synthesized numerous studies and present detailed information on agriculture practices from all over the Mediterranean region and throughout many periods.[91]

Food Shortages

While few first-century sources exist for endemic food shortages, numerous inscriptions exist in Asia Minor describing usually positive responses made by individuals to extreme food shortages.[92] Ancient authors, such as Joshua the Stylite, Josephus, Libanius, and Orosius,[93] described the affects of famines. They were not so interested in endemic food shortages experienced by households in the lower socio-economic segments of the population. Two later sources, Galen[94] and rabbinic writings, touch on endemic food shortages.

First-Century Diets

Three secondary sources provide detailed descriptions of diet, food preparation, and nutrition of the ancient world. John Wilkins and Shaun Hill

---

89. Hesiod, *Works and Days*, c. 750 to 650 BCE; Theophrastus, *Enquiry into Plants*, circa 370 BCE; Varro, *On Agriculture*, in 116–27 BCE; and Columella, *On Agriculture*, in late first century CE.

90. Garnsey, *Famine and Food Supply*; Garnsey, *Food and Society*.

91. Horden and Purcell, *The Corrupting Sea*.

92. Winter, "Responses to Corinthian Famines," 86–87. Better known inscriptions in Biblical studies are ones from Corinth from the first century that laud Tiberius Claudius Dinippus for his multiple benefactions during periods of food shortages. I provide more examples in chapter 6.

93. Joshua the Stylite, in 507 BCE; Josephus, late first century CE; Libanius, born in Antioch in 314 CE; Orosius, in early fifth century CE.

94. Galen, 129–99/217 CE.

provide a quite detailed discussion on diets of not just the aristocracy, but also rural peasants and urban non-aristocrats.[95] Joan Alcock, in addition to discussing diet-related issues, provides a good description of the eating establishments that provided food for many city dwellers.[96] Andrew Dalby identifies and defines in alphabetical order many foods and herbs used in ancient times. He also includes classical sources for each entry.[97] Moreover, later rabbinic sources from Galilee describe diets that suggest that available food was probably at, or below, subsistence level for the poorer people.

Concluding Remarks on Data Sources

In summary, I use late primary sources from Antioch and sources from the first century Galilee, when available. I supplement those few sources with material from different times or geographic areas within the Roman East. The sources provide invaluable information for selected types of food-access practices, but the data is insufficient for a comprehensive analysis of food-access practices in the first-century Roman East. Secondary sources on agricultural practices and diets are part of the solution to the problem of limited primary data for making the argument that the Gospel advocates for sufficient food for everyone. The other part of the solution lies in modeling.

Modeling Food Access in the First-Century Roman East

I have argued that the Roman Empire is the general context for the Gospel and that there is limited primary data related to food access across a spectrum of socio-economic segments of the population, especially rural households, in the first-century Roman East.[98] In this section, I argue that a well-designed model can overcome limitations in data.[99] In addition to the paucity of primary sources, two factors influence the use of modeling to present the salient conditions and features of food access. The first factor is the complexity of the web of societal practices that affected the ability of people in the lower socio-

---

95. Wilkins and Hill, *Food in the Ancient World*.
96. Alcock, *Food in the Ancient World*.
97. Dalby, *Food in the Ancient World from A to Z*.
98. Carney, *Shape of the Past*, 320–21, 317. Carney notes the difficulty with quantifiable sources for the first century. He says that analysis is still possible through well-constructed models. He suggests that existing sociological models of similar societies be used to draw inferences on the first-century situation to "patch out" the scanty data which is available.
99. Morley, *Theories, Models and Concepts in Ancient History*, 58.

economic segments of the population to acquire sufficient food. Second, first-century societies operated in quite different ways than twenty-first century western societies. Social structures, economics, kinship, and governance were different from corresponding structures now, and all affected food access. A model facilitates understanding those differences.

A person's having enough to eat is the result of a complex web of actors, decisions, and actions. The ability of a person to get enough food begins with the capabilities of the land, sea, and air to produce sufficient desired[100] and needed food items. However, sufficient food generated by natural resources was not enough to ensure that all socio-economic segments of the population actually receive enough food items to sustain life. Access to food, as discussed in chapter 1, involves who controls the production and distribution, and how they control these functions. Both *who* and *how* are intertwined in the exploitative entitlement system.[101] For now suffice it to say that the entitlement systems, and hence one's ability to gain access to sufficient food, were enmeshed in kinship, politics, economics, and status. A descriptive model of food-access processes in the first century can help untangle this complex web.[102] The model used for this study builds on the framework developed by Jack Goody, available primary sources, secondary source analyses, and existing models of pieces of the web.

In the sub-sections below, I explore briefly the benefits of pursuing this method, and note some pitfalls in the use of models. I then turn attention to the two leading classicists used by biblical scholars in modeling the imperial context of the New Testament. I examine their work and its usefulness for this study. I conclude that a new model is desirable.

The Benefits of Modeling and a Word of Caution

Thomas Carney advocates for modeling to understand the first century and contends that without a model "it would be difficult to think of all these pressures, let alone keep them all in mind."[103] Carney describes a model as follows.

---

100. "The cultural system here has its own 'cultural logic'. Only by reference to such a calculus can we explain the eating habits of, say, the Americans, who reject the flesh of horse and dog on grounds that cannot be explained by any variety of utilitarian theory" (Goody, *Cooking, Cuisine, and Class*, 32–33).

101. Entitlement systems are a topic of chapter 6.

102. Goody, *Cooking, Cuisine, and Class*, 40–48.

103. Carney, *Shape of the Past*, 21, 73.

> A model is an outline framework, in general terms, of the characteristics of a class of things or phenomena. This framework sets out the major components involved and indicates their priority of importance. It provides guidelines on how these components relate to one another. It states the range within which each component or relationship may vary. A model is something less than a theory and something more than an analogy.[104]

Scholars, using social-science criticism, support his position and go further by asserting that all biblical scholars use models, whether they are conscious of them or not.[105]

Modeling has a number of advantages along with some limitations. Carney argues that models stimulate thinking and give clarity to relationship configurations that were previously too complicated and confused, which would lead to mental overload.[106] A key for the data source situation described above is that the use of a model extends conscious control over the manner of handling the disparate data sources.[107] As a heuristic device to reduce complexity, it acts like "a pair of blinkers" by limiting the number of variables and relationships under consideration.[108] Consequently, a model cannot explain everything. Frederiksen argues that there will always be room for doubt about any model no matter how complex one makes the categories.[109] I suggest that doubt abates through repeated application of the model with positive results. I suggest that one must be mindful that models are only approximations when drawing conclusions for interpretation of a text. Moreover, modeling is an art form as there are no prescribed rules for making the leap from data to inferences.[110] New data may indicate another factor or relationship.[111] Hence, Carney insists that the use of a model is not

104. Carney, *Shape of the Past*, 7.

105. Elliott, *What Is Social-Scientific Criticism?*, chap. 4; Ling, "Virtuoso Religion and the Judean Social World," 238. Ling asserts that the value system of the researcher is always found in the researcher's model. He is correct. The point is not that his assertion is correct, but that one needs to provide some transparency with respect to one's context.

106. Carney, *Shape of the Past*, 9, 20.

107. Ibid., 4–6.

108. Ibid., 35.

109. Frederiksen, "Theory, Evidence and the Ancient Economy," 165.

110. Carney, *Shape of the Past*, 36; Moxnes, *The Economy of the Kingdom*, 23.

111. Malina, "Interpretation: Reading, Abduction, Metaphor," 259–60, discusses this process under the rubric of abduction: "Abduction is reasoning that begins with data and moves toward hypothesis with the introduction of a new idea. It is reasoning toward a hypothesis.; it deals with how a hypothesis is adopted on probation, with reasons for suggesting a hypothesis in the first place." He continues, "The verification process makes known the approximation to reality of the suggested hypothesis."

static, but is open to whether new data confirms the model, requires a shift in the model, or discards the model entirely.

Some scholars, though, are not convinced that social-scientific modeling in biblical studies is useful, but instead, see its use leading to misleading interpretations.[112] Long-standing issues and misconceptions can be categorized three ways. First, use of models predetermines results since it is hard to consider viewpoints that do not fit the model. Second, reification of pivotal social values, such as honor-shame, leads to them being assumed *a priori*. Third, the assumption is invalid that the culture controls the actions of people (that is, a static or structured model) and humans have no agency.[113] Most criticisms are without basis for correctly constructed models. The first complaint is valid if the modeler intentionally ignores data that contradicts the model. Such a scenario describes poor modeling method.[114] Instead of ignoring data that does not fit the model, the modeler adjusts the model to fit the new and emerging information.[115] Criticism of static, rigid models that portray an individual having no agency is also valid.[116] The model that I will employ is not static but is able to trace multiple possible responses to events of the first-century Roman East. In chapter 4, I use the model to assess the impact of increased military presence in Antioch on access to food by both rural and urban lower socio-economic segments of the population (PS 5– PS 7).

Some detractors of modeling see no value in applying sociology, on which models are built, to biblical texts. Early theoretical positions and other concerns about applications appear in a collection of studies in the 1986 volume of *Semeia*. Cyril Rodd, for example, argues that applying sociological analysis to biblical texts is philosophically impossible to do. He accurately describes the manner in which biblical scholars apply social-scientific theories and models:

---

112. Morley, *Theories, Models and Concepts in Ancient History*, 1, noted that the emotions still surrounding this issue "[m]ake it clear that this is not a purely technical, methodological issue."

113. Crook, "Structure Versus Agency in Studies of the Biblical Social World," 252.

114. Morley, *Theories, Models and Concepts in Ancient History*, 65.

115. Ibid., 16. Morley argues that one can never prove a model (theory). It can become more plausible as more data comes to light that confirms it. On the other hand, one can prove a model to be wrong by a single contrary example. He goes on to say that since historical data arises through a process of interpretation, it can be reinterpreted with the introduction of new data, which initially seems contradictory.

116. Crook, "Structure Versus Agency in Studies of the Biblical Social World," 253; Ling, "Virtuoso Religion and the Judean Social World," 228–35. Some scholars criticized the honor-shame model, as first introduced in Biblical studies, from this perspective. For a substantial criticism, see Ling's discussion.

(1) Accept the theory and use it to interpret the data or (2) use the theories to suggest lines of research. He claims the first manner is illegitimate.[117] Yet, he does accept the use of the theories as heuristic devices to suggest lines of research, which then have to stand or fall on their own merit. For the second case, he argues that incorporating the assumptions derived from the theory in one's study is inappropriate.[118] Unfortunately, often the assumptions are essential for an explanation of the setting of the biblical text.

I do not accept Rodd's radical position, but his argument does caution against blindly applying social-scientific models inappropriately, or blindly accepting work done by previous scholars who use models that are not suited for cross-cultural work.[119] I accept the position of Carney who would not agree with Rodd. Yet, Carney does caution that the greater the distance between biblical studies, in this case, and the disciplines and cultures from which the models are being borrowed, the greater the risk in using a model. On the other hand, he adds that the situation is worse if one does not borrow at all.[120] Vigilance is especially required in not over-extending work done for other times and places to the first century.[121] Finally, modeling cannot be used in isolation from previous work that has been in use, under scrutiny, and modified to fit particular scenarios.[122]

Gerhard Lenski and John Kautsky are the two modelers of ancient societies most often turned to by biblical scholars.[123] Their work provides

---

117. Rodd, "On Applying a Sociological Theory to Biblical Studies," 101–5; Tolbert, "Social, Sociological, and Anthropological Methods," 266–67. Tolbert makes the same point. She notes that Biblical scholars reverse the sociological approach. The model or theory is accepted, and applied to the data instead of data verifying the model or theory.

118. Rodd, "On Applying a Sociological Theory to Biblical Studies," 104.

119. Malina, "Social Scientific Approaches and the Gospel of Matthew," 160–63; Fuglseth, *Johannine Sectarianism in Perspective*, 40n90; Elliott, *What Is Social-Scientific Criticism?* Elliott gives numerous examples of modeling incorrectly when the researcher does not understand the chosen model.

120. Carney, *Shape of the Past*, 35; Duling, "Theories, Methods, Models." In section 4 of chapter 1, Carney discusses many pitfalls of modeling under the heading "When Models Mislead."

121. Crossley, *Why Christianity Happened*, 36. Crossley makes a similar argument and lauds the model developed by John Dominic Crossan depicting early Christianity, but disagrees with his conclusions based on the model.

122. Carney, *Shape of the Past*, 361.

123. The work of Mann on structures of social power provides excellent insights into the first-century entitlement structures. However, biblical scholars have not used his work as extensively as Lenski and Kautsky. I do not address his work here, but I do use it occasionally in my own arguments. Mann, *The Sources of Social Power*.

many good insights into the possible workings of the first-century Roman East and some rationales for food shortages. It is to their models I now turn.

Lenski's Advanced Agrarian, Extractive Society

In his classic book, *Power and Privilege*, Lenski addresses the principles that govern distribution of goods in a society: who gets what, when, and how. He argues that the examination of those principles permits one to understand social strata as well as what he refers to as power classes.[124] His concentration on how power works in a society is a key element to this study because power controls privilege and prestige that, in turn, control the distribution of goods, including food. His inquiry reveals principles behind the dominant entitlement system, which directly affected access to food. Lenski's model of an advanced, agrarian, extractive society fits the first-century Roman East at many points. The term *agrarian* connotes the principal economic factor being agriculture, and the majority of the population being involved in agricultural production.[125] The term *extractive* acknowledges that cities were surrounded by large agricultural areas that fed the city inhabitants and provided for many of their needs.[126]

Lenski identified twelve characteristics of advanced agrarian societies,[127] which I do not itemize here, but instead follow David Fiensy. He summarizes some aspects of Lenski's analysis into three categories connected to the first-century Roman Empire.

> First, agrarian societies were controlled by monarchs who gained and held power by their military. They imposed their will on their subjects (and enriched themselves) usually by brute force. Thus, the economy almost always produced a certain political reality as well. Second, due to technological advances, diversity of labor, and improved trade, there was a collective surplus of

---

124. Lenski, *Power and Privilege*, 75.

125. Ibid., 193–95. Lenski notes that war was a close second as a major industry. The Levant was not immune to war, which interrupted and disrupted agricultural production.

126. Stegemann and Stegemann, *The Jesus Movement*, 11, 17–18; Lenski, *Power and Privilege*, 198–200; Grimshaw, *Analysis of Matthew's Food Exchange*, 38; Fiensy, "Ancient Economy and the New Testament," 196. Grimshaw cites archaeological data from around Jerusalem that indicates that cities could only expand if there was assurance of an adequate food supply from the surrounding areas. Fiensy uses the term *extractive* to observe that the structure of advanced agrarian societies had two groups: the takers and the givers.

127. Lenski, *Power and Privilege*, 192–210.

food beyond what was needed merely to subsist. Most of the surplus, however, was siphoned off by the rulers. Third, since there was a surplus, urban communities could exist and the population in general could increase. In most agrarian societies about one tenth of the population lived in urban centers, the rest in small villages which worked the land.[128]

To Fiensy's summarization, I would add the following important observation from Lenski's characteristics, namely control of land use was an important factor in access to food. Under the rubric of Lenski's "proprietary theory of the state," the emperor owned the state and could use it—including all land—for his personal advantage. He gave lands to others, and the appointee likewise ruled for his personal advantage. The economic gain normally came about from the right to levy taxes[129] and not from ownership *per se* since different entities could simultaneously own the same piece of land.[130] However, high taxes drove crop selection toward cash crops and away from food crops. The result was less food for the cultivator.

Scholars apply Lenski's work to social stratification[131] and to societal structures[132] affecting distribution of goods, of which food was an important good. The model has been widely and fruitfully employed, yet scholars are moving away from a blind application of it. For example, analysis of archeological data is calling into question whether rural areas fit the pure Lenski description with respect to trade.[133] Another adjustment involves a

---

128. Fiensy, "Ancient Economy and the New Testament," 195–96.

129. Mitchell, "Requisitioned Transport in the Roman Empire: A New Inscription from Pisidia," 131; Carney, *Shape of the Past*, 118. Mitchell and Carney cite an example for 14 CE when the emperor Tiberius admonished his prefect in Egypt that he "preferred to see his provinces shorn, not shaved to the bare skin or flayed."

130. Lenski, *Power and Privilege*, 214–18; Kautsky, *Aristocratic Empires*, 100. In chapter 6, I explicate multiple ownership of land.

131. Duling, "The Matthean Brotherhood and Marginal Scribal Leadership," 642–71; Duling, "Theories, Methods, Models;" Duling, *A Marginal Scribe*, 96–103. Fiensy, *The Social History of Palestine in the Herodian Period*, chap. 5. In the second reference, Duling presents a careful evaluation of models used for the first-century Roman Empire. Fiensy discusses Lenski's models as it applies to Palestine in the first-century.

132. For examples of scholars who expand insights from Lenski to further their own arguments and models, see Saldarini, *Pharisees, Scribes, and Sadducees in Palestinian Society: A Sociological Approach*, 35–49; Finger, *Of Widows and Meals: Communal Meals in the Book of Acts*, multiple places and arguments; Hanson and Oakman, *Palestine in the Time of Jesus*, 101; Wire, "Gender Roles in a Scribal Community," multiple places and arguments.

133. Lenski, *Power and Privilege*, 205; Fiensy, "Ancient Economy and the New Testament," 200. Lenski suggests only luxury items were transported long distances. Fiensy discusses discoveries in Galilee showing major export businesses in common pottery

more nuanced understanding of the relationship between the city and the rural population that surrounded it.[134] In the evolving view, the city is less a pariah consumer entity,[135] but the city and the countryside are in a reciprocal relationship.[136]

Lenski's classic representation of classes in agrarian societies dispels the notion of a pyramid of social control, while at the same time it portrays a few people with enormous power and privilege and many people with little of either. Yet, Lenski's multi-dimensional social stratification scheme suggests that some peasants had more power and privilege than some merchants, and more power and privilege than some in the governing classes.[137] Scholars are giving more attention to the big bulge in his model by

---

and in stoneware vessels.

134. Wrigley, "Parasite or Stimulus: The Town in a Pre-Industrial Economy." Wrigley was an early voice who argued that the dichotomy of views on the city-rural relationship is improper. His principal argument is that the economic relationship is too complex to have such simple distinguishable categories. Other scholars advocating for a more nuanced examination are Hopkins, "The City Region in Roman Palestine," 102; Osborne, "Pride and Prejudice, Sense and Subsistence," 120; Edwards, "Socio-Economic and Cultural Ethos of the Lower Galilee," 54; Freyne, "Urban-Rural Relations in First-Century Galilee."

135. Abrams, "Introduction." Abrams writes that this issue has lost its momentum. A problem with trying to make the claim is the inability to delineate precisely what constitutes a city or town; Lenski, *Power and Privilege*, 206, describes the relationship as "essentially symbiotic in character, but with definite overtones of parasitism." He does continue, in footnote 66, that the military superiority of the city enabled it to extract more crops, or force the peasant to accept lower prices, than if the power imbalance had not been so great. Examples of scholars of the parasite view include: Clark and Haswell, *The Economics of Subsistence Agriculture*, 212; MacMullen, *Roman Social Relations*, 15–21, 33–35, 38–39, 55–56; Applebaum, "Judaea as a Roman Province: The Countryside as a Political and Economic Factor," 370, 663–64; Garnsey, *Famine and Food Supply*, 61; Corbier, "City, Territory, and Taxation," 213–19, 234; Rohrbaugh, "The Preindustrial City," 108–9; Finger, *Of Widows and Meals: Communal Meals in the Book of Acts*, 100–101.

136. Hopkins, "The City Region in Roman Palestine," 25–30; Oakman, *Jesus and the Economic Questions*, 147; Garnsey and Saller, *The Roman Empire*, 98; Moxnes, *The Economy of the Kingdom*, 88; Wallace-Hadrill, "Elites and Trade," 243; Edwards, "Socio-Economic and Cultural Ethos of the Lower Galilee," 56–62; Horden and Purcell, *The Corrupting Sea*, 91–96.

137. Lenski, *Power and Privilege*, 284, Figure 281: a graphic representation of the relationship among classes in agrarian societies; see also ibid., 216, 223. Pertinent to the argument in chapters 6–8 on the realm of the heavens versus the Roman Empire, Lenski makes two points germane to access to food. First, the system of stratification is an expression of the value system of the society. Second, inequalities are inevitable. The difference in the two realms may not be inequality but sufficiency that occurs in the realm of the heavens and that is missing in the Roman Empire.

adding more detail and finer categorizations.[138] Lenski continues to influence strongly biblical studies. Scholars are expanding his work with more nuances with the advent of more data while others are moving entirely away from some aspects of it. Richard Horsley cites a problem with the stratification model, and its subsequent interpretation and use. He observes that the model obscures the conflict in the power relations. He advocates for the work of John Kautsky as he sees that work more usefully showing the "subordination of one society to another and one ruling class to another . . . held together by an ideology of a god and/or king/high priest at its center as a symbol of the whole."[139]

Lenski's model provides the foundation for the broad-brush concepts of the first-century Roman East, which I expand to a more detailed and nuanced view in the model described below. His stratification model does not have enough detail for the argument of this study. Yet, he opened the door for this analysis with his chapter on "The Structure of Distributive Systems," and particularly his figure illustrating that a person's ability to command resources was dependent on a number of factors related to the person's roles in the society.[140]

Kautsky's Aristocratic Empires

John Kautsky developed a model of the aristocratic empire. The term *aristocrat* refers to "a ruling class in an agrarian economy that does not engage in

---

138. Freyne, "Herodian Economics in Galilee," 42. Freyne contends that Lenski fairly well matches what we know about the Galilee. The leading works adding detail to Lenski are by these scholars: Fiensy, *The Social History of Palestine in the Herodian Period*, 157–70; Friesen, "Poverty in Pauline Studies," 341; Longenecker, *Remember the Poor*, chap. 3; Scheidel and Friesen, "The Size of the Economy and the Distribution of Income in the Roman Empire," 83.

139. Horsley, *Scribes, Visionaries, and the Politics of Second Temple Judea*, 60–62, 61. Horsley examines the second-temple period of Ben Sira. Horsley's full critique covers several chapters.

140. Lenski, *Power and Privilege*, chap. 4, p. 284, Figure 1: graphic representation of the structure of the power dimensions of the distributive system of a fictional society; Duling, *A Marginal Scribe*, 248–64. Duling applies and expands Lenski's model to a discussion of the social ranking and marginality of scribes within the Matthean community. See in particular, Duling's Chart 9.1: "A Fictional Distributive System for the Roman Empire" (ibid., 248). Duling's discussion on marginality provides excellent theoretical material on the stresses of the Matthean community to live both in the Roman empire and the "not yet totally manifested" realm of the heavens.

productive labor but lives wholly or primarily off the labor of peasants."[141] Kautsky describes peasants as

> those engaged in agriculture in aristocratic empires, though they also produce their necessities other than food, for example, their cloth and clothing, their tools and their dwellings. Thus, I include in the peasantry those in the village who carry on crafts, like weaving, carpentry, and pottery, on a part-time basis and even the relatively full-time village craftsmen that develop in some peasant societies. Hence, aristocratic empires must contain not only aristocrats but also peasants who, in turn, live in agrarian primitive societies.[142]

His model correlates with Lenski's agrarian category[143] in that it acknowledges Lenski's agrarian society within the aristocratic empire.

Kautsky's work on aristocratic empires is important for examining food processes from two perspectives. First, he argues that within an empire there would be at least a few agrarian primitive societies, which function differently than urban societies.[144] Making a distinction between rural and urban is important for identifying the different approaches to the distribution of food items. Rural society was strongly reciprocal-based with some market (redistribution) accommodations whereas urban society was less reciprocal-based with stronger market distributions. At the most basic level, distribution involved sharing between households within a kinship group. At the other end of the spectrum, one finds redistribution. Reciprocal relations, unlike redistribution, ensured two things: distribution of goods would be equitable, and help would be available. When the economy of a village is reciprocity-based, the maintenance of social relationships is more important than economic motives. Solidarity of the village would be undermined if one villager profited at the expense of food for another. Social motives were also behind redistribution, but with profit-driven decisions. Redistribution involved the extraction, storage, and eventual distribution of crops to further political goals not necessarily in the best interests of the

---

141. Kautsky, *Aristocratic Empires*, 24.

142. Ibid., 270.

143. Ibid., 20. Kautsky also includes Lenski's horticultural society.

144. With respect to what could be perceived as a pejorative description, Kautsky writes, "Obviously also, the term 'primitive' is used here without any necessary implication of simplicity, crudeness, or backwardness, but merely it suggests that primitive societies appear first, that is, before aristocratic empires" (ibid., 24). Mann writes, "Societies are constituted of multiple overlapping and intersecting sociospatial networks of power . . . Societies are not unitary" (*The Sources of Social Power*, 1).

small landowners or non-aristocrats in the city.[145] Although the Matthean community was urban-based, it did not exist apart from the countryside. The Gospel reflects this interaction with the inclusion of many parables and actions related to food deriving from rural societies.

Second, Kautsky's model addresses the demands of the aristocrats on rural peasants, and villages, in the form of tributes and rents that affect food access. He identifies exploitative practices that lead to loss of life because of insufficient food. For example, he writes:

> Thus, it is quite possible for aristocrats to tax peasants (or to raise taxes on peasants) who are barely surviving. This is done by forcing some to die and the rest to produce more or by forcing all of them to produce more ... How then can 90 percent of the peasants produce what 100 percent produced before? They can, if the 10 percent who are eliminated by death produced little or nothing to begin with. This may well be the case because, when the aristocrat takes 10 percent of the food supply from the village, it will probably be the least productive peasants—the old and the sick—who will die first.[146]

For a number of years, biblical scholars accepted his harsh view of the first-century Roman East. More recently, scholars have argued against his extreme exploitation stance,[147] while still holding to the tenet that a majority of the population lived close to a subsistence level and affirming that actions by the aristocracy often had harmful effects on people in the lower socio-economic segments of the population.

A New Model Describing Food-Access Processes Fills a Current Void

While both Lenski and Kautsky have contributed significantly to understanding of agrarian societies and aristocratic empires, their models have certain deficiencies as noted above. Primarily for this argument, neither model engages the issue of food-access processes at the level needed for this study. Lenski begins his book with a chapter promisingly entitled

---

145. Sahlins, *Stone Age Economics*, 189–90; Polanyi, "The Economy as Instituted Process," 37, 90, 254; Fusfeld, "Economic Theory Misplaced: Livelihood in Primitive Society," 349; Temin, "Market Economy," 177.

146. Kautsky, *Aristocratic Empires*, 106.

147. Garnsey, *Famine and Food Supply*, 43–63; Horden and Purcell, *The Corrupting Sea*, 271.

"The Problem: Who Gets What and Why?"[148] Unfortunately, he does not address directly food-access issues or practices. He does address many of the aspects of distribution systems that the model must be able to address (for example, land ownership, extractions by privilege, property as a right not as a thing).[149] Kautsky writes expansively about exploitative distribution practices, yet his categorizations—aristocrat and peasant—are at too general a level to be of much help. Neither Lenski nor Kautsky speaks to specific practices of the first-century Roman East. The models by scholars doing variations on Lenski and Kautsky suffer from the same problem of specificity. With a few exceptions,[150] their models are at a macro level. As such, the models offer little help in addressing which particular practices and entitlements contributed to particular socio-economic segments of the population having, or not having, access to sufficient food.

A model using a more nuanced level of specificity permits examining access to food, for example, according to socio-economic status and according to where one lived. All parts of the food-access processes were in symbiotic relationships in which pressure on one process led to readjustments in others.[151] The descriptive model described in the next chapter enables the tracing of the shock waves and ripples of an event through the food-access system.

A new model will account for the structures, actors, practices, products, and histories of the Roman East[152] that affect access to food. These factors

---

148. Lenski, *Power and Privilege*, chap. 1. Lenski reviews the history of what principles drove the answer to this question over time and what principles drove the interpreters of this question.

149. Ibid., 213–16.

150. The principal exception is Oakman, who has been modeling peasant-related issues for a number of years. His work has been invaluable. Oakman, *Jesus and the Economic Questions*; Oakman, *Jesus and the Peasants*, 4; Davies, "Linear and Non-Linear Flow Models for Ancient Economies"; Scheidel and Friesen, "The Size of the Economy and the Distribution of Income in the Roman Empire." The latter two works are theoretical in nature but provide enough detail to be quite useful to the argument of this study.

151. Carney, *Shape of the Past*, 74; Buckley, *Sociology and Modern Systems Theory*, 41, 58. Buckley goes further than Carney in describing societies as complex adaptive systems. The relationships form a casual network in which some stability exists within some parts at any given time (41). He notes that responses are not simple and direct like a billiard ball coming off the cushion, but more complex in mediating between the external forces and behaviors that may cause the society to reorganize to deal with its new environment (58).

152. Ling, "Virtuoso Religion and the Judean Social World," 228–35, 235–38. In the first set of pages noted here, Ling writes a blistering critique of what he perceives to be static modeling by members of the Context Group, especially Malina. He then turns to a discussion of the need for modeling which takes into consideration that people have agency.

include items such as peasant, aristocrat, city-rural, crop selection, entitlement, gender and age, land, market exchange, patronage, peasant, reciprocity, redistribution, storage, taxes, Temple, tenant, and trade. The model will accommodate an examination of relationships among such disparate factors in a conceptually clear manner. Societies change and the model will view society as a complex system of fluid associations and dissociations producing practices and structures to accommodate the forces of a specific event.[153] In particular, it will permit assessment of which socio-economic segments control the power, and ideology that support their vested interests.[154] It will assist in highlighting the strategies, practices, and attitudes, critiqued by the Gospel that hindered and helped access to food by various groups from the lower socio-economic segments of the population.[155] It will support and elucidate the argument of this study that the Matthean Jesus was proposing a realm of the heavens that was different from the Roman imperial order in that it ensured access to adequate food for everyone. The model will enable discussions concerning such deviance from the imperial norm.[156] My goal is a descriptive model that accounts for most of the needed data by the most probable explanatory mechanisms.

Chapter Summary

I discussed the evolution of SRI, and described the various textures (methods) that make up its exegetical process. I argued that the method would enable examination of the argumentation and description of the social context of the full Gospel text itself related to the realm of the heavens and food-access practices. Understanding the practices in the first-century that led to some people not having enough to eat leads to understanding the critique the Gospel makes of the world in which the Matthean community lived where people went hungry, which is different than the realm of the heavens that Jesus brought near. I argued that modeling is an effective method for engaging with the first-century societies found in the Roman East. First, it simplifies the description of the complex social environment of the first century that affected the ability of different socio-economic segments to have access to food. Second, it provides possibilities of how the first-century operated for those

---

153. Buckley, *Sociology and Modern Systems Theory*, 8–9.
154. Ibid., 18–30, 167.
155. Freyne, "Galilee and Judaea in the First Century," 41.
156. Kloppenborg, *Q, the Earliest Gospel: An Introduction to the Original Stories and Sayings of Jesus*, 21, 40. Kloppenborg notes that, in the development of a model, the scholar generates hypotheses about the subject that the model then accommodates.

processes that have limited verification from primary sources. I discussed the limited primary data that are available for use. I argued that the previously developed models by Lenski and Kautsky and the later adaptations by biblical scholars are beneficial, but their categories are too general to model practices that affected specific socio-economic segments of the population. The shortcomings indicate a need for a specialized model.

3

How Did People Get Access to Food?

THE SUB-TITLE OF THIS study is "The Pragmatics of Food Access in the Gospel of Matthew." A strong, clear paradigm that paints a picture of how people from various socio-economic segments of the population acquired food is essential for understanding the arguments in the remainder of this study.[1] Acquisition of food by specific groups of population in the Roman East involved a complex web of processes and power dynamics. To facilitate the development of a paradigm of food access for the first-century Roman East I use a descriptive model that focuses on the pragmatic aspects of food access for particular types of households. For example, the paradigm can explain how peasant land used for food and household needs can be diverted to generate cash for aristocrats who want more ostentatious lifestyles. The model helps to build a paradigm that permits one to see how peasants needed to balance the nutritional needs of their households with external obligations and other household demands.

In the next sections, I first discuss the Goody Framework. It is a useful tool for organizing into a coherent picture the factors related to households of varying socio-economic status acquiring food. I then describe how food access worked in the first-century Roman East by using a model especially designed to depict the important factors and relationships. The discussion is in broad strokes so the relationships between the components are clear. In latter chapters, discussions of practices critiqued by the Gospel focus in more depth on the details. Finally, I use a scenario to show how the model

1. Morley, *Theories, Models and Concepts in Ancient History*, 9. Morley discusses the aim of modeling such as done for this study as offering "a particular sort of knowledge about the past—a way of thinking about it and imagining it, rather than simply information about it."

facilitates understanding of the pragmatics of food access when external events cause food supplies to be diminished. I examine the effects of military occupation forces on both rural and urban households. Although not always explicitly mentioned in latter chapters, this model paradigm is assumed and does undergird the arguments used throughout this study.

Goody Framework for Food Processes

A complex process accounts for people having enough to eat. The process begins with the capabilities of the land, sea, and air to produce sufficient desired[2] and needed food items. It is not enough that the natural resources generate sufficient food items because other factors control whether all socio-economic segments of the population actually receive enough food items to sustain life. Decisions related to crop selection, for example, affect how much food is available to be distributed. A web of decisions and societal-sanctioned actions determines who receives how much of the produced food. To begin to clarify this complex process, Jack Goody developed a generic framework for food processes shown in the table below.[3] The framework provides a mechanism for generating questions to ask and for collecting and comparing information from a number of sources and disciplines that influence food processes, but for which food processes are only of secondary importance or of tangential interest. The answers to the questions lead to a paradigm of how food access works in the society of interest, such as the first-century Roman East.

Table 3. Goody Framework for food processes

x. Processes	x.1. Phases	x.2. Aspects
1. Production	1.1.1 preparation	1.2.1 items of production
	1.1.2 plant	1.2.2 division of labor
	1.1.3 cultivate	1.2.3 natural resources
	1.1.4 harvest	1.2.4 technology and techniques
	1.1.5 conserve	1.2.5 quality and quantity
		1.2.6 ownership of land

2. "The cultural system here has its own 'cultural logic'. Only by reference to such a calculus can we explain the eating habits of, say, the Americans, who reject the flesh of horse and dog on grounds that cannot be explained by any variety of utilitarian theory" (Goody, *Cooking, Cuisine, and Class*, 32–33).

3. Ibid., 40–48.

x. Processes	x.1. Phases	x.2. Aspects
2. Distribution	2.1.1 allocation within producing unit	2.2.1 nature of transfer (within)
	2.1.2 gift	2.2.2 nature of transfer (without)
	2.1.3 reciprocal exchange	2.2.3 equality of distribution within
	2.1.4 market	2.2.4 technology of storage
	2.1.5 obligatory transfer	2.2.5 technology of transfer
	2.1.6 destruction	2.2.6 periodicity of distribution
3. Preparation	3.1.1 preliminary work	3.2.1 who cooks with whom for whom
	3.1.2 cooking	3.2.2 technology
	3.1.3 dishing up	
4. Consumption	4.1.1 assembling participants	4.2.1 distribution in time
	4.1.2 distribution of cooked / prepared food	4.2.2 structure of meal
	4.1.3 eating	4.2.3 ways of eating
	4.1.4 clearing away	4.2.4 technology
		4.2.5 eating group
		4.2.6 differentiation of cuisine
5. Clean-up	5.1.2 disposal of excess	

The Goody framework spans the full spectrum of food processing: production, distribution, preparation, consumption, and clean-up. Before turning to more detail on the framework, some generalized observations are in order. Goody notes that the focus of the analysis changes with the particular process. For example, the focus for production is the farm (land); for distribution, granary or market; for preparation, kitchen or bakery; for consumption, table or banquet; and for clean-up, scullery.[4] Goody makes additional observations about food processes that one needs to bear in mind when examining them in the first-century Roman East with its wide disparities in political power and wealth. Economic factors dominate the production phase since

4. Ibid., 37.

it involves aspects of land control, the work organization, and storing food, leading to the distribution of what is produced. The process of distribution is overtly political because the aristocracy could demand rent, tribute and tax revenues. Even within the domestic unit, decisions were made concerning conservation of seed, sale in the market, and above all who gets how much food until the next harvest, especially if the domestic unit were to run short.[5] The framework enables one to examine such issues with clarity.

To guide the formulation of a paradigm of any society's food processes, Goody developed what he refers to as *phases* and *aspects* for each process. *Phases* come close to being sub-processes. For example, production of agricultural items involves preparation (table 3, 1.1.1) of the land through tilling or plowing before the actual planting (table 3, 1.1.2) of the seed. The phases of distribution are more modes of distribution than phases of distribution. *Aspects* are key topics used to think about the phases of a process. For example, in the first century, some crops (table 3, 1.2.1) required more labor (table 3, 1.2.2) than others did, but may have been able to grow on more marginal land (table 3, 1.2.3). When examining the mechanisms that helped and hindered people having enough to eat, the aspects of the phases suggest avenues of exploration.

Disturbances in production or distribution can lead to food shortages. Consumption and clean up do not relate strongly to access to food. In the cities, slow down in preparation could cause food shortages. For example, in Ephesus in the second century, a strike by the bakers plunged the city into disorder. The proconsul of Asia "brought them to their senses" with an edict, which ran, in part:

> Wherefore, I forbid the bakers to assemble in association and their officers to make inflammatory speeches, and I order them to give complete obedience to those in charge of the community's welfare, and to provide the city fully with the necessary production of bread. (27 SEC IV 512 = Abbott and Johnson 124)[6]

Yet, such episodes are rarely attested in the extant sources and not attested in Matthew's Gospel. Consequently, I only use the framework to establish a paradigm for food access based on production and distribution phases and aspects.

Production questions revolve around who made decisions on what use was to be made of the arable land. For example, what effect did the Roman presence in the Mediterranean East have on use of land for food crops

---

5. Ibid., 37.
6. Garnsey, *Famine and Food Supply*, 259.

versus cash crops to meet the tax demands? What effect did the unpredictable weather patterns have on ownership patterns? What was the relationship between the farmers and the pastoralists?

The phases of the distribution process indicate specific sets of relations within a society.[7] Food can be distributed as gifts (table 3, 2.1.2),[8] through reciprocal exchanges (table 3, 2.1.3), and market mechanisms (table 3, 2.1.4). How big a safety net would gifts in the form of alms be? During periods of severe shortages, what happened to the traditional forms of exchange? What were safety nets for such periods, and who benefited? Does one find more reciprocal relations in the rural segments and more market exchanges in the cities and how would the two systems co-exist?

Given the oppressive situation in the first century, distribution as obligatory transfer (table 3, 2.1.5) is extremely important. This phase includes items such as taxes, rents, tithes, and debt reduction. I place taxes into the category of *transfer* versus *exchange* because there is little balance (that is, the producer gets little of value—present or future—for the loss of the product). Kautsky discusses that an ideology of the society may indicate that the peasant is getting something in return (that is, the relationship is one of reciprocity), when in reality the peasant gets virtually nothing. He writes, "The relationship between the aristocrat and the peasant is about as reciprocal as that between the shepherd and his animal. The shepherd will protect it from attack and let it live on and eat from his land; 'in return;' he takes its milk or wool and even its meat." The two things often cited as being of value to the peasant were the use of the aristocrat's land—which once was the peasant's—and protection from robbers. Kautsky does point out the irony of protection from "robbers" when the aristocrat is exploitative and acts generically as a robber.[9] I place *tithes* here for the same reasons. There is little balance.

What happened to the kinship group already on the land when the ruler gave the land to a city or a friend? What happened when taxes were increased which took a surplus that in reality did not exist?[10] Less obvious are the transfers related to social obligations, which in some primitive

---

7. Goody, *Cooking, Cuisine, and Class*, 45.

8. Firth, *Primitive Polynesian Economy*, 11–12. Firth's whole book lends insights into how the rural societies of the first century may have handled gifts and reciprocity. On the cited pages he discusses how the pay for harvesting depends on the social relationship between the worker and owner of the land and whether money was the preferred method of payment or grain itself.

9. Kautsky, *Aristocratic Empires*, 114, 111.

10. Ibid., 106. According to Kautsky, an increase in tax results in a death rate increasing proportionately to the tax increase.

societies today occur even if the household has to forego eating. Raymond Firth writes,

> Nothing illustrates so well the contrast between primitive and civilized economic ideologies as the psychology of food. Its primary value is of course nutritional, but primitive cultures often impute to it further values of a non-nutritional order; for example, when it is employed as a means of meeting kinship responsibilities and other social obligations, or when it is displayed or even allowed to rot because of the non-material satisfactions this gives. This must be stressed in order to refute the popular misconception that the savage is occupied primarily with filling his belly. The range of values which lead to economic activity are socially determined and are not arranged in what might be termed a "natural scale." The "primary" want of hunger is often subordinated to other less tangible economic wants which are traditionally dictated.[11]

Although not exactly an obligatory transfer in the sense of externally imposed, the expenditures of aristocrats to portray themselves as honorable citizens and patrons of a city need to be accommodated in the model.[12] This need to generate funds for such activities affected both the items of production (table 3, 1.2.1) moving to cash crops and the distribution of crops—both food and cash—to the aristocracy. What controls, if any, restricted the aristocracy simply siphoning off crops from the producing units?

To recap, the Goody Framework itself does not offer insights into how various segments of the population in the first-century Roman East obtained access to food. It does facilitate the development of a strong model and paradigm of food access in the first-century Roman East by highlighting factors that were in play in the web of practices and by suggesting ways in which to think about the relationships.

---

11. Firth, *Primitive Polynesian Economy*, 37–38.

12. "Let kings and royal stewards and those who would be foremost in their cities and hold office engage in money-getting" (Plutarch, *On Love of Wealth* 525D, 521 [in *Moralia*, trans. De Lacy and Einarson, LCL]). Such people need liquid wealth to give banquets, buy gladiators, bestow favors, raise armies, pay court, and send presents to superiors (patrons).

Descriptive Model of Food Access in the First-Century Roman East

The design issue for any model is to balance simplicity of expression (that is, not too many components) with the strength of descriptive capability (that is, straightforward indications of relationships among the components). In developing a model to support an argument, the most important components are those for which a small change can effect large over-all changes in the system.[13] In the first century, access to sufficient food depended on two major factors: location and distribution-acquisition of enough food of varying types. The place of residence—rural or urban—dictated the means of access and the mechanisms available to survive short-term food shortages. Likewise, the resources available to acquire food depended in large measure on location. The rural peasant depended on his crop production for food and for income to discharge obligations. The city resident depended upon his employment for income and upon the largess of aristocrats. Within and between these two major factors is a host of secondary factors (for example, wealth and status within the social group; rent, tax and tithe, and financial obligations; alternative food sources) that are also important to an argument that addresses practices. Secondary factors exhibit the most variability with respect to the various socio-economic segments of the population. To accommodate these design issues, the model is composed of layers to demonstrate how land use affected crop selection and distribution and to demonstrate that crops supported secondary factors in addition to food consumption. By looking at how the secondary factors intersect with land and distribution issues, one can see where decisions and actions non-uniformly affected different socio-economic segments of the population.

The model depicted in figure 1 is composed of five levels to show broad dependencies between the levels and to highlight secondary factors. The levels are: (1) use of land, (2) distribution of cultivated land between aristocrats and peasants, (3) apportionment of crop yield between household needs and any surplus to accommodate cash requirements, (4) functions supported by crop yield, which include storage against a bad year, and (5) city as a consumer of rural products.

The first four levels shown below constitute the rural aspects of food access. The boxes on the left specify functions supported by crops grown on estates. The boxes on the right depict the equivalent functions for peasants. The middle boxes (in dashed lines) depict uses of revenue from cash crops.

---

13. Buckley, *Sociology and Modern Systems Theory*, 79.

The last level constitutes the urban aspect of food access. On the left, the boxes represent the urban household of an estate owner, which includes family, staff, and artisans attached full time to the household. Its rural counterpart supports this urban household (indicated by the box at level three labeled *for city use*). On the model are boxes labeled *Bakers* and *Eating Places* that show where poorer urban residents acquired their food. I highlight three specific groups of urban residents: *Merchants*, *Day Laborers*, and *Peddlers / Beggars*. These three general groups used different methods to acquire food. As I argued in chapter 1, these groupings can vary substantially in the ability of an individual to command enough food. The acquisition of food by these people requires resources from market-driven mechanisms, such as eating establishments. I describe each level in more detail and relationships between levels in the remainder of this section.

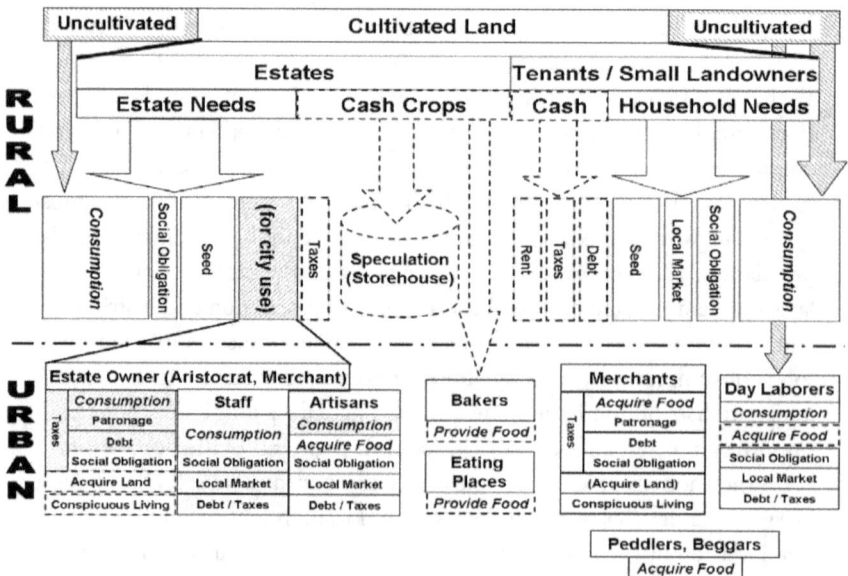

Figure 1. Full model

The boxes are for illustration only. The size or length of the box is not calibrated to percentages found in the first century. For example, at level two there are two boxes. One is labeled *Estates* and the other is labeled *Tenant / Small Landowners*. The length of the boxes suggests that land controlled by estate owners was approximately 55 percent. Drawing such a conclusion from this model is unwarranted. In fact, the percentages would have varied over time and by location. The boxes are strictly notational to facilitate argument.

how did people get access to food? 65

Level 1: Use of land

The first level of figure 1 shows that some land is cultivated and other land is uncultivated.[14] The *Cultivated Land* was used for production of food crops and non-food crops, such as flax.[15] Crops in this sense include orchards and vineyards as well. *Uncultivated Land* (boxes with left-to-right diagonal stripes) is often viewed as wasteland, but it was a source of food, especially in times of shortages. Peasants pastured herds on it. The forest provided foods—nuts and berries—for anyone taking the trouble to gather them.[16] Wild game and birds provided supplemental food. Sources do not indicate how much the peasant population consumed wild game and birds, although the sources indicate game and birds were a source of food.[17] Peasants also exploited seasonal bird migrations.[18] Some actions (for example, giving land to veterans) shifted uncultivated land to cultivated status.[19] Such action resulted in the potential removal of food from the tables of the existing residents of the area.

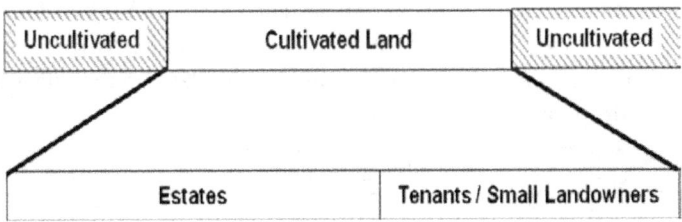

Figure 2. Model levels 1 and 2

14. I am concerned with land-based food sources in subsequent chapters because the Gospel focuses more on practices related to agricultural production than the other food sources. Fish was also a source of food for some. Hanson provides an excellent description of the fishing industry in the Galilee area. Hanson, "The Galilean Fishing Economy."

15. Geyer, "Evidence of Flax Cultivation from the Temple-Granary Complex Et-Tell (Bethsaida/Julias)," 231. The high percentage of flax pollen in the granary indicates it was a major cash plant during the first century, yet its export is not documented until well over 200 years later.

16. Corbier, "City, Territory, and Taxation," 222.

17. Dio Chrysostom, *Discourses* 69.

18. Horden and Purcell, *The Corrupting Sea*, 187.

19. Applebaum, "Economic Life in Palestine," 638; Stegemann and Stegemann, *The Jesus Movement*, 112; Oakman, *Jesus and the Economic Questions*, 67; Mann, *The Sources of Social Power*, 143–44. Applebaum and the Stegemanns speak to a general lack of unused land good enough for cultivation in Palestine.

Level 2: Distribution of land between aristocrat and peasant landowners

This level focuses attention on the distribution of the *Cultivated Land* only. It indicates that aristocratic estate owners and small peasant landowners were competing for control of cultivated land and, by extension, control of crop selection. The image of farmlands in the United States would conjure up images of large to abundantly large tracts of land with one crop growing on the tract. The best image of agricultural lands for the first-century Roman East would be a series of gardens, not expanses of fields. According to Horden and Purcell, the average size of a plot was .123 hectares. Garnsey argues that the size of a farm varied over time and by location, but a good average size was 3–4 hectares. With that size, a typical farm consisted of 23 to 32 plots.[20] Thus, even a small landowner could have over twenty plots. Some biblical scholars have posited that a shift in the allocation percentage favoring the aristocracy (increasing the length of the *Estates* bar) was a major impetus leading to below-subsistence-living conditions for many peasants.[21] At a macro-level argument, that proposition is true, but the mechanisms that the Gospel critiques need more detail. Subsequent levels of this model permit explication of the required details.

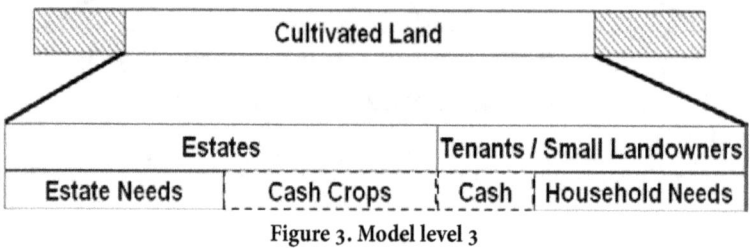

Figure 3. Model level 3

Level 3: Apportionment between household and cash needs

As I argued above, the first level of the model indicates that the land can be divided into land under cultivation and everything else, which is also a source for food. The second level traces the crops grown on the cultivated land to their owners. The third level of the model shows owners made

---

20. Horden and Purcell, *The Corrupting Sea*, 201, 221; Garnsey, *Famine and Food Supply*, 46.

21. Stegemann and Stegemann, *The Jesus Movement*, 112; Oakman, *Jesus and the Economic Questions*, 38–46; Davis, *Scripture, Culture, and Agriculture*, 123. Based on archaeological data, Fiensy suggests that there were medium sized estates, specifically in the valley controlled or owned by aristocrats living in Sepphoris. Unpublished paper presented at SBL 2009, New Orleans, Louisiana.

decisions with respect to the use of the land they controlled. It was necessary to produce food for *Household Needs* (such as different cereal grains, legumes, carobs, figs, olives, grapes, herbs) of the producers and owners, and to produce *Cash Crops* (such as wheat, olives, flax, figs, and grapes for wine). Geographic aspects affected what types of plants could be planted. For example, grains did best in valleys, whereas orchards and vineyards did best on hillsides.[22] Some crops could grow on the same area of land, such as olives and grains.[23] Both estates and small landowners allocated part of their crop production to generating cash, but an increase in the percentage of cash crops adversely affected availability of food.[24] The next level of the model demonstrates how the decisions to put land into cash crops affected the ability of lower socio-economic segments of the population to have access to sufficient food. However, before discussing the next level, a few comments are in order concerning tenants.

The tenant is a special category of small landowner. Tenants were in some type of lease agreement with the estate owner.[25] They worked the land for their household needs as well as the needs of the estate owner. A major difference between tenants and small landowners was control of crop selection. In the case of tenants, the estate owners, to generate cash for their civic obligations and conspicuous lifestyles, could dictate how much of the land worked by tenants would be placed in *Cash Crops*. The result would be that the *Household Needs* bar for the tenant would get shorter as the *Cash Crops* bar got longer, which obviously meant less food available for tenant households. Primary sources from the first century show that the estate owners were aware of the problem of pushing their tenants too far, particularly if it meant tenants would no longer work the land. For example, Pliny cautions that one is better off with local cultivators whose households have worked the land for generations. He says having turnover in tenants is bad

---

22. Oakman, *Jesus and the Economic Questions*, 20.

23. Columella, *On Agriculture* 2.9.6. Columella notes that more seed is required when planting grain in vineyards.

24. Horden and Purcell, *The Corrupting Sea*, 201, 205, 229, 261. For example, they write, "Subsistence monoculturals bring disaster in most Mediterranean environments" (201), and, "concentration on monocultures [is] to the ultimate detriment of local society, institutions, and the environment" (229).

25. Stegemann and Stegemann, *The Jesus Movement*, 111; Oakman, *Jesus and the Economic Questions*. The Stegemanns write that the boundary between the small landowner and tenant is hard to define since the independent small landowner was also available during the harvest season to work for the estate owner. In effect, all peasants worked for some aristocrat in the sense that they paid taxes assessed by the aristocrats in the urban areas. See Oakman for a comprehensive treatment of tenants.

business.²⁶ Varro advocates for treating workers with respect and, perhaps even providing a few side benefits.²⁷

To recap, apportionment of land to crops to support household needs and cash needs affected the amount of food available for consumption by peasant households. Pressures, such as increased taxes or rents, that cause peasants to increase the percentage of their crops in grains created a situation that often resulted in less food to eat. How this situation occurred is the topic of the next section.

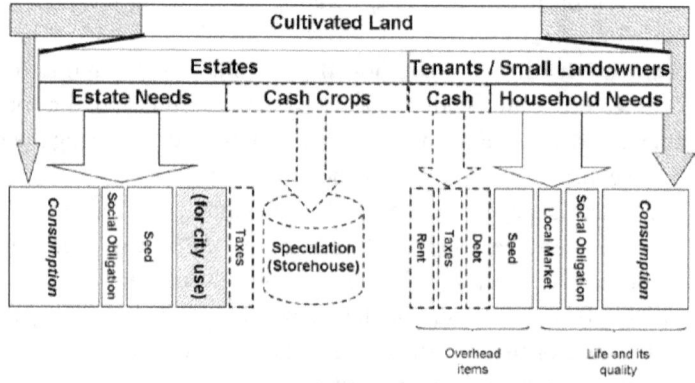

Figure 4. Model level 4

Level 4: Functions supported by crop yields

This layer shows who and what the crops supported—including consumption by household members. On the right, the boxes indicate crops supporting a small landowner, or tenant. Crucial *Seed* for the next-year planting would come from either the *Cash Crops* or the *Household Needs* depending on how good the current-year crop yield was. The *Household Needs* crops were not only for consumption, but also supported, through trade in-kind, many secondary functions such as procurement of tools and pottery that the household did not make. For a person to live at a subsistence level involved more than having enough to eat. At a minimum, a person needed clothing and usually needed shelter.²⁸ Often other items such as provisions for *Taxes*, *Rent*, and

---

26. Pliny, *Letters* 3.6. In discussing the advisability of purchasing some land, Pliny notes that the previous owner had continually put his tenants in debt and then seized their property on the ensuing default. Pliny considers a risk to his purchase to be having to find good laborers.

27. Varro, *On Agriculture* 1.17.14–16.

28. Oakes, "Constructing Poverty Scales for Graeco-Roman Society," 368; Horsley, "Little Tradition and Hidden Transcripts," 248–49; Scott, *Weapons of the Weak*, 236.

Debt obligations took precedence over food.[29] In good years, the *Cash Crops* (primarily wheat for small landowners) would provide the necessary amounts for taxes, rents, and debt relief.[30] In bad years, the cash requirements would come from selling the *Household Needs* crops (primarily cereals and legumes, and sometimes herbs). As the bar for *Household Needs* gets shorter, fewer food crops are available for the other items, such as *Consumption* by the household.

Distribution of food within a household would have provided for the varying needs of its members as long as food was sufficient. In a rural setting, production involved all members of the household.[31] During shortages which cause the total allocated to the producing unit to fall below the amount needed to keep everyone alive, allocation of food becomes complex. John Kautsky points out that even if the producing unit were to try to spread its allocation among everyone, the elderly and children would probably still die first because they are normally weaker to start.[32] Carol Meyers argues that women, as chief preparers of cooked food, would exert control over when, how, and how much food was consumed.[33] Men might be privileged.[34] Yet, a woman was essential in food production as she would also have tended a small garden, which would include herbs and spices for cooking and preserving, and she probably raised chickens.[35]

The model treats small landowners and tenants as individual households. However, as a rule in the first-century Roman East, kinship was a primary focus in all decision-making. Even a remote homestead would be associated with a village and kinship groups. The economics of the village were primarily reciprocal-based within and among households.[36] The category *Social Obligation* would have been very important, even to the extent

---

29. Oakes, "Constructing Poverty Scales for Graeco-Roman Society," 368; Firth, *Primitive Polynesian Economy*, 17–19.

30. Jones, *The Greek City*, 263. Jones discusses merchants who bought agricultural produce from peasants and then sold it to wealthier urban dwellers. Cash was the medium of exchange, which peasants then used to pay their taxes and rents.

31. Jobling, "Feminism and 'Mode of Production' in Ancient Israel," 242.

32. Kautsky, *Aristocratic Empires*, 107; Morley, *Theories, Models and Concepts in Ancient History*, 89–100. Morley discusses the problems with insufficient data to identify sex and gender distinctions, principally because women were not considered significant to many of the authors of primary data.

33. Meyers, *Discovering Eve: Ancient Israelite Women in Context*, 145–47.

34. Garland, *The Eye of the Beholder*, 19, 21.

35. Safrai, *The Economy of Roman Palestine*, 105; Cato, *On Agriculture* 143.

36. I discuss reciprocity in more detail on pp. 108–15. Its underlying principle involves sharing with others when they need help or when an event has occurred to celebrate or to mourn.

that a person might go hungry to meet their social obligations.[37] An example is hosting, or materially participating in, celebrations. The parable of the lost coin (Luke 15:8–9) provides such an example. A woman loses a coin and goes to great lengths to find it. The irony is that she invites friends and neighbors to a celebration of finding the coin, and the celebration probably cost more than the value of the lost, but now found, coin. Fulfilling this social obligation may have taken food off her table. In a modern economic paradigm, this action makes little sense, but in the ancient economy marked by social obligation, such an obligation was an important and crucial activity.[38] James Scott writes, "To fall below this level is not merely to be that much poorer economically; it is to fall short of what is locally defined as a fully human existence. It is as much a socially devastating loss of standing as it is a loss of income."[39]

On the left of figure 4, the *Estate Needs* crops (such as grains, legumes, olives, grapes for wine) supported both people living on the estate and, from a functional point of view, people living in the city (level 5) in the household of the estate owner. The rural members of the estate had needs and social obligations similar to their small landowner counterparts.

The middle box shows *Cash Crops* (usually wheat which stored well) grown for market, or to retain for *Speculation*, that are stored in *Storehouses*. Producers did not consume this grain, but made it available for urban, non-agricultural workers or for people suffering from severe food shortages. The owner sold it to local markets (level 5) or to markets away from the local areas. One such local market included the bakers and food establishments in the city. The price of the grain would affect the price of bread from the *Bakers* or the *Eating Places*. When owners held back the grain from local markets, an artificial food shortage occurred. When prices rose, people in the lower socio-economic segments of the population would go without food, or would consume at levels below subsistence.[40] While they usually would not die of starvation, their health declined and mortality increased

---

37. Firth, *Primitive Polynesian Economy*, 17–18, 37–38. The work by Firth is an excellent example of such studies from the past seventy-five years. The social uses and obligations that are based on food is a theme of his entire book. He argues that the focus of subsistence economies is not only on food to support bodily needs at a low level but on food to serve virtually every social function within the social group.

38. Ibid., chap. 2 especially.

39. Scott, *Weapons of the Weak*, 237; see also Neyrey, *Honor and Shame in the Gospel of Matthew*, 170–71.

40. Duncan-Jones, *Structure and Scale in the Roman Economy*, 144–45; Garnsey, Gallant, and Rathbone, "Thessaly and the Grain Supply of Rome During the Second Century B.C.," 38. On page 96 for a discussion of healthy diets and the consequences of undernourishment and malnutrition.

from under-nourishment and malnutrition-related causes.[41] The owners also shipped and sold their cash crops to areas experiencing crop losses where prices warranted the cost of transport. Storage was a business in itself. Merchants built granaries that they rented out to smaller landowners. With the rental came protection from attack.[42] Pulling crops from food distribution and storing them for speculation was a particular sore point among people in the lower socio-economic segments of the population.[43] Primary sources attest attacks on granaries and their owners.[44]

Level 5: Urban consumers

Level 5 includes nine typical groupings of people who live in the city: estate owner, his staff (including slaves[45]), artisans, bakers, eating-place owners, merchants, day laborers, peddlers, and beggars. Only *Day Laborers* (on the far right) are directly involved in agricultural production. *Merchants* (right side) and *Peddlers* (bottom) might be secondarily involved if they provided materials needed by peasants.

URBAN	Estate Owner (Aristocrat, Merchant)				Bakers	Merchants	Day Laborers
	Consumption	Staff	Artisans	Taxes		Acquire Food	Consumption
	Patronage	Consumption	Consumption		Provide Food	Patronage	Acquire Food
	Debt		Acquire Food			Debt	
	Social Obligation	Social Obligation	Social Obligation		Eating Places	Social Obligation	Social Obligation
	Acquire Land	Local Market	Local Market			(Acquire Land)	Local Market
	Conspicuous Living	Debt / Taxes	Debt / Taxes		Provide Food	Conspicuous Living	Debt / Taxes

Peddlers, Beggars
Acquire Food

Figure 5. Model level 5

On the left is a large unit of boxes labeled *Estate Owner (Aristocrat, Merchant)*. Most aristocrats lived in the city and not on their estates. They received

---

41. Dando, *Geography of Famine*, 44.

42. Lewis and Reinhold, *Roman Civilization*, 2, 127; Rickman, *Roman Granaries*, 209. Lewis catalogues an inscription from the second century describing such a rental agreement: *CIL*, vol. VI, no. 33,860 (= Dessau, no. 5,913 = FIRA, vol. III, no. 145b).

43. Josephus, *Life* 70–71, 117–20. I discuss this point with other examples on pages 216–21.

44. Dio Chrysostom, *Discourses* 46; Philostratus, *Apollonius* 1.15; Garnsey, *Famine and Food Supply*, 77; Jones, *The Roman World of Dio Chrysostom*, chap. 3.

45. Braund, *Augustus to Nero: A Sourcebook on Roman History, 31 BC–AD 68*, 258, 259. Owners were required to feed their slaves. In order to get out of that obligation masters would manumit slaves. The practice was so prevalent that Rome passed laws limiting the percentage of one's slaves that could be freed in a single year (Digest, 48.12.2 pr.[Ulpian]; Gaius, Institutes, 1.42–46 [Lex Fufia Caninia, 2 BC]).

support at least in part by the products of their estates.[46] The gray boxes, *Social Obligation*, *Acquire Land*, and *Conspicuous Living*, are the functions that require revenue from the *Cash Crops* at Level 4. *Social Obligations* were very costly, and like their rural counterparts, the ability of aristocrats to participate in society was associated with their status and honor. Plutarch and Dio Chrysostom described the situation saying that if aristocrats could not display their wealth they might as well be deprived of their wealth.[47] Their social obligations included civic responsibilities such as building projects and underwriting festivals or providing free handouts of food.[48] Most aristocrats were wealthy, but some aristocrats became so deeply in debt[49] from *Conspicuous Living* that they resorted to evading scheduled civic duties.[50]

Aristocratic households often fully employed *Artisans*. Other artisans would function more as independent workers. Within this classification are both individual artisans and small businesses that employed a number of crafts persons. Artisans would receive both food and wages for their services. Some artisans commanded substantial wages, but most lived closer to subsistence level. For example, a Temple artisan in Jerusalem earned 1,200 *denarii* per year compared to a vineyard worker earning 200–250 *denarii* per year.[51] When times were not good, the artisans would need to acquire food from street peddlers, from peasants who have come to the city to sell their food products, from the public eating establishments, or from bakers.

The boxes labeled *Consumption* and *Acquire Food* represent the end-stage of actually getting food to eat for non-agricultural workers living in the city. Given that food was available, the questions are "How was this allocation made?" and "Would a person get enough to sustain life?" Non-agricultural workers acquired food from the local *Eating Places* mentioned below. The group of people varied substantially in economic makeup.[52]

---

46. On Level 4, the box labeled *For City Use* indicates this support.

47. MacMullen, *Roman Social Relations*, 62. Plutarch, *Cato major* 18.4, and Dio Chrysostom, *Discourses* 46.3.

48. Duncan-Jones, *Structure and Scale in the Roman Economy*, 160; MacMullen, *Roman Social Relations*, 61; Garnsey and Saller, *The Roman Empire*, 115.

49. MacMullen, *Roman Social Relations*, 62; Osborne, "Pride and Prejudice, Sense and Subsistence," 140.

50. Garnsey and Scheidel, *Cities, Peasants, and Food*, 8; Hopwood, "Bandits, Elites and Rural Order," 177; Jones, *The Roman World of Dio Chrysostom*, 23. Jones describes a situation in which Dio Chrysostom pleads poverty in order to avoid his duty. Jones assumes Dio Chrysostom would not be alone.

51. Heichelheim, "Roman Syria," 182–83.

52. See the discussion on pages 125–27 for more information on the resources of people in different categories of occupations.

how did people get access to food? 73

The ability to access food depended on financial resources and social standing such as how active a man, or woman, was in civic affairs. Wealthy *Merchants* who owned land resemble aristocrats but without their political power. Some merchants do not own land but had financial resources.[53] Less wealthy merchants, called *Peddlers*, represent the one-family businesses prevalent in first-century cities. *Day Laborers* led precarious lives since work was not necessarily steady.

Another source of food came from the patronage system.[54] A patron would distribute actual food baskets (*sportula*) to clients who were in need, or would give them small coins with which to purchase food. The *sportula* coins were worth six sesterces in Martial's day. While this amount would not provide sufficient food, a person could be the client of more than one patron. Consequently, he or she might be able to receive this type of assistance from more than one patron.[55] *Beggars* had a short life expectancy and they needed to rely on the beneficence of strangers[56] or any food they could scrounge.[57] Almsgiving involved gifts in the forms of coins given the destitute.[58]

Bakers were very important for providing food to the city—not only baking, but also grinding. Some bakers became quite wealthy, as evidenced from their funerary inscriptions.[59] They banded into bakers associations for price fixing and, more importantly, as a powerful force in the political arena since they controlled a primary food source.[60]

---

53. Robinson, "Re-Thinking the Social Organization of Trade and Industry in First Century AD Pompeii," 89. His theme is that "there were fortunes to be made by the economic lower classes."

54. I discuss patronage in more detail on pages 118–121.

55. Garnsey and Saller, *The Roman Empire*, 151; Carcopino, *Daily Life in Ancient Rome: The People and the City at the Height of the Empire*, 171–72.

56. Osborne, "Introduction: Roman Poverty in Context," 5–6. I discuss almsgiving in more detail on pages 115–17.

57. Wilkins and Hill, *Food in the Ancient World*, 137.

58. Longenecker, *Remember the Poor*, chap. 4; Parkin, "You Do Him No Service." Longenecker presents a thorough and succinct discussion on different types of charitable giving in the first century. He supplements the essay by Parkin.

59. Petersen, "The Baker, His Tomb, His Wife, and Her Breadbasket: The Monument of Eurysaces in Rome."

60. Garnsey, *Famine and Food Supply*, 259; Goodman, *State and Society in Roman Galilee, A.D. 132–212*, 56.

Figure 6. Grinding room in commercial baking establishment at Ostia

Figure 7. Baking room in commercial baking establishment at Ostia

Eating Places were prevalent in cities. Joan Alcock mentions six types of food establishments, denoted by the Latin terms: *taberna, thermopolia, popina, caupona, stabula,* and *mansiones*.⁶¹ She classifies the first three as fast food establishments and the last three as hotels with varying levels of food service. The *taberna*, located at the front of a large house, was both a shop and a bar recognizable by its masonry counters with openings to hold large vats, at least in the case of Pompeii. The vats held dry foods such as grains, legumes, beets, chickpeas, fruits, and nuts.⁶² Inscriptions show bars hanging from the ceiling holding hams, sausages, and vegetables. The *thermopolia* was a bar with snacks and drinks. The *popina* was a greasy spoon, to use modern vernacular. They were often located next to baths, and the menu from one in Pompeii lists chicken, fish, ham, and peacock.⁶³ These establishments not only provided food and drink, but were also the social bases for the urban poor, as well as for gambling and competitive drinking. Some men of higher socio-economic status also frequented such establishments.

The *mansiones* were stopping places along a road. They provided extremely safe lodging with good food. The *stabula* was like a modern motel with provision for the safekeeping of horses. The *caupona* provided the worst accommodations. They provided rooms with shared beds and fast food. Menus of such inns in Pompeii listed grains, chickens, dried and smoked fruits, vegetables, sausages, cheese, and fruit.⁶⁴

To recap, members of aristocratic households and wealthy merchant households would have eaten food prepared at the household. Other urban residents would rely mostly on bakers and eating establishments for their

---

61. Alcock, *Food in the Ancient World*, 125–32.
62. Ibid., 126.
63. Ibid., 127–28.
64. Ibid., 126.

food. Day laborers may have also received food as part of their compensation. Beggars would need alms to purchase food and would scrounge from waste products. Urban residents were also known to leave the city and forage for food in the uncultivated land like their rural counterparts.

Model Paradigm Summary

In summary, in the first-century Roman East, access to food began with how much land was under cultivation and what types of crops were grown. The uncultivated areas of land were a secondary source of food for both rural and urban households. Rural households ate what they grew, raised, or caught. However, the crops they grew also covered non-food-related needs such as seed for the next year, taxes, and social obligations. In a bad year when crop yields were low, a peasant household would not have enough to eat because of the other obligations. In a good year, the household might store some of its surplus against a future bad year. Most urban residents relied on food sold in the city for their meals, help from patrons, foraging, or begging. Day laborers acquired food sometimes when they performed agricultural work, but otherwise were like their other urban neighbors. When the incomes of urban residents were high enough and the food prices were reasonable, they could acquire enough food to sustain their lives. Aristocrats and wealthy merchants used food from their estates and food they bought to provide meals for their families and household staff. Their need for conspicuous living drove them toward cash crops to underwrite their life styles. The move toward cash crops caused food prices in the city to rise and amount of food produced for consumption in the rural areas to fall. In both situations, less food would be available for the lower socio-economic segments of the population.

Having used the model to explore in general terms how people in the first century acquired food, the question arises as to how adequate the model is for explaining the ripple effects of decisions that affect the food supply? Peter Temin states the obvious answer. "A good model fits the observed facts more closely than a poor one."[65] Moreover, a model is not convincing unless it bears enough resemblance to historical reality.[66] Obviously one cannot validate the model by direct observation of the first century, but one can validate it to some degree by archaeological data, inscriptions, and primary sources. I have provided some data in the discussion above and I present much more data to support the details in the next chapter, which

65. Temin, "Market Economy," 170.
66. Garnsey and Saller, *The Roman Empire*, 49.

deals with specific mechanisms helping provide sufficient food. The validation problem is somewhat mitigated since I am looking for patterns of social dynamics and not trying to reconstruct a particular historical situation.[67] Nonetheless, as I demonstrate in the next section, one can use the model to bring understanding to particular historical situations, such as the military presence in Antioch.

Using the Model to Trace the Impact of an External Event on Access to Food

A military action occurred during the Jewish War of 66–70 CE that would have had an impact on access to food for many living in the Antioch area. Josephus writes that the number of troops increased to 20,000.[68] Since the Romans were massing for war, their requisition techniques would be more ruthless. Many more mouths to feed and more ruthless actions should have devastated the countryside and peasants' supply of food. Josephus relates that Titus amassed food to take with his army when it went to lay siege to Jerusalem. As many in Jerusalem starved to death, the Romans had abundant food.[69] Hence, the amount taken with them would have been considerable.

The question is, "What effect did the stationing of Roman troops at Antioch have on access to food by the lower socio-economic segments of the population?" Garnsey and Saller write, "Quantifying the needs of the army is a formidable undertaking. To be comprehensive, it would have to take in, among other things, raw materials such as iron, timber, animals for cavalry, transport, meat and leather, products of the clothing industry, other equipment and weaponry, before we come to basic food rations."[70] Scholars have assessed the overall economic effect, but not the impact on particular socio-economic segments of the population. The analyses normally assume the usual occupation levels, but military and political actions, such as staging troops for a war, could decrease the amount of grain available to the poorer rural segments or the poor in the cities who had few resources with which to purchase grain. There are three possible economic outcomes from provisioning the army: (1) increased local economy, (2) no effect, and

---

67. Moxnes, *The Economy of the Kingdom*, 25.
68. Josephus, *J.W.* 3.28, 23.68.
69. Josephus, *J.W.* 5.520.
70. Garnsey and Saller, *The Roman Empire*, 89; Temin, "Market Economy," 176. Temin cites an inscription indicating that the price of grain rose when an army was passing through the area.

(3) depressed local market. I will briefly outline the arguments of proponents for the three positions. Then I will use the model to trace the possible effects military build-up had on access to food for various segments of the population in Antioch.

Keith Hopkins argues the first outcome. What is known is that some of the wages earned by the soldiers went for their own food, clothing and weapons. Moreover, the army purchased and requisitioned food. Hopkins argues that the army was a boost to the economy because of increased trade contracts for food and wages spent for clothing and other items.[71] Fergus Millar, however, examined data from Syria to estimate the cost of housing a legion and decided that, for Syria, stationing of Roman troops was economically neutral.[72] Thomas Carney takes the negative stance when he writes, "Soldiers appeared everywhere . . . as tax extractors. They used their favored legal status and tax exemptions to promote their loan sharking, rentier and entrepreneurial activities."[73] These three scholars offer three different analyses as to the effect of military occupation forces in Antioch on the food supply.

In this section using the model I have proposed, I argue that at a macro-level, the economic effect of an on-going military presence in Antioch was probably neutral. Yet, the effect on specific segments of the population was variable and adversely affected access to food for a number of people. Using the model, I demonstrate how the need to feed and supply the army affected the normal food distribution flow.

The box in figure 8 labeled *Military* indicates the soldiers who need food and supplies. I placed the block between the rural level and the urban level in the model because the effect of the provisioning of the army affected both rural and urban households. The questions for this study address what was the source of food for the soldiers? How did the army acquire its food? In addition to special requisitions and foraging expeditions, the army bought local grain at a fixed price, below the market rate,[74] in a system called *frumentum emptum*.[75] The purchased grain would come from grain previously stored by the local estate owners in granaries, or from current crops as

71. Hopkins, "Economic Growth and Towns in Classical Antiquity," 110, 152–53.
72. Millar, *The Roman Near East, 31 B.C.–A.D. 337*, 45.
73. Carney, *The Economies of Antiquity*, 83.
74. Garnsey and Saller, *The Roman Empire*, 92.
75. Duncan-Jones, *Structure and Scale in the Roman Economy*, 32; Garnsey and Saller, *The Roman Empire*, 96; Rickman, *Roman Granaries*, 71; Pliny, *Panegyricus* 29; Tacitus, *Agricola* 19.

levies.[76] Both approaches had negative effects on food supply for the lower socio-economic segments of the population.

When the army bought from granaries, the grain would come from the stored grain supply as indicated by the large arrow from *Below Market* to *Military—Acquire Food*. The arrow from *Market* to *Bakers* indicates normal sale of grain for city consumption continued as before, if grain were still available. The price to the bakers, eating establishments, and urban residents possibly elevated[77] as the grain owner took advantage of the perceived, or actual, scarcity caused by the army and recouped lost income pressed on him by the army purchase of his crops at below market prices.[78]

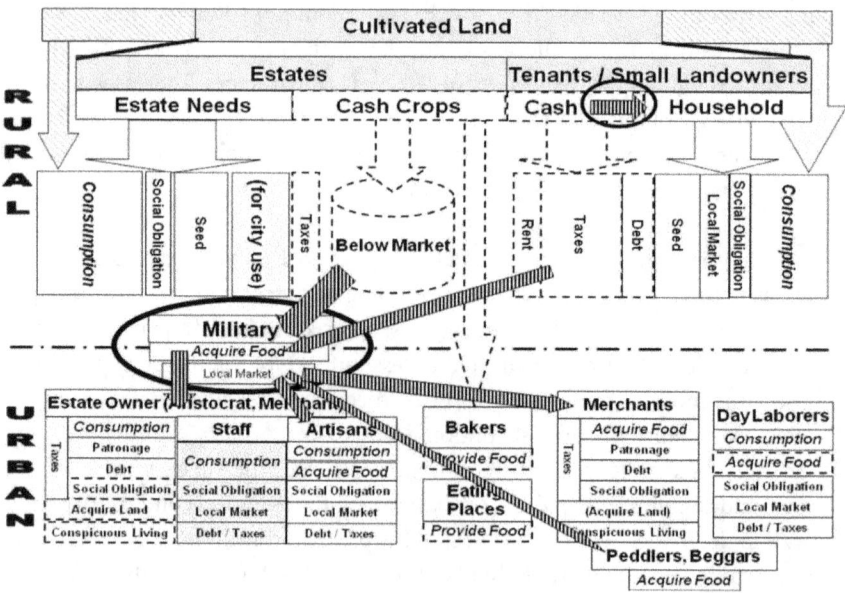

Figure 8. Effect of military occupation presence

The purchasing power of the soldiers brought money into the region, particularly the cities, but the result could be that common items became scarcer causing an increase in prices (see the dark arrows). Entire industries arose, or expanded, to support the military (for example, textiles).[79] The number of people who supported the troops increased, although they might have

76. Hopkins, "Economic Growth and Towns in Classical Antiquity," 47.

77. Cicero, *Ver.* 2.3.93.217. Cicero writes about Gaius Sentius returning home with a sizeable sum of money he had made by selling his rations when the prices were high.

78. Duncan-Jones, *Structure and Scale in the Roman Economy*, 145; Hopkins, "Economic Growth and Towns in Classical Antiquity," 48. Duncan-Jones writes of variability in grain prices over days and weeks in the order of 10–93 percent.

79. Hopkins, "Economic Growth and Towns in Classical Antiquity," 110, 152–53.

come from neighboring villages, which swelled the number of people in the city (merchant, artisan, peddlers). The land-owning merchants profited with increased demands for their products. Since they owned land, they could rely on their own crops and did not need to pay higher prices for grain, or bread. The aristocrats would especially benefit because the entitlement structure would guarantee them any military contracts they wanted. However, this increase in non-food producing people put more demand on the cash crops that fed the cities through the *Bakers* and *Eating Places*. Bakers needed more grain to produce more bread for those with money to buy it. In advanced agrarian societies, the actual production of food could rarely be increased.[80] Hence, increases in population, especially population in cities, would strain the existing balance of food production to food consumption.[81] The total amount of crops produced was limited, but there were more mouths to feed. The lower socio-economic segments of the population would not get as much as before.

When the army acquired grain through purchase and through taxes or levies, small landowners were required to use their grain as taxes in-kind. (Note the arrow from *Small Landowners Taxes* to the *Military Acquire Food* box.) Their households would have less grain to support their needs. Decisions concerning allocation of the household's dwindling grain supply became tougher since seed for planting took precedence, but taxes and debt were still there.[82] Social obligations would have finally started to crumble because there was nothing to share with a neighbor who lost crops from natural causes. Tenants would be in worse shape than would peasants. Tenants would have the same additional drain on resources as peasants, but owe part of their crop productions to their landlords. Over time, the estate owner of tenants' lands would probably force an increase in the percentage of cultivated land to go to cash crops, which led to a further decrease of food crops for tenants working the land.

The situation for the lower socio-economic segments of the urban population is not much better. The *Day Laborer* had a fixed income because

---

80. Moxnes, *The Economy of the Kingdom*, 78; Garnsey and Saller, *The Roman Empire*, 64, 82. Most of the data for agricultural productivity comes from Italy because of a lack of detailed information for the Roman provinces. Garnsey and Saller say that the data does not support arguments that the yields were too low. They state that "smallholders, especially where settlement was dispersed and farmers lived and worked on or near their properties, were in a position to obtain good returns from their crops by intensive methods of production" (ibid., 82).

81. Kautsky, *Aristocratic Empires*, 289–91.

82. Braund, *Augustus to Nero: A Sourcebook on Roman History, 31 BC–AD 68*, 282 (Small, 439). Sometimes when debt became too heavy, peasants walked off their land (called *migration through poverty*) as evidenced by a petition from tax collectors for relief of their obligation since several village populations had dwindled to nothing.

the amount of land under cultivation remained fixed. However, prices for bread and other necessities of life would increase. The *Peddler* might have more income from selling to the soldiers, but prices for food would have gone up (the thin arrow). The beggars had access to nothing since most of their dole came from the non-aristocratic strata that were the hardest hit.[83]

Hence, at a macro level scholars may well be right when they argue that the effect was economically neutral. Nevertheless, my argument indicates that not all was equal across the socio-economic segments of the population. Using the model, I have shown the unequal effects by the additional arrows that represent resources leaving some groups and resources accruing to other groups. As indicated by the direction of the arrows in figure 8, the small landowners, peasants, and day laborers bore the burden of the military presence by having less access to food while others got richer.

To recap, the imperial presence in Antioch in the late first century probably caused the Matthean community—the majority of whom belonged to the lower socio-economic levels—to experience more serious endemic food shortages brought about by heavy taxes and food supplies going to support the Roman army stationed in the area.

Chapter Summary

In summary, a complex web of relationships and processes affected access to food in the first-century Roman East. The Goody Framework helps to formulate and to clarify this web. A specially designed model describes how various groups of people in the first century acquired food by analyzing production and distribution processes and key factors that contributed positively and negatively to access to sufficient food. The model permits analysis for different socio-economic segments of the population. It permits locating practices, critiqued in the Gospel, on the appropriate levels, which leads to insights into why the Gospel critiques the practices that it does. The model strikes a balance between enough complexity to say something meaningful without making claims that available data cannot support. This model will facilitate discussions in subsequent chapters about food-access practices in the first century at, and between, various socio-economic levels. Using the model, I examined the impact on food access for households at varying socio-economic levels from the presence of the Roman occupation forces in Antioch. The discussion showed how such a presence would have contributed to the experiences of the Matthean community. The discussion in this chapter was broad brush so that the paradigm could be firmly established.

83. Longenecker, *Remember the Poor*, 77–80.

4

Most People Could Eke Out a Living

PREVIOUS SCHOLARLY WORK RAISED consciousness concerning the precarious nature of living in the first century. John Wilkins and Shaun Hill summarize the emerging consensus: "The majority of ancient populations lived the hard life of the subsistence farmer or landless labourer, which was insufficient to guarantee enough food for the family unit in all years."[1] The brief section in chapter 1 on economic analysis of food shortages, however, suggested that while food shortages were a problem, the situation was not so severe as claimed by earlier scholarship. This chapter expands on this modification to the consensus by highlighting the survival mechanisms that households in the lower socio-economic segments of the population employed to avoid slipping into more dire situations.

To enable a deeper understanding of the context of the survival mechanisms, I revisit in more detail the question of what constitutes subsistence-level living and argue that most households could eke out a living. I sustain this argument with four claims. First, I discuss what constitutes a healthy diet (that is, calories, proteins, minerals, vitamins, and amino acids). Second, I argue that diets were theoretically healthy for all but the most destitute. I argue the major contributor to unhealthy diets was inconsistency in consuming enough of the types of food necessary to sustain one's body. Third, I argue that to have sufficient food consistently required survival mechanisms. While there was some overlap, the survival mechanisms for urban households were different from those for peasant households. I argue here against the dominant view of subsistence living that does not consider alternate food sources by noting survival mechanisms that provided

---

1. Wilkins and Hill, *Food in the Ancient World*, 51.

additional food items in times of stress. Fourth, I bring together the survival mechanisms with the poverty scale from chapter 1 to show that the most destitute not only had little food but they had few, if any, survival mechanisms available to them. Consequently, their continued survival depended on other people who were willing to share their own sparse resources.

Finally, I conclude the chapter with a description of the horrific conditions experienced when situations of severe food shortages occurred. None of the survival mechanisms of the lower socio-economic segments of the population could protect them in such situations. The situation was truly one in which the vast majority of people died from starvation, or disease due to their weakened condition from too little food. In this scenario, the wide difference in wealth between the few and the many was a major factor in survival.

Diets Were Marginal for Sustaining Physical Life

To be healthy a diet must provide enough calories for energy so the body does not break down body tissues to provide the missing calories. The diet must provide carbohydrates, proteins, minerals, amino acids, and vitamins necessary for the body to repair itself and to keep vital organs functioning properly. A diet can have enough calories, and still malnutrition occurs because a person cannot get enough healthy food. Two questions arise. What kind of diet would sustain life? Could a person in the first century, in theory, consistently get enough calories and enough nutrients[2] for at least subsistence living? Peter Garnsey and Walter Scheidel have addressed these issues,[3] and I use their data. I argue that the diet of all but aristocrats was principally grain-based, supplemented by vegetables, eggs, and occasionally wild game and fish. I argue that this diet was healthy if a person had access to enough food.

What Kind of Diet Would Sustain Life?

With Jesus teaching his disciples to pray for their daily bread, an image is invoked of the majority of the people relying on bread for their diet needs with wine or water to wash it down. Grains were the staple food source across the entire Roman Empire,[4] with estimates between 50 percent and 75 percent

---

2. Dando, *Geography of Famine*, 42. A person can consume enough calories and still suffer from malnutrition.

3. Garnsey and Scheidel, *Cities, Peasants, and Food*, chap. 14, 226–52; Borowski, "Eat, Drink and Be Merry: The Mediterranean Diet," 99–104.

4. Garnsey, "Grain for Rome," 118–19; Safrai, *The Economy of Roman Palestine*, 128;

of the food consumed by a poor urban resident.[5] People consumed grains in the form of bread,[6] porridge, or flat cakes. People ate bread for both of their meals. Bread was often prepared with herbs or honey and sprinkled with poppy seeds or flavored with spices.[7] Porridge[8] had the advantage over bread in that it could be dried and kept for several years,[9] as a source of food when the current-year crops were insufficient. Flat cakes (*plakous*) were common among rural peasants and poorer urban residents as well as desserts for aristocrats.[10] The common ingredients were flour, cheese, and honey.[11]

Wheat is good for providing necessary calories for energy. Somewhat surprising is the fact that the required calories in grain would also provide more than enough protein, with two glaring exceptions: growing children and women who are pregnant or lactating.[12] Protein insufficiency contributes to increased susceptibility to diseases such as tuberculosis, typhoid fever and dysentery and weakens the person's ability to survive diseases.[13] Wheat also provides thiamin and niacin—both B vitamins—as well as vitamin E. On the other hand, wheat is not good for riboflavin (vitamin B2) and vitamins A, C, and D. Deficiency in vitamin A results in eye problems, including blindness (Matt 9:27–28; 11:5; 12:22; 15:14, 30–31; 20:30; 21:14). Deficiency in vitamins C and D can cause problems with bones and teeth (Matt 11:5; 15:30; 18:8; 21:14). Wheat and barley both potentially provide adequate calcium and iron, except in all probability for pregnant or lactating women who would need more than twice the usual amount of calcium required for other adults. Unfortunately, more primitive processing, by the

Horden and Purcell, *The Corrupting Sea*, 201.

5. Garnsey, "Grain for Rome," 119; Safrai, *The Economy of Roman Palestine*, 128; Garnsey and Scheidel, *Cities, Peasants, and Food*, 229; Horden and Purcell, *The Corrupting Sea*, 203.

6. Wilkins and Hill, *Food in the Ancient World*, 126. Peasants also made bread from non-grain flours (for example, acorn and pulse).

7. Alcock, *Food in the Ancient World*, 169; Wilkins and Hill, *Food in the Ancient World*, 118. Wilkens and Hill note that Athenaeus mentions seventy-four types of bread, but his number would have been too low.

8. Wilkins and Hill, *Food in the Ancient World*, 115. Porridge would have been similar to Italian polenta.

9. Ibid., 125.

10. Ibid., 127; Dalby, *Food in the Ancient World from A to Z*, 68. Dalby says that symposia participants ate cakes. Symposia were not venues of rural or urban poor. He also notes the use of cakes in religious rituals.

11. Dalby, *Food in the Ancient World from A to Z*, 68–71.

12. Clark and Haswell, *The Economics of Subsistence Agriculture*, 7; Garnsey and Scheidel, *Cities, Peasants, and Food*, 229–30.

13. Dando, *Geography of Famine*, 44.

people in the lower socio-economic segments of the population, of grains for food obviates much calcium or iron being in a form that can be absorbed by the body.[14] Mineral deficiencies, in general, can cause a plethora of undesirable conditions ranging from poor growth and bone issues to temporary nausea and muscle weakness. To make up the deficiencies in all the needed nutrients, the other 25 to 50 percent of the diet would need to be composed of foods that provide the missing nutrients needed for a healthy body.

Roman diets actually consisted of quite a variety of foods.[15] With the exception of wealthy households, people were mostly vegetarian and typically ate garden vegetables and herbs, chickpeas, beans, apples, figs (delicacy), and cicadas and locust.[16] The legumes (that is, lentils, chickpeas and broad beans) were sources of protein, but more importantly, provided the amino acids and vitamin A missing from a grain diet.[17] Peasants often sold the *better* grains (wheat) for cash and ate *inferior* grains (barley) and other foods.[18] The inferior grains did, in fact, have less of the basic nutrients. An often-made compromise was to extend wheat flour with flour from legumes to make bread, which would have been actually healthier.[19] In the urban areas, people in the lower socio-economic segments of the population also had access to chickpeas, lentils, beans, as well as cheap vegetables such as cabbage, leeks, garlic, and onions.[20] For example, Martial writes about a pudding made of chickpeas and beans that was sold as a hot dish from street vendors.[21]

Breakfast for the majority of people consisted of bread dipped in olive oil or bread with some vegetables. Poor people made do with bread and garlic, but wretchedly poor people ate bread with salt. The evening meal for the non-aristocracy consisted of bread and some hot food, including vegetables, pulses, and legumes with possibly eggs.[22] They occasionally ate

---

14. Alcock, *Food in the Ancient World*, 233–34.

15. Wilkins and Hill, *Food in the Ancient World*, 114.

16. Ibid., 54–56. There were regional variations, of course. In Egypt, people also ate wood grubs.

17. Garnsey and Scheidel, *Cities, Peasants, and Food*, 242.

18. Garnsey, *Famine and Food Supply*, 51; Wilkins and Hill, *Food in the Ancient World*, 52, 135; Alcock, *Food in the Ancient World*, 238, 169. Both authors base their observations on the writings of Galen, a second-century physician, in *On the Powers of Foods*, vol 2. They mention a large range of fruits and vegetables, along with onions and garlic, which peasants could consume immediately, or dry and preserve.

19. Garnsey and Scheidel, *Cities, Peasants, and Food*, 242.

20. Ibid.; Juvenal, *Satires* 3.293; Martial, *Epi.* 13.13.11.

21. Martial, *Epi.* 1.41.46 and 41.103.110.

22. Safrai, *The Economy of Roman Palestine*, 105; Cato, *On Agriculture* 143. Cato insists that the farmer manager's wife should keep plenty of hens for eggs.

meat that they could catch or raise,²³ or at special occasions such as a wedding festival.²⁴

A person's diet depended on the region in which he or she lived²⁵ and on social and political factors. For example, rural peasants living far from larger cities were more apt to consume milk than wine and to use butter instead of olive oil and they would eat different cereals.²⁶ What constituted acceptable food depended on one's social position. For example, a prominent person did not eat barley, which was a staple of people in the lower socio-economic segments of the population.²⁷ The taboo was so strong that, as Joan Alcock reports, Augustus punished soldiers who broke rank by executing every tenth man and making the rest eat barley.²⁸ Sometimes, a city official issued decrees concerning food prohibited from sale at eating establishments. The decrees might be for political reasons, but in other instances, the basis might have arisen from moral issues concerned with consuming some foods.²⁹

In a city, economic means determined specific foods consumed and balances between the food types.³⁰ The beggars ate mallow shoots and withered radish leaves and anything else they could scrounge,³¹ including grain out of horse manure.³² The urban poor ate food purchased from street vendors and fast food establishments that included many of the same types of food as the rural poor.³³ The urban poor rarely ate meat, except possibly

---

23. Wilkins and Hill, *Food in the Ancient World*, 147–53; Varro, *On Agriculture* 2.5.11. Birds were the most common meat for the poor. Pigs were a common, cheap source of meat. Varro mentions that some meat was raised for the market.

24. Wilkins and Hill, *Food in the Ancient World*, 123.

25. Pastor, *Land and Economy in Ancient Palestine*, 5; Richards, *Land, Labour and Diet in Northern Rhodesia: An Economic Study of the Bemba Tribe*, 8–9. Richards discusses the difficulty of studying diets of primitive peoples due to regional variations and preferences.

26. Wilkins and Hill, *Food in the Ancient World*, 22, 41, 24.

27. Ibid., 53. The wealthy did like barley for flavoring, which could have led to decreased availability as food for the poor.

28. Alcock, *Food in the Ancient World*, 229.

29. Ibid., 128–29.

30. Garnsey and Scheidel, *Cities, Peasants, and Food*, 240.

31. Wilkins and Hill, *Food in the Ancient World*, 137.

32. "Nothing was wasted in the ancient world: not an abandoned baby, not the cloth that kept the rag picker in business, not the empty fisherman shack on the beach, not even the grains of barley in horse manure on the streets. There were always people poor enough to fight over another's leavings" (MacMullen, *Roman Social Relations*, 14).

33. Wilkins and Hill, *Food in the Ancient World*, 133–35; Alcock, *Food in the Ancient World*, 169; Garnsey and Scheidel, *Cities, Peasants, and Food*, 241; Goodman, *State and Society in Roman Galilee, A.D. 132–212*, 54–55; Pleket, "Urban Elites and Business in the Greek Part of the Roman Empire," 140. Goodman discusses food coming from

at some public festivals, although the poorer people rarely received meat.[34] The wealthy urban person had a superior diet in the sense that they could acquire and consume foods other than cereals and pulses. They had more variety in their diet, ate the better cereals, exotic imported food, fish, and meat.[35] A lavish ten-day feast in the Iron Age included beef, lamb, stags, gazelles, ducks, geese, doves, fish, eggs, bread, wine, vegetables, fruit, nuts, garlic, onions, and turnips.[36] A mosaic in Antioch depicts a table laden with cakes, eggs, pig's feet, and artichokes.[37]

Thus far, I have argued that the diet of all but the destitute or wealthy was vegetarian with grain prepared in various ways, pulses, legumes, vegetables, herbs, fat from oil or butter, wine or milk, and insects. Most people only occasionally ate fish or meat. The urban and rural non-aristocratic households had similar bread and vegetarian diets. The wealthy households consumed fish and meat regularly. The destitute ate whatever they could scrounge or beg. The diets of all but the destitute were more varied than an emphasis on "daily bread" might suggest. The diets of all but the most destitute were theoretically healthy unless something impinged on a person or household from consistently getting the quantity and quality needed. The question is "Did most people consistently eat the diets described above and, hence, sustain a somewhat healthy body?"

Signs of Undernourishment and Malnutrition

Scholars generally agree that there was widespread undernourishment and malnutrition[38] in the first century.[39] David Fiensy writes that a broader base

peasants supplying the urban eating establishments. On the other hand, Pleket cites a Greek inscription from Lyon of a trader who operated a large general store.

34. Nijf, *The Civic World of Professional Associations in the Roman East*, 157–64, 187. Nifj examined numerous inscriptions about public meals. The entitlement system determined the position of a person relative to public-meal disbursements. The poor person might only receive watered down wine served with a few small pieces of bread.

35. Alcock, *Food in the Ancient World*, 233.

36. Borowski, "Eat, Drink and Be Merry: The Mediterranean Diet," 99.

37. Bockmuehl, *Jewish Law in Gentile Churches: Halakhah and the Beginning of Christian Public Ethics*, 60.

38. Dando, *Geography of Famine*, 42. Dando makes the technical distinction between two terms. Undernourishment refers to lack of sufficient calories. Malnutrition refers to the lack of sufficient essential nutrients.

39. Garnsey, *Food and Society*; Carter, *The Roman Empire and the New Testament*, 116; Carter, "Matthew's Gospel: An Anti-Imperial/Imperial Reading," 427; Whittaker, "The Poor," 286; Sen, *Poverty and Famines*, 14.

of data would help substantiate the claim, and yet, he claims that the average person suffered from malnutrition.[40] One argument points to the high incidence of disease as a sign of malnutrition.[41] A second argument involves emerging research that assesses skeletal remains for signs of malnutrition. Some studies of skeletal remains from ancient times support the assertion of malnutrition in both adults and children.[42] Robert Garland cites studies of remains from Herculaneum that demonstrate female diets were less nutritional than male diets. Children were more likely deprived of food during food shortages, with females suffering more than males.[43] Yet, Estelle Lazer's recent study of skeletal remains from Pompeii suggests the opposite. She cautions that drawing conclusions based on skeletal remains is problematic.[44] After a detailed discussion of medical conditions that might be indicated by bone, skull, and dental materials, she concludes that the people whose skeletons she assessed had not been exposed to major stresses in the form of malnutrition or illnesses in the growing years.

A surprising conclusion of Lazer's study was that life spans for the Pompeii sample were comparable to Western populations. Her conclusions are in conflict with the more commonly held positions on life expectancy. The common claim is that the imbalance in wealth contributed in part to high mortality rates in the lower socio-economic segments of the population. By the age of six approximately one third of children would be dead. By age twenty-six, three-fourths were dead, and 90 percent by age forty-six.[45] The destitute person living in structural poverty,[46] who had no reserves of grain or other resources, would find any food shortage to be

40. Fiensy, *The Social History of Palestine in the Herodian Period*, 98.

41. Clark and Haswell, *The Economics of Subsistence Agriculture*, 23; Garnsey, *Food and Society*, 45–60; Carter, *Matthew and the Margins*, 123–25; Garland, *The Eye of the Beholder*, 21.

42. Alcock, *Food in the Ancient World*, 240; Fiensy, *The Social History of Palestine in the Herodian Period*, 97. Fiensy discusses the problems with using skeletal remains to deduce diet insufficiency. The problems are (1) do not know what type of peasant, (2) geographical differences, and (3) skeleton may be from famine or siege. He observes that another estimate of the prevalence of malnutrition is the ratio of children to adults in tombs. Children are more susceptible to dying from malnutrition. Unfortunately, he provides no data to confirm or deny malnutrition in Antioch.

43. Garland, *The Eye of the Beholder*, 19, 21. Female skeletons showed iron deficiency in forty-one percent of the cases whereas males were at twenty-eight percent. He concedes that the iron deficiency could be from malaria and not malnutrition, which indicates one of the problems with using this type of data.

44. Lazer, *Resurrecting Pompeii*, 220.

45. Carney, *Shape of the Past*, 88.

46. Morley, "The Poor in the City of Rome," 29. Structural poverty refers to people who were born into a situation of mere subsistence living and remained poor.

serious.[47] Consequently, the expected life span for such a person was only twenty to thirty years.[48] The two claims might not be wholly in opposition since Lazer observes that her sample was not necessarily representative of a usual population.[49] The conflicting claims do point to the need for further work in this area to make more nuanced arguments on malnutrition and life expectancies.[50]

Based on this information, I suggest that, while the diets were varied enough to be healthy for the majority of the people, there is no guarantee that people in the lower socio-economic segments of the population consistently had enough of the foods day in and day out, or even year in and year out.[51] For example, food was normally quite scarce immediately before the harvest for peasant households.[52] Moreover, wheat prices are quite volatile in agrarian societies.[53] Cicero writes about a situation in which the price of bread before harvest was almost twice what it was after the harvest.[54] The price increases would have made it impossible for the poorer urban residents to purchase sufficient food.[55] Moreover, I will argue on pages 168–87 that people in the lower socio-economic segments of the population had

---

47. Stark, "Antioch for Matthew's Gospel," 195.

48. Whittaker, "The Poor," 288; Duncan-Jones, *Structure and Scale in the Roman Economy*, 103–4.

49. Lazer, *Resurrecting Pompeii*, chap. 8.

50. Duncan-Jones, *Structure and Scale in the Roman Economy*, 92. He devotes his entire chapter 6 to Roman life expectancy. He notes that the customary life expectancies are not controversial. He also argues that the age expectancies would be highly class dependent. In addition, he postulates that the life expectancies between urban residents and rural residents might be shorter for the former, although the variation is impossible to determine.

51. Carter, *The Roman Empire and the New Testament*, 110; Garnsey and Scheidel, *Cities, Peasants, and Food*, 241.

52. Clark and Haswell, *The Economics of Subsistence Agriculture*, 22. They refer to the phenomenon as *pre-harvest hunger*. People would gain weight after the harvest and then lose it in the pre-harvest period.

53. Duncan-Jones, *Structure and Scale in the Roman Economy*, 144–45; Garnsey, Gallant, and Rathbone, "Thessaly and the Grain Supply of Rome During the Second Century B.C," 38; Livy, 30.38.34–36. Duncan-Jones notes price variations in 45–78 CE within days and weeks ranging from 10 to 93 percent. Livy describes a situation in 202 BCE in a post-war time situation. Prices collapsed in Rome when more grain arrived than was expected.

54. Duncan-Jones, *Structure and Scale in the Roman Economy*, 144; Cicero, *Ver.* 91.214–15. Sacerdos arrived and requisitioned grain before the harvest. The farmers asked to pay in money since they had no surplus grain. Sacerdos, at the request of the farmers, commuted the price to post-harvest levels.

55. Garnsey and Scheidel, *Cities, Peasants, and Food*, 240.

less access to the diversity of food sources described here because of decisions of the aristocracy.

Did a Household Have Access to Sufficient Food?

A healthy diet depends on the consumption of 1,000 to 3,500 calories per day,[56] of the proper mix of foods to provide the necessary vitamins and minerals. The range is quite large because the number of calories varies depending of types of activity performed,[57] as well as the age and gender of the person. Other factors include such conditions as "Is the person fighting a disease" or "Is the woman pregnant or nursing?"[58] Wilkins and Hill estimate that for very active people, such as most of the people in the first century, calorie requirements would have been 2,434 per day for women and 3,337 per day for men.[59] Rabbinic sources specify that a divorced woman should receive enough food to provide 2,700–3,300 calories per day.[60] Using a comparable, current society in which village people eat a similar diet to the one described above, Wilkins and Hill write the diet yields about 2,550 calories per day. Their point indicates that even if a person of the first century consumed the diet outlined above, he or she might still not consume enough calories every day. If a person consumes less than the calories or nutrients she needs, she usually does not succumb to starvation but dies prematurely because her body is not strong enough to fend off disease.[61]

Obviously, one cannot know how many calories a person, or group of people, consumed in the first century. Yet, estimates of subsistence-level income based on calorie requirements form the bases for the economic analyses referenced in chapter 1 and discussed in more detail in the following section. Scholars estimate total yearly grain production in the Roman Empire and then work backwards to arrive at possible levels in kilograms of grain available to categories of people. Based on the calories generated from

56. Friesen, "Poverty in Pauline Studies," 343; Whittaker, "The Poor," 275. Whitaker says that there are no value-free scientific estimates of minimum caloric and nutritional needs.

57. Wilkins and Hill, *Food in the Ancient World*, 61; Cato the Elder, *On Agriculture* 56. Cato stipulates allotments for field workers should be more than the overseer receives. The field workers should get more at times of the year when their labor is heavier.

58. Friesen, "Poverty in Pauline Studies," 343.

59. Wilkins and Hill, *Food in the Ancient World*, 114.

60. Oakman, *Jesus and the Economic Questions*, 61. Oakman is referencing *M.Ket* 5:8.

61. Clark and Haswell, *The Economics of Subsistence Agriculture*, 21.

a kilogram of grain, scholars can then estimate the calories available per person in a category over the course of a year.

Based on the work of Walter Scheidel and Steven Friesen, I have argued in chapter 1 that access to sufficient food was a problem in the first century for many people. I gave no basis for my calculations. In this section, I present my calculations that the majority of households could have lived at or above subsistence level. Table 4 is the original Friesen scale, but using Bruce Longenecker's percentages.[62] Applicable to the argument of this study, Friesen deals with economic, not purely social, stratification in urban contexts. He argues that the previous emphasis by biblical scholars on social status[63] undermines economic analysis of the factors in the first-century society that contributed to the exploitation of the lower social segments of the population. Therefore, he created his poverty scale to encourage other scholars "to stop ignoring the silent majority of the inhabitants of the Roman Empire when we reconstruct Roman imperial society."[64]

Table 4. Poverty Scale

Scale	Description	Includes	Percent of population
PS 7	Below subsistence level	some farm families, unattached widows, orphans, beggars, disabled, unskilled day laborers	25%
PS 6	At subsistence level (and often below minimum level to sustain life)	small farm families, laborers (skilled and unskilled), artisans (esp. those employed by others), wage earners, most merchants and traders, small shop/tavern owners	30% (55%)
PS 5	Stable near subsistence level (with reasonable hope of remaining above the minimum level to sustain life.)	many merchants and traders, regular wage earners, artisans, large shop owners, freedpersons, some farm families	25% (80%)

62. Friesen, "Poverty in Pauline Studies," 341; Longenecker, *Remember the Poor*, 44–59.

63. Friesen, "Poverty in Pauline Studies," 325, 323–37. Friesen gives a good overview of the scholarship trends, which arrived at this position.

64. Ibid., 337; Barclay, "Poverty in Pauline Studies: A Response to Steven Friesen," 363; Barclay correctly takes umbrage with Friesen asserting that scholars are not addressing issues such as exploitation. Twenty years earlier, Frederiksen, "Theory, Evidence and the Ancient Economy," 165, wrote: "The emphasis on 'stratification' has the advantage of reminding us of a total society, in which the great majority were the voiceless poor; the image [layer cake] conveys visually that statuses always existed, and were based on huge discrepancies of wealth."

Scale	Description	Includes	Percent of population
PS 4	Moderate surplus	some merchants, some traders, some freedpersons, some artisans (especially those who employ others), and military veterans	17% (97%)
PS 3	Municipal elites	most *decurial* families, wealthy men and women who do not hold office, some freedpersons, some retainers, some veterans, some merchants	2% (99%)
PS 2	Regional or provincial elites	equestrian families, provincial officials, some retainers, some *decurial* families, some freedpersons, some retired military officers	1%
PS 1	Imperial elites	imperial dynasty, Roman senatorial families, a few retainers, local royalty, a few freedpersons	.04%

Scheidel and Friesen provide categories that are more detailed than Friesen's original analysis. Using three separate methods, they estimate the size of the total Roman economy for the mid-second century.[65] Working backwards, they estimate *per capita* income for segments of the population for different scenarios. The scenarios include minimally sufficient (bare bones basket) and living a respectable life (respectability basket). They divided the categories PS 2 through PS 7 into more detail,[66] with the most gradations for the PS 5 category. The granularity is important since it gives a better picture of the precarious life of the lower socio-economic segments of the population. Table 5 below is a reproduction of their *Table 8: Civilian non-elite gross income distribution: 'pessimistic' scenario (overall per capita mean ~ 460 kg[67] of wheat equivalent per year)*. They then apportion the remaining Roman economy in grain equivalents.[68] Instead of occupational

---

65. Their calculations have to do more with income of a city dweller. They acknowledge rural residents would have had access to food sources not included in the calculations.

66. Scheidel and Friesen, "The Size of the Economy and the Distribution of Income in the Roman Empire," 83. Table 7, Non-elite income scale.

67. Scheidel and Friesen, "The Size of the Economy and the Distribution of Income in the Roman Empire," 84. The economic analysis behind this table is complex and explained in detail in the essay. The *460 kg* number is the overall average for all the Roman Empire, from which they subtract out an amount attributable to the higher social orders.

68. Scheidel and Friesen, "The Size of the Economy and the Distribution of Income in the Roman Empire," 84. The first century did not have a monetary-based economy.

classes, they estimate the percentage of population that would have specific incomes. Table 5 is their pessimistic estimate. They also produce an optimistic estimate, which has 10 percent of the population in *middling* or above status versus 5 percent for the pessimistic estimate.[69]

Table 5. Scheidel and Friesen: Table 8

Level	Wheat (in kg)	Percentage of population	Mean per capita income	Aggregate income (in M kg)
5	3275—3920	0.4	3602.5	978
4	2620—3275	0.6	2947.5	1,201
3	1965—2620	1.0	2292.5	1,557
2	1310—1965	1.5	1637.5	1,668
1	655—1310	3.5	982.5	2,335
0.75—0.99	491—655	8.0	573.0	3,113
0.50—0.74	327—491	60.0	409.0	16,663
0.25—0.49	164—327	22.0	245.5	3,667
TOTAL		97.0	459.0	31,182

I created table 6 to map their grain-equivalent figures to the descriptions of the original Poverty Scale in table 4 above to bring together qualitative and quantitative data. Table 6 has eight columns divided into three sections. The first section is the Friesen Poverty Scale with percentages based on the work of Longenecker from table 4 above. The second section pulls together various columns of table 5 and the analysis by Scheidel and Friesen. I aligned the first two sections based on cumulative percentages of the population. I used two estimates for subsistence incomes in grain equivalents: 335 kg and 300 kg. Both are higher than the 200 kg estimate often used, which does not take into account rent and higher food costs for urban residents.[70] For the last section, I divided the estimated income levels by the levels suggested for subsistence, which yields the ratio of subsistence level to income. If the ratio is below one, the category is below subsistence level.

Scholars of ancient economics use the hypothetical grain equivalents as the measure to compare things economically. Instead of saying, the subsistence level for a family of four living in a city is *x dollars*, they say *y kg of grain*.

69. Scheidel and Friesen, "The Size of the Economy and the Distribution of Income in the Roman Empire," 85. If they add in military, the "middling class" percentage rises about two percentage points.

70. Stegemann and Stegemann, *The Jesus Movement*, 79–86. The cost of living varied across the Roman Empire with some cities, like Rome, being substantially more expensive than other cities.

Table 6. Poverty Scale to subsistence needs

PS Level	% Pop	Cum %	S-F % Pop	Cum % Pop	S-F Range in kg Grain Equivalent	Range as Ratio of Subsistence at 335 kg	Range as Ratio of Subsistence at 300 kg
PS 7	25	25	22	22	164—327	.49—0.98	.55—1.09
PS 6	30	55					
PS 5	25	80	60	82	327—491	.98—1.47	1.09—1.64
			8	90	491—655	1.47—1.96	1.64—2.18
			3.5	93.5	655—1310	1.96—3.88	2.18—4.37
(PS 4)[1]			1.5	95	1301—1965	3.88—5.87	4.37—6.55
			1	96	1965—2620	5.87—7.82	6.55—8.73
			0.6	96.6	2620—3275	7.82—9.78	8.73—10.92
PS 4	17	97	0.4	97	3275—3920	9.78—11.73	10.92—13.07

1. The description of PS 4 as a moderate surplus would indicate it should be positioned more here than at a higher grain equivalent. However, the percentages are quite small and the impact of the move would be negligible.

Two factors influence the analysis. The first observation is that the plight of the 30 percent in the PS 6 category has become ambiguous. The original description says "At subsistence level (and often below minimum level to sustain life)." In the worst-case scenario (335 kg column), all of the households in PS 6 would be below subsistence since the bottom range of PS 5 is already below subsistence. The best-case scenario (300 kg column) indicates all people in PS 6 are hovering just above subsistence. The PS 6 category includes small farm households, day laborers, independent artisans, and most merchants and shop owners. These groups, especially the first two, are those for whom the Gospel portrays Jesus performing most of his ministry of healing and feeding. If the Matthean community had a composition similar to some Pauline communities,[71] the Matthean community would be composed principally of people from the PS 6 category with a few from the PS 4 and PS 5 levels. They would be the ones most at risk of not sustaining a subsistence level if even small changes are imposed. They would be the ones most likely to worry about life in terms of eating and drinking (Matt 6:25).

As much as 30 percent more people would be pushed below subsistence when the number of kilograms needed for subsistence made a 12

71. Friesen, "Poverty in Pauline Studies," 348–58; Carter, "Matthew's People," 139. For a synopsis of Friesen's analysis, see his figure 5: Economic profile of Paul's assemblies. The highest category in which he places any people is PS 4. Carter describes the Matthean community as poor and poorer. On the other hand, the argument on pages 146–55 for the location of Matthean community uses the assumption that it had at least one wealthy person since it was costly to produce a book such as the Gospel.

percent rise from 300 kg to 335 kg. This observation demonstrates the precariousness of many people's lives, and the damage inflicted by rises in food prices in the city or rises in taxes and rents to peasants. Douglas Oakman agrees with this observation. He contends that the diet of the typical first-century person would meet modern estimates of minimal subsistence but barely. If extractions increased, the person would drop below the minimum food requirements.[72] On the other hand, the calculations made no accommodation for alternative food sources, such as wild game, insects, nuts, and berries. The rural households would be better off than the estimates above, while at the same time, PS 5 and PS 6 categories were comprised of people who could easily slide into the PS 7 level if they were out of work, had part of their crop fail, or were assessed more taxes or rent.

The PS 4 households fit the descriptions of a vigorous middling segment that made up 17 to 20 percent[73] of the population.[74] PS 4 would appear to be at little risk of falling below subsistence level since their income was four to almost six times subsistence level.

To recap, the estimates from table 6 show that the majority of the people of the first-century Roman East would have had access to resources permitting them to acquire sufficient food. Yet, segmenting the population into different levels did not dispel the commonly held view of a few having almost everything. That fact notwithstanding, the analysis by Scheidel and Friesen demonstrates that the part left for the masses would have been sufficient for a small middling segment of the population, a large segment near subsistence level, and a small, but still significant, segment at subsistence and under risk of falling into destitution. Since PS 7 accounts for 22 to 25 percent of the population, access to sufficient food was a serious issue. The conclusion accords with Peregrine Horden and Nicholas Purcell, as well as Neville Morley, who observe that, were the majority of a population on the cusp of starvation in good years, the vast majority would not survive their bad years. That scenario did not seem to be the case in the first century.[75]

---

72. Oakman, *Jesus and the Economic Questions*, 62.

73. Given the percentages at the upper end of this grouping were small, it would be easy enough to slide the PS 4 marker back to the 95 percent level to be more in line with its description in table 4 as a moderate surplus.

74. Robinson, "Re-Thinking the Social Organization of Trade and Industry in First Century AD Pompeii," 89, would support this type of analysis: "In the rush to emphasize the scale of upper class economic activity, the presence of any potential independent mercantile group has been largely forgotten. Again, this ignores the fact that there were fortunes to be made by the economic lower classes."

75. Horden and Purcell, *The Corrupting Sea*, 271; Morley, "The Poor in the City of Rome," 32.

These estimates are for a steady-state scenario based on examining the whole of the Roman Empire in broad categories. The Mediterranean was anything but a steady state from year to year across all its regions. Disaster could occur at any time for a particular household or area. It would not affect the aggregate PS level of the tables, but would have adversely affected particular households. The question now becomes, "What resources and mechanisms would any particular household have to survive short-term disaster?"

Survival Mechanisms

The people hovering at the subsistence level practiced various mechanisms to help them have enough food to prevent starvation during short-term interruptions of their food supply. Interruptions for rural peasants included the normal *pre harvest famine* or loss of a few farm plots to hail or spotty rain. Interruptions for the urban resident included prices of food temporarily going up, as in pre-harvest periods, or not finding work. In the sections below, I outline survival mechanisms used in the first-century Roman East to ensure access to sufficient food. I begin with rural households, move to methods common to both, and end with urban households.

Mechanisms for Rural Households

In this section, I argue that peasants employed mechanisms to mitigate the vagaries of the climatic conditions in the Roman East that wreaked havoc with agricultural production. On the average, rainfall would be sufficient, but in any given year for many small areas, the rainfall would not be sufficient.[76] The concept of a *normal year* without shortages somewhere and at some level is a misplaced concept.[77] Equating the concept of a normal year for a particular location, or a particular household, to the concept of

---

76. Hopkins, "Agriculture," 127.

77. Horden and Purcell, *The Corrupting Sea*, 120, 179–80, 262; Garnsey, *Famine and Food Supply*, 9; Columella, *On Agriculture* 3.20.21; Theophrastus, *Enquiry into Plants* xii. Garnsey, along with Horden and Purcell, proposed the concept of micro-regions with their unique characteristics. This is not a new concept since Columella described how much and what kind of seed the farmer should plant in what kind of soil. In 3.20.1, he says all areas have their own variety. With respect to grain, Theophrastus discusses the effects of climatic issues in 8.1.6–7. Horden and Purcell make the observation that the agricultural writers were not proposing better methods but, basically, just enumerating best practices across a number of micro-regions.

self-sufficiency is also not helpful.[78] There were years of glut and years of severe shortage and everything in between.[79] Climatic conditions caused crop shortages to range from transient, localized, and short-term shortages due to spotty rains and hailstorms to protracted, multi-year, widespread severe food shortages.[80]

The work of Garnsey on grain production and yields and percentages of crop failures during the first century is an essential piece of the puzzle surrounding access to food. From his work, one can get a good sense of the fickleness of grain-crop success with data showing some types of wheat failing as often as one year out of three.[81] Fortunately, failure rarely occurred in the same place for a second consecutive year.[82] Garnsey argues that survival depended on peasants following a low-risk production strategy (43) and establishing a social network (43, 55–63). He notes that the estimated farm size was too small to support a typical household on its own production. Therefore, crucial to survival was access to uncultivated land, and other employment (47). In addition, Garnsey discusses dispersal of fragmented land holdings (48–49), planting of a variety of crops—some for consumption and other for sale (52), and storage as an economic necessity (52–55).[83]

Horden and Purcell argue throughout their book that the populations of the Mediterranean had developed survival strategies over time to weather the highly variable climate and social conditions. Alternate sources of food were always present, although the sources of the alternatives varied by the micro-region in the circum-Mediterranean.[84] These alternative food sourc-

---

78. Horden and Purcell, *The Corrupting Sea*, 151; Morel, "The Craftsman," 226; Varro, *On Agriculture* 1.53. Horden and Purcell, as well as Morel, suggest that the ancient literary tradition which lauded self-sufficiency may not have reflected reality—especially for the smaller landowner. Writing of Italy, Varro notes that the landowner could expect to find day laborers for the harvest but if their cost was too high, the field should be pastured instead.

79. Horden and Purcell, *The Corrupting Sea*, 152; Garnsey, *Famine and Food Supply*, 9.

80. Garnsey, *Famine and Food Supply*, 271; Clark and Haswell, *The Economics of Subsistence Agriculture*, 126. The information in the following discussion covers situations in more than the Antioch or Galilee areas. However, Clark and Haswell contend that food production and seasons were similar across the Mediterranean.

81. Garnsey, *Famine and Food Supply*, chap. 1. Garnsey bases his arguments on literary and epigraphic data from Athens covering 600–322 BCE and Rome from 509 BCE through 250 CE. He also uses comparable modern statistics on agricultural yields and climate.

82. Garnsey, *Famine and Food Supply*, 17.

83. Ibid., 43–63. I specify the particular page references in the parentheses.

84. One can describe the mechanisms generically. For example in one micro-region, the inhabitants might net migratory birds, and in another region, they might net

es routinely provided sustenance during the *pre-harvest famine* between planting and reaping when grain supply was at its nadir, as well as years of poor crop yields. The methods of survival included: (1) planting a diversity of crops in garden-size plots across a wide area, (2) animal husbandry, (3) storage of food products, and (4) using uncultivated food sources found in the wild.[85] Storage of food products was crucial to peasants but also for the urban poor. The situation was not bleak but it was still precarious. Having survival mechanisms helped but they were not fail-proof, and a single bad year could wipe out individual households.[86]

Diversity of Food Sources

A principal method for survival was to plant a diversity of crops on small plots of land located in many different areas to mitigate the total loss of crops.[87] Cereals, especially different types of wheat, were the dominant crop for food.[88] Given the remarkably high rate of failure for grains noted above, cultivators sowed mixed crops to mitigate risk.[89] Columella, a first-century agriculturalist, addressed this topic extensively.[90] Farmers planted legumes because, like grain, legumes stored well, provided fodder for any livestock, and some provided food for people.[91] A few examples suffice to illustrate

---

migratory fish. In both cases, they are taking advantage of access to seasonal, non-plant food sources to supplement crops.

85. Horden and Purcell, *The Corrupting Sea*, chap. 4.
86. Garnsey, *Famine and Food Supply*, 23.
87. Horden and Purcell, *The Corrupting Sea*, 201–4; Applebaum, "Economic Life in Palestine," 650–56, 663; Garnsey, *Famine and Food Supply*, 48–53; Grimshaw, "Luke's Market Exchange District," 39–40; MacMullen, *Roman Social Relations*, 5–6; Hanson and Oakman, *Palestine in the Time of Jesus*, 119; Columella, *On Agriculture* 1.preface.22–26. MacMullen, quoting a treatise on surveying by Siculus Flaccus, writes "in many regions we find persons holding lands not contiguous but individual lots in various places, separated by several holdings" (*Roman Social Relations*, 152); Pliny, *Letters* 3.19.14, to Calvisius Rufus. Pliny wrote that he wanted to buy a tract of land abutting his current property, but that action could result in large losses in a single year since both would have the same weather.
88. Garnsey, *Famine and Food Supply*, 50.
89. Ibid., 49; Applebaum, "Economic Life in Palestine," 654; Horden and Purcell, *The Corrupting Sea*, 152. Horden and Purcell note that the production of wine and oil was also variable and could affect the price of grain and thus its availability to the lower socio-economic segments of the population.
90. Columella, *On Agriculture*. In Books 2 and 3, Columella discusses many types of plants that farmers could, or should, plant. For example, in 2.6.4 and 3.20.1, he suggests planting plots with different varieties of vines to ensure a successful crop.
91. Horden and Purcell, *The Corrupting Sea*, 203; Hopkins, "Agriculture," 125;

the variety of legumes used. In some places, rural people subsisted on panic (made into a porridge) and millet (made into bread), which was cheap but required lots of hoeing. On the other hand, lupine required little labor, was cheap, and built up poor soil. Navew and turnips were a staple food for rural populations.[92]

Horticulture, which was less sensitive to rainfall, complemented crops mentioned above. Horticultural crops, such as olives, figs and carobs, and grapes, had their own set of climatic hazards resulting in meager and erratic yields. For example, olives only produce every other year.[93] Nevertheless, many horticultural products were storable for use in bad years of grain production.[94] Olives were particularly good because the cultivator could plant other crops around them[95] and the olive plants survived in years when there was no one to work them.[96] Olive oil was easily stored for future conversion to a cash product in the local market in a bad year.[97] Figs were a prominent orchard crop, which could grow in less desirable corners of the farm garden plots. They were also much more caloric than grain or olives. Carob grew in marginal areas and did not disturb other crop production. It could serve as a food source in hard times and made good animal fodder.[98] Grapes could produce wine or raisins. Both forms were storable.[99] Wine played a part in

---

Fiensy, *The Social History of Palestine in the Herodian Period*, 95; Columella, *On Agriculture* 2.7, 2.10; Flint-Hamilton, "Legumes in Ancient Greece and Rome: Food, Medicine, or Poison?," 372–75. In looking at the long history of cultivation in the Levant, Hopkins notes that grains and legumes were often grown together as complementary crops. Flint-Hamilton has detailed comments on various types of legumes: lentils ("Legumes in Ancient Greece and Rome: Food, Medicine, or Poison?," 375–77), chickpeas (377–78), bitter vetch (378–79), broad beans (379–81), and grass and garden peas (381–82).

92. Columella, *On Agriculture* 2.9.17–18, 12.10.22.

93. Oakman, *Jesus and the Economic Questions*, 27. Farmers divided the groves, which meant that one grove was producing each year. Olives take a long time to produce from seeds—15 years.

94. Hopkins, "Agriculture," 127.

95. Columella, *On Agriculture* 2.9.6.

96. Ibid., 3.1.4.

97. Horden and Purcell, *The Corrupting Sea*, 209–11; Kloppenborg, *The Tenants in the Vineyard*, 297; Freyne, "Herodian Economics in Galilee," 34; Aristotle, *Politics* 1.10.18–10. Aristotle considered them a shrewd investment strategy, if one had a local monopoly. Freyne speaks to the olive oil industry in western lower Galilee furnishing Phoenician cities.

98. Horden and Purcell, *The Corrupting Sea*, 210.

99. Hopkins, "Agriculture," 128; Columella, *On Agriculture* 3.1.10. Columella writes that grapes in grape form did not make a good cash crop unless the farmer lived close to a city.

meeting the nutritional needs of the people, although its production was labor intensive and its yield often moved to a cash-crop status for local consumption by the aristocracy.[100] The need for labor provided a market for peasants to supplement their incomes by working in vineyards.[101]

The discussion thus far has been about cultivated crops that served as food sources, but the prudent peasant used other food sources. Dio Chrysostom describes the varied diet of rural people who lived on public land as coming from hunting and from a small garden with fruit trees.[102] In addition, perhaps to having their own fruit trees, farmers would gather fruit from trees growing in the marginal, uncleared forest areas (*Uncultivated*). Galen described farmers foraging for both supplementary foods and alternative foods (that is, foods eaten normally and those eaten only in times of more extreme food shortages).[103] In the former category are things like apples and pears, which provided rural households with a major winter food when the season was good.[104] Rural households cultivated a kitchen garden of herbs and vegetables and plants used for eating or for preserving other foods.[105] Peasants might also raise birds both for their meat and for their eggs.[106] Last, but not least, Columella writes that honey from wild bees was a source of nutrition and a universal fruit preserver.[107]

To recap, primary sources indicate a strong interest in the need for effective agricultural practices that could ensure at least some plots producing food crops. The writings indicate a variety of crops, which correlates with the description of the diets on pages 83–96. First-century cultivators

100. Horden and Purcell, *The Corrupting Sea*, 215–19; Hopkins, "Agriculture," 128.

101. Horden and Purcell, *The Corrupting Sea*, 216.

102. Dio Chrysostom, *Discourses* 7.11–20, 43–47, 75–76. He has his host describe the life of a herdsman. Although the presentation was stylized, one may assume it bore some resemblance to reality or it would not have been a plausible story; Plutarch, *Mor.* 4.4.1 (667). Plutarch notes that people caught game and fowl in Euboea in abundant numbers.

103. Garnsey, *Food and Society*, 52–53. Garnsey is referencing Galen, VI 513, 517, 522–23, 620.

104. Columella, *On Agriculture* 12.10 and 12.14, especially 12.14.12.

105. Garnsey, *Famine and Food Supply*, 53; Frayn, "Wild and Cultivated Plants," 33; Columella, *On Agriculture* 10, 11.19–53, 12.17.11. The passage in Columella's Book 11 discusses particular vegetables and plants and the timing of their cultivation.

106. Safrai, *The Economy of Roman Palestine*, 105; Malina and Rohrbaugh, *Social Science Commentary on the Synoptic Gospels*, 354; Alcock, *Food in the Ancient World*, 233; Wilkins and Hill, *Food in the Ancient World*, 18; Dio Chrysostom, *Discourses* 7.76. Safrai argues that the consumption of eggs was quite high for peasants in Galilee.

107. "There is no kind of fruit which cannot be preserved in honey" (Columella, *On Agriculture* 9, except 9.1, and 12.10.15–16 [Forester and Heffner, LCL]).

also saw the benefits of non-crop food sources, especially to supplement cultivated food when disasters did happen.

Fish and Wild Game

Biblical scholars have mostly neglected fish as food sources for the Mediterranean. Fish were significant sources for food, especially when they were pickled.[108] The pickling process itself was beneficial from three perspectives. First, all of the parts of the fish were used, even those that would not have been eaten as fresh fish. Second, pickled fish weighed less than fresh fish, which made it easier to transport. Third, the pickle itself was nutritional and supplied nutrients missing in a high-cereal diet. Like crop cultivation, particular fish and their harvesting were unique to micro-regions.

The area surrounding the Sea of Galilee had strong fishing and pickled fish industries, which the Romans licensed for fishing and taxed the catch.[109] The person catching the fish could use it for food, or could sell it for processing. Like grain, fish as a cash crop was part of the survival strategies since fish could be stored against crisis and then sold. The revenue from the sale of the fish could purchase other forms of less expensive food.[110] Plutarch describes fish as a delicacy, howbeit, a quite expensive one. "Sea food is out of all proportion the most expensive."[111] Fish as a major food source in Antioch is unknown, although it would be possible since Antioch was located on a river.

Wild game and birds provided nutrients—especially protein—necessary for a healthy diet. Sources do not indicate how much the peasant population consumed wild game and birds although the sources indicate this was a source of food.[112] Some evidence points to the hunting of mammals such as gazelles.[113] Columella advised larger landowners about creating a game preserve.[114] Hunting inside a preserve was more predictable than hunting in the wild. The owner of the game preserve also exploited seasonal bird migrations.[115]

---

108. Horden and Purcell, *The Corrupting Sea*, 194–96.
109. Hanson, "The Galilean Fishing Economy," passim.
110. Horden and Purcell, *The Corrupting Sea*, 194–95.
111. Plutarch, *Mor.* 4.4.2 (668 [Hoffleit, LCL]).
112. Dio Chrysostom, *Discourses* 46.
113. Hopkins, "Agriculture," 125.
114. Columella, *On Agriculture* 9.1.
115. Horden and Purcell, *The Corrupting Sea*, 187. Migratory birds were sometimes the primary source of food for island societies.

Thus far, I have shown that rural households planted a diversity of crops in multiple, dispersed plots. This technique did two things. First, it mitigated the total loss of crops for food. Second, it provided a relatively healthy diet. Further, rural households made use of naturally occurring food sources from *Uncultivated Land*. Some of these sources were wild game and birds.

Animal Husbandry

Subsistence agriculture in the Levant included subsistence pastoralism,[116] which was a strategy of breeding and herding camels, cows, goats, and sheep,[117] as well as bees, pigeons, and poultry.[118] Domesticating animals offered the same nutritional advantage as hunting wild animals in the summer slump between sowing and reaping, but with less probability of failure.[119] Livestock did require effort because they needed to be "grazed, milked, protected, medically attended, sheared, bred, and exchanged (bought and sold or bartered); they are vulnerable to disease, theft, predation, and wandering."[120] Keeping animals only made sense when their grazing did not impinge on land used for human food crop production.[121] There was usually enough marginal land that some livestock could be kept.[122] In times of unexpected crop shortages, peasants could sell or slaughter their animals for food.[123] Livestock, in this sense, took the place of storage of grain for redistribution in times of shortages.[124]

In the Levant, strong kinship ties across centuries formed a bond of cooperation between subsistent farmers and subsistent pastoralists.[125] The

---

116. Hopkins, "Agriculture," 124; Applebaum, "Economic Life in Palestine," 656; Horden and Purcell, *The Corrupting Sea*, 200.

117. LaBianca, "Subsistence Pastoralism," 116; Columella, *On Agriculture* Books 1, 6, 7.

118. Applebaum, "Economic Life in Palestine," 654; Columella, *On Agriculture* 8.

119. Horden and Purcell, *The Corrupting Sea*, 198.

120. Varro, *On Agriculture* 2.Intro.4–6.

121. Pastor, *Land and Economy in Ancient Palestine*, 10. One estimate says a typical farm household had ten to fifteen goats and sheep along with one or two cows.

122. Horden and Purcell, *The Corrupting Sea*, 198; Davis, *Scripture, Culture, and Agriculture*, 31; Hopkins, "Agriculture," 125.

123. Derrett, *Jesus's Audience*, 96; Safrai, *The Economy of Roman Palestine*, 170; Horden and Purcell, *The Corrupting Sea*, 355; Heichelheim, "Roman Syria," 182–87. The last two sources cited here give sample prices for sheep and goats and other items for comparison.

124. Horden and Purcell, *The Corrupting Sea*, 199.

125. LaBianca, "Subsistence Pastoralism," 118. In exceedingly difficult circumstances, farmers might walk off their land and join their more nomadic pastoralist kin.

approach to pastoralism relied on rain but in a different way than for farmers. For the farmer, rainfall was necessary not only for crops, but also for human and livestock consumption in the dry season. Farmers collected rainwater using human-made cisterns and reservoirs. On the other hand, during the rainy season, nearby deserts produced pastures that could support thousands of animals. The flocks would not compete for arable land with crop production. When the desert became too dry, the pastoralists brought their herds to graze on the stubble and weeds left growing in the fields.[126] Having a herd graze was beneficial to the farmer because it was a non-labor intensive way of keeping weeds from pulling residual moisture and nutrients from the soil that would be necessary in the next planting season.[127] The grazing was beneficial to the pastoralist because it provided food for the herd. The symbiotic relationship between agriculturalist and pastoralist benefitted both and took advantage of climate features of the Levant.

Shared Mechanisms

Two of the most important survival mechanisms, storage and social networks, were practiced by both rural and urban residents. The implementation strategies varied somewhat but the goals were identical. Storage was the first line of defense against temporary setbacks in access to current-year food. Social networks were the second line of defense for the household experiencing a food shortage, and served to bind the extended community together. The third shared survival mechanism was almsgiving.

Storage

Storage of a portion of the crop yield was routine and necessary for survival until the following reaping season.[128] The stored surplus provided seed for the following year and provided food until the harvest the following year.[129] Storage of non-crop foodstuffs (for example, fruit or pickled fish) was also routine and necessary for survival. Storage was critical enough that Hesiod

---

126. Ibid., 117–19; Oakman, *Jesus and the Economic Questions*, 27; Applebaum, "Economic Life in Palestine," 645.

127. Applebaum, "Economic Life in Palestine," 654; LaBianca, "Subsistence Pastoralism," 119. While describing different times, both authors note that goats, more than sheep, were particularly destructive if they got into a cultivated field. On the other hand, the destructive uprooting of plants was beneficial in the stubble and weeds.

128. Garnsey, *Famine and Food Supply*, 77.

129. Ibid., 53–54.

portrayed it idealistically as a moral imperative.[130] At the same time, he gives practical reasons for it when he writes, "lest a bad intractable winter catch you up together with Poverty, and you rub a swollen foot with a skinny hand."[131] Agriculturalist handbooks cautioned farmers to dole out their stored reserves and, if possible, keep back enough for a second year in case the coming year was bad.[132] Unfortunately, grain did deteriorate. Theophrastus noted that seed over two or three years of age is only good for food.[133] The fact that as seed aged it was less likely to sprout was a risk if a peasant household sustained multiple-year failures for a number of its crop plots. Its subsequent yield would be less than usual. One might assume the household could make some trade of old seed for food for new seed for planting.[134]

Successful storage of food products required properly constructed storage vehicles,[135] or places with proper ventilation and temperature. Moisture and pests were a major concern.[136] The storage area for grain for a household consisted of a loft in the house[137] or an upper floor in an *insula* in the city. Other preserved items were stored in specially designed jars.[138] Temperature control might take the form of wine cellars that would

---

130. Hesiod, *Work and Days* 3–4. Hesiod wrote that the gods bless hard work (473–78) and he asserted that poverty brought shame (315–19). To avoid shame he suggested saving, which would fend off hunger (361). If one worked hard, one would avoid going hungry (393–96, 402, 410–13). Sowing and tending carefully would enable the farmer to have enough from season to season (469–79).

131. Hesiod, *Work and Days* 493, 503 (Most, LCL). The final phrase is a description of malnutrition. In 503, Hesiod says that people suffering from hunger should have built storage huts in the summer.

132. Pastor, *Land and Economy in Ancient Palestine*, 175n35.

133. Theophrastus, *Enquiry into Plants* 8.11.14; Varro, *On Agriculture* 1.57.2. In section 11, Theophrastus discusses variations between germination of seeds with respect to age and temperature during storage as well as grubs and worms that occur as seeds age and decay. Varro makes the exaggerated claim that wheat can store for 50 years and millet for 100 years.

134. See the discussion on reciprocity under social safety networks.

135. Horden and Purcell, *The Corrupting Sea*, 204; Columella, *On Agriculture* 12.15–10. The storage technique obviously depended on the plant or animal and how it was harvested and processed. For example, Columella discusses particulars for preserving items from the kitchen garden and their use.

136. Garnsey, *Famine and Food Supply*, 55.

137. Columella, *On Agriculture* 12.12.11–12. It would seem that such situations would not deter moisture and pests, but this was the favored approach by Columella. He even speaks against other approaches.

138. Columella, *On Agriculture* 2.4–5. Columella describes storing food items in a jar with straight walls—not like amphora for wine—so that the stored item would not float to the top but could be packed down and liquid placed on top to keep pests out.

be cooler and have a more stable temperature than aboveground storage.[139] For smaller farming households, an effective approach against insects was sealing an underground store.[140] Scholars know very little about the losses by smaller landowners and households in the cities in the lower socio-economic segments who could not afford better storage techniques. Clark and Haswell estimate loss as high as 35 to 50 percent, which would be a serious blow to those already with barely enough to eat.[141]

Thus far I have argued that rural households did not need to store a full year's food requirements since they could use alternate food sources that usually occurred all through the year. Nevertheless, they used a variety of methods to preserve and store food stuffs to mitigate loss through decay and from pests. Some of the techniques preserved food for multiple years and would be a crucial source of food for a bad year, or for giving to a neighbor who had a bad year. Urban households principally relied on the availability of stored food at reasonable prices.

Storage was also necessary to sustain the populations of cities year round,[142] but not all surpluses of stored grain was available for residents (see figure 9). Storage by the large landowner became a counter-survival mechanism for many urban people in the lower socio-economic segments of society when landowners held back their grain from the market.[143] Moreover, the Roman government took grain from the market to support its military and the life style of its officials. Some cities, through their local agents, took grain from the market.[144] They stored grain that they received as tax and rent payments from the independent landowners,[145] and sold it to achieve political ends. Archeological evidence and primary sources attest to such storehouses

---

139. Arav, "Bethsaida Excavations: Preliminary Report, 1994–1996," 97–102. Arav reports on a courtyard house with triclinium indicating a well-to-do household. Excavators found a subterranean structure holding a number of wine amphora as well as pruning hooks. They dubbed the house "the House of the Vintner"; Columella, *On Agriculture* 12.18–25 on wine-making, 12.26 on what to do if wine soured, and 12.31 on what to do if an animal died in it.

140. Horden and Purcell, *The Corrupting Sea*, 205.

141. Clark and Haswell, *The Economics of Subsistence Agriculture*, 62.

142. Horden and Purcell, *The Corrupting Sea*, 208.

143. I take up this assertion in more detail on pages 189–93.

144. Rickman, *Roman Granaries*, 180–81, 163. Funerary inscriptions for men who were responsible for the operation of storehouses provide some of the data.

145. Kloppenborg, *The Tenants in the Vineyard*, 323.

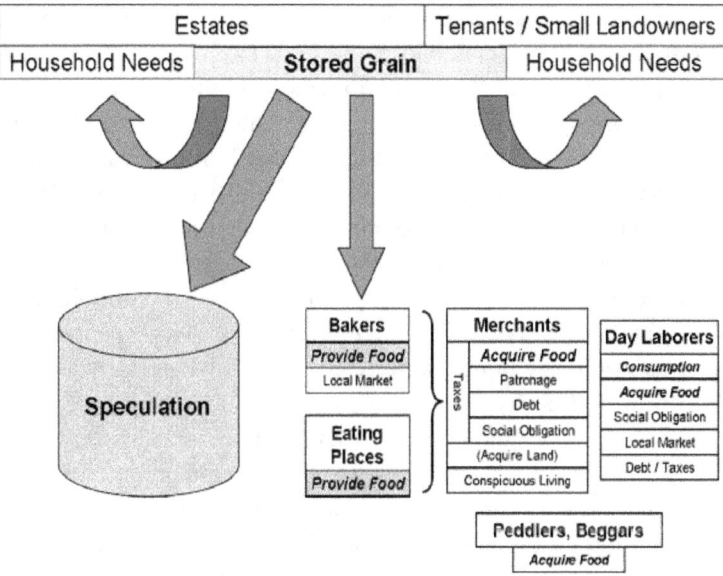

Figure 9. Uses of stored grain

(*horrea* is the more general term)[146] both near Antioch and in the Galilee area near Sepphoris, Tiberius, and Bethsaida.[147] Large estates may have had their own *horrea*, but medium to small landowners could not afford either to build a *horrea* or to defend it. Merchants built commercial *horrea* and rented space to smaller estate landowners.[148] With the rental of

---

146. Varro, *On Agriculture* 42; Columella, *On Agriculture* 1.6.9–20 and other places to a lesser extent; Rickman, *Roman Granaries*, 61, 62. Storehouse, or granary, might bring to mind the silo of current farming areas in the United States. However, the *horrea* would have looked more like a large, rectangular warehouse with multiple rooms around the sides and perhaps even more than one floor. Various agricultural writers devoted space to describe the construction of *horrea*. Rickman notes that the Roman military *horrea* had a standard design. He lists no military *horrea* for Antioch or the Galilee, despite troops stationed in Antioch.

147. Rickman, *Roman Granaries*, 209; Freyne, *Galilee: From Alexander the Great to Hadrian*, 7; Freyne, "Galilee and Judaea in the First Century," 44; Jonathan L. Reed, "The Social Map of Q," 25; Applebaum, "Economic Life in Palestine," 647, 660, 696; Geyer, "Evidence of Flax Cultivation from the Temple-Granary Complex Et-Tell (Bethsaida/Julias)," 231. Freyne attests imperial granaries in both upper and lower Galilee. Reed asserts sizable granaries in both Sepphoris and Tiberius. Applebaum places granaries on the maritime plain at Jabneh and Jamnia on imperial land. Geyer discusses the granary at Bethsaida.

148. Lewis and Reinhold, *Roman Civilization*, 2, 127. Lewis catalogues an inscription from the second century: *CIL*, vol. VI, no. 33,860 (= Dessau, no. 5,913 = FIRA, vol. III, no. 145b); Gardner and Wiedemann, *The Roman Household: A Sourcebook*, 74–75. They catalog an inscription from Pompeii concerning the provision of foodstuffs securing a loan.

the rooms came protection, although with caveats on liability under some circumstances.[149] Both public and private *horrea* were targets of people who were desperate for food.[150] The attack might be in the form of pilfering by workers or through direct violent attack.[151] The *horrea* were also targets during war.[152] The grain stored, that was not used for political purposes or for speculation,[153] became available for bakers and eating establishments to provide food for the lower socio-economic segments of the population who had money with which to purchase the offered foods.

To recap, survival techniques for peasants involved production and storage of many different types of food crops; keeping a kitchen garden; raising domesticated animals, birds, and bees; capture of wild game and birds; and collection of wild plants. They needed a variety of techniques because the climate in the Mediterranean was fickle and could cause local losses of crops on a frequent basis. The fickleness of the climate could prevent day laborers from having jobs to earn money to purchase food and could cause food prices to rise beyond the capabilities of PS 5 and PS 6 households to purchase food. Sometimes even these survival mechanisms were not sufficient and peasants fell back on a social safety network of kin and neighbors.

Figure 10. Inner room of a *horrea* in Ostia

Figure 11. Outside view of *horrea* in Ostia

149. Rickman, *Roman Granaries*, 209. An example of a caveat is robbery with violence.

150. Braund, *Augustus to Nero: A Sourcebook on Roman History, 31 BC-AD 68*, 288. Braund catalogues a petition to the chief of police complaining about the theft of twenty loads of anise from a storehouse and the apparent inactivity of the village elder to discover those responsible for the theft.

151. Scott, *Weapons of the Weak*, 32.

152. Josephus, *Life* 118–20.

153. I take this topic up in more detail on pages 189–93.

Social Safety Networks

When the other methods failed, reallocation of food stores was an imperative of survival.[154] Reallocation was the primary social safety network for people and households in all socio-economic segments of society in the first-century Roman East. The relationships underlying reallocation were quite complex in character.[155] To understand the place of reallocation in the survival strategies, I describe the two major competing systems—reciprocity and redistribution—individually and then bring them together. A key point is that economic systems, of which reallocation was a part, were embedded in the first-century society.[156] These systems both drove and reflected social organization. Exchanges established new relationships and reinforced existing relationships.[157]

These exchanges had a moral foundation (that is, rule abiding that society defined).[158] For example, in a village there would be a moral expectation that those with more should share with those having less. This expectation might not extend to the absentee landowner who did not share with the tenant because the social distance was too great.[159] The example shows that the social distance between the two entities involved (that is, by kinship, social rank and wealth) did affect the types of exchanges.[160] Garnsey and Saller write, "The place of a Roman in society was a function of his position in the social hierarchy, membership of a family, and involvement in a web of personal relationships extending out from the household. Romans were obligated to and could expect support from their families, kinsmen and dependants both inside and outside the household, and friends, patrons, protégées and clients."[161] Basically, the closer the distance, the less exploitative was the exchange.

---

154. Horden and Purcell, *The Corrupting Sea*, Chaps 6 and 9; Garnsey, *Famine and Food Supply*, 55.

155. Goody, *Cooking, Cuisine, and Class*, 45; Davies, "Linear and Non-Linear Flow Models for Ancient Economies," 142–54, particularly figure 6.14 on p. 150. Davies shows the myriad of different types of economic flows in the Roman period.

156. Sahlins, *Stone Age Economics*, 301; Polanyi, "The Economy as Instituted Process," 253.

157. Weiner, "Reciprocity," 1060; Polanyi and Pearson, *The Livelihood of Man*, 36. Polanyi and Pearson do state that the movement and integrative effect of these exchanges requires definite structures in society. The argument is close to being circular.

158. Sahlins, *Stone Age Economics*, 198; Scott, *Weapons of the Weak*, 184; Stark, "Antioch for Matthew's Gospel," 191.

159. Oakman, *Jesus and the Economic Questions*, 152.

160. Sahlins, *Stone Age Economics*, 191, 197.

161. Garnsey and Saller, *The Roman Empire*, 148.

At the most basic level, reallocation involved reciprocity between households within a kinship group.[162] For example in the *Euboean Discourse*, Dio Chrysostom describes the exchange between the grown daughter and her husband with her father. She and her husband provided wheat, and her father provided game, fruit and vegetables.[163] At the other end of the spectrum where social distance was great, one finds redistribution. Aristocrats sold grain out of the local area for a profit with little consideration of the effect of the sale on the local inhabitants who might no longer have had access to affordable grain. Patronage occurred in between these two ends.[164]

Exchanges[165] took two forms: redistribution (market-exchange) and reciprocity.[166] Alicia Batten writes, "Although conceptually reciprocity and market exchange may be opposed they not only coexist in reality but interact continuously. While the market economy profoundly influenced the operation of reciprocity relations and networks, the latter in turn influenced the market system."[167] Redistribution involved the extraction, storage, and eventual distribution of crops to further political goals[168] not necessarily in the best interests of the small landowners or non-aristocrats in the city.[169] The direction of the flow of goods was from the rural areas to the

---

162. Firth, *Primitive Polynesian Economy*, 11. Firth reports two findings from his field work that are germane to this discussion. First, the landowners paid their female laborers more if the women were kinsfolk. Second, laborers preferred to be paid in grain, but the landowners preferred to pay in coin. Kinfolk were more likely to be paid in grain.

163. Dio Chrysostom, *Discourses* 69.

164. On the issue of patronage in the rural areas, see: Hanson and Oakman, *Palestine in the Time of Jesus*, 73; Garnsey, *Famine and Food Supply*, 58.

165. Polanyi, "The Economy as Instituted Process," 266, defines exchange as "the mutual appropriative movement of goods between hands." He writes that all exchanges have a rate associated with them. The difference between redistribution and reciprocity lies in how the rate is established.

166. Firth, *Primitive Polynesian Economy*, 313. Firth's book contains an excellent discussion on the difference between these economic approaches by a society. He illustrates the points with observations and descriptions of the practices and values of a tribal group in a setting with many characteristics in common with the rural first-century Roman East.

167. Batten, "The Degraded Poor and the Greedy Rich: Exploring the Language of Poverty and Wealth in James," 68n68; Carney, *The Economies of Antiquity*, 73; Weiner, "Reciprocity," 1066.

168. Sahlins, *Stone Age Economics*, 189–90; Moxnes, *The Economy of the Kingdom*, 39. Moxnes notes that war is a basic form of redistribution.

169. Polanyi, "The Economy as Instituted Process," 254. Redistribution can also apply to a household or a village. Extending this thought, one might observe that this type of redistribution came into play during periods of extreme food shortages when decisions were made about who in the household received how much food.

aristocracy.[170] Society defined and maintained the rights and obligations sanctioning the movements from the poor to the politically powerful. The power to determine the rights and obligations resided with the aristocracy[171] and ultimately with the emperor.[172]

Two distinctions between reciprocity and redistribution concern the period before the return and the value of the return. In reciprocity, the receiving party might delay the return until the giving party needed a return. The return might not be the same value as the original exchange, as our market-based economy would expect.[173] On the other hand, redistribution has immediacy about it (for example, taxes are due now). Redistribution has a negotiated value (for example, rent is a certain percentage of the crop and is due at harvest). K.C. Hanson and Douglas Oakman suggest that redistribution denotes more "the person gets what the elites allow" and reciprocity leans toward "the person gets what he needs."[174]

Reciprocal relations, unlike redistribution, ensured two things: distribution of goods would be equitable,[175] and help would be available.[176] When the economy of a village is reciprocity-based, the maintenance of social relationships is more important than economic motives.[177] Solidarity of the village would be undermined if one villager profited at the expense of food for another.[178] Social motives were also behind redistribution, but with

---

170. "The institutionalization and the 'setting up' of the rules is primarily a work of the elite on the basis of their conceptions and visions" (Moxnes, *The Economy of the Kingdom*, 38).

171. Polanyi and Pearson, *The Livelihood of Man*, xxxiv; Polanyi, "The Economy as Instituted Process," 253; Firth, *Primitive Polynesian Economy*, 233.

172. Oakman, "The Ancient Economy in the Bible," 35; Oakman, *Jesus and the Economic Questions*, 78. Oakman emphasizes that politics was personal and not institutional.

173. Temin, "Market Economy," 170. Temin states that the return would be balanced in a manner determined by tradition and society.

174. Hanson and Oakman, *Palestine in the Time of Jesus*, 113.

175. Polanyi, "Aristotle Discovers the Economy," 90.

176. Scott, *Arts of Resistance*, 131. The exception was when a household had incurred the contempt of its neighbors. A household held in contempt would not be able to exchange labor, borrow a draft animal, find spouses for the children, make a loan, or otherwise participate in typical social interactions.

177. Fusfeld, "Economic Theory Misplaced: Livelihood in Primitive Society," 349.

178. Polanyi and Pearson, *The Livelihood of Man*, 37; Temin, "Market Economy," 177. In Egypt, records indicate that, within an estate, market exchanges occurred. Temin, who advocates for market-based economy, bases his observation on prices recorded for services and goods, including grain. However, he does not discuss how the prices were set.

profit-driven decisions.[179] For example, the aristocracy needed large sums of money to maintain their status.[180] To achieve this end, they would make economic decisions with little regard for their social inferiors.[181]

Reciprocity encompasses a continuum from general reciprocity between close kin and friends[182] at one end to balanced reciprocity with other people in the village to negative reciprocity with strangers[183] at the other end of the continuum.[184] Negative reciprocity is "doing unto others as you would not have them do unto you." It is an ethos of distrust of or hostility to an enemy. It may include hostility to any non-kin person,[185] including people dwelling in the city to which the rural area is associated.[186] An example of negative reciprocity is a situation in which a peasant soaks the grain before taking it to market in the city so that it will weigh more and its sale will garner more money. *Quid pro quo* best describes balanced reciprocity where the recipient may receive wheat but return the favor with helping to build a shed.[187] General reciprocity encompasses giving of a gift without thought of return,[188] although socially defined expectations would encourage the

---

179. Polanyi and Pearson, *The Livelihood of Man*, xxxiv, 40.

180. Osborne, "Pride and Prejudice, Sense and Subsistence," 125–31.

181. Malina, "Wealth and Poverty in the New Testament and Its World," 360.

182. Sahlins, *Stone Age Economics*, 191,194; Moxnes, *The Economy of the Kingdom*, 62; Saller, *Personal Patronage under the Early Empire*, 82; Hanson and Oakman, *Palestine in the Time of Jesus*, 113; Varro, *On Agriculture* 1.16.13. Varro encourages a small landowner to set up a local network to share implements he could not afford alone.

183. Sahlins, *Stone Age Economics*, 194–95; Moxnes, *The Economy of the Kingdom*, 62; Firth, *Primitive Polynesian Economy*, 310.

184. Stegemann and Stegemann, *The Jesus Movement*, 36. This page contains an excellent figure showing the different types of reciprocal relationships applied to the first century.

185. Ohrenstein, "Talmud and Talmudic Tradition," 253. The Hebrew Scriptures frequently speak against negative reciprocity and speak for the provision for the alien and stranger.

186. Sahlins, *Stone Age Economics*, 195–97, 203; Horsley, *Galilee*, 177. Sahlins talks to kinship distance being defined by the community. According to Horsley, the situation by which the area around the city became the property of the city did not occur in Galilee before the second century.

187. Polanyi, "Aristotle Discovers the Economy," 90, notes that "the indigent who possessed no equivalent to offer in exchange had to work off his debt (hence the great social importance of the institution of debt bondage)."

188. Hanson and Oakman, *Palestine in the Time of Jesus*, 113, describe the gift as being freely given; Weiner, "Reciprocity," 1062–1064, traces the history of scholarship concerning gift giving. She notes that Marcel Mauss, in his groundbreaking book *The Gift*, argues that, under the umbrella of reciprocity, a person freely gives a gift. Since his work, other anthropologists, such as Levi-Strauss, have shown that a person often gives the gift with ulterior motives, especially if the gift is a woman in marriage. The more

most people could eke out a living 111

recipient to find some way to thank the donor.[189] In fact, the moral reputation of a person depended somewhat on whether he returned favors.[190]

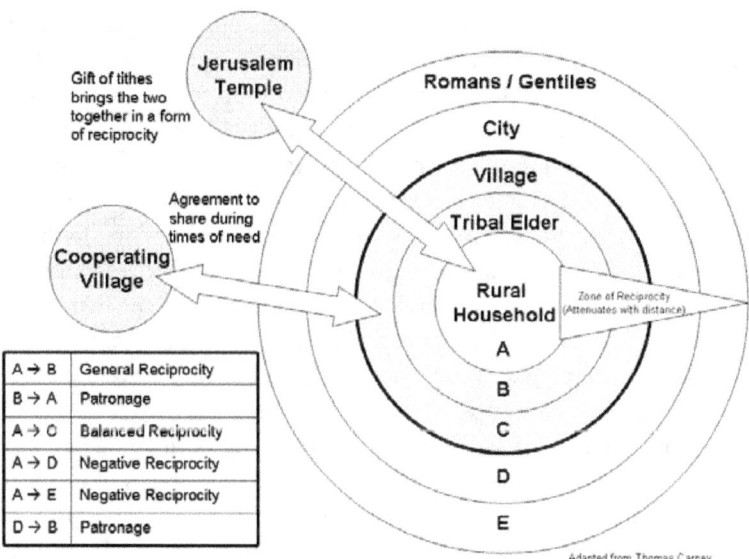

Figure 12. Reciprocal relations

Figure 12 depicts in a simple manner reciprocal relations between different segments of the society. General reciprocity is "the cement of life" for rural societies since it operates in a group in which members respond to each other in compassion and with willingness to help another even if it means denying themselves. They know that if the situation reversed, the person they are helping would help them.[191] They not only share tangible items such as

commonly accepted view is that the gift is not freely given but the expected return is more fluid than in reciprocity.

189. Oakman, *Jesus and the Economic Questions*, 78–79; Firth, *Primitive Polynesian Economy*, 310–11; Lendon, *Empire of Honour*, 63; Sahlins, *Stone Age Economics*, 202.

190. Lendon, *Empire of Honour*, 68; Moxnes, *The Economy of the Kingdom*, 62; Sahlins, *Stone Age Economics*, 221. Sahlins notes that the returned favor might not be a material transfer. The return could be in the form of a feast or celebration.

191. Derrett, *Jesus's Audience*, 67, 38; Moxnes, *The Economy of the Kingdom*, 77; Sahlins, *Stone Age Economics*, 210. Moxnes argues against general reciprocity by evoking the concept of limited good. The problem with his argument is that he assumes individualism and so moves to negative reciprocity with everyone being an enemy or an outsider. On the other hand, Sahlins correctly notes "the habit of share and share alike is easily understandable in a community where everyone is likely to find himself in difficulties from time to time, for it is scarcity and not sufficiency that makes people more generous, since everybody is thereby ensured against hunger" (*Stone Age Economics*, 210).

food and utensils but they share their time to help a neighbor.[192] Such a social organization was a key survival factor to a small farmer whose livelihood could easily be damaged (for example, by a wild animal rooting in his crop). For that year, the farmer would need assistance from a kinsman or village friend. In another year, when the helper experienced such an event, the farmer would come to the aid of his former helper to overcome the shortfall.[193] Within the city, ethnic precincts could act somewhat like villages with similar social safety networks for established members. On the other hand, in times of more severe food shortages, the sudden influx of rural people into a city would overwhelm the reciprocity system.[194] The people flocking to the city would need to rely on the aristocracy—not kin or friends—to feed them.[195]

In tribal oriented societies found in the rural areas of the first-century Roman East, the relationship between the household and tribe, of which it was a member, was quite strong based on common lineal descent dating to prehistoric times, which engendered a strong sense of loyalty.[196] This loyalty formed the basis for various forms of cooperation between kin in periods of poor food availability. On pages 102–3, I note the cooperation of pastoralist and agriculturalist. The relationship of the household to its tribe is primarily general reciprocity tempered with balanced reciprocity.[197] Karl Polanyi goes so far as to say, "the community keeps all its members from starving unless it is itself borne down by catastrophe, in which case interests are again threatened collectively, not individually."[198] In practical terms, such a utopia did not exist. There was no idealization of community, and there were definite ideas about who owned what and how far compassion extended.[199] For example,

---

192. Oakman, *Jesus and the Economic Questions*, 23.

193. Garnsey and Woolf, "Patronage of the Rural Poor in the Roman World," 156. This type of reciprocity does not work on the basis that the first farmer received two *modii* of grain when he needed it. He will later give the second farmer two *modii* of grain even if he needs three. Instead, it operates based on both receiving necessary aid from each other when needed. If the second farmer needs three *modii*, the first farmer will give him three.

194. Finger, *Of Widows and Meals: Communal Meals in the Book of Acts*, 131; Meggitt, *Paul, Poverty and Survival*, 169.

195. Garnsey and Woolf, "Patronage of the Rural Poor in the Roman World," 157.

196. LaBianca, "Subsistence Pastoralism," 118–19.

197. Lev 25:14 supports this concept when it cautions that people involved in economic transactions should not wrong one another. Deut. 15:7–8 says a person should not only extend his hand to the needy neighbor but should loan him enough to cover his need.

198. Polanyi, *The Great Transformation: The Political & Economic Origin of Our Time*. 46.

199. Firth, *Primitive Polynesian Economy*, 59.

Hesiod cautioned that a household in need could only approach a neighbor for a limited number of times without reciprocating in return.[200]

Food was part of the general manner in which people exchanged goods, but more restrictions were in place for food, which was essential for life, than for non-food goods.[201] In time of need, a person might exchange food with another person or group with whom no other exchanges would normally occur.[202] Villages, towns, and cities had standing reciprocal agreements to help each other out when needed and the other village, town, or city was not suffering the same fate.[203]

These more benign forms of reallocation should not blind one to the fact that for the most part many of the relationships were "usually mediated through control exercised by the powerful—landlords, entrepreneurs, or officials—who seek out the areas of shortfall in order to dispose advantageously of what they have accumulated."[204] For example, farmers coming to the city voluntarily to satisfy their households' needs were in a positive relationship with the city.[205] Whereas, the converse is a negative relationship when a city initiates the action to extract taxes and rents,[206] which might be beyond the ability of a peasant's means to pay.[207] In this

---

200. Hesiod, *Work and Days* 400, 344–50.

201. Carney, *The Economies of Antiquity*, 60; Finger, *Of Widows and Meals: Communal Meals in the Book of Acts*, 128; Fiensy, "Ancient Economy and the New Testament," 199–205; Davies, "Linear and Non-Linear Flow Models for Ancient Economies." Adapting models by Davies to the Galilee, Fiensy describes deeply and succinctly the flow of goods to explicate the Galilean economy. This essay is an excellent discussion of a typical Roman East economy that is coming from a market-based perspective.

202. "Among goods exchanged, food is most often used in generalized reciprocity, and because of standards of hospitality, food is extended to a wider sphere of human relationships than are other things" (Sahlins, *Stone Age Economics*, 217).

203. Garnsey, *Famine and Food Supply*, 55, 73.

204. Horden and Purcell, *The Corrupting Sea*, 206; Oakman, *Jesus and the Economic Questions*, 79. Oakman holds a similar position.

205. Garnsey, *Famine and Food Supply*, 56, 43; Jones, *The Greek City*, 263. In some cases, peasants would sell items from their kitchen gardens to acquire things that they were deficient in such as salt. In other cases, peasants would sell to pay obligations. Garnsey suggests that the smaller farming households produced most of the food for a city. He does also say that in times of more severe shortages the citizens expected the elite of the city to protect them. Jones argues that merchants bought from peasants and sold to aristocrats. Merchants paid a peasant in cash, which the peasant used to pay taxes and rent.

206. Julian, *Misopogon* 352C. A city itself could own land that it leased out to villages, or tenants, to cultivate. A late example comes from Julian describing Antioch as owning 10,000 lots of land.

207. Oakman, *Jesus and the Economic Questions*, 57–72. Oakman's section on "Level of Subsistence, Taxes, and Rents" is a good source for examining this relationship in more detail.

latter case, redistribution was power-based and disrupted flow of goods based on reciprocity.[208]

To recap, reallocation could be a key survival mechanism when based on a reciprocal social organization. It helped to mitigate the year-to-year imbalances.[209] The city population would be more heavily market-based but still have strong vestiges of reciprocity through patron-client relationships (see below). The rural population operated more on a reciprocity base in their daily lives although entering into the market at the fringes.[210]

Almsgiving

Almsgiving involved gifts in the forms of coins given the destitute.[211] While scholars may not understand how almsgiving functioned prior to the expansion of Christian writings on the topic[212] and rabbinic writings,[213] almsgiving must have functioned in some manner since primary sources attest to the presence of beggars. Advice concerning almsgiving was not uniform. Epictetus advocates that one should ignore beggars, if possible.[214] Seneca described aristocrats flinging coins at the beggars in order to keep as far away from them as possible.[215] Aristocrats may have been reacting to the squalid condition of the destitute,[216] or they were repulsed because many beggars were deformed.[217] Cicero wrote that giving alms to the poor would corrupt them and encourage disorderly, idle mobs.[218] Seneca writes that a Stoic wise man should not feel pity, but he should give to the anonymous poor.[219]

208. Ibid., 79.

209. Garnsey and Woolf, "Patronage of the Rural Poor in the Roman World," 156.

210. These are generalized comments. I am not reopening the dual economy model question. I am suggesting that within the economic structures some people operated more from a reciprocal orientation than others did. See Abrams for a short discussion of the topic. Abrams, "Introduction" in *Towns in Societies*.

211. Longenecker, *Remember the Poor*, chap. 4; Parkin, "You Do Him No Service." Longenecker presents a thorough and succinct discussion on different types of charitable giving in the first century. He supplements the essay by Parkin.

212. Parkin, "You Do Him No Service," 6, 70.

213. Hamel, *Poverty and Charity in Roman Palestine*, 216–19.

214. Parkin, "You Do Him No Service," 61; Epictetus, *Discourses* 3.22.89.

215. Seneca, *Moral Essays on Mercy* 2.6.2.

216. Parkin, "You Do Him No Service," 69.

217. Garland, *The Eye of the Beholder*, 24–25, 39.

218. Cicero, *Off.* 2.54.

219. "The wise man, therefore, will not pity, but will succour, will benefit, and since he is born to be of help to all and to serve the common good, he will give to each his

most people could eke out a living 115

Is there any evidence that begging was productive? Seneca describes a debate concerning a situation in which a man made his living on the begging of children and whether it harmed the state. The man took abandoned children, mutilated them, and sent them out to beg.[220] One does not know how long the children survived, but apparently, they collected alms. Seneca wrote that women who had exposed a child often gave alms to a beggar.[221] Longenecker presents several examples including a frieze depicting a well-dressed woman and youth handing out a coin to a beggar.[222] Beggars performed acts of self-denigration for the amusement of passer-bys whom they hoped would give them alms. They did such things as chewing on shoes and banging nails into their heads.[223] John Chrysostom describes such activities and instructs his congregation not to watch or to contribute to such activities.[224]

Anneliese Parkin summarizes the situation. "Elite self-representation and lack of interest in our sources mask a reality of desultory, but habitual, giving. There is more interaction between the elite and the structural poor in the early imperial period than appears in the primary sources if casually read."[225] Shortly after the first century, rabbinic sources strongly encourage almsgiving.[226] Despite the paucity of supporting data, Parkin notes that most almsgiving came from the lower socio-economic segments of the population.[227] Paul describes such sharing of limited resources in the Corinthian

---

share thereof. He will extend a due measure of his goodness even to the unfortunates who deserve to be censured and disciplined; but more gladly will he come to the rescue of the distressed and those struggling with mishap . . . And, too, he will not avert his countenance or his sympathy from anyone because he has a withered leg, or is emaciated and in rags, and is old and leans upon a staff; but all the worthy he will aid, and will, like a god, look graciously upon the unfortunate" (Seneca, *Moral Essays on Mercy* 2.6.2–3 [Basore, LCL]).

220. The Elder Seneca, *Controv.* 10.14; Parkin, "You Do Him No Service," 70–71. In a similar, contemporary setting, able-bodied males mutilate themselves to secure more alms. However, Parkin notes little evidence of this practice for the first century.

221. Garnsey and Saller, *The Roman Empire*, 143; The Elder Seneca, *Controv.* 10.14.20–21. Garnsey and Saller state that wealthy females exposed infants for financial reasons. They cite a fragment from Musonius Rufus (15b, ed. O. Hense). Several statements by Seneca reflect this sentiment. "A woman hands alms to a beggar when she is asked—particularly if she has had a child, and exposed it. How wretched the thought as she hands the money over: 'Maybe this is my son'!" (Basore, LCL)

222. Longenecker, *Remember the Poor*, 78.

223. Parkin, "You Do Him No Service," 77.

224. John Chrysostom, *Ep. I ad Cor.* 21.5–6; Parkin, "You Do Him No Service," 77.

225. Parkin, "You Do Him No Service," 81.

226. Hamel, *Poverty and Charity in Roman Palestine*, 216–19.

227. Parkin, "You Do Him No Service," 69–70.

community: "gave out of the depths of their destitution" (2 Cor 8:2).[228] The receipt of alms would have been a survival mechanism for the destitute. Almsgiving was not restricted to cities, but mechanisms were in place for villages also.[229] Magistrates of the village, called *parnasim*, collected money from villagers to give to local and vagrant beggars, including Gentiles.[230] One could surmise that almsgiving did not reverse the plight of the person in the PS 7 category, and it was not a sustainable strategy.

Summary of Shared Mechanisms

To recap, both rural and urban people stored food when they could against bad future times when crops were scarce or no jobs were available. This mechanism became compromised seriously when rents and taxes took more of households' surpluses and left them little in reserve. Giving alms to the destitute was part of the landscape for cities and villages. Often, PS 4 to PS 6 level people gave alms and not the wealthy. The giving of alms relates to the most important line of defense against compromised access to food: social safety networks. Social safety networks not only provided food for the hungry, but it also bound extended communities together. As surpluses became scarcer, the ability of peasants to share with their neighbors became more difficult.

Mechanisms for Urban Residents

Urban residents in the lower socio-economic segments of the population were under different pressures than their rural counterparts to have consistent access to sufficient food. While food was available year round, the income of the household may not have been stable and prices varied. In a city, people had six options for acquiring food. First, they were associated with a wealthy household and received meals as part of their remuneration. Second, they were independent but had ties with patrons. Third, artisans, day laborers,[231] and peddlers bought food on the street. Fourth, they went outside the city to obtain food from non-cultivated areas in the same manner as rural peasants. Urban residents had fewer options to preserve non-

---

228. Friesen, "Poverty in Pauline Studies," 351; his translation.

229. Davis, *Scripture, Culture, and Agriculture*, 123. Davis describes the situation in villages where the wealthier members of a village would encounter indigents who would have claims on assistance.

230. Goodman, *State and Society in Roman Galilee, A.D. 132–212*, 122.

231. When day laborers performed agriculture work and received payment in kind, they could store some food for short periods.

crop food items. They did not have kitchen gardens for the herbs and spices used in preservation, although spices and herbs were sold in the markets.[232] Fifth, some urban residents had access to crops from cultivated fields in the same manner as rural destitute. Galen described what he referred to as a universal practice by which urban residents went to the fields after the harvest to collect food crops—wheat, barley, beans, and lentils—to store for use during the year.[233] Last, they begged in the streets, stole, and ate garbage. People who received part of their food from patrons would probably also have purchased food on the street. In the sections below, I describe three mechanisms that permitted an urban dweller to have access to food year round: (1) patronage, (2) doles, and (3) eating establishments.

Patronage

Patronage was a central social construct of the first century.[234] Peter Oakes writes, "[I]ts core characteristics are that there is a non-market relationship between socially unequal people in which dissimilar benefits are exchanged. The most characteristic exchange involves the patron providing access to resources normally unavailable to the client."[235] Patronage is one mechanism for a person with more resources (patron) to help a person with fewer resources (client). Clients often had multiple patrons,[236] and patronage had multiple levels.[237] A person who was a client could also be a patron to others.[238] A

232. Cooley and Cooley, *Pompeii: A Sourcebook*, 164, 167. *CIL* IV 4888 lists prices for food items including mustard, mint, and salt. Found in pottery vessels were bay, honey, pepper, and pickling brine.

233. Hopwood, "Bandits, Elites and Rural Order," 172. Hopwood references Galen, *Peri Eucumais kai Kakochumas* 1, translated by de Ste. Croix. This practice deprived the rural residents of food they needed. Galen writes that by the following spring many rural residents were sick.

234. Scholars have written extensively on patronage during the Roman period. Saller, *Personal Patronage under the Early Empire*; Braund, "Function and Dysfunction: Personal Patronage in Roman Imperialism"; Garnsey and Woolf, "Patronage of the Rural Poor in the Roman World"; Elliott, "Patronage and Clientage"; Lendon, *Empire of Honour*; DeSilva, *Honor, Patronage, Kinship & Purity*; Stewart, "Social Stratification and Patronage in Ancient Mediterranean Societies."

235. Oakes, "Urban Structures and Patronage," 178.

236. Hanson and Oakman, *Palestine in the Time of Jesus*, 72; Braund, "Function and Dysfunction: Personal Patronage in Roman Imperialism," 148. Braund writes that at the higher echelons of society, patrons vied for particular clients.

237. Oakes, "Urban Structures and Patronage," 182–83. An analysis of town and city layouts indicated that patronage enclaves might have existed throughout a city.

238. Ibid., 179. Oakes notes that archaeological excavations showed a bench outside the home of a cabinet-maker. The archaeologists believe that the bench implies the

key feature of patronage was that it did require the client have something to offer.[239] Consequently, the destitute of PS 7 and probably most people of PS 6 would not have qualified.[240] Below, I highlight a few aspects of patronage that impinge on food access.

Reciprocity, as discussed above, was primarily horizontal in relationships while patronage was vertical with the implied difference in status.[241] Reciprocity contributed to cohesion within a group (that is, the social safety network), but patronage undermined cohesion.[242] Gift giving and sharing of reciprocity had an expectation of return,[243] but patronage changed the expectation to an obligation.[244] Further, the client could never repay the gift fully. The relationship encompassed an on-going series of gifts and returns.[245] Patronage involved the simultaneous exchange of both concrete and symbolic items. Symbolic items were important and related to the entitlement system with the transfer of power and influence to the recipient.[246] Concrete items might include recommending a client for a job.[247] This relationship would be very important for an artisan at the PS 5 or PS 6 level. Steady employment led to consistent access to food. Peasants had little likelihood of success in the judicial system, and a patron as creditor or adjudicating on his behalf would probably work out better.[248] Lesser members of a segment of society would voluntarily enter into the service[249] of a more powerful person in order to reap the benefits of the patronage relationship.[250] A patron would distribute actual food baskets (*sportula*) to clients who were in need,

---

cabinet-maker was a patron.

239. Whittaker, "The Poor," 291; Hands, *Charities and Social Aid in Greece and Rome*, 78–80. Whitaker writes that patron clients were "respectable poor."

240. Meggitt, *Paul, Poverty and Survival*, 168, esp. n64, takes to task New Testament scholars who portray patronage in very pervasive terms.

241. Saller, *Personal Patronage under the Early Empire*, 11. Romans used language carefully at this point. The language of friends was ambiguous enough not to imply social inferiority that the word client conveyed. Nevertheless, the concept of lesser friends did evolve.

242. Garnsey and Woolf, "Patronage of the Rural Poor in the Roman World," 157.

243. Lendon, *Empire of Honour*, 68.

244. Carter, *The Roman Empire and the New Testament*, 115.

245. Hanson and Oakman, *Palestine in the Time of Jesus*, 72.

246. Ibid.

247. Longenecker, *Remember the Poor*, 73.

248. Hanson and Oakman, *Palestine in the Time of Jesus*, 119.

249. D'Arms, *Commerce and Social Standing in Ancient Rome*, 165. One should not confuse business partnerships with patronage.

250. Lenski, *Power and Privilege*, 244–45; Saller, *Personal Patronage under the Early Empire*, 38.

or would give them small coins with which to purchase food.[251] Thus far, I have argued that patronage was a survival mechanism for urban dwellers provided they were not too far down the poverty scale and had nothing to offer the patron. Benefits would include actual food at times or money to buy food, as well as possible employment opportunities.[252]

A question remains concerning patronal relationships between urban residents and rural residents. Garnsey and Gregory Woolf mention several areas where patronage is positive. First, when shortages affect an entire village and reciprocity could not function, the patron can provide relief. Second, peasants need equipment that they cannot afford to purchase. The question is whether one considers such a relationship to be dependency or patronage. Garnsey and Woolf distinguish based on whether the relationship is involuntary (for example, bound by legal sanctions) and how much decision making remains with the weaker member of the pair.[253] Tenancy is an ambiguous relationship because not all such relationships had contracts associated with them.[254]

James Grimshaw describes the relationship between an aristocrat and his tenant in terms of patron-client. He notes that the relationship is asymmetrical with respect to power, but asserts that the tenant had agency to choose his patron.[255] Aristocrats would probably have viewed their relationships with peasants as a patron-client. From their perspective, they gave peasants two things: land to work and protection. Yet peasants often already *owned* the land, although a ruler or official to a third party may have gifted upper level control of it.[256] As far as protection was concerned, Kautsky describes the relationship using the analogy of a shepherd to his animal. "The shepherd will protect it from attacks and let it live and eat from his hand; 'in return;' he takes milk or wool and even its meat."[257] In this scenario,

---

251. Garnsey and Saller, *The Roman Empire*, 151. *Sportula* were worth six sesterces in Martial's day. This amount would not be enough to live on; Carcopino, *Daily Life in Ancient Rome: The People and the City at the Height of the Empire*, 171–72. A person could be the client of more than one patron. Consequently, he might be able to receive this type of assistance from more than one patron; Hands, *Charities and Social Aid in Greece and Rome*, 188–89 D.130. Hands catalogues an inscription from the first half of second century CE; Nacolia, Phrygia (Asia Minor); Dessau, 7196 (TAM, V, 95f; Laum, No. 121, Lewis and Reinhold, Re, n, 340), chapter of the will of Publius Aelius Onesimus, imperial freedmen. The freedman was providing for the corn dole but also wanted half of the proceeds of the endowment to be for *sportula*.

252. Garnsey and Woolf, "Patronage of the Rural Poor in the Roman World," 154.

253. Ibid., 160.

254. Ibid.

255. Grimshaw, "Luke's Market Exchange District," 40.

256. Moxnes, *The Economy of the Kingdom*, 43.

257. Kautsky, *Aristocratic Empires*, 111, 114.

patronage was not positive, but perhaps necessary when other mechanisms failed. Peasants may have shared the view expressed by Kautsky when debt obligations took too much food off their tables.[258]

Doles for the Poor

Given the substantial percentage of the people below subsistence, one can deduce that the poor were everywhere. Gildas Hammel writes that very little in the extant literature would suggest that the wealthy felt any obligation to assist the poor, and that any generosity on their part would be for their "love of brilliance and glory."[259] From an economic perspective, giving to the poor was redistribution (that is, giving back some of what had been previously extracted).[260] Doles for the poor took two general forms, euergetism and almsgiving, which I discussed above. Almsgiving functioned similarly to patronage but did not require the recipient to be of value.[261]

Euergetism is different from both patronage and almsgiving. It normally was in the form of a large grant whose target was not the destitute, although the poor may have sometimes benefited. Paul Veyne describes the climate of euergetism as one "which gives edifices and pleasures to citizens rather than alms to the poor."[262] Euergetism related to food took the form of feasts, office of *sitones*, and *alimenta*. Wealthy people would sometimes conduct a public feast in honor of a god or emperor,[263] which would have normally provided food and drink more for the higher socio-economic segments of the population than the lower segments. Joan Alcock writes that the "poor ate scraps left over from feasts given by the wealthy."[264] I discuss

---

258. Carter, *The Roman Empire and the New Testament*, 47. Carter argues these relationships were ultimately exploitative.

259. Hamel, *Poverty and Charity in Roman Palestine*, 219. See Matt 6.

260. Moxnes, *The Economy of the Kingdom*, 116, 120.

261. Hamel, *Poverty and Charity in Roman Palestine*, 219; Hands, *Charities and Social Aid in Greece and Rome*, 80. The wealthy normally thought the poor to be in that condition due to laziness. Consequently, any aid would not help such persons recover from their condition.

262. Veyne and Murray, *Bread and Circuses*, 20.

263. Corbier, "City, Territory, and Taxation," 215; Cotter, "Cornelius, the Roman Army and Religion," 292, 295; Derrett, *Jesus's Audience*, 60; Klauck, "The Roman Empire," 80; Wilkins and Hill, *Food in the Ancient World*, 61–62; Warmington, *Remains of Old Latin*, 4, 149; Julianus 362. Warmington cites an interesting inscription for a public work that involved the building of a public kitchen (*Remains of Old Latin*, 1471). Julian describes the aristocracy of Antioch spending lavishly on feasts during the May festival.

264. Alcock, *Food in the Ancient World*, 239.

the function of the *sitones* in detail on pages 201–6. The function involved providing food during severe food shortages.

Alimenta was a fund to provide food to children. Most *alimenta* schemes were in Italy. Only two are known for the East and the emperor Hadrian established one of those.[265] The scheme began with Augustus' occasional support of children via his *minores pueri*. The practice gained preeminence in the time of the emperor Trajan,[266] whose statue in the Roman Forum has him seated on a platform with two children before him, which is similar to depictions on coins.[267] Pliny, the Younger, writes:

> Let the gods only grant you, Caesar, the long life which you deserve and preserve the spirit you owe to them, and the lists of children entered at your bidding will ever multiply! These grow increasingly day-by-day, not so much because parents care more for children, as because every citizen is cared for by his prince. Go on with subsidies and allowances if it is your wish, but the true reason for these births lies in yourself.[268]

Often the fund was underwritten by interest from loans forced on landowners.[269] David Johnston argues that the underwriting would not have taken all of the income from the land, and a city would not undertake such a legacy unless it was of benefit to the city.[270] Naphtali Lewis and Meyer Reinhold describe the scheme as follows. Cities participating in the imperial scheme would make loans at five per cent against a small portion of the land under their jurisdiction and they reserved the income for the *alimenta*.[271] Private individuals also set up such funds,[272] as the following inscription shows.

265. Hands, *Charities and Social Aid in Greece and Rome*, 110, 112–13.

266. Brunt, *Roman Imperial Themes*, 516.

267. Hands, *Charities and Social Aid in Greece and Rome*, 109–10; Mattingly, *Roman Coins: From the Earliest Times to the Fall of the Western Empire*, 166, Plate XLV.

268. Pliny, *Panegyricus* 28.26–27 (Radice, LCL).

269. Longenecker, *Remember the Poor*, 89–95; Hands, *Charities and Social Aid in Greece and Rome*, 110–13; Garnsey and Woolf, "Patronage of the Rural Poor in the Roman World," 153–70; Carney, *The Economies of Antiquity*, 94; Wiedemann, "The Patron as Banker," 22; Pliny, *Letters* 7.19. There is some disagreement among these scholars as to whether the loans were for the benefit of the cultivators or not. All agree that the interest funded the *alimenta*.

270. Johnston, "Munificence and Municipia," 115.

271. Lewis and Reinhold, *Roman Civilization: Selected Readings*, 2, 255.

272. Hands, *Charities and Social Aid in Greece and Rome*, 108, 114, 184, 197; Garnsey, *Famine and Food Supply*, 262; Johnston, "Munificence and Municipia," 117. Hands cites several inscriptions from which I draw two here. D.17: Pliny set up a scheme in Corum. Hands notes that not all children may have been included since a scheme in Milan (D. 51) expected the parents to send their sons to Milan for education. Garnsey

> T. Helvius Basila left to the people of Atina 400,000 sesterces, the revenue from which was to be used for providing corn to their children until their coming of age, upon which they were to receive the sum of 1,000 sesterces.[273]

Limitations may have existed on the number of children from a single household who could receive the benefit, which resulted in boys being favored over girls.[274]

> She also left 1,000,000 sesterces to the town of Tarracina in memory of her son Macer, so that out of the income from this money child-assistance subsides might be paid to one hundred boys and one hundred girls–to each citizen boy 5 *denarii* each month, to each citizen girl 4 *denarii* each month, the boys up to sixteen years, the girls up to fourteen years–in such a way that the payments should always be received by groups of a hundred boys and a hundred girls.[275]

Scholars debate the motives for setting up these schemes.[276] Garnsey and Woolf note that these schemes differed from other benefactions because they were based on poverty and not on citizenship.[277] From the perspective of food access, while it was not a universal solution, it did provide for children in specific locations.

Eating Establishments

Cities had establishments that sold drink and hot food.[278] Street vendors crowded the streets and hawked their wares: wine, fish, sausage, pastries, and

---

cites the Pliny fund as being for Como, Pliny's hometown, and states the amount of the grant from Pliny to be one-half million sesterces. Johnston notes that Pliny took special legal actions to ensure that mismanagement by the local council could not undermine his intent for the grant.

273. Hands, *Charities and Social Aid in Greece and Rome*, 184. Hands catalogues this inscription from the second half of the first century from Atina in southern Italy: Dessau, 977 (Lewis and Reinhold, RC, II, 348f.).

274. Garnsey, *Famine and Food Supply*, 67.

275. Lewis and Reinhold, *Roman Civilization: Selected Readings*, 2, 268. Lewis and Reinhold catalog this inscription from *CIL*, vol. X, no. 6,328 (= Dessau, no. 6, 278)

276. Garnsey and Saller, *The Roman Empire*, 77. For example, Garnsey and Saller do not offer a reason but do assert that the motives were most probably not humanitarian in nature.

277. Garnsey and Woolf, "Patronage of the Rural Poor in the Roman World," 161.

278. Sperber, *The City in Roman Palestine*, 28. Sperber notes that the city derived income from rental space for shops and stalls and from taxes on the income of the

most people could eke out a living 123

cakes.[279] *Eating Places* included the equivalent of fast food restaurants, called in Latin, *taberna, thermopolia*, and *popina*. In addition, three types of hotels existed that provided food. They were *caupona, stabula*, and *mansions*, which I have described on pages 63–76.[280] Apuleius offers a description of buying food in the market during which he ineffectually haggled over the price of fish. A friend who was an *aedile* of the market arrived and shamed the seller by saying he had taken advantage of his friend.[281]

From Pompeii, principally, and other sources, one can get a sense of what food cost. Inscriptions show that the price of bread varied between areas in Pompeii and distinctions were made between types of bread.[282] Stegemann and Stegemann list representative prices of many items: loaf of bread at 1 *as*, liter of wine at 1 *as*, 1 lb. ginger at 6 *denarii*, simple dishes at 1–2 *asses*, and meat at an inn at 2 *asses*. The costs did vary from city to city.[283] For example, Antioch had the highest cost of living in the Roman East.[284] With respect to survival, food was available in all seasons for the person having money, or being associated with a wealthy household. Prices might increase in natural shortage periods related to the agricultural cycle. To recap, the diet could be as varied and nutritious as money permitted.

Survival Mechanisms Helped Some People More Than Others

So far, I have shown that consistent access to sufficient food was a serious problem for many people. I have identified survival mechanisms for rural and urban settings. In this section, I give greater clarity to the issue of unequal survivability by bringing together the discussion of the Poverty Scale

---

shops and stalls. Occasionally there would be tax-free days, which usually honored an individual.

279. Martial, *Epi.* 7.61.

280. Alcock, *Food in the Ancient World*, 125–32. Distinctions between the types are noted in chapter 3.

281. Apuleius, *Golden Ass* 1.24.25.

282. Cooley and Cooley, *Pompeii: A Sourcebook*, 163. CIL IV 5380 catalogues a list of food, found by the door going into an eating establishment, whose price changes by the day of the week. It lists bread at 8 asses, plain bread at 2, porridge at 3, and bread for slaves at 2 and 4. No explanation of the differences between bread, plain bread, and slave bread is given. One could assume that the people of Pompeii knew what distinguished the types of bread.

283. Stegemann and Stegemann, *The Jesus Movement*, 41; Heichelheim, "Roman Syria," 189. Heichelheim cites the price of bread in Palestine as 50 to 600 percent higher than in Egypt.

284. Heichelheim, "Roman Syria," 189.

occupational groups with the discussion of survival mechanisms that I have outlined. Extending the Poverty Scale by adding components that affected a household's ability to acquire food permits a more nuanced argument. On this very point, Oakes levels a criticism of the Friesen scale for using a single criterion of wealth. "By thinking of these [resources] in income-equivalent terms, this gives him a one-dimensional, and very concrete, variable to use—as opposed to problematically multi-dimensional variables such as status."[285] Oakes continues by pointing out the problem of using a monetary-based measure when applying the scale to New Testament communities: the text rarely says anything about the resources of the characters or people, but describes behaviors.[286] Oakes suggests that scholars should move beyond the Friesen scale to an "ordered poverty scale" which would include more factors than economic ability. Such factors would include socially perceived necessities for an acceptable life.[287] The argument of this study does not go as far as Oakes suggests, but does extend the Friesen work and does describe behaviors. Table 7 on page 127 below relates the survival mechanisms, discussed on pages 96–124, to the Friesen Poverty Scale. In the following section, I will explain the columns.

Description of Mechanisms Used in Expanded Poverty Scale

The following mechanisms are directly related to surviving endemic food shortages: (1) social network, (2) patron, (3) alms, (4) Jewish laws, (5) direct access to food crops, (6) access to uncultivated land, (7) growing a kitchen garden, and (8) access to livestock.

Social networks (1) are important for both rural and urban residents. As discussed in a previous section, the networks spanned extended households and occurred between friends. They were extensive enough to prompt Libanius to write that the rural inhabitants had little need for a city because of the exchange among themselves.[288] Within the cities, precincts often formed based on ethnicity and sometimes based on other factors such as shared business.[289] The communal nature of the first-century circum-Mediterranean

---

285. Oakes, "Constructing Poverty Scales for Graeco-Roman Society," 367–68; Malina, "Wealth and Poverty in the New Testament and Its World," 300. Malina supports this notion when he writes that scholars should examine "the basic social structures people use to realize and express their values."

286. Oakes, "Constructing Poverty Scales for Graeco-Roman Society," 368.

287. Ibid., 370–71.

288. Libanius, *Or.* 11.230.

289. Harland, *Associations, Synagogues, and Congregations*; Kloppenborg and Wilson, *Voluntary Associations in the Graeco-Roman World*. These two books are excellent

would create a village within the city, in which the social network would resemble its rural counterpart.

Having a patron (2) in the city provided security except during unfavorable economic situations. In such circumstances, for example, the independent artisan would be the first to lose a daily bequest.[290]

The receiving of alms (3) was probably more prevalent in cities and towns than villages. In villages, the usual reciprocal relations should come into play in times of need.

The Jewish laws (4) concerning "gleanings" and "corners of fields" was a common practice in rural areas of the Lower Galilee and, perhaps, in rural areas populated with Jewish settlers. The Jewish quarter in Antioch may have had ties with a rural Jewish settlement near Antioch.[291] Later rabbinic writings established various criteria related to income to determine if a person was eligible to participate in the practice.[292] Access to land is fundamental in agricultural-based societies. Access to a variety of crops (5) provided a healthy diet. Access to uncultivated land (6) provided alternate food sources such as wild game, birds, nuts, and berries. A kitchen garden (7) provided herbs for cooking and for preserving foods. Access to livestock (8) and poultry provided on-going food products such as milk and eggs and provided a food source in dire circumstances. In times of shortages, the estate owners could withdraw to their estates to get away from food shortages in the city.[293]

The final two factors reveal the familiar wealth criteria, which is part of the original Poverty Scale calculations. Fulfilling social obligations (9) was very important to maintaining one's status and honor even if it meant going hungry, or going into debt. A household not being able to meet its financial obligations (10) from taxes or loan payments was a primary reason that members of the household might go hungry and eventually become destitute.

I omit two factors from the table because a relatively few men (PS 1 through PS 3) could exercise those functions: decision-making authority for

---

sources for information on the various types of voluntary associations.

290. Blue, "The House Church at Corinth and the Lord's Supper: Famine, Food Supply, and the Present Distress," 233.

291. Meeks et al., *Jews and Christians in Antioch in the First Four Centuries of the Common Era*, 40n43. The Jewish community in Antioch was organized with an *archon*: ἄρχων τῶν ἐπ Ἀντιοχείας Ἰουδαίων (Josephus, *J.W.* 7.47) who could activate perhaps special help from the Jewish farmers of the Hulat of Antioch (*t.Dem* 2:1).

292. Heichelheim, "Roman Syria," 181. *M. Peah* 8.8, 9: "If a man has two hundred denarii he may not take gleanings, the forgotten sheaf, peah or poor man's tithe . . . If a man has fifty denarii and he trades with them, he may not take gleanings, the forgotten sheaf, peah, or poor man's tithe."

293. Whittaker, "The Poor," 285.

crop selection and influence in the legal system. Both factors play a prominent role in the dominant entitlement system.[294] Independent landowners also had decision-making authority for their land to the extent they were not forced to plant cash crops for debt and tax burdens.

Table 7. Poverty Scale with survival mechanisms

P: positive mechanism
?: may or may not have the mechanism
E: a city resident could go to the estate

PS Level	City / Town	Rural	social network	patron	alms	Jewish laws	direct access crops	uncultivated food	kitchen garden	livestock	social obligations	financial obligations
7	farm families		P	?	-	?	P	P	-	-	-	-
	unattached widows / orphans / beggars		-	-	P	?	-	-	-	-	-	-
		small farm families	P	-	-	?	P	P	P	?	-	-
		attached widows	P	-	-	P	-	-	?	-	-	-
		orphans	P	-	-	P	-	-	-	-	-	-
	attached widows		P	-	P	-	-	-	-	-	-	-
	unskilled day laborers		?	-	?	P	P	P	-	-	-	-
6		unskilled day laborers	P	-	-	P	P	P	-	-	-	-
		medium farm families	P	-	-	-	P	P	P	P	?	?
		small tenant farmers	P	?	-	-	P	P	P	P	?	?
		migrant artisans	-	-	P	-	-	-	-	-	?	-
	skilled day laborers		P	?	-	?	P	P	-	-	?	?
	independent artisans		P	P	-	-	-	-	-	-	?	-
	small local business		P	P	-	-	-	-	-	-	?	-
	small traders		P	P	-	-	-	-	-	-	?	P
5	merchants & traders		P	P	-	-	-	-	-	-	P	-
	wage earners		P	P	-	-	-	-	-	-	P	-
	large shop owners		P	P	-	-	-	-	-	-	P	-
		local artisans	P	P	-	-	-	-	P	-	P	P
		medium farm families	P	P	-	-	P	P	P	P	P	P
		larger tenants	P	P	-	-	P	P	P	P	P	P
4	large business		P	P	-	-	?	?	?	P	P	P
	artisan shop owners		P	P	-	-	-	-	-	-	P	P
	international traders		P	P	-	-	E	E	E	P	P	P
	skilled laborers		P	P	-	-	-	-	-	-	P	P
		village elder	P	P	-	-	P	P	P	P	P	P
		larger farm families	P	P	-	-	P	P	P	P	P	P
3	usual players + Augustales		P	P	-	-	E	E	E	P	P	P
1-2			P	P	-	-	E	E	E	P	P	P

---

294. I discuss entitlement systems in chapter 6.

Interpretation of the Expanded Poverty Scale

When dealing with food access, a key to understanding the situation involves the avenues available to the person and the level of agency available to that person to take care of the household. Two primary factors affected a person's sustained access to food. The first is wealth as expressed in the original Friesen Poverty Scale of table 4. The second is access to supporting mechanisms which is shown in table 7 as a *P* or a ? in the cell. The more categories available, the more likely the person and his household could survive from year to year. Table 7 demonstrates that the ability of different socio-economic segments to have access consistently to sufficient food varied dramatically. For example, the PS 7 rural small farmers would stave off starvation longer than others in this category could because they had more access to a variety of foods, especially from uncultivated areas. However, if they were assessed more taxes, they would lose more of their cultivated crops and need to rely more heavily on alternative food sources as would all of the neighbors. They would have no more survival mechanisms to fall back on and they might simply walk off the property[295] or be forced to turn to banditry.[296]

Concluding Remarks

I have shown that the diets could be healthy and that poor health related to problems with access to food was both a function of insufficient quantity of food as well as quality of food. The latter occurred especially when principal food sources were unavailable during more extreme food shortages. Food shortages were a continuing problem in the first century for many people but about as many people lived comfortably above subsistence level as below or on the cusp. Survival mechanisms were in place to weather the less severe food shortage episodes, but people who were already at risk had fewer mechanisms available to them. The crucial social networks were stronger in the rural environment than the urban environment. Reciprocity in a village offered support longer than patronage did in a city. Having access to kitchen gardens and uncultivated land for food sources was an advantage of rural location over city inhabitation. On the other hand, the

---

295. Oakman, "Jesus and Agrarian Palestine," 64; Theissen, *Sociology of Early Palestinian Christianity*, 34, 47; Braund, *Augustus to Nero: A Sourcebook on Roman History, 31 BC–AD 68*, 282. Braund catalogues a petition from a tax collector in which the tax collector is complaining that the population of some villages has declined to just a few people because "some have migrated through poverty."

296. Hanson and Oakman, *Palestine in the Time of Jesus*, 88–90; Josephus, *Ant.* 15.346, 320.113–314; Josephus, *J.W.* 2.228.

city provided a steadier availability of food when the person had money or a patron. Rural inhabitants were susceptible to a shortage of food before the harvest. Periods of insufficient food cycles like this may have made rural peasants more susceptible to diseases from malnutrition. People above the PS 5 level would rarely suffer from lack of access to food, except in times of significant disasters. Rural households in levels PS 5 and PS 6 had more mechanisms to fall back on than city households at the same levels. To this point, I have discussed periods of short-term and transient disasters that affected a person's access to sufficient food. Unfortunately, more severe disasters occurred and most of these survival mechanisms would have been insufficient for any but households in PS 2 and 3 categories.

Severe Food Shortages Were Devastating

In the previous sections, I identified various means by which many households were able to survive from year to year. Some people did die from starvation, although the majority of the people had at least enough to eat most of the time. The exception to this normal situation was severe food shortage. In this section, I describe the devastating famines during which thousands of people actually died of starvation and thousands of others died from illnesses, because their bodies were too weak to combat most maladies. Starvation was a painful death. Quoting the Grecian Muses, Columella wrote, "To die of hunger is the bitterest of fates."[297] In Rome in 441–40 BCE, numerous people who were starving chose suicide instead of starvation by drowning themselves in the Tiber.[298]

Droughts and pestilence (locust) were the principal causes of severe food shortages.[299] The ancients considered famine itself the worst evil of the triad: "pestilence, sword, famine."[300] The protracted multi-year famines were quite serious and often resulted in the loss of tens of thousands of lives in cities[301] and unnoted losses of life in rural areas. Cicero wrote that the

297. Columella, *On Agriculture* 2.2.7 (Ash, LCL).

298. Livy, 4.12.11. Lucius Minucius was the prefect of the corn supply but had trouble finding grain to buy anywhere so he forced locals to sell any surplus above the current month's needs and he deprived slaves of their daily bread. He brought charges against dealers, but there was still a shortage and the poor of Rome lost hope.

299. Garnsey, *Famine and Food Supply*, 18–19. Garnsey argues that the vocabulary covering famines in ancient literature is of marginal use in determining the severity of the reported event. I chose the examples used here based on the actual description of the event and not a Greek term used to reference the event.

300. Hamel, *Poverty and Charity in Roman Palestine*, 45. See also Rev 6:1–7.

301. Dando, *Geography of Famine*, 77.

fear of famine was enough to bring on riots in a city.[302] There is no reason to assume peasants did not share this fear because even in a good year there was little to eat. The numerous inscriptions lauding people who provided food during dire periods demonstrate the frequency of severe food shortages during the first century.[303] For example, seventeen inscriptions for the Corinth area attest to people assuming such responsibilities beginning with the reign of Claudius and extending through the reign of Trajan.[304] Inscriptions by different organizations laud Tiberius Claudius Dinippus at multiple times for supplying grain in the 40s and 50s.[305]

Josephus describes a two-year drought during the reign of Herod.[306] Drought reduced crop production, which in turn caused diet changes leading to distemper and some deaths.[307] In the second year the crop failed again; the grain for food was gone; and neighbors had none to share or to sell. Josephus simply says that the poorer socio-economic segments of society had "to find many new ways of sustaining themselves."[308] Josephus

302. Cicero, *Dom.* 4.11-12.

303. Dmitriev, *City Government in Roman Asia Minor*, 123, 224; Garnsey, *Famine and Food Supply*, 14, 261; Liebeschuetz, *Antioch in the Later Roman Period*, 121; Chancey, *Greco-Roman Culture and the Galilee of Jesus*, 176; Di Segni, "Dated Greek Inscriptions from Palestine"; Lehmann and Holum, *The Greek and Latin Inscriptions of Caesarea Maritima*; McLean, "Epigraphical Evidence in Caesarea Maritima," 57. Garnsey mentions Perge, Apamia, Epidaurus, and Megalopolos. The inscriptions cited are not from the Galilee or from Antioch. One should not conclude that the lack of such inscriptions in the Galilee or Antioch meant no such actions existed. There are almost no inscriptions of any type from the first century in Galilee. Liebeschuetz notes the lack of inscriptions in Antioch and its surrounds lauding benefactions on behalf of village folk. McLean notes that a full catalog of inscriptions from Caesarea Maritima has not been published, but he has published 215 inscriptions known as ICaesarea.

304. Danylak, "Tiberius Claudius Dinippus and the Food Shortages in Corinth," 236. Twenty of the inscriptions are in Latin and the remaining six in Greek.

305. Danylak, "Tiberius Claudius Dinippus and the Food Shortages in Corinth," 242-44; Winter, "Responses to Corinthian Famines," 86-87; Blue, "The House Church at Corinth and the Lord's Supper: Famine, Food Supply, and the Present Distress," 235; Carter, *The Roman Empire and the New Testament*, 111. Nine of the inscriptions are identical except for the organization that funded the tribute. Danylak argues convincingly that Dinippus only served once and not the three times often accorded to him. On the other hand, Winter, Blue and Carter suggest three times. I cite more examples on pages 201-6.

306. Josephus, *Ant.* 15.299-317.

307. "Large numbers die not directly from the disease, but from dehydration and lack of calories because they become too weak to obtain food and liquids" (Stark, "Antioch for Matthew's Gospel," 195, 203).

308. Josephus, *Ant.* 15.503 (Marcus and Wikgren, LCL); Goody, *Cooking, Cuisine, and Class*, 59. Josephus does not define what these *sources* were, but in other writings, such things as cats, rats, horses, fecal matter, and human flesh are noted.

reports that Herod was deprived of his tribute and acquired the hate of his subjects. Consequently, he petitioned Caesar and received permission to buy grain.[309] Herod provided bread and clothing to the poor to buy the good will of his subjects and to acquire fame among foreigners. His actions were not common among Roman rulers, with the exception of the Emperor and the regular grain dole in Rome.[310]

Ps.-Joshua the Stylite described a multi-year famine caused by locust in Edessa in the 400s CE. His work offers one of the more detailed descriptions of severe food shortages. Grain and legumes, in addition to wine, rose in price more or less simultaneously. In the summer of the first famine year, they tried a summer crop of millet, but it failed. The inflation in the prices of staples caused the skyrocketing of the prices of other foodstuffs while non-edible commodities were worth less than half their normal price. Getting virtually nothing for non-edible commodities and not having work because of crop failures, poorer people in the cities turned to begging. People abandoned their farms, flooded the city, and overwhelmed the bakers. By the second year, they supplemented an inadequate grain ration with miserable scraps of vegetable matter and consecrated bread. They were driven to eating human flesh. Mothers abandoned their children. Even with bread supplements and some emergency accommodations, they died of painful starvation that had wasted them away. The dead were lying exposed on every street and were so numerous that their disposal was a major problem.[311]

Orosius succinctly described a locust-caused famine that had occurred around 125 BCE. The intersection of human-based shortages from war and natural shortage from a locust plague exacerbated this particular event. Orosius may have exaggerated the numbers below, but the severity was not exaggerated.

---

309. Josephus, *Ant.* 403, fn c (Marcus and Wikgren, LCL); Garnsey, *Famine and Food Supply*, 99; Winter, "Responses to Corinthian Famines," 91. The principal grain growing regions supplied Rome. To buy grain from them required permission from the Emperor. Josephus petitioned the prefect of Egypt and was apparently able to obtain a permit. An inscription from Ephesus (*I. Ep.* 215, 11) tells of a second-century incidence in which the city wanted to buy wheat: "[B]earing in mind the necessity that first the imperial city should have a bounteous supply of wheat procured and assembled for its market . . . then you will be among the first after the homeland."

310. Fiensy, *The Social History of Palestine in the Herodian Period*, 114; Garnsey and Saller, *The Roman Empire*, 98–99. Fiensy suggests Herod's action was not humanitarian. If peasants starved, Herod would have needed to replace them, which would have cost him money. Garnsey cites evidence of Egyptian grain used for shortages in the Levant: CIG 2927 and 2938.

311. Joshua, *The Chronicle of Joshua the Stylite*.

5.11: ¹In the consulate of Marcul Plautius Hypsaeus and Marcus Fulvius Flaccus, a horrible and unaccustomed disaster befell Africa when she had hardly recovered from the ravages of war. ²Great swarms of locusts gathered all over Africa, not only destroying any hope of a crop, but also eating every sort of grass, including part of their roots, and the leaves of trees along with their younger branches. They even gnawed through bitter bark and dry wood. Then, suddenly, they were swept up into bunches by the wind, and, after being carried through the air for a long time, were drowned in the African Sea. ³After the currents had driven great heaps of them onto the shore far and wide along the coast by the action of the waves, these decaying, putrid masses exuded a stench so foul that it could not be imagined. From it so great a plague descended on all of animal-kind alike that everywhere the rotting corpses of birds, domesticated, and wild animals which had been killed by the disease as it was borne through the air, increased the disease's potency. ⁴My whole body trembles as I record how many men perished. Indeed, in Numidia, where at that time Micipsa was king, 800,000 men are said to have perished, along with some 200,000 who lived on the coast, especially in the areas around Carthage and Utica. In the city of Utica itself, 30,000 soldiers who had been stationed there to protect all Africa were killed and blotted out. ⁵This disaster befell them with such sudden violence that it is said that at Utica more than 1,500 corpses of the young were taken out for burial through a single gate in a single day.[312]

Many different food sources collapsed simultaneously: food crops, domesticated animals and birds, as well as wild birds. One may assume that the drought would also have affected wild animals. In effect, the primary survival mechanisms of the rural population described above all failed together. Orosius made no mention about reallocation efforts, but the widespread nature of the plague was noted which would have limited opportunities for acquiring food nearby.

The examples above show how catastrophic were the less frequent, extreme food shortages in the first-century Roman East. These shortages would usually be the result of a naturally occurring event such as a multi-year drought or locust infestation. Their effect could be devastating especially if the area affected was large enough that the normal survival accommodations failed. Famine affected all socio-economic segments of society, but the lower socio-economic segments of society were the most vulnerable to actual hunger and

---

312. Joshua, *The Chronicle of Joshua the Stylite*, chap. 38.

starvation.[313] The rabbis would later succinctly put the issue, "While the fat one becomes lean, the lean one is dead."[314]

Chapter Summary

I have argued that the fickleness of the Mediterranean climate led to inconsistent crop productions, particularly grain. Although grain was a staple food source, other food sources were usually available both to rural and urban residents. These food sources mitigated the vagaries of grain production and helped bridge the gap in agricultural food sources between the planting and reaping seasons. They also provided for a potentially healthy diet.

The primary problem with diet was getting enough nutritionally adequate food, which scholars have asserted was a serious problem in the first century. Economic analyses have verified that the problem was serious, but not as serious as once thought. Part of the shift in view on the magnitude of the problem is the result of examining the bigger picture to include not just grain production but survival mechanisms practiced by the lower socioeconomic segments of the population. Both rural and urban residents had mechanisms, although the rural residents seemed to have a slight edge. I have demonstrated that the majority of the population could eke out a subsistence living unless a major negative event took place. Their lives hung precariously on the border between subsistence and below-subsistence. Any loss of resources or erosion of survival mechanisms would put many people below subsistence. Further, I have argued that survival mechanisms were in place to prevent people on the margins from slipping into destitution.

Having described the social conditions of the first century in general, the question should arise as to whether the Matthean community experienced events that would have caused their safety mechanisms to break down. Did it experience food shortages during the period in which it was solidifying its understanding of the teaching and actions of Jesus? I will argue that the community experienced traumatic events and their gospel would engage in a critique of both the exploitative practices of the aristocracy but perhaps more importantly, the deterioration of the social safety network of sharing that was at the heart of the embodied realm of the heavens.

---

313. Gapp, "The Universal Famine under Claudius," 261; Morley, "The Poor in the City of Rome," 33; Friesen, "Injustice or God's Will," 240. Gapp notes that little documentation exists concerning how the famine affected the social structures of the ancient world;

314. Hamel, *Poverty and Charity in Roman Palestine*, 55. Hamel quotes from a Midrash on Lamentations: LamR. 3.10.

5

The Gospel Reflects the Trauma of Experienced Food Shortages

THUS FAR, I HAVE argued that many people in the first-century Roman East lived at, or just above, subsistence level, and had developed survival mechanisms to help them remain above the subsistence line. The argument covered three previous chapters. In chapter 1, I have argued briefly that food shortages were a problem for a sizeable number of people in the first-century Roman Empire. In chapters 2 and 3, I have clarified the complex web of food access through the use of a model. The model displays relationships between the two most prominent factors of food access: production and distribution, and the different socio-economic segments of the population. I demonstrated the power of the model by examining what effects a military presence in Antioch would have had on the food supply to residents, both urban and rural. In chapter 4, I have taken up in more detail the argument that food shortages were a problem. I have concluded that 25 percent of the population lived below subsistence level and another 30 percent lived on the cusp.

The argument now shifts attention to the Matthean community and its gospel. In this chapter, I argue that the Matthean community most probably experienced food shortages during the period in which the community developed its identity. Further, I argue that the trauma of these shortages affected the way the Matthean community remembered the teaching and actions of Jesus relative to food shortages. To sustain these two claims I argue five points. (1) The Gospel was written for a specific community. (2) The Gospel was finalized between c. 80 and c. 100 CE. (3) The Matthean community was probably located in Antioch in Syria. (4) Food supply in

Antioch was not consistent in the period before 80 CE. (5) The trauma of food shortages influenced the Matthean community's view of the appropriate pragmatic responses sanctioned by Jesus. In the following section, I argue these points in order.

The Gospel Was Written for a Specific Community

Richard Bauckham and contributors to his book[1] question the assumption that there was a Matthean community. A long strand in twentieth-century scholarship had posited specific communities addressed by each Gospel. Burnett Streeter strongly advocated such a view of gospel communities.[2] Redaction criticism of the Gospel of Mark, in the 1960s and 1970s, reinforced his work. Similar work on Matthew came later.[3] Pauline scholarship strongly influenced the community paradigm that correctly assumes Paul wrote letters to specific communities.[4] Willie Marxsen raised an early caution to this paradigm when he wrote, "The community ought not to be unqualifiedly viewed as located in a specific place, though we shall keep in mind the possibility of defining it exactly."[5] Bauckham and associates contend that the author of each gospel did not write for a specific community[6] but wrote for general circulation. The implied audience is "indefinite rather than specific" and included "every Christian community of his [the author's] time in which Greek was understood."[7] They want to force one to decide between the intent of the Gospel being for a wider audience and the Gospel as arising out of and meeting the needs of a specific

---

1. Bauckham, *The Gospels for All Christians*.

2. Streeter, *The Four Gospels: A Study of Origins*; Wrede, *The Messianic Secret*, 5. The concept did not originate with Streeter, but he argued it more explicitly. For example in 1901, William Wrede wrote, "I should never for an instant lose sight of my awareness that I have before me descriptions, the authors of which are later Christians, be they never so early—Christians who could only look at the life of Jesus with the eyes of their own time and who described it on the basis of the belief of the community, with all the viewpoints of the community, and with the needs of the community in mind."

3. Bauckham, "For Whom Were Gospels Written?," 15, 17–18.

4. Ibid., 27.

5. Marxsen, *Mark the Evangelist; Studies on the Redaction History of the Gospel*, 20.

6. Bauckham, *The Gospels for All Christians*, 16; Burridge, "About People, by People, for People: Gospel Genre and Audiences," 128, 129–30: "These four individual accounts, each concerned with the resolution of their particular themes, suggest that they have been composed, not by communities, but by four single writers each of whom wants to portray a particular view of Jesus in his Gospel in the manner of an ancient biography."

7. Bauckham, *The Gospels for All Christians*, 4; Gerhardsson, *The Reliability of the Gospel Tradition*, 137–39, expresses a similar sentiment.

community. These concepts are not mutually exclusive and, indeed, scholars have criticized the proposition for confusing the intent of the writers with the ultimate use of the gospels.[8] In the paragraphs below, I argue against the assumptions underlying Bauckham's arguments using the arguments in large part from David Sim's extensive rebuttal of Bauckham's work.[9]

Bauckham argues that the gospel authors wrote their gospels for general circulation and for a general audience, and the gospels dealt with issues that would have been of general, widespread interest.[10] He concedes that not all topics of a gospel would be applicable to all Christian communities but suggests that enough of any gospel would be of interest for other communities to embrace it.[11] Bauckham contends that the differences between the gospels occurred because each Evangelist wanted to portray his own theological and Christological views.[12] Sim counters that one cannot argue that the Evangelist intended to write to a general audience based solely on many of the issues existing widely.[13] Further, Sim argues that saying a gospel is a relatively open text is not compatible with saying each Evangelist had a particular message to be read in a particular way.[14]

Bauckham's argument is predicated on a single person writing down his story of Jesus based on his own knowledge as he traveled from place to place. While I do not necessarily agree that a school is involved, Raymond Brown and John Meier make an argument that would counter Bauckham's position of a single person as the author of the Gospel.

> When one considers the wide knowledge of different text-forms represented in the Matthean citations of the Old Testament, it seems almost impossible that one man, starting on his own, could have enjoyed such a vast knowledge and command of textual variants. If one instead sees Matthew as coming at the end of and inheriting the work of a whole Christian scribal school, which in turn grew up on Jewish learning children through Jewish Christians in the community, his achievement becomes more intelligible.... in a larger sense, of course, Matthew inherits not

---

8. Incigneri, *The Gospel to the Romans: The Setting and Rhetoric of Mark's Gospel*, 32.
9. Sim, "The Gospels for All Christians?" The reader is encouraged to read this work in its entirety. Sim argues in detail, but I only highlight his arguments in this discussion.
10. Bauckham, "For Whom Were Gospels Written?," 3, 24.
11. Ibid., 22–25.
12. Ibid., 47–48.
13. Sim, "The Gospels for All Christians?," 23.
14. Ibid., 16–17.

just the work of the scribal school but of all the bearers of tradition at Antioch.[15]

Krister Stendahl suggests that the Gospel has too close an affinity to other writers from early Christianity to have been written by "a converted rabbi who succeeded in combining the old forms and the new faith."[16] The current work on orality also goes against the concept of a single person being behind a particular gospel.[17] Recent scholarship emphasizes the oral-scribal nature of the first-century Roman East.[18] In his early work, Werner Kelber, a pivotal scholar examining the issue of orality in the first century, saw a great chasm between the literary and the oral.[19] Recent work argues for the both-and nature of the situation. Oral transmission and written transmission existed beside each other and sometimes complemented each other.[20] Against Bauckham's position, Terence Mournet argues that it would be difficult to envision a situation where a single author would gather the various written sources, sit at a table, and compose a gospel without the benefit of oral traditions, which he had heard.[21]

Bauckham's second assumption is that the Gospels were directed at Christians rather than non-Christians. He argues that the early Christian movement was monolithic and worldwide, and Christian communities kept in close communication with one another.[22] Bauckham makes the follow-

15. Brown and Meier, *Antioch and Rome*, 56–57.

16. Stendahl, *The School of St. Matthew, and Its Use of the Old Testament*, 30.

17. Dunn, "Jesus in Oral Memory"; Weren, "The History and Social Setting of the Matthean Community," 51; Derrenbacker, *Ancient Compositional Practices and the Synoptic Problem*, 37, 44. Dunn argues that there was a long maturation process for the Gospel and, further, that tensions can be discerned in the received text between earlier and later layers.

18. Kloppenborg, *Q, the Earliest Gospel: An Introduction to the Original Stories and Sayings of Jesus*, ix; Gerhardsson, *The Reliability of the Gospel Tradition*, 113–18.

19. Kelber, *The Oral and the Written Gospel*, xvi, 14.

20. Derrenbacker, *Ancient Compositional Practices and the Synoptic Problem*, 27; Dunn, "Jesus in Oral Memory," 301–3; Oivind Andersen, "Oral Tradition," 51; Petrov, "Memory and Oral Tradition," 79–81; Kelber, "The Generative Force of Memory: Early Christian Traditions as Processes of Remembering," 20; Gamble, *Books and Readers in the Early Church: A History of Early Christian Texts*, 19. Gamble addresses the issue of orality versus literacy and argues that empirical studies show that one should not make sharp distinctions between the two. He writes "Evidence for the production, use, and appreciation of texts in early Christianity, even before the composition of the Gospels, is too strong to allow oral tradition and literary activity to be set off against one another."

21. Mournet, *Oral Tradition and Literary Dependence: Variability and Stability in the Synoptic Tradition and Q*, 195, 148. See also Derrenbacker, *Ancient Compositional Practices and the Synoptic Problem*, 6.

22. Bauckham, "For Whom Were Gospels Written?," 33; Sim, "The Gospels for All

ing points. (1) Books, particularly ancient biographies,[23] were written to be circulated. (2) The author of Matthew was probably like other early Christian leaders who traveled widely and worked in more than one community. (3) An extensive network of Christian communities was in constant and close communication.[24] (4) Christian literature did in fact circulate quite rapidly.[25] (5) If the author of Matthew used Mark as a source, would not the author assume that his gospel would also circulate?[26] Bauckham's arguments support his hypothesis, but they do not prove his hypothesis. With the exception of point four that I do not contest, I discuss and contest each other point in the following paragraphs.

Richard Burridge develops and supports the first point concerning the gospel as a biography, βίος. Indeed, he shows that often an author wrote intending his biography to be in general circulation. Biographies could have different functions, and he argues that the gospels fall into the apologetic or polemic functions, which indicate a wide audience was the target.[27] The weakness in Burridge's argument is that his context is not parallel to that of the Evangelists since all the authors in his essay are described as writing to further their personal agenda for personal gain.

The premise that books in general were written to be circulated is not fully supported. Loveday Alexander, a co-contributor, contradicts the easy distinction that oral presentation was for local communication and books were used for general audiences.[28] She does suggest that once written, the

---

Christians?," 9–11. Sim argues strongly that there was diversity and conflict early in the Christian movements, which is clearly evident in the Pauline letters. Further, the communities with similar beliefs networked with each other, but not with outside Christian communities. He comes back to his argument concerning rival Christian networks in rebutting other arguments; ibid., 11, 14, and 16.

23. Bauckham, "For Whom Were Gospels Written?," 29; Sim, "The Gospels for All Christians?," 18, makes the claim that, "Even if we grant that the Gospels belong in general terms to the genre of Graeco-Roman biography, there is little similarity between the Evangelists and the classical biographers." See discussion on pages 36–37 that addresses the strong similarities between the Gospel and ancient biographies. The Gospel being in biography form does not necessarily support the circulation argument.

24. Bauckham, "For Whom Were Gospels Written?," 30–33.

25. Ibid., 3–4, 43; Thompson, "The Holy Internet: Communication between Churches in the First Christian Generation," 53–58, 60. Thompson picks up and expands Bauckham's notion. He claims that conflict and differences over theology and practice fueled further communication within the network of Christian communities.

26. Bauckham, "For Whom Were Gospels Written?," 3, 13.

27. Burridge, "About People, by People, for People: Gospel Genre and Audiences," 131–35.

28. Alexander, "Ancient Book Production and the Circulation of the Gospels," 90, 100.

text could circulate to other Christian groups.²⁹ She also notes that written texts based on oral lectures circulated widely, but such circulation may have been without the author's consent.³⁰ Hence, one cannot use the effect of a tradition moving to written form to argue the intent of an author. Further, Joel Marcus argues against Bauckham's position by offering several counter examples. Qumran texts targeted the local community despite the Qumran community being part of the larger Essene movement. The Jewish residents of Heliopolis lent support to legitimating the temple there with the generation of the Jewish text, *Joseph and Asenath*. A Christian text, *The Teaching of Addai*,³¹ presents the foundational legend of the community in Edessa (Syria). Alexander also contends that circulation required existing social networks³²—a point espoused by Bauckham but argued against by Sim.

Examination of the Pauline epistles counters the next two arguments concerning mobility and communication. It is true that in the Greco-Roman world people had many opportunities for travel. The epistles show mobility of some Christians and communication between some communities. Sim argues that mobility and communication are restricted to those who are like-minded with Paul and who are located in Greece and Asia Minor. For example, Sim notes that Paul limited his exposure to Jerusalem for twelve years. Finally, Sim concludes that to infer the mobility of each Evangelist based on the mobility of some Christian leaders is not justified since the textual evidence we have does not show James leaving Jerusalem.³³

Bauckham poses his final argument as a question. If the author of Matthew used Mark as a source, would not the author assume that the gospel would circulate? The obvious answer is yes. The more subtle answer involves a different question. Given that Matthew made extensive changes to Mark's gospel to conform to his own perspective, would Matthew have wanted his gospel to circulate? Would not the Evangelists "therefore have been mindful of the inherent dangers associated with writing for a general audience and

29. Ibid., 90, 95.
30. Ibid., 94.
31. Marcus, *Mark: A New Translation with Introduction and Commentary*, 27, 27.
32. Alexander, "Ancient Book Production and the Circulation of the Gospels," 99.
33. Sim, "The Gospels for All Christians?," 11–15. His arguments are persuasive despite his arguments from silence on page 13 to support the point of little contact outside the Pauline network. In arguing against Bauckham's positive example of Ignatius, Sim (ibid., 14) says that the geographical area involved was predominantly Pauline. At ibid., 12, he states that Paul had no direct contact with Antioch during the period of the epistles following the episode described in Galatians. The two positions seem to be conflict with respect to whether Antioch would have been part of a Pauline network.

expecting their message to be preserved intact?"³⁴ Sim's conclusion is that Matthew may have hoped for a limited audience.

At this point in the discussion, the concept of a Matthean community is temporarily back in consideration. Stephen Barton argues that the text can only take one to a readership and not to a Matthean community. He describes the term *community* as a "slippery, ideologically 'loaded' word." Later he observes that many variant descriptions of the Matthean community have been derived by looking at the text. He concludes that one should consider Matthew's readership or audience and not his community.³⁵ The fact that one cannot now define or reconstruct the Matthean community from the Gospel text is not sufficient to say that such a community did not exist but only that scholars do not have enough information to define precisely the community.³⁶

Sociological work in the area of the use of narratives in small groups as community defining works against the Bauckham position. Warren Carter picks up Burridge's earlier work³⁷ in which Burridge examines the function of βίος within groups surrounding a charismatic leader, a close parallel to the Gospel context. Part of the function was community definition, and Carter notes that βίος overlaps with *encomia* genre.³⁸ Carter and Jerome Neyrey each demonstrate that the Gospel evidences support for many of the ways that groups use *encomia* to define themselves as a distinct group,³⁹ that is, delineation of the community's origin, its accomplishments, and its deeds. Carter argues that the opening chapters of the Gospel locate the community's origin in the purposes of God and the ministry of Jesus, who has brought the community into existence. The accomplishments take the form of theocratic governance in the sense of a community of disciples that does the will of God as revealed by Jesus, who is described as fulfilling the Law and the prophets, and who authorizes Peter to determine which laws are

34. Ibid., 16.

35. Barton, "Can We Identify the Gospel Audiences?," 176, 181.

36. Harland, *Associations, Synagogues, and Congregations*, 26–28. Harland shows that voluntary associations are a good model for understanding the composition and functioning of early Christian groups. However, he also shows that there is great variation in the associations for which we have primary sources. The same type of variability prevents one from deriving a precise and comprehensive model for any given Christian group.

37. Burridge, *What Are the Gospels? A Comparison with Graeco-Roman Biographies*.

38. Carter bases his arguments on the work of Balch, "Two Apologetic Encomia: Dionysius on Rome and Josephus on the Jews," 102–22.

39. Carter, "Community Definition and Matthew's Gospel," 637–42; Carter, *Matthew and the Margins*, 11–14; see also Neyrey, *Honor and Shame in the Gospel of Matthew*, chaps. 4 and 5.

binding in the future. Finally, the deeds of the disciples are greater than their opponents are in righteousness, and their deeds are not hypocritical like the deeds of the scribes and Pharisees.[40] Carter's work implies that the Gospel was not written for general circulation and, more likely, that it functioned as a rhetorical artifact that helped define the Matthean community.

To recap, I reject Bauckham's hypothesis that individuals wrote the gospels for general circulation and for a general audience. The counter arguments are stronger than Bauckham's arguments that early Christian leaders traveled around and wrote books for general circulation to a unified Christian movement, or that the end use of the Gospel represents its intended purpose. The arguments showing that the Gospel exhibits community-defining functions are in line with sociological studies about the development of communities. They counter Bauckham's arguments that the form of the Gospel indicates the author intended it for general audiences. Sim summarizes our mutually held position, "While it [Bauckham's argument] contains some valid criticism of traditional Gospel scholarship, it does not in the final analysis succeed in proving it wrong. Nor does it make a plausible alternative case that the Gospels were composed for each and every Christian church."[41] I assert that the Gospel of Matthew arose out of a particular early Christian community who wrote it primarily for their own use.

The Gospel of Matthew Was Put in Written Form c. 80 CE—c. 100 CE

Dating the period during which the stories of the Matthean community solidified into their written gospel involves establishing a lower date and an upper date. Candidates for the lower dates argued by scholars are before and after the Jewish War of 67-70 CE. The upper date most commonly proposed is before 110 CE. The arguments involve textual and contextual analysis. I present both positions for the lower date, but argue for the post-war date. I present the common arguments for the upper date and note some issues with the dating process.

The arguments concerned with establishing the lower date involve interpretations of Matt 22:1-14, synoptic ordering, and textual analysis of other Matthean passages tied to possible contexts. Matt 22:1-14 describes the destruction of a city, commonly assumed to be Jerusalem. Three arguments speak against associating this passage with Jerusalem. First, Robert

---

40. Carter, "Community Definition and Matthew's Gospel," 642-54, particularly 649-52 for the three arguments.

41. Sim, "The Gospels for All Christians?," 4.

Gundry rejects associating this passage with the actual destruction of Jerusalem because such an assumption would indicate that the Gentile mission did not begin until after 70 and other Matthean texts imply an earlier dating of the Gentile mission.[42] The next two arguments assert that the passage was not related to any historical event. It was a *topos* common to the period,[43] or was a general theological statement about how God would punish Jerusalem.[44] On the other hand, the passage specifically says that the king burned the city, and Josephus writes an apologetic for Titus burning Jerusalem. Josephus attributes its destruction to God, who incited Roman soldiers to set the fire. Titus was unable to undo what God had ordained when his soldiers could not hear Titus' command to quench the fire.[45] The Josephus passage ties to the Matthean passage in that Matt 22:7 refers to the burning of the city indicating a possible link to Jerusalem. The possibility is strengthened in that the reference to the burning of the city is absent from the Lukan version of the parable (Lk 14:15–24). Further, according to Carter, the insertion in Matt 22:7 interrupts the flow of the Matthean parable creating the unrealistic scenario of a wedding banquet occurring in the smoldering ruins of the city. Carter concludes that Matthew added the verse as a theological statement about God using Rome to destroy Jerusalem, which accords with the view of Josephus.[46] The Matthean insertion of verse seven strongly implies that the lower date for the Gospel should be post-70. Meier also argues for a date after the destruction of Jerusalem based on Matt 22:1–14, which he sees reflecting a period not immediately after the destruction. He picks an early date of 80–90 CE.[47]

Arguments supporting a pre-70 date also rely on correlating Matthean texts to historical situations. For example, Gundry argues that Matthew makes more frequent references to the Sadducees than Mark or Luke. The Sadducees lost influence after 70 CE, and using them as a foil for Matthew implies a date before 70 CE when they were still influential. Matthew

---

42. Gundry, *Matthew: A Commentary on His Literary and Theological Art*, 600. Gundry also states that to associate this passage with the destruction of Jerusalem is to associate the king Caesar with God, which "would require much daring." He makes more arguments based on an analysis of passages related to the debate on the position of the community vis-à-vis the synagogue.

43. Robinson, *Redating the New Testament*, 20–21.

44. Wansbrough, *St. Matthew, A New Catholic Commentary*, cited in Kealy, *Matthew's Gospel and the History of Biblical Interpretation*, 742–43.

45. Josephus, *J.W.* 6.250, 252–66.

46. Carter, *Matthew and the Margins*, 16–17.

47. Meier, *Law and History in Matthew's Gospel: A Redactional Study of Mt. 5:17–48*, 71, 7.

5:23–24 references gifts before the altar, which would imply that the Temple was still standing at the time of composition.[48] While these arguments appear strong, they do not take into account scholarship that points to the Gospel being the product of a long maturation process. For example, Wim Weren argues that the Gospel displays layers of traditions: (1) pre-70 in which the community was still a full member of a Jewish community, (2) period of 70–80 in which the community was in conflict with Pharisees, and (3) the period of 80–90 in which the community makes the final redaction of its gospel.[49] Based on Weren's layers, Gundry's argument uses passages from the second stage of the development of the Gospel. As such, Gundry's argument cannot be used to date the Gospel.

Also favoring a date after 70 is the argument based on the ordering of the synoptic gospels. A commonly held view is that Matthew used Mark as one of its sources, and scholarly consensus dates Mark to around 70. Hence, Matthew must have come after Mark, and by extension, after 70.[50] Allowing some time to elapse for the Gospel of Mark to circulate and to be accepted would point to the 80–90 CE period. I do not find the arguments for a pre-Jewish War date to be persuasive in the face of an analysis of Matt 22:1–14 and the extensive work on the ordering of the synoptic gospels.

Most, but not all, scholars base the upper date on the possible relationship of the Gospel to the writings of Ignatius that appear to use it, or at least to share common material with it.[51] This position establishes the upper date no later than 107-8 CE. Scholars make a similar argument using the Didache as the foil to set the early date for Matthew. Hubertus van de Sandt notes the consensus on dating the Didache to the end of the first century. According to the arguments, the Gospel would need to have been in final form prior to the generation of the writings of Ignatius or of the Didache. As I show, the argument for Ignatius is stronger than that for the Didache.

A consensus does not exist concerning parallels between the Gospel and the Didache:[52] the Didache used Matthew[53] or similarities are attributable

---

48. Gundry, *Matthew: A Commentary on His Literary and Theological Art*, 602, 604.

49. Weren, "The History and Social Setting of the Matthean Community," 53.

50. Contra Gundry, *Matthew: A Commentary on His Literary and Theological Art*, 602. Gundry observes that one can accept an earlier date for Matthew without claiming anything about which gospel came first. The date for Mark only has to move earlier than is customarily asserted.

51. Schoedel, "Ignatius and the Reception of the Gospel of Matthew in Antioch," 130.

52. Sandt, *Matthew and the Didache: Two Documents from the Same Jewish-Christian Milieu?*, 1. He also notes the growing unease in attributing use of Matthew by the authors of the Didache. Syria as the origin of both documents is accepted.

53. Varner, "The Didache 'Apocalypse' and Matthew 24"; Tuckett, "The Didache

to shared common materials.[54] Scholars are divided on whether the same passage is or is not related (for example, Did 9:5d || Matt 7:7a).[55] Given the scholars have not reached a consensus on this relationship, I reject basing the upper date on the use of the Gospel by the Didache.

The possible use of Matthew by Ignatius remains a point of contention among patristic scholars.[56] The scope of this study prohibits a detailed review of the arguments, but I offer a brief description of the various positions and draw a conclusion. The proponents of the Ignatius argument cite several passages showing Matthean material. Possible parallels to Matthean passages cited are (1) *Eph* 5.2 || 18:19–20; (2) *Eph* 6.1 || 10:40, 21:33–41; (3) *Eph* 10.3 || 13:25; (4) *Eph* 11.1 || 3:7; (5) *Eph* 14.2 || 12:33; (6) *Eph* 15.1 || 23:8; (7) *Eph* 16.2 || 3:12; (8) *Eph* 17.1 || 26:6–13; (9) *Eph* 19 || 2:2, (10) *Magn* 5.2 || 22:19;(11) *Magn* 8.2 || 5:11–12; (12) *Magn* 9.1 || 27:52; (13) *Trall* 9.1 || 11:19; (14) *Trall* 11.1 || 15:13; (15) *Rom* 9.3 || 10:41–42; (16) *Phld* 2.2 || 7:15; (17) *Phld* 3.1 || 15:13; (18) *Phld* 6.1 || 23:27; (19) *Phld* 7.2 || 7.2 || 16:17; (20) *Sm* proem || 12:18; (21) *Sm* proem 1.1 || 3:15; (22) *Sm* proem 6.1 || 19:12; (23) *Sm* proem 6.2 || 6:28; (24) *Pol* 1.2–3 || 8:17; and (25) *Pol* 2.2 || 10:16.[57] Not all of these passages carry the same weight.[58] For example, using word and grammar usage, Meier argues that (9) *Eph* 19.2–3, (17) *Phld* 3.1, and (25) *Pol* 2.2 demonstrate clearly a dependence on Matthew.[59] While acknowledging that other scholars disagree with him, Meier argues that *Eph* 19.2–3 is a homiletic midrash on the star motif of Matt 2:2.[60] Clayton Jefford brings up the question of how Ignatius used the Matthean materials. After his review of the possible parallels, he concludes that Ignatius based his theological and ethical teachings on Matthean materials, but that Ignatius

---

and the Synoptics Once More: A Response to Aaron Milavec," 509–18.

54. Milavec, "Synoptic Tradition in the Didache Revisited"; Kloppenborg, "Halakhic Evidence of Didache 8 and Matthew 6 and the Didache Community's Relationship to Judaism"; Williams, "Social Memory and the Didache."

55. Sandt, "'Do Not Give What Is Holy to the Dogs' (Did 9:5d and Matt 7:6a): The Eucharistic Food of the Didache in Its Jewish Purity Setting," 225–26. He argues the saying has a cultic ring and does not depend directly on the Matthean parallel.

56. Jefford, "Did Ignatius of Antioch Know the Didache?," 334.

57. Ibid., 338n319.

58. Kèohler, *Die Rezeption des Matthèausevangeliums in der Zeit vor Irenèaus*, 73–96; Schoedel, "Ignatius and the Reception of the Gospel of Matthew in Antioch," 154. Kèohler categorizes passages as probable, quite possible, and theoretically possible but unlikely. Schoedel suggests that such comparisons focus the discussion on the Ignatius-Matthew connection too narrowly.

59. Meier, "Matthew and Ignatius: A Response to William R. Schoedel," 180.

60. Ibid., 186. Meier argues that in some cases the passage by Ignatius matches its Matthean parallel almost word for word

did not tend to use quotations. He does concede that Ignatius used words or phrases found in Matthew (for example, the *coming wrath* in (4) *Eph* 11.1 or a tree known by its fruit in (5) *Eph* 14.2).[61] The list of possible parallels, whether strong or weak, is substantial and covers a number of the writings of Ignatius.

John Meier argues against the proposition that Ignatius used materials similar to Matthew[62] rather than the Gospel itself. He cites as an example, (17) *Phld* 3.1: "Keep yourselves from the evil plants, which Jesus does not cultivate, because they are not a planting of the Father," with its parallel to Matt 15:13–14. He argues that the two admonitions share the same context, the noun φυτεία occurs only in the New Testament in Matt 15:13 and only in Ignatius in early Christian literature. Moreover, the passage is most likely a Matthean redaction. He concludes that such similarities would be unlikely if Ignatius only used a similar M tradition.[63]

Scholars argue against the connection between Ignatius and Matthew based on differences in theology and social milieu. They ask, "How can such apparently different churches as the Church of Paul and Peter, the church of Matthew, and the Church of Ignatius all be progressive developments of one, and the same, local church?"[64] The principal caution centers on accommodating a strong shift in ecclesiastics and orthodoxy in a relatively short period. For example, Ignatius does not display the strong Jewish flavor of the Gospel.[65] William Schoedel concedes considerable differences in the contexts and he argues that the theological stance of Ignatius was closer to John and the notion of the sufficiency of Jesus Christ (for example, *Ph* 8.2) is Pauline.[66] Yet, keeping his analysis textually based, he argues that the "good news" proclaimed by Ignatius has a lot in common with Matthew. He asserts that Matthean materials formed "the backbone of the gospel materials in Ignatius."[67] Despite reservations from the skeptics, the arguments showing

---

61. Jefford, "Did Ignatius of Antioch Know the Didache?," 339.

62. "It was not the Gospel of Matthew itself on which Ignatius relied, but that he depended in whole or in part on materials of a Matthean type that continued to circulate apart from the Gospel" (Schoedel, "Ignatius and the Reception of the Gospel of Matthew in Antioch," esp. 129).

63. Meier, "Matthew and Ignatius: A Response to William R. Schoedel," 182–83.

64. Robinson and Koester, *Trajectories through Early Christianity*, 125; Brown and Meier, *Antioch and Rome*, 113.

65. Kilpatrick, *Origins*, 134.

66. Schoedel, "Ignatius and the Reception of the Gospel of Matthew in Antioch," 151–53.

67. Ibid., 154.

dependence on Matthew in the writings of Ignatius seem more convincing. Thus, c. 100 CE becomes an upper date of final redaction of the Gospel.

Antioch Was the Probable Location of the Matthean Community

The varying proposals for the location of the Matthean community rely on textual analysis of the Gospel itself and the necessity of the community out of which it arose having enough prominence in early Christian communities for the Gospel to have gained some widespread acceptance so quickly.[68] Textual analysis has led scholars to posit the Matthean community in a large, wealthy,[69] culturally diverse Greek-speaking city[70] on a trade route with a large Jewish population in conflict with some other group. While no certainty is possible, I argue for Antioch as the most likely location by addressing three questions: (1) "Was the Matthean community located in a city?" (2) "Where was the community located geographically?" (3) "Based on the answers to questions one and two, out of what specific city might the Gospel have emerged?"

Matthean Community Located in a City

Scholars make four different arguments to place the Matthean community in a city. (1) The usage and emphasis of πόλις is different than in Mark. (2) The variety of coins referenced indicates a wealthy city on a trade route.[71] (3) The Gospel was written in Koine Greek that was spoken primarily in the cities.[72] (4) Wealth, which was found primarily in cities, was necessary to write a book as lengthy as the Gospel of Matthew. In the paragraphs below, I expand each argument in turn and make my counter arguments.

The first argument for the Matthean community being located in a city relies on Mark and Matthew using the terms *city* and *town* differently,[73] shown by frequency of use of the terms and redactions to emphasize the im-

---

68. Streeter, *The Four Gospels: A Study of Origins*, 486, 502–4.

69. Kingsbury, "Verb Akolouthein ("to Follow")," 66–67.

70. There is a minority of scholars (for example, Eduard Schweizer and Gerd Theissen) that sees the community as itinerant charismatics. While the earliest followers of Jesus might have been wandering charismatic groups, I accept the arguments against such a setting being the one out of which the Gospel would have arisen.

71. Kilpatrick, *Origins*, 125.

72. Gale, "Antioch Versus Sepphoris," 143.

73. Kilpatrick, *Origins*, 124–25.

portance of cities. The frequency argument as presented has methodological problems, although the conclusion is correct. Jack Kingsbury, for example, states that Matthew uses πόλις more times than Mark—twenty-six versus eight—but without noting that Matthew is longer.[74] A better metric is the percentage of verses containing πόλις for each Gospel. This metric shows Matthew with a stronger use of πόλις than Mark—2.341% versus 1.189%. The metric of the percentage of occurrences of the term—number of occurrences divided by the total number of words in the Gospel—yields a similar almost two-to-one ratio: Matthew at 0.147% and Mark at 0.071%. A similar metric can be applied to the uses of κώμη. Using the metrics above relative to κώμη, the ratios are Matthew at 0.375% and 0.022% with Mark at 1.040% and 0.062%, respectively. Hence, Mark favors κώμη more than Matthew. In summary, these two analyses confirm that Matthew favors the term *city* over the term *town*. The question remains whether this emphasis is the result of the Matthean community being city-based.

Aaron Gale and Michael Crosby each offer an interesting observation concerning Matthew linking οἶκος with πόλις. Crosby lists Matt 10:14, 12:25, 17:24–25, 23:38, 26:18, to which Gale adds Matt 2:8–11, 10:11–12, 26:6, in which this pairing occurs. They conclude the community's permanent dwelling is in or near a city.[75] The problem with their argument is that the specified passages do not link the two terms as strongly as one might expect. Gale and Crosby identify Bethany, Capernaum, and Bethlehem as cities. Matthew explicitly cites Bethany as a city. Contrary to their argument, Matthew never refers to Capernaum or Bethlehem as cities. Matthew, explicitly locating Jesus at home in Capernaum (Matt 4:13),[76] does not support their household-in-the-city argument since Capernaum could be a village and not a city. Matthew changed Mark to a city-focus in Matt 9:35 when Matthew adds *city* to the Markan version (Mk 6:6). Gale claims Matthew shows an urban stance in verses where Mark pairs *city* and *town*, but Matthew replaces the entire expression with *all of* a geographical area.[77] While the assertion may be true, Gale only cites two instances: 4:23 and 4:24 (listed as 14:24). Hence, scrutiny shows all these promising arguments relying on redactions to be weak. Many of the references are indirect (that is, the verse mentions a place name, but nowhere in the text does one find whether

---

74. Kingsbury, *Matthew as Story*, 125.

75. Gale, "Antioch Versus Sepphoris," 142; Crosby, *House of Disciples: Church, Economics, and Justice in Matthew*, 40.

76. The fact that some scholars believe that Capernaum was a city does not obviate the fact that Matthew is silent on this point. See for example, Saldarini, "The Gospel of Matthew and Jewish-Christian Conflict," 27.

77. Gale, "Antioch Versus Sepphoris," 142.

Matthew thought the place was a city).⁷⁸ When the analysis is restricted to explicit city references, it cannot sustain their argument.

The general methodological problem is the unspoken assumption concerning the location for Mark. If the origin of Mark is not a city, the arguments that the redactional changes may indicate a city scenario for the Matthean community are valid. If the place of origin for the Gospel of Mark were Rome, as is often suggested, one would need to show why Mark had not used city terminology for the same reasons suggested for Matthew using city terminology. A different assumption could be that Mark is more reflective of earlier, untrammeled versions of the Jesus tradition, but scholars do not commonly hold such an assumption. Claiming redaction of the term *city* is not a strong argument for the Matthean community being located in a city. Most importantly, the assumption that the use of πόλις in the narrative must reflect the place of origin is very suspect in and of itself.

A stronger, but still not strong, argument for an urban location is the use and description of coins found in the text. Coins, especially larger denominations, were mostly a city phenomenon. Kingsbury argues that Matthew used a variety of coin types, except the low-value *lepton*. Matthew references the high value coins—gold, silver, and talent—twenty-eight times versus once in Mark and four times in Luke.⁷⁹ Kingsbury concludes that Matthew's use of coin terminology reflects a community that is well acquainted with a variety of coins, and people with this familiarity would live in a city.⁸⁰ In rural economies, in-kind transactions occurred more often than money exchanges,⁸¹ and archeological excavations outside of cities find few coins.⁸² These facts sustain his argument. One weakness in the argument is that one can know about a gold coin and its use without ever having owned one. A second weakness shows up with the an examination of the references (denarius [2x]: Matt 18:28; 22:19; copper [1x]: Matt 10:9;

---

78. Strickert, "The Coins of Philip," 84. Strickert notes that Mark refers to Bethsaida as a town, which was correct early on. He does not speak to Matthew but does indicate that Luke and John are correct to refer to Bethsaida as a πόλις, which is a status it received later. His observations caution about placing too much emphasis on redaction relative to terminology without knowing if the change is just a reflection of an actual terminology change over time.

79. Once again, the argument is made with counts and not percentages. However, the disparity in counts is wider here than in the city argument above, which would result in percentage differences strongly favoring Matthew.

80. Kingsbury, "Verb Akolouthein ('to Follow')," 67–68.

81. Oakman, *Jesus and the Economic Questions*, 25.

82. Evans, *Coins and Economy in Palestine*, 8. Most of the coins dating between 40 BCE and 96 CE were located near Roman structures such as theaters, amphitheaters, and hippodromes.

silver [6x]: Matt 10:9; 26:15; 27:3, 5, 6, 9; gold [4x]: Matt 2:11; 10:9; 23:16, 17; talent [10x]: Matt 18:24; 25:15, 16, 17, 18, 20, 22, 24, 25, 28). All but one reference to talents come in one parable. All but one reference to silver comes in the narrative of the betrayal by Judas. When the lack of spread across the Gospel is taken into account, the Gospel does not display much of a large-coin bias.

Scholars have also argued for a city setting based on context in the first century: use of Koine Greek and the expense related to writing such a long text. The argument that the use of Koine Greek requires a city setting cannot be sustained since Greek was understood and spoken as a second language in rural areas.[83] However, a final point in favor of an urban setting is that wealth was necessary to write such a lengthy text. Wealthy people normally lived in cities,[84] although they spent some time at their rural estates.

None of the individual arguments for an urban setting is strong. Further, it is interesting that with respect to food-access issues, the Gospel often deals with rural-based examples. This observation does not counter the possibility of a city setting. In rural-based societies, some landowners live in the city and go to their fields from there (Matt 20:1–16). Day laborers,[85] as well as people from farms who had come to the city to beg,[86] could also live in the city. Despite most arguments being weak, I accept an urban setting since no arguments have been presented for a non-city milieu.

Syria Is the Probable Geographic Area

Scholars have suggested five possible geographic areas for the Gospel's origin: Egypt, Phoenicia, trans-Jordan, Galilee, and Syria. The order reflects increasing scholarly support for each candidate area. In this section, I will present arguments made for each geographic area, and conclude that Syria is the strongest candidate.

S. van Tilborg and S. G. F. Brandon have proposed Egypt, specifically Alexandria as a place of origin. Both argue that Alexandria had an established Jewish community, and the city was known to be highly anti-Jewish.[87]

---

83. Mussies, "Greek in Palestine and the Diaspora," 1053.

84. Saldarini, "The Gospel of Matthew and Jewish-Christian Conflict," 27; Derrenbacker, *Ancient Compositional Practices and the Synoptic Problem*, 24–25. Derrenbacker notes the expense of manuscripts on papyrus. In one citation, *P.Oxy.* 1654, the cost for a single sheet is roughly one-third of a day's wage for a laborer.

85. MacMullen, *Roman Social Relations*, 42. The discussion concerns Italy and not the Roman East, but the point is made that there were seasonal migrations of laborers.

86. Finger, *Of Widows and Meals: Communal Meals in the Book of Acts*, 131.

87. Tilborg, *The Jewish Leaders in Matthew*, 172; Brandon, *The Fall of Jerusalem and*

the gospel reflects the trauma of experienced food shortages 149

Additionally, Brandon argues that there was a flourishing Christian church by the second century that had early beginnings in alignment with the Jerusalem church and not with Paul. He sees Alexandria being a place of refuge for Christian Jews fleeing Jerusalem in 70 CE, and hence, the Gospel's portrayal of Egypt as a refuge against those wishing to kill Jesus, the Messiah.[88] Against Alexandria as an option are several factors. Matthew shows no influence from Philo, the well-known Jewish philosopher and writer in Alexandria.[89] The Gospel does not read like any of the substantial body of literature surviving from Alexandria.[90] By the end of the first century, the church in Alexandria had not achieved prestige and influence.[91] The counter-arguments are persuasive and, hence, I reject Alexandria, and consequently Egypt.

Another proposed location is the Phoenician coast, particularly the cities of Tyre or Sidon, or Caesarea Maritime. Textual arguments suggest a coastal location since Matthew distinguishes between the Mediterranean Sea and the Sea of Galilee (Matt 8:32, 14:28–29, 18:6). Matthew changes the description of the Canaanite woman (Matt 15:22 || Mk 7:26) in line with common usage of Canaan referring to Phoenicia.[92] A non-textual argument is that Caesarea Maritime had an established Christian community early on (Acts 10) which was prominent after 189 CE. The strongest counter arguments are that the church in Caesarea Maritime arose from the conversion of a pagan centurion and that such a church would be difficult to reconcile with some of the narrowly Jewish passages of the Gospel.[93] Caesarea Maritime does not satisfy the criterion of having a large Jewish population at the end of the first century.[94] Tyre and Sidon are not candidates because so little information is available about them in the first century. In addition, there is no indication of their influence in the early church.[95]

Another textual analysis moves a possible place of origin away from the coast to the east side of the Jordan. H. Dixon Slingerland makes this proposal based on two verses, Matt 4:15 and 19:1. He carefully argues that

---

the Christian Church, 221; Barclay, *Jews in the Mediterranean Diaspora: From Alexander to Trajan (323 BCE—117 CE)*, 158.

88. Brandon, *The Fall of Jerusalem and the Christian Church*, 221–27.
89. Kilpatrick, *Origins*, 133.
90. Overman, *Church and Community in Crisis*, 16.
91. Brown and Meier, *Antioch and Rome*, 19.
92. Kilpatrick, *Origins*, 131–32.
93. Brown and Meier, *Antioch and Rome*, 20.
94. Josephus, *J.W.* 2.457, 452.507–9, 457.361–63. The residents of Caesarea Maritima massacred Jews in 66 CE.
95. Brown and Meier, *Antioch and Rome*, 21–22.

Matthew redacted them intentionally to reflect his own geographical perspective. Matthew refers to western locations as being on the other side of the Jordan, because Matthew is on the eastern side.[96] While presenting a strong argument on the geographical area, Slingerland is tentative in suggesting Pella for the actual city.[97] He bases the suggestion principally on a possible influx of Jerusalemites after the Jewish War and the period of the 90s, which corresponds to the height of activity of the Christian church there.[98] While conceding that the tradition must point to some Jewish Christian group being there at some time, Brandon argues strongly that Pella as a place of refuge for Christians from Jerusalem would have been highly unlikely based on many factors. Two factors are the strong historically Greek nature of the city and the sack of Pella by Jews in 66 CE.[99] The sack of the city was devastating and would have rendered the inhabitants inhospitable to Jews of any persuasion coming from Jerusalem.[100] Slingerland's arguments for the geographic area of the trans-Jordan area are thought provoking. A point against this location is that it is not touted as having a prominent Christian church whose prestige would have underpinned the widespread acceptance of a gospel arising from it.

Lower Galilee, a patristic favorite,[101] is also a candidate as a geographical area for the Gospel's origin.[102] Matthew portrays most of the ministry of Jesus in Lower Galilee, with the primary exception being the move to Jerusalem in chapter 19 and following. Matthew 4:13 emphasizes the Galilee by specifying Capernaum as the home of Jesus. Eight out of ten miracles

96. Slingerland, "The Transjordanian Origin of St. Matthew's Gospel," 18–22.

97. Weren, "The History and Social Setting of the Matthean Community," 54. Weren argues that the Gospel is the result of a long maturing process for the Matthean community, which he describes as a network of house churches. He says there were three phases and three different locations for the development of the Gospel. More importantly, he says that the first stage could have been located in Slingerland's trans-Jordan area although he favors the border area between North and South Galilee near Capernaum. Weren argues that the community would not have been there after 70.

98. Slingerland, "The Transjordanian Origin of St. Matthew's Gospel," 26.

99. Josephus, J.W. 2.458.

100. Brandon, *The Fall of Jerusalem and the Christian Church*, 169–73.

101. Streeter, *The Four Gospels: A Study of Origins*, 500; France, *The Gospel of Matthew*, 15; Miller, *Studies in the History and Traditions of Sepphoris*, 2–3.

102. Freyne, *Galilee: From Alexander the Great to Hadrian*, chap. 4 and 5, 323–29; White, "Crisis Management and Boundary Maintenance," 229–31; Romeny, "Hypothesis on the Development of Judaism and Christianity in Syria in the Period after 70 C.E.," 33. Flying in the face of many scholars who posit Syria based on affinities of Matthew to the Didache, Romeny suggests Galilee could be a possibility or at least a location close to Palestine. Upper Galilee is not a candidate since it was a non-urbanized village culture with no free cities.

the gospel reflects the trauma of experienced food shortages 151

occur in Galilee.[103] Anthony Saldarini makes the following five arguments for Galilee. (1) It has the large cities of Sepphoris and Tiberius as well as the lesser cities of Bethsaida and Capernaum. (2) Archeological finds, and the writings of Josephus, suggest that there were Jews and Gentiles who spoke Greek. (3) A Christian community residing in one of the large cities would have the resources to educate and support a writer such as Matthew. (4) Galilee is also a region where Jewish culture was dominant and Matthew would not have to explain Aramaic expressions. (5) The Matthean community could come into conflict with other expressions of Judaism, especially at Jamnia.[104] Saldarini makes a strong case for Galilee as being a candidate for the gospel location when he writes:

> Thus, there is no need to locate Matthew in Antioch in order to find a literary, linguistic, and cultural milieu rich enough to support the gospel. The Galilee, with its complex and cosmopolitan society and its tightly woven cultural network, could easily have supported the nascent rabbinic Jewish and Christian Jewish movements, as well as the other apocalyptic, priestly, messianic, revivalist, and revolutionary currents running through society.[105]

Sean Freyne, however, rejects Galilee as the place of composition of the Gospel. He argues that the new focus at the end of the Gospel is on a gospel for all nations, and this new focus would exclude Galilee since Galilee would be associated with the failed mission of the past.[106] Meier argues against Galilee. He sees the Matthean community at the intersection of Jewish and Gentile worlds and asserts that the Jewish-Christian communities were destroyed in all of Palestine after the fall of Jerusalem.[107] Unfortunately, he gives no collaborating evidence, and Brandon argues against Meier's position. Brandon looks at the textual evidence supporting this view of the destruction of Jewish-Christian communities and concludes the evidence is not satisfactory to postulate a mass exodus of Christians from Palestine.[108] At this point, I find Saldarini's argument to be more persuasive than arguments against Galilee as a location for the Matthean community.

---

103. Kingsbury, "Verb Akolouthein ("to Follow")," 66.

104. Saldarini, "The Gospel of Matthew and Jewish-Christian Conflict," 26–27; Davies, "A Different Approach to Jamnia: The Jewish Sources of Matthew's Messianism."

105. Saldarini, "The Gospel of Matthew and Jewish-Christian Conflict," 27.

106. Freyne, *Galilee: From Alexander the Great to Hadrian*, 360–64.

107. Meier, *Law and History in Matthew's Gospel: A Redactional Study of Mt. 5:17–48*, 71, 8.

108. Brandon, *The Fall of Jerusalem and the Christian Church*, 175–77.

The use of Koine Greek not being widespread in Galilee is the basis of another objection. Freyne argues that Greek was widely spoken there,[109] but Mark Chancey argues convincingly that Greek was not widely spoken, and written even less.[110] Kingsbury supports Chancey's position.[111] The arguments for Galilee as a possible geographical area are not strong, but neither are the counter-arguments.

If Lower Galilee is a geographic possibility, then what city is a candidate? Aaron Gale and J. Andrew Overman are proponents of Sepphoris, or maybe Tiberias, in Galilee.[112] Sepphoris was the largest city in Galilee,[113] was located on the major trade route in that area, and minted money. Archaeology and primary sources locate the city in a fertile agricultural region, possibly with storehouses.[114] It had a substantial Jewish population.[115]

Yet, both Galilee and Sepphoris suffer the same criticism as other areas and cities: little evidence that they had a Christian community that achieved the necessary prestige and influence to have its gospel accepted widely.

Syria is a frequent candidate for the geographical location based both on textual and non-textual arguments. The same argument that Saldarini made for Galilee can be made for Syria. It had Antioch as a major city. A long-standing Roman occupation would indicate that Greek was spoken there. Meier describes Syria as a "meeting place and melting pot of Jewish and Gentile Christians," and it had a well-developed scribal tradition.[116] Textual analysis points to the geographical area of Syria. Matthew 4:24 says of Jesus "his fame spread throughout all Syria," a reference that has no parallel in Mark.[117]

A non-textual based reason offered for Syria is the use of the Gospel by the Nazoraioi and the Ebionites in the area[118] and by the Didache, all

109. Freyne, *Galilee: From Alexander the Great to Hadrian*, 139.

110. Chancey, *Greco-Roman Culture and the Galilee of Jesus*, 161–65.

111. Kingsbury, "Verb Akolouthein ('to Follow')," 67–68.

112. Gale, "Antioch Versus Sepphoris," 145–56; Overman, *Church and Community in Crisis*, 18–19. I will be principally following Gale's arguments.

113. Josephus, *J.W.* 3.34.

114. Freyne, "Herodian Economics in Galilee," 32; Negev, "Sepphoris Later Diocarsarea," 827. According to the *Notitia Dignitatum*, Sepphoris was a military center. There would normally be granaries in the area to support the army food requirements.

115. Overman, *Matthew's Gospel and Formative Judaism*, 159.

116. Meier, *Law and History in Matthew's Gospel: A Redactional Study of Mt. 5:17–48*, 71, 8.

117. Carter, *Matthew Storyteller*, 21; Streeter, *The Four Gospels: A Study of Origins*, 504. Carter notes that this change is surprising given the focus on Galilee in this section of Matthew.

118. Freyne, *Galilee: From Alexander the Great to Hadrian*, 364; Edwards, "The Gospel of the Ebionites and the Gospel of Luke," 568–70. Edwards argues that the work

attested to Syria.[119] On pages 141–45, I argued that a consensus does not exist concerning the Didache relying on the Gospel. Even if one accepts the reliance of the Didache on the Gospel, it does not follow necessarily that the two texts came from the same setting. Sandt opposes this position and argues that the Didache and the Gospel shared the same historical and geographical setting.[120] Attempts to establish location based on the use of Matthew by groups in the geographical area is weak. Since scholars accept that some form of the Gospel of Mark had arrived in Antioch from its place of origin, I cannot dismiss the same scenario for the relationship between the Matthean materials and other documents found in Syria. The arguments of similarity to other documents attested to the area are not persuasive.

To recap, Egypt is not a candidate because Alexandria is not a viable candidate. Phoenicia is not a candidate because it did not have a large Jewish population in the late first century. The trans-Jordan is an intriguing candidate but fails the criterion of hosting an influential Christian community. Lower Galilee, a patristic favorite, likewise fails the criterion of hosting an influential Christian community and a possible issue surrounding the prevalence of the use of Koine Greek. Syria remains as the only viable candidate, and it has textual and other traits to recommend it.

Antioch Is the Strongest Candidate

Traditionally, Antioch has been, and continues to be, the location most often cited.[121] While no certainty is possible, scholars posit several reasons for Matthew arising specifically from Antioch. The significant role Peter plays in the Gospel (Matt 10:2; 16:16) could be a reflection of Peter's prominence in the community at Antioch (Gal 2:11–14).[122] Antioch fits the ascribed traits of being an urban center with an early history of Christian community set in a Hellenistic-Jewish cultural milieu, which was on a major trade route, with a large Jewish population.[123] Antioch was both a strongly Roman city and

---

has a stronger affinity to Luke than to Matthew. If this is the case, using an affinity of Matthew to the Ebionites to argue location becomes non-convincing.

119. Streeter, *The Four Gospels: A Study of Origins*, 507–11.

120. Sandt, *Matthew and the Didache: Two Documents from the Same Jewish-Christian Milieu?*, 1–2; Romeny, "Hypothesis on the Development of Judaism and Christianity in Syria in the Period after 70 C.E.," 33. On the other hand, Romeny argues in a similar fashion, but he suggests the same neighborhood is close to Palestine, and may even be Galilee.

121. Senior, "Directions in Matthean Studies," 8.

122. Carter, *Matthew Storyteller*, 21; Brown and Meier, *Antioch and Rome*, 23–24.

123. Schoedel, "Ignatius and the Reception of the Gospel of Matthew in Antioch,"

a strongly Jewish city. Jews received citizenship from its founder and were called Antiochenes.[124] Diaspora Jews were particularly numerous in Syria but congregated in Antioch due to favorable treatment.[125] As the first major Christian center outside of Jerusalem,[126] it would have had the prestige and influence required. A further significant argument centers on the earliest citations of the Gospel being written by Ignatius early in the second century. I reject any city other than Antioch in Syria, including Edessa, due to Syriac and Aramaic, and not the required Greek, being spoken predominantly.[127]

Food Supply Was Not Consistent in Antioch

I will now argue that Antioch in the late first century as the location and time for the Matthean community has several important implications for this study. Antioch was on a trade route,[128] which would be conducive to aristocrats stockpiling grain as they participated in the grain trade. As I will argue on pages 189–193, this practice placed peasants at greater risk for crop failures and raised food prices in the city. In this section, I argue that Antioch was located in a fertile plain, which would usually provide sufficient food for the city and its environs. However, Antioch had a strong imperial presence,[129] which affected food supply. Furthermore, traumatic events in the first century at Antioch caused the Matthean community to experience severe interruptions in access to food and strengthened their vision of the realm of the heavens providing sufficient food for everyone.

Antioch Was Situated in a Fertile Plain

The Antioch area could support a variety of food sources since it was located on a fertile plain, and the slopes of Mt. Silpius, with good water from springs and the nearby Orontes River.[130] J. H. W. G. Liebeschuetz mentions

---

129; Kraeling, "The Jewish Community at Antioch," 132–33. Based on rabbinic sources, Kraeling asserts the Jewish population was the third largest in the early Roman period.

124. Josephus, *Ag. Ap.* 2.39.
125. Josephus, *J.W.* 7.43–44.
126. Brown and Meier, *Antioch and Rome*, 12.
127. Ibid., 21. For example, Brown and Meier note that the inscriptions in general, and funerary inscriptions in particular, are in Syriac. This objection is not countered when the general geographical area is proposed versus Antioch in particular.
128. Downey, *History of Antioch in Syria*, 21.
129. Carter, *Matthew and Empire*, 41.
130. Downey, *History of Antioch in Syria*, 21.

vegetables in spring, grapes and melons in summer supplemented by eggs, dried fruit, and meat as a luxury.[131] Glanville Downey cites wheat and barley, olives, olive oil and wine in abundance, and garden vegetables.[132] Archaeological analysis of shards from a farm area show traces of emmer, hulled barley, oat grasses, and rye grasses.[133] Specific information on crops exists for the Galilee and Samaria, and for purposes of the argument here, I assume the crop production was at least similar to that found in Antioch. Safrai writes, "Talmudic literature mentions over 500 types of produce. Of these, about 150 types of cultivated crops, 8 types of grain, 20 types of legumes, 24 types of vegetables, 30 types of fruit and about 20 types of spice plants have been identified."[134] Legumes were a regular part of the diet in Galilee and the more important varieties were lentils and green beans for human consumption.[135] Peasants grew vegetables for consumption, but not for storing or selling.[136] In Samaria, archaeological surveys show cultivated crops with 26.4 percent in grains, 20.2 percent in grapes, and 12.9 percent in olives.[137] To recap, crops reported for Antioch and the Levant confirm the recommendations made by the first-century agriculturalists, as discussed in the previous chapter. One would also expect the usual crop losses on particular plots 30 percent of the time, as discussed in the previous chapter.

Human-Based Threats to Sufficient Food

Human-based threats to food access include factors such as a severe tax situation that often led to loss of land by smaller landowners[138] and a strong Roman presence that drew on the food resources for the area. By the time of the composition of the gospel, the tax situation was generally bad enough that Domitian issued an order that the emperor must approve any new taxes or requisitions.[139] The public reason given was couched in terms of justice

---

131. Liebeschuetz, *Antioch in the Later Roman Period*, 69–70n69.

132. Downey, *History of Antioch in Syria*, 19–21.

133. Braidwood and Braidwood, *Excavations in the Plain of Antioch*, Appendix II, 540–44.

134. Safrai, *The Economy of Roman Palestine*, 104. Safrai writes a detailed description in chapter 2 of cultivation in Palestine just after the first century.

135. Ibid., 145.

136. Ibid., 144.

137. Ibid., 108.

138. Oakman, *Jesus and the Peasants*, 4, chaps. 1 and 2.

139. Lewis and Reinhold, *Roman Civilization*, 2, 321. Lewis catalogues Inscr. Gr. Lat. Syriae, vol. V, no 1,998, 81–96 CE.

and of coming to the aid of provincials, who were already exhausted trying to provide the necessities. The economic reason was that peasants starving or walking off the land would result in uncultivated land.[140] No cultivation is unacceptable on at least two levels for the ruling group: no tax income on the produce and no food for Antioch aristocracy or Roman soldiers, as well as people in the lower socio-economic segments of the population. Carter estimates that the total loss to the rural population surrounding Antioch could be up to 70 percent taking into account rents, taxes, and grain requisitions.[141] Making these payments was neither easy nor sustainable over time for smaller landowners and farming households. Withholding payments was not an option. Philo and Plutarch each describe the terrible punishments, including torture and death that tax collectors meted out on people in arrears.[142] It is no wonder that the cause of the fire in Antioch in 70 CE was a man attempting to burn the tax and business records.[143]

Antioch had a substantial Roman presence as evidenced by prominent Romans living in Antioch and a sizeable military detachment stationed in Antioch.[144] Antioch hosted prominent Romans as young men. The future emperor Trajan lived in Antioch while his father was governor in 76–79 CE. Pliny the Younger was in residence 81–82 CE.[145] No explicit epigraphic evidence exists to indicate a permanent Roman garrison in Antioch. One can infer this situation[146] from Antioch being a major Roman city on a trade route in an unstable part of the Roman Empire.[147] Josephus places the entire twelfth legion at Antioch, which would be approximately five thousand

---

140. Carter, *Matthew and Empire*, 41.

141. Ibid., 114, 148.

142. Stegemann and Stegemann, *The Jesus Movement*, 49–51; Philo, *Spec. Leg.* 3.159–62; Plutarch, *Lucullus* 20. According to Plutarch, slavery was peace compared to the tortures (20.2).

143. Josephus, *J.W.* 7.54–61; Dio Cassius, *Hist.* 67.66; Goodman, "The First Jewish Revolt: Social Conflict and the Problem of Debt," 418. Burning of tax records was not the only avenue of resistance. Cassius describes a massacre of tax collectors in Numidia in Egypt when money was being forcibly extorted. Goodman says that Josephus might have been wrong since creditors kept their own loan documents as evidenced from documents recovered from the Judean desert.

144. Klauck, "The Roman Empire," 76; Isaac and Roll, "A Milestone of A.D. 69 from Judaea," 17–19; Jones, "The Roman Army," 210; Josephus, *J.W.* 2.500. Josephus writes that the twelfth legion was stationed in Antioch, which if at full strength would be about 5,300 soldiers.

145. Downey, *Ancient Antioch*, 97–98.

146. Isaac and Roll, "A Milestone of A.D. 69 from Judaea," 17–19; Jones, "The Roman Army," 210.

147. Lassus, "Antioch on the Orontes," 61.

soldiers plus camp followers,[148] who do not contribute to the production of food. In preparation for the Jewish War of 66–70 CE, the number of troops increased to 20,000.[149]

The question is whether the presence of troops in Antioch was good or not. The answer depended on one's perspective. Romans were inclined to view themselves in a favorable light. For example, Tacitus writes an account of an incident around 69 CE when Vespasian was threatening to move the soldiers from Antioch to a less favorable assignment. "For the provincials were accustomed to live with the soldiers and enjoyed association with them; in fact, many civilians were bound to the soldiers by ties of friendship and of marriage."[150] On the other hand, the locals might have viewed five thousand Roman soldiers, along with their servants[151] and auxiliary cohorts, in a city with a population of one hundred fifty thousand[152] with a less friendly lens. Benjamin Isaac says, "at times, a military command centre was the cause of great misery for its inhabitants. Occasional munificence was not enough to compensate for the rapaciousness of the soldiers and the greed of officials."[153]

Natural Threats to Food Supply: Famines, Floods, and Earthquakes

The Matthean community most likely existed for some time before the finalizing of its gospel. A dating of the finalizing of the Gospel between c. 80—c. 100 CE positions the Matthean community in a period of more severe than usual food shortages. Famines, floods, and earthquakes occurred often and would have affected food supplies and the price of grain in the period leading up to the final redaction of the Gospel.[154] The Matthean community,

---

148. Josephus, *J.W.* 2.500.
149. Ibid., 3.28, 23.68.
150. Tacitus, *Hist.* 2.80.84 (Moore, LCL).
151. Josephus, *J.W.* 3.69.
152. Stark, "Urban Chaos and Crisis," 149. Stark is estimating the population within the walls of the city and does not include villagers associated with the city.
153. Isaac, *The Limits of the Empire*, 276.
154. "In closing, let me note that earthquakes, fire, plagues, and invasions did not appear for the first time at the start of the Christian era. People had been enduring catastrophes for centuries without the aid of Christian theology or Christian social structures. I am by no means suggesting that the misery of the ancient world caused the advent of Christianity. I am arguing that once Christianity did appear, its superior capacity for meeting these chronic problems soon became evident and played a major role in its ultimate triumph" (Stark, "Antioch for Matthew's Gospel," 204).

as residents of the Antioch area, would have experienced these traumatic events and conditions.

Floods of the Nile in 44–47 CE raised the price of grain in Antioch for several years.[155] Figures from Josephus have led scholars to calculate the price of bread at thirteen times its normal price.[156]

There was a major earthquake in the Antioch region on 9 April 37 CE[157] and again between 41 and 54 during the reign of Claudius, who provided some relief to the city.[158] Minor earthquakes and frequent flooding hit Antioch since the city was located on the slopes of Mt. Silipius between the mountain and the Orontes river, into which water drained from the mountain slopes.[159] Earthquakes interrupted the normal processes involved in food production especially if they occurred during the harvest or planting seasons. Likewise, floods often disturbed the crop production cycle. Unmentioned in the record would be grain crop failures, which Peter Garnsey estimates as occurring one in three years.[160] All of these events could exacerbate the already endemic food shortage situation found under Roman rule and provoke more severe food shortages.

Thus far I have argued in this section that the Matthean community probably experienced endemic food shortages as the result of Roman occupation, high taxes, and difficult weather conditions. They would have experienced several traumatic extreme food shortage situations. I argue below that such traumas are reflected in the Gospel narrative.

The Trauma of Food Shortages Affected the Gospel Text

My argument is that traumatic situations, like food shortages, affected how the Matthean community remembered the ministry of Jesus as conveyed in the Gospel. In this section, I give a brief overview of the theory framing this argument. I describe traumatic events that occurred in Antioch during the time that the Gospel text solidified. Finally, I argue that effects of the traumas on the Gospel text are discernible.

---

155. Gapp, "The Universal Famine under Claudius," 262; Garnsey, *Famine and Food Supply*, 21; Lassus, "Antioch on the Orontes," 61.

156. Josephus, *J.W.* 3.320–21; Mealand, *Poverty and Expectation in the Gospels*, 9–10.

157. Downey, *Ancient Antioch*, 89.

158. Downey, *History of Antioch in Syria*, 195–96. Specifying the precise date is problematic, but since Claudius granted relief to the city, the earthquake had to have occurred in the 41–54 period.

159. Lassus, "Antioch on the Orontes," 62.

160. Garnsey, *Famine and Food Supply*, chap. 1.

Trauma and Social Memory Theory

Sociologist Jeffrey Alexander argues that when a group is under extreme stress, it attempts to make sense of its present by turning to its past. When a community feels it has been subjected to a horrendous event such as a famine, cultural trauma occurs. Such an event leaves lasting marks upon group memories and changes group identity in fundamental and irrevocable ways. The meaning of the trauma may be constructed over time by re-remembering past events through the process of storytelling.[161] Making sense of the trauma uses both present circumstances and a construction of a past dependent on the present focus.[162] The venue of sense making is storytelling that constructs a new reality for the community and convinces it that such a trauma did indeed occur, and someone or something caused it. This narrative venue permits the community to assign motives and responsibility, praise and blame, and arouse feelings.[163] Finally, the narrative tells the community how it should face the present and the future in the aftermath of its current trauma.[164] I suggest that as the Matthean community reflected on its past, the community collectively constructed memories[165] of Jesus dealing positively with endemic food shortages to think about what to do in their current situations of food shortages—both endemic and episodic.

John Gillis describes the phenomenon in this manner. "Memories are not things we think about but things we think with."[166] Although social

---

161. Alexander, "Toward a Theory of Cultural Trauma," 1, 12–15, 22.

162. Olufowote, "Rousing and Redirecting," 464–65.

163. Bormann, "Symbolic Convergence," 104.

164. Alexander, "Toward a Theory of Cultural Trauma," 12–15, 22; Gillis, *Commemorations*, 5. Alexander's discussion of cultural trauma places his theory within the more general theory of Social Memory. Gillis argues that a current issue always brings to mind and shapes the memory of the item being commemorated to safeguard the community.

165. Schudson, "Dynamics of Distortion in Collective Memory," 351; Aguliar, "Archaeology of Memory," 65; Hodgkin and Radstone, "Introduction: Contested Pasts," 1–2. The issue of constructing memories is not as flexible as one might think but memories do change. Remembering events is a construction process. In a new situation, the memories may be different than the group remembered previously although neither memory may be *factual* from a historical view point. Further, different groups living through the same history can have vastly different memories that shape their values and practices (for example, the different gospel communities producing different gospels). Hodgkin and Radstone discuss the need for the present to accommodate the past so that the people in the present can move on. In addition, they note that while there may be agreement on the course of events that took place, the *truth* of the events must be negotiated.

166. Gillis, *Commemorations*, 5.

memory is malleable, it is also persistent in that "the structure of available pasts presents only some pasts and poses limits to the degree that they can be changed, while placing other pasts beyond our perceptual reach."[167] A modern day illustration of how the group controls the modification of its social memory comes from Kenneth Bailey, based on his personal experiences observing storytelling in village settings. Any member of the village could retell a traditional story, although normally the village gave deference to an elder. A key restriction was that only members of the community who had grown up with the stories could tell them.[168] The community would exercise control over the story at three levels: (1) no flexibility such as with poems and proverbs, (2) some flexibility as with parables and recollections of people and events important to the identity of the community, and (3) total flexibility such as with jokes and casual news.[169] It is possible that such controls existed in the Matthean community as members told and retold stories of Jesus feeding the multitudes when he had almost no food (Matt 14:13–21; 15:32–38), or teaching them to pray for daily bread (Matt 6:11) while condemning stockpiling of grain that took away their daily bread (Matt 6:19–20). The stories let them make sense of their past and current situation and know what was expected of them when new food shortage situations occurred.

The Gospel Reflects the Trauma of Severe Food Shortages

Alexander argues that while a group may distort historical facts, the moral frameworks remain real and constant.[170] The *re-remembering* sustains the very values which the group holds dear and which group members may feel are being threatened.[171] According to this theory, if the Matthean community experienced traumas related to food shortages (which I have argued above that it probably did),[172] they would remember the stories about Jesus feeding people in situations of endemic food shortages. According to the

---

167. Olick and Robbins, "Individual and Society—Social Memory Studies: From 'Collective Memory' to the Historical Sociology of Mnemonic Practices," 128.

168. Bailey, "Informal Controlled Oral Tradition," 40. Bailey relates an experience of a man in his sixties who had lived in the village for thirty-seven years. The village prohibited the man from reciting its tradition because he was not from the village.

169. Ibid., 42–50.

170. Alexander, "Social Construction of Moral Universes," 262; Schwartz, "Social Context of Commemoration," 377, 395.

171. Olick, Review of *Frames of Remembrance*, 267, 269.

172. The Matthean community probably suffered through food shortages associated with floods, earthquakes, regular crop failures, and the presence of Roman troops.

the gospel reflects the trauma of experienced food shortages 161

theory, the Matthean community *distorted* the memories by adding to those memories what was necessary in the recurring situations of more extreme food shortages. For example, the story of the rich young man exhorts the wealthier members of the community to sell possessions and give to the poor, who could then buy food (Matt 19:16–22). This action mimics a practice of civic leaders during times of extreme food shortages.[173] These constructed memories in the Gospel mimic practices that provided access to food and condemn practices in use in the Roman East that limited people having access to sufficient food.

To recap, the Gospel portrays Jesus in situations that occur during periods of extreme food shortages. Those memories that were captured in the Gospel reflect the distortion in the social memory of the Matthean community. These *rememberings* strongly reinforce values central to membership in the community. The judgment scene in Matthew 25 implies that membership in the Matthean community requires members to provide food and drink to those in need and to visit people in prison. The scenario describes the situation of need that the poor experienced during times of food shortages (Matt 25:34–46). The judgment on those who do not do these things is harsh.[174] This assumption underlies my argument that access to food was an important feature of the realm of the heavens. The value placed on no one going hungry was prominent as a result of the Matthean community suffering through frequent food shortages.

Chapter Summary

In this chapter, I argued two major claims. First, the Matthean community probably experienced food shortages due to widespread crop failures, floods, earthquakes, and Roman military presence. Second, I argued the trauma of such experiences would have affected the way the Matthean community remembered the teaching and actions of Jesus relative to food shortages. These *distorted* memories are found in the Gospel. I began by identifying four framing assumptions. (1) A Matthean community existed (2) probably in Antioch. (3) It solidified its gospel c. 80 CE—c. 100 CE that (4) followed a plethora of events in Antioch that negatively affected the population of Antioch, especially people in the lower socio-economic segments of the population, probably like many in the Matthean community. The theory

---

173. I address this practice in chapter 6 and I give examples from inscriptional data.

174. Barth, "Matthew's Understanding of the Law," 58–60. Barth argues that one sees a much stronger judgment theme in Matthew than in other Synoptic Gospels. This theme is coupled with a stronger exhortation to do the will of God.

of trauma and social memory suggests that a gospel narrative would reflect traumas experienced by the community out of which it arose. In the next two chapters, I will argue that the Gospel does indeed critique specific practices and attitudes that mostly hindered, but occasionally helped, people have access to sufficient food in periods of endemic food shortages, as well as traumatic periods of more extreme food shortages.

6

Not Enough Food and the Dominant Entitlement System

I HAVE ARGUED IN chapter 4 that despite a climate that wreaked havoc with food production, most people in the Mediterranean were able to live at least at subsistence level, although approximately 25 percent of the people lived below subsistence level (PS 6 and PS 7), and another 30 percent lived precariously on the cusp of subsistence (PS 5). I further argued in chapter 4 that survival mechanisms helped to provide sufficient food in periods of stress for those households on the cusp of subsistence-level living. The principal survival mechanisms for peasants were polyculture, storage of food, and social safety networks. The principal survival mechanisms for urban dwellers were social safety networks and being employed in order to have money to buy food from the various food establishments.

As participants in its social system, the Matthean community experienced directly the practices presented later in this chapter that were causing problems with access to food for its member households. I have argued in chapter 5 that the Matthean community experienced both endemic and severe food shortages described in chapter 4. In chapter 5, I also argued that the Gospel, the community's foundational story, reflected the trauma of those food shortages.[1] Among the practices mentioned in the Gospel are the tactics

---

1. I assert that, as its foundational document, the Gospel stories would reflect the socio-economic composition of the Matthean community. This is a complex issue, but for the sake of the arguments presented in this chapter and the following chapter, I assume the community and authorial audience (that is, the auditors that the actual author(s) posited when composing the Gospel) to be composed of a mix of poverty levels similar to that found in typical cities, including Antioch. There would be members of enough wealth to be patrons of the house churches and to have underwritten the

used by aristocrats to wrest control of land from peasants and force them away from polyculture, storage of food causing shortages and providing relief, employing people, and sharing limited resources.

In this chapter, I examine practices that were undermining the principal survival mechanisms. I argue that actions taken by aristocrats undermined survival mechanisms and increased the drain on resources needed for access to sufficient food for the lower socio-economic segments of the population. I argue that peasant practices and attitudes were contributing to the breakdown of general reciprocity that was the underpinning of the social safety network of the lower socio-economic segments of the population. In this chapter and the following one, I attend to the critiques that the Gospel of Matthew makes about such practices that undermined the principal survival mechanisms (that is, polyculture, food storage, and social safety networks).

I begin this chapter with an overview of land ownership. With this focus, I describe the entitlement systems that permitted aristocrats to take actions with impunity that wrested control of crop selection from peasants. I note Matthean verses or phrases that allude to the dominant entitlement system and its exploitative practices. In general, peasants were losing control of their land and falling into debt. I noted in chapter 2 that Biblical scholars rely on two anthropologists—Gerhard Lenski and John Kautsky—to understand conditions in the Roman East. About debt, Kautsky writes,

---

substantial costs of the writing and publication of the Gospel. I assert that the highest applicable level of the Poverty Scale is the PS 4 level. Most of the membership would be in the lower categories, PS 5 through PS 7. If the community were practicing the exhortations of their gospel, the PS 7 people should be better off than the norm since they would be on the receiving end of acts of mercy and justice. As I argued in chapter 5, severe food shortages occurred in the Antioch area. One could expect the Matthean community to have members who were displaced from the rural areas during those periods and who stayed in the city, along with their households. Little textual information is available to prove, or disprove, these assertions that lie behind my analysis and exegesis. The Gospel has stories involving PS 4 landowners with vineyards, perhaps merchants who travel and deal with substantial amounts of money, small landowners, day laborers, and beggars, some of whom are physically disabled. Most of the work on a possible socio-economic composition of an early Christian community has concentrated on Pauline communities. Other research involves examining *voluntary associations* from the period, as good models for early Christian communities. None of my statements above contradicts the findings of these types of studies. For a discussion of authorial audience and its relationship to actual auditors, see especially Carter, *Matthew Storyteller*, 3–5; Anderson, "Matthew: Sermon and Story," 506; Duling, *A Marginal Scribe*, 53–54. For other discussions of the possible make-up of the Matthean community, see the following: Friesen, "Poverty in Pauline Studies," 348–58, especially Figure 345: Economic profile of Paul's assemblies; Ascough, *Paul's Macedonian Associations*; Harland, *Associations, Synagogues, and Congregations*; Love, *Jesus and Marginal Women: The Gospel of Matthew in Social-Scientific Perspective*, 21.

> In a money economy, the peasant may well fall into debt, partly because of the taxes and dues he owes to the aristocracy are easily increased, partly because of the cyclical nature of agriculture that permits the peasant to sell his product only once or twice a year, while he still needs to buy things and therefore requires money all year . . . [I]f, as is common, he cannot repay his bill, he will lose his land.[2]

My argument is that the pressures that debt placed on peasants forced them away from polyculture. I look at the Parable of the Talents (Matt 25:14–30) for clues that provide insights into this situation.

The next section explores grain storage, which was another principal survival mechanism. I explore both the negative and positive sides of grain storage and examine Matthean passages that speak to the two sides. For the negative side, I examine the admonition concerned with storing up treasures (Matt 6:19–21). For the positive side, I look at Jesus presented as a *sitones* (Matt 14:13–21; 15:29–38) who feeds people in times of food shortages.

The next chapter examines the crucial social safety network that was being stressed because food was withheld from local markets and lost to debt. I argue that the Parable of the Householder and Workers (Matt 20:1–15) strongly condemns attitudes that undermined the crucial social safety network, while at the same time portraying positive actions to be emulated.

Ownership of Land and Control of Food Production

Physical survival of members of peasant households was strongly dependent on access to lands and selection of crops.[3] Control of land and decisions concerning production and distribution of food were foundational for ensuring access to food. To understand the dynamics at work, one needs to

---

2. Kautsky, *Aristocratic Empires*, 291; Oakman, "Jesus and Agrarian Palestine"; Oakman, *Jesus and the Peasants*, 4; Goodman, "The First Jewish Revolt: Social Conflict and the Problem of Debt," 427; Pastor, *Land and Economy in Ancient Palestine*. Debt is often cited as an underlying cause of starvation for many people in the first-century Roman East. Yet, the views of Biblical scholars on the pervasiveness and seriousness of debt are not uniform. Space does not permit me to address the topic of debt itself. Instead, I address some of the practices that drove peasants into debt situations. Applying a food-access lens to the debt-forgiveness passages does not enhance the interpretative stance of scholars looking at forgiveness of debt from an economic perspective. Freyne, Horsley, and Davis make the argument that this condition existed since the earlier Israelite periods. Freyne, *Galilee: From Alexander the Great to Hadrian*, 44; Horsley, *Jesus and Empire*, 402; Davis, *Scripture, Culture, and Agriculture*, 123.

3. Oakman, *Jesus and the Economic Questions*, 141–42; Osborne, "Introduction: Roman Poverty in Context," 4.

understand ownership and control of land in the first-century Roman East. Lenski writes, "*property consists basically of rights, not of things*, particularly of rights to things which are in short supply."[4] Land was naturally limited and, hence, in short supply.[5] Both an aristocrat[6]—or a city[7]—and a peasant often had rights to the same piece of land.[8] Each could be entitled to some part of the value of the land with aristocrats having more rights than peasants.[9] Roman law distinguished between land usage (*possessio*) and land ownership (*dominium*). For peasants, their primary interest was *possessio*. They considered land to be an inalienable heritage:[10] theirs to work to support their households. They considered the loss of land to an outsider, even legally, to be theft.[11] On the other hand, aristocrats were interested in *dominium* (ownership) of the land. An important factor in status of aristocrats was the amount of land owned in the legal sense and profit from agriculture

---

4. Lenski, *Power and Privilege*, 216.

5. Applebaum, "Economic Life in Palestine," 692; Josephus, *Ant.* 20.22–23. Applebaum describes hostile actions between groups over cultivable land. In one example, Josephus writes about a conflict that occurred between Jews of Perea and Greeks of Mia, in 44 CE in the territory of Philadelphia.

6. MacMullen, *Roman Social Relations*, 38–39. MacMullen describes large villas near Antioch that would have required intensive agriculture and would imply concentration under control of one household of hundreds or thousands of peasant households.

7. Hamel, *Poverty and Charity in Roman Palestine*, 217; Oakman, *Jesus and the Economic Questions*, 46; Osborne, "Introduction: Roman Poverty in Context," 5; Corbier, "City, Territory, and Taxation," 219, 222; Crosby, *House of Disciples: Church, Economics, and Justice in Matthew*, 37. A city would have owned the land around it. The land provided income to the city through leasing to large landowners, but the city did not usually lease all of its land. When it surveyed land for tax purposes, a city would exclude some land (called *saltus* in Latin, which I refer to as *Uncultivated Land* in the model of chapter 3), which became available for communal use by residents. A typical use of the land was common pasturing of herds. Peasants, and city residents, might use it for collection of nuts and wild berries. Hence, the city owned the land but residents had rights to use the common land.

8. Kautsky, *Aristocratic Empires*, 99, writes that, later than the first century, Roman law moved toward the modern concept of "private property as an absolute right to use and abuse."

9. Polanyi, "Aristotle Discovers the Economy," 75; Kautsky, *Aristocratic Empires*, 100; Oakman, *Jesus and the Economic Questions*, 51–52; Hamel, *Poverty and Charity in Roman Palestine*, 217.

10. Lenski, *Power and Privilege*, 214–16; Sean Freyne, *Galilee: From Alexander the Great to Hadrian*, 176; Oakman, *Jesus and the Economic Questions*, 37–38; Duling, *A Marginal Scribe*, 100.

11. Oakman, *Jesus and the Economic Questions*, 38, 47, 80; Josephus, *Ant.* 14.313–18. Josephus relates the return of confiscated land to its original owners.

was not a primary goal.¹² This division of rights to the land often worked if an aristocrat left the peasants to decide what to plant and restitution to the *owner* aristocrat for usage was negligible.

I argue that two factors contributed to the balance between peasant and aristocrat use of the land breaking down, which resulted in decreased access to food among peasants. First, aristocrats wanted land owned by free peasants and took any means possible to obtain the coveted land.¹³ Since they controlled the legal part of the dominant entitlement system, very few checks on aristocratic power were in place to benefit peasants. Wresting ownership of the land created extra burdens on the peasants who still occupied the land they had previously owned and possessed. Second, aristocrats became interested in the lucrative grain markets and began to interfere with decisions of what crops should be planted. This move especially lessened access to food and crops for peasant needs.¹⁴

Dominant Entitlement System and the Push Away from Polyculture

In his classic book, *Power and Privilege*, Gerhard Lenski addresses the principles that govern distribution of goods in a society: who gets what, when, and how. He emphasizes that a discussion of distribution needs to begin with processes and bring structures into the discussion later.¹⁵ A primary

---

12. Garnsey and Saller, *The Roman Empire*, 74. Garnsey and Saller discuss that the value system underlying land ownership included profit-seeking when selling, but not profit maximization when farming.

13. Lendon, *Empire of Honour*, 30. Lendon writes that personal influence enabled the cheap purchase of a farm. It was so pervasive that "what a great man wanted, he frequently turned to his influence to gain."

14. In describing the model in chapter 3, I have discussed the various household needs and functions supported by crops.

15. Lenski, *Power and Privilege*, chap. 1, 7–8. Lenski is moving toward a synthesis of the earlier two approaches to the issue of distribution and social stratification. The two approaches arise primarily depending on whether one views the inequality as being just (conservative position) or unjust (radical position). His argument continues in the guise of functionalists versus conflict theorists. Instead of battling over categories, he suggests that scholars should transform categories into variables and take a dialectical approach. Coming back to my argument, Lenski writes, "In its earliest phases, Christianity represented an interesting mixture of both radical and conservative elements, undoubtedly a reflection of the fact that social inequality *per se* was not of major concern to Jesus and his early followers. Nevertheless, their teachings and actions are by no means wholly irrelevant. The goals which Jesus set before men, and his criticism of the popular goals of his day, reflect a clear rejection of the latter. The communism of the early church in Jerusalem clearly constituted an implicit criticism of the inequalities

function of all societies is to feed the population. The processes involved vary with the environmental issues related to food production of the society. Social structure determines who has the power and authority to make decisions related to crop production and its distribution.

I argue in this section that, in the first-century Roman East, peasants lived under two competing entitlement systems:[16] the dominant aristocratic system and their local[17] system. In chapter 4, I have argued that physical survival of members of peasant households was strongly dependent on access to lands and selection of crops.[18] I argue in this section that the dominant entitlement system enabled aristocrats to wrest control of land and its crop production from peasants with little impunity. After a brief overview of entitlement systems in the first-century Roman East, I turn to practices condoned by the dominant entitlement system that were wreaking havoc with peasants having access to sufficient food.

In an agriculturally based society, access to food is at the heart of the entitlement systems. Amartya Sen writes

> [an entitlement system] concentrates on the ability of people to command food through the legal means available in the society, including the use of production possibilities, trade opportunities,

---

present in society . . . But in the writings of St. Paul, who was destined to have such a profound influence on later Christian thought, a much more conservative spirit is evident" (ibid., 7). Lenski continues, "As the Church gained in power and influence, the more radical tendencies in Christianity gradually lost ground, at least among church leaders. The conservative viewpoint came in time to be regarded as virtually a matter of doctrine" (ibid., 8).

16. Kautsky, *Aristocratic Empires*, 269, 271–75; Scott, *Arts of Resistance*, xi; Redfield, *Peasant Society and Culture*, 1956, 68–84. Kautsky does not discuss a peasant entitlement system, but he does write that it needs to be studied. He also says the reason peasants have so little power is because the Roman Empire consisted of multiple societies, about which I assert that each one had its own entitlement system. Scott does not refer to competing entitlement systems, but he does speak to different societal controlling systems. Each system has its own structure for distribution of goods and services and for appropriating labor. The system of aristocrats dominates, but that "subordinates in such large-scale structures of domination nevertheless have a fairly extensive social existence outside the immediate control of the dominant. It is in such sequestered settings where, in principle, a shared critique of domination may develop" (*Arts of Resistance*, xi). My argument is that the Gospel would be part of such a critique by the Matthean community.

17. I use the term *local entitlement system* to refer to the system operating at the village level. From village to village, the entitlement systems might display variations in the details of specific practices, but all local entitlement systems should share the characteristics of peasant social systems (for example, general reciprocity).

18. Oakman, *Jesus and the Economic Questions*, 141–42; Osborne, "Introduction: Roman Poverty in Context," 4.

not enough food and the dominant entitlement system 169

> entitlements vis-à-vis the state, and other methods of acquiring food. A person starves either because he does not have the ability to command enough food, or because he does not use this ability to avoid starvation. The entitlement approach concentrates on the former, ignoring the latter possibility. Furthermore, it concentrates on those means of commanding food that are legitimized by the legal system in operation in that society.[19]

A person's ability to have access to enough food to sustain one's life over time depended on a number of interrelated power and status issues that rippled throughout the entire fabric of the society. Biological needs determined neither food crop selection nor the distribution of food. The determination came more through a socially conditioned context and through entitlements claimed by the aristocracy.[20] A peasant household on the fringes of the entitlement system was at the mercy of aristocrats more ensconced in the dominant political and economic systems.

Both systems of entitlements—dominant and local—were tied strongly to kinship, politics, economics, and status. These factors are not separate. Kinship was the primary factor. Politics was embedded in kinship.[21] Economics was embedded in kinship and politics.[22] Status depended on one's family and how much land one owned. The two entitlement systems varied in the processes through which status, politics, and economics operated, but the two entitlement systems shared kinship ties as the fundamental characteristic.

David Schneider describes the pervasiveness of kinship, as it functioned in the first-century Roman East.

> Explicit in the idea of the kin-based society is the conception of the kinship unit or group as multi-functional, or functionally minimally differentiated. That is, the kin group or unit is at the same time the economic, political, religious unit, and may assume other functions as well . . . [E]conomics is not something like an institution, a group acting in a particular way, but is rather something which kinship and family groups do . . . It

---

19. Sen, *Poverty and Famines*, 45.

20. Gapp, "The Universal Famine under Claudius," 261; Garnsey, *Famine and Food Supply*, 45.

21. Lendon, *Empire of Honour*. Lendon provides an excellent discussion of the Roman Empire governed based on kinship structures.

22. McGowan, *Ascetic Eucharists: Food and Drink in Early Christian Ritual Meals*, 1; Garnsey and Saller, *The Roman Empire*, 43–63; Badian, *Publicans and Sinners: Private Enterprise in the Service of the Roman Republic, with a Critical Bibliography*, 98; Moxnes, *The Economy of the Kingdom*, 27.

is kinship that is the organizing principle. It is kinship that is valued as fundamental and unbreachable. It is kinship that is held to be the basic referent and touchstone for everything else. It is the bonds of kinship which either alone or above all else hold the society together.[23]

In the first century, the idea of kinship extended beyond *blood* and *marriage kin* to include others who behaved and were treated as if they were family. The Latin term *domus* referred to a larger kinship group than a nuclear family. The term included husband, wife, children, servants, slaves, and others living in the house.[24] Political alliances and friendships were thought of in kinship terms.[25] For example, to leave a friend out of a will was an insult.[26] When asked who his family was, Jesus responded that it was composed of those who did the will of the father (Matt 12:46–50). His answer is an apt description of extended kinship and patriarchal household of the first-century Roman East.

While the two entitlement systems shared a strong kinship basis that worked in a similar manner within the social circle, the legal aspect of the dominant system negatively affected people not in the controlling social circle. An oft-used word to describe this situation is *exploitation*.[27] The legal system did indeed permit aristocrats to operate with little liability for their actions that harmed people in the lower socio-economic segments of the population.[28] Yet, John Kautsky argues that no matter how cruel and greedy

23. Schneider, *A Critique of the Study of Kinship*, 47–49.

24. Garnsey and Saller, *The Roman Empire*, 128.

25. Josephus, *Ant.* 17.321–23. Caesar made presents to Herod's daughters and found husbands for them.

26. Garnsey and Saller, *The Roman Empire*, 155; Fronto to Antoninus Pius Augustus (pp 254–59); Pliny, *Letters* 2.20 (to Calvisius Rufus); Seneca, *Ben.* 4.20.23; Josephus, *Ant.* 17.190. Josephus reports that Herod bequeathed to Caesar ten million *drachma* in addition to silver and gold vessels and costly garments to Julia, Caesar's wife.

27. Lenski, *Power and Privilege*, 210–20; Kautsky, *Aristocratic Empires*, 6, 112; Hanson, "The Galilean Fishing Economy," 100; Firth, *Primitive Polynesian Economy*, 171. The term *exploitation* usually carries with it a moral connotation. The term often occurs in an inflammatory sense of "to take advantage of" instead of its other meanings such as "to make use of," "utilize," or "make the most of." All of these aspects are present in the relationship between those in power and all others, particularly the relationship of the landowner to the peasant or tenant. Firth strongly suggests replacing the term with a more neutral expression.

28. Kautsky, *Aristocratic Empires*, 103; Foxhall, "The Dependent Tenant: Land Leasing and Labour in Italy and Greece," 112, discusses the legal disadvantages of being a tenant, who probably agreed to lease terms because of few alternatives for survival. Yet, he observes, "a tenant was likely to be kept from starvation in the worst years by the intervention of the landlord."

one might think a landowner to be, exploitation was limited.[29] Pliny suggests that workers should be given benefits to keep them happy.[30] Columella writes,

> When twilight has come on, he [overseer] should leave no one behind but should walk in rear of them, like a good shepherd, who suffers no member of his flock to be left in the field. Then, when he has come indoors, let him act like that careful herdsman and not immediately hide himself in his house but exercise the utmost care for every one of them; and if, as generally happens, any one of them has received some hurts in the course of his work, and is wounded, let him apply fomentations.[31]

Landowners, in practice, could not deprive peasants and tenants of all their products and surpluses because landowners needed peasant and tenant labor and their goods to survive. Moreover, it took too much effort to control the production and distribution processes. Peasants and tenants devised ways to hold on to some of their surplus.[32] The legality of actions of peasants and tenants would seem to depend on which entitlement system formed the basis of the opinion (Matt 21:33–41).[33] A basic conflict between the two entitlement systems involved the question "What is a fair division of the product?"[34]

The overarching structure and ideology of the dominant entitlement system shifted dynamics away from most people getting what they needed to some people in power getting what they wanted.[35] Sen makes a point about the twenty-first century that is germane to the Roman Empire. "Starvation is the characteristic of some people not having enough to eat. It is

---

29. "That limit is reached when the goose that lays the golden egg is killed" (Kautsky, *Aristocratic Empires*, 105).

30. Pliny, *Letters* 3.19.16 (to Calvisius Rufus).

31. Columella, *On Agriculture* 11.11.18.

32. Lenski, *Power and Privilege*, 100; Columella, *On Agriculture* 1.1.20, 11.21.16.

33. "Land could also be lost through indebtedness, usucaption, and occupation by a more powerful party. Seen in this light, the parable's [Matt. 21:33–41] underscoring of the legitimacy of inheritance is not simply an innocent reflection of an old Israelite practice of land tenure but an *assertion* of the importance of inheritance in a world where it could no longer be taken for granted" (Kloppenborg, *The Tenants in the Vineyard*, 39).

34. Scott, *Arts of Resistance*, 100; Kautsky, *Aristocratic Empires*, 105–15. While Kautsky acknowledges that such questions would have arisen, he concludes that both sides accepted the rights and duties connected with the exploitative relationship supported by an established custom. Against Kautsky's position, Scott argues that while peasants were cognizant of their place in the rather rigid social hierarchy, they developed strategies to evade control through a variety of means.

35. Horden and Purcell, *The Corrupting Sea*, 268.

not the characteristic of there being not enough food to eat. While the latter can be the cause of the former, it is but one of many possible causes . . . [S]tarvation statements translate readily into statements of ownership of food by persons."[36] The key concept for economics in the first-century Roman East is that the use of the resources extracted and redistributed through the dominant entitlement system was not for the good of society *per se*, but to further political agenda, which normally benefitted a select few.[37] Crops, particularly grain, became the means for aristocrats to get what they wanted at the expense of enough food to eat for the poor. By acquiring more land and ownership of more food held in storage, the large landowning aristocrats affected negatively the lives of peasants they would never see.

The local entitlement system for peasants included legal systems and politics. Unlike the dominant system, the local entitlement system only had legal jurisdiction over the local community (for example, village organization led by a village elder or group of elders).[38] Although a village scribe was responsible for the ruler's interests.[39] The range of control highlights a principal difference between the two systems. The aristocratic entitlement system affected peasants, but rarely was the converse true.[40] Yet, even the poorest peasant could have a hearing, although not everyone was equal.[41]

In the city, almost all residents were also outside the dominant entitlement system. Qualification for city council included the expectation that the councilors had respectable birth, wealth, and moral worth.[42] Wealth was

---

36. Sen, *Poverty and Famines*, 1; Dando, *Geography of Famine*, 42. Dando makes a similar point when discussing hunger as being a social disease, not a medical problem.

37. Baloglou, "Hellenistic Economic Thought," 112–17, discusses the term *political economy* as found for the first time in Book II, 1345b, 12–14, of Pseudo-Aristotelian *Oeconomica* where it defines *political economy* as the revenue of the polis. Carney, *The Economies of Antiquity*, 90–91, adds the point that the aristocracy controlled the political economy, but not "the invisible hand of the market." Oakman, "The Ancient Economy in the Bible," 34, comments that the political economy "involves the politically or religiously induced extraction of a percentage of local production, the store housing of that product, and its eventual redistribution for some political end or another." Malina, *Christian Origins and Cultural Anthropology: Practical Models for Biblical Interpretation*, 85, describes the first-century society as having a political economy as well as a domestic economy.

38. Kautsky, *Aristocratic Empires*, 32; Oakman, *Jesus and the Economic Questions*, 45.

39. Oakman, *Jesus and the Economic Questions*, 45; Duling, *A Marginal Scribe*, 264–65.

40. Moxnes, *The Economy of the Kingdom*, 79.

41. Kautsky, *Aristocratic Empires*, 32.

42. Veyne and Murray, *Bread and Circuses*, 52–53; Giardina, "The Merchant," 245–48. Merchants could be wealthy but usually they were not socially acceptable. To

occasionally enough to qualify a person, such as the son of a freedman, for the council.[43] Very few city residents qualified. Instead, proliferation of associations, which were structured like the local government,[44] became local entitlement systems for many craftsmen and artisans.[45] Some associations were ethnic- or neighborhood-based and offered their members citizenship in the association when citizenship in the city was not accessible to them.[46] Sometimes, the association exerted political power as a group.[47] Occasionally, an association would contribute funds to help a member who had fallen on hard times.[48] The various forms of associations often had patrons who set up funds to help their members in times of crisis, although death benefits for the family were more prevalent than food benefits other than banquets.[49] Although they often had meals, being a social safety network in the sense of sharing one's resources is only sometimes attested.[50] A wealthy woman, Antlante, made food provisions for the inhabitants of Termessos in Pamphylia in the time of a famine. Yet, ensuring that its members had work, and hence could buy food, was the more normal venue. On the other hand, strong friendship within the association might mean that at the intra-association level, a friend helped a friend, or became a patron.[51] Rodney Stark argues that one of the reasons

---

overcome their lack of regard, they bought land.

43. Garnsey and Saller, *The Roman Empire*, 114–15; Pleket, "Urban Elites and Business in the Greek Part of the Roman Empire," 141. Pleket writes that wealth only qualified one when other more acceptable candidates were lacking. He found only one instance where a person involved in international trade, despite such trade being a lucrative business, was permitted to be on a council.

44. Kloppenborg, "Collegia and *Thiasoi*: Issues in Function, Taxonomy and Membership," 26; Clarke, *Serve the Community of the Church: Christians as Leaders and Ministers*, 6; Harland, *Associations, Synagogues, and Congregations*, 8, 35. Ascough, *Paul's Macedonian Associations*, 18. Ascough notes that inscriptions for associations occurred in villages as well as cities.

45. Nijf, *The Civic World of Professional Associations in the Roman East*, 40; Ascough, *Paul's Macedonian Associations*, 22.

46. Harland, *Associations, Synagogues, and Congregations*, 102; Kloppenborg, "Collegia and *Thiasoi*: Issues in Function, Taxonomy and Membership," 18.

47. Harland, *Associations, Synagogues, and Congregations*, 107–9; Ramsay MacMullen, "A Note on Roman Strikes," 269.

48. Ascough, *Paul's Macedonian Associations*, 25–26.

49. Ibid., 25.

50. Harland, *Associations, Synagogues, and Congregations*, 99; Nijf, *The Civic World of Professional Associations in the Roman East*, 256. Harland catalogues TAM 3.4,62, which is described in the text. Nijf catalogues inscriptions connecting associations with grain distributions. IK 17.1, 3080 (Ionia, Ephesus) and TAM 3.1, 4 and 3.1, 62 (Pisidia, Termessos).

51. Ascough, *Paul's Macedonian Associations*, 30.

Christianity spread was that Christian communities provided a social safety network with the sharing of resources.[52]

Scholars have documented the manner in which aristocrats used the dominant entitlement system to wrest control of land from peasants.[53] Often aristocrats who wanted land were members of the ruling council. They could use tax levies (Matt 17:25) to force the less powerful[54] into debt situations (Matt 5:25; 18:23–34) that caused peasants to lose control of their land.[55] Payment of taxes was, of course, not new in the first century,[56] but under the Romans, collection became more efficient.[57] Keith Hopkins writes that

---

52. "To cities filled with the homeless and impoverished, Christianity offered charity as well as hope. To cities filled with newcomers and strangers, Christianity offered an immediate basis for attachments. To cities filled with orphans and widows, Christianity provided a new and expanded sense of family" (Stark, "Urban Chaos and Crisis," 161).

53. Garnsey and Saller, *The Roman Empire*, 64; Duncan-Jones, *Structure and Scale in the Roman Economy*, 142; Osborne, "Pride and Prejudice, Sense and Subsistence," 132; Stegemann and Stegemann, *The Jesus Movement*, 42–43, 112; Oakman, "The Ancient Economy in the Bible," 35.

54. Kautsky, *Aristocratic Empires*, 325; Derrenbacker, *Ancient Compositional Practices and the Synoptic Problem*, 23. Derrenbacker cites P Oxy. 71 (ca. 303 CE) from the catalog in *The Oxyrhynchus Papyri*, ed. Renfell and Hunt, 1:134. Aurelius Demetrius, who was defrauded because he was "illiterate," addressed the petition to prefect Clodius Culcianus. It states, "When therefore I asked him for the money [owed to me] while Heron was *strategus*, he attempted, owing to my being illiterate (ἀγράμματον), to commit a fraud to my detriment."

55. Davis, *Scripture, Culture, and Agriculture*, 93, 123. This situation and its condemnation were not new in the first century. Davis argues that Lev 25 traces the stages of economic loss that an Israelite small landowner might experience. She writes, "Farmers felt the burden and constraints imposed by the government in several ways. Taxation-in-kind of agricultural products (e.g., 'exactions of wheat,' Amos 5:11; 'the king's mowings,' Amos 7:1) was compounded by conscription for labor gangs and military service, and also by appropriation of valuable metals for military purposes; iron that might have been used for plowshares was turned into swords' (see Isa. 2:4; Mic. 4:3; Joel 4:10). Altogether, the demands of the centralized government may well have consumed half or more of a family's labor and production capacity. In a bad agricultural year (about three years out of ten in that semiarid land), many families would have been unable to feed themselves and also meet the demands of the state. So the crown literally gained ground for centralized agriculture through acquisition of the ancestral lands of small farmers who went into debt and put up their land as collateral. Land thus extracted from freeholders was reassigned to the new aristocracy in the process known as *latifundialization* ('the making of wide estates'). In the old rural economy, those who were relatively well-off would have resided in the villages. As members of the same community with the indigent, they would have been immediately confronted with the claim of the needy, who were probably their kin" (ibid., 123).

56. Polanyi and Pearson, *The Livelihood of Man*, 64–65; Oakman, *Jesus and the Economic Questions*, 40; Josephus, *Ant.* 12.180–85.

57. White, "Finances," 234; Hopkins, "Taxes and Trade in the Roman Empire (200 B.C.—A.D. 400)," 121; Garnsey and Saller, *The Roman Empire*, 103; Horsley, "Little

the use of local aristocracy,[58] who were members of the council, to collect taxes led to maldistribution of the tax burden.[59] He argues that the Romans established the amount of the tax, but the local government determined how to apportion the tax. For example, Caelius requests that Cicero remove taxes paid to a city on lands of Caelius' friend, M. Feridius.[60] Hopkins suggests that taxes on aristocratic land may have been proportionately less than on peasant land. Such incongruity could arise simply because taxes were on the use of land and not ownership of land. Hence, the tenant paid a land use tax and not the property owner.[61] Scholars do not know the exact level of taxes (for example, proposed levels vary from twelve to fifty per cent[62]), but even small increases would have been devastating for households on the cusp of subsistence.

Aristocrats also used illegal tactics, and their control of the legal system protected them. Beatings,[63] maulings, and murders were a frequent complaint. Peasants could make complaints to the council but rulings were usually in favor of aristocrats.[64] Sometimes the authorities participated in violence to maintain an exploitative relationship.[65] Less violent means

---

Tradition and Hidden Transcripts," 254–55. The more strident collection of taxes in Galilee began after Herod. An increase in taxes may have occurred in both Antioch and Galilee, but no definitive data proves the point. Yet as I have noted in chapter 4, even small increases in taxes could move thirty per cent more people from PS 6 (at subsistence) to PS 7 (below subsistence). White writes that Vespasian raised taxes in order to stabilize the economic system, including valuation of coins in circulation.

58. Overman, "Matthew's Parables and Roman Politics: The Imperial Setting of Matthew's Narrative with Special Reference to His Parables," 426.

59. Kautsky, *Aristocratic Empires*, 325; Braund, "Function and Dysfunction: Personal Patronage in Roman Imperialism," 141.

60. Cicero, *ad Familiares* 8.9.4.

61. Oakman, *Jesus and the Economic Questions*, 46; Corbier, "City, Territory, and Taxation," 226–27. Corbier writes that, in the year of the census, large landowners were more able to leave land fallow and avoid taxes than were smaller landowners.

62. Stegemann and Stegemann, *The Jesus Movement*, 48, 119–23.

63. Braund, *Augustus to Nero: A Sourcebook on Roman History, 31 BC–AD 68*, 289. Braund catalogs [762] *Small 440*, which concerns a dispute over the lease of a factory that was in need of much repair and the petitioner being behind in rent because of expending monies for repairs. His petition is "that you require those in charge not to molest me over the rent."

64. Friesen, "Injustice or God's Will," 241; Fiensy, *The Social History of Palestine in the Herodian Period*, 79; MacMullen, *Roman Social Relations*, 10–12. MacMullen notes some seventy pleas for redress, mostly in the first and second centuries. The data he uses is from Egypt, but I suggest that similar practices probably existed in places where records did not survive, such as most of the Roman East.

65. "On an imperial estate in north Africa (*saltus Burunitanus*), the emperor's procurator provided force to maintain the exploitation of the subtenants at the hands of

involved letting one's cattle ransack a neighbor's field that was ready for harvest or planting weeds in a field[66] (Matt 13:24; 13:31). A large-estate owner could move boundary stones on adjoining property[67] owned by a widow or other helpless individual.[68] Wealthy people could bribe people to bear false witness in court.[69] A peasant was helpless in court battles (Matt 5:25–26).[70]

Sometimes, a tactic affected large numbers of peasants simultaneously such as when a ruler gave land to friends, or towns, which had supported him[71] (perhaps the context of Matt 21:33–41). An example occurred during

---

the wealthy lessees. When the humble subtenants protested that more than the agreed rent and days of labour were being demanded of them, the procurator sent in soldiers, 'ordering some of us to be seized and tortured, others fettered, and some, including even Roman citizens, beaten with rods and cudgels'" (*CIL* VIII. 10570 + 14464, cited in Garnsey and Saller, *The Roman Empire*, 112).

66. MacMullen, *Roman Social Relations*, 150n134. *P. Mich.* V 228 and 230; *P. Mich.* VI 421; P. Cairo Goodspeed 15; *P. Oslo* 22; *P. Oxy.* 903 and 2234; *P. Tebt.* 331; SB 7205; BGU 759; *P. Hamb.* 10; P. Ryl. 136, 141, 144f., 151; *P. Fay.* 108; and BCH 7 (1883) 63 f. (9 BCE in Cnidus); Braund, *Augustus to Nero: A Sourcebook on Roman History, 31 BC-AD 68*, 288, [759] catalogs *PRyl* 138 from 34 CE, which is a petition to the chief of police concerning crop damage. It reads in part: "Orsenouphis, son of Heracleus, and Heracles, son of Ptollis, let their flocks into the newly-planted oliveyards of the said estate in the farmstead of Dromeus and they grazed down 200 olive plants, among those which previously belonged to Falcidius . . . I therefore request that the accused be brought before you so that I may get justice. Farewell."

67. Deuteronomy 19:14 and 27:17 specifically prohibit such practice. Isaiah 8:8 and Micah 2:2 speak against the seizing of another's land. Many of the inscriptions catalogued by DiSegni were boundary markers. Di Segni, "Dated Greek Inscriptions from Palestine."

68. Fiensy, *The Social History of Palestine in the Herodian Period*, 79.

69. While not specifically related to food or land issues, Matt 26:14–16; 27:3–8; 28:12–15 depict those in power buying testimonies. "Do not contend with the powerful, or you may fall into their hands. Do not quarrel with the rich, in case their riches outweigh yours; for gold has ruined many, and has perverted the minds of kings" (Sir 8:1–2).

70. Hanson and Oakman, *Palestine in the Time of Jesus*, 119, write that the Matthean passage "reflects a situation in Roman Palestine where it is at least perceived that informal justice is better than official justice. It is better to have a patron in the creditor ('make friends') than to face the courts controlled by the landlord class."

71. Applebaum, "Economic Life in Palestine," 643; D'Arms, *Commerce and Social Standing in Ancient Rome*, 145; Duncan-Jones, *Structure and Scale in the Roman Economy*, 122; Strickert, "The Coins of Philip," 182; Stegemann and Stegemann, *The Jesus Movement*, 111; White, "Finances," 227; Oakman, *Jesus and the Economic Questions*, 46, 67. In the Shechem area, Herod gave to one of his ministers approximately 2,500 acres on which 175—200 households lived. Applebaum and Strickert have similar discussions. White argues that expropriation of land and then its transfer to local aristocrats who would pay taxes on it was a strategy Rome adopted to support its colonial administration. "Let each subjugated state pay the cost of its subjugation." Oakman contends that imperial ownership of land in Judea (that is, *ager publicus populi Romani*) did not occur until after 70 CE. After that time, there would be more foreign ownership and

the reign of Claudius when such an action transformed a population of free farmers into tenant farmers, *coloni*, owned by the town Grophina in Palestine.[72] In another example, Josephus writes that Herod gave surrounding land to Tiberius.[73] Such moves negatively affected access to food because peasants could be liable for more taxes.[74] When villages and land of free peasants were given to a town, the town could legally collect taxes from the villages it now owned,[75] which prompted the elders of a village[76] to collect resources from the households who farmed and lived in the village.[77] Demands for taxes and tributes in coin[78] (Matt 17:24–25; 22:19–20; 21:12) caused a ripple effect that, in the end, harmed availability of food for peasants. The cities required coins from aristocrats leasing the city land (that is, doing tax farming[79]), from merchants and traders[80] (that is, marketing rights, anchorage for ships[81]), for tolls (Matt 9:9), and from villages that the city owned.[82] The villages taxed their resident producers such as cultivators, herders, and households involved in the fishing industry.[83] Aristocrats

---

more exploitation of peasants working the land.

72. Di Segni, "Dated Greek Inscriptions from Palestine," 186–87; MacMullen, *Roman Social Relations*, 21; Mealand, *Poverty and Expectation in the Gospels*, 5; Josephus, *Life* 46–47. DiSegni explicates a boundary marker and writes that the town's name on the marker was probably a distortion of Agrippina. Jewish sources mention this town. MacMullen writes that it was not unusual for substantial parts of village lands to be temporarily given to citizens in cities. The locals would meet their new owner's representatives with hostile actions. Josephus reports that Philip was concerned about fleeing to the villages he owned.

73. Josephus, *Ant.* 18.36–38; Stegemann and Stegemann, *The Jesus Movement*, 110.

74. Josephus, *Ant.* 12.169, 175.

75. Oakman, *Jesus and the Economic Questions*, 78; Corbier, "City, Territory, and Taxation," 222; Herzog, "Why Peasants Responded to Jesus," 50; Josephus, *Ant.* 19.25–26. Herzog notes that Romans retaliated with violence to any resistance to payment of taxes. Josephus relates such an instance.

76. Oakman, *Jesus and the Economic Questions*, 46. Native chiefs governed villages.

77. Edwards, "Socio-Economic and Cultural Ethos of the Lower Galilee," 67.

78. Evans, *Coins and Economy in Palestine*, 53–54; Hopkins, "Taxes and Trade in the Roman Empire (200 B.C.—A.D. 400)," 101. Hopkins argues that the imposition of taxes paid in coin contributed to increases in international trade.

79. Corbier, "City, Territory, and Taxation," 219, 232.

80. Kautsky, *Aristocratic Empires*, 325.

81. Polanyi, "The Economy as Instituted Process," 262; Corbier, "City, Territory, and Taxation," 224.

82. Hanson and Oakman, *Palestine in the Time of Jesus*, 117.

83. Hopkins, "Taxes and Trade in the Roman Empire (200 B.C.—A.D. 400)," 101; Oakman, *Jesus and the Economic Questions*, 76; Garnsey and Saller, *The Roman Empire*, 56; Hanson, "The Galilean Fishing Economy," 102; Horsley, *New Documents Illustrating*

involved in the tax farming[84] required their tenants to pay their leases in coin.[85] To obtain the necessary coins, peasants obviously had to raise more crops that were marketable and less crops for their food consumption.[86] They then had to sell enough crops at prices set by the city.[87] The effect was peasants moving more of their acreage to cash crops—grain.

To recap, peasants had reduced access to food because the dominant entitlement system exacted taxes and rents from them. Peasants lost crops that they could have used for seed[88] for the following year or food for their households to pay tributes, taxes, and rents to the other *owner* of the land.[89]

Early Christianity, 5, 105; Hanson and Oakman, *Palestine in the Time of Jesus*, 117. Hanson and Oakman write that the villages were primarily focused on collection of taxes-in-kind.

84. Corbier, "City, Territory, and Taxation," 232.

85. Hopkins, "Taxes and Trade in the Roman Empire (200 B.C.—A.D. 400)," 103, 101; Polanyi and Pearson, *The Livelihood of Man*, 64; Carter, "Resisting and Imitating the Empire: Imperial Paradigms in Two Matthean Parables," 265. A better term would be *cash equivalents* since peasants often paid obligations with part of their crop yields. On the other hand, sometimes they were required to pay in coins, including the tax that replaced the Temple tithe. Vespasian imposed this tax post-70 and, in probably an insulting fashion, it went to help maintain the temple of the victorious Jupiter Capitolinus in Rome.

86. Hopkins, "Taxes and Trade in the Roman Empire (200 B.C.—A.D. 400)," 101.

87. Carney, *The Economies of Antiquity*, 102–3; Carney, *Shape of the Past*, 199; Hopkins, "Taxes and Trade in the Roman Empire (200 B.C.—A.D. 400)," 104.

88. Heichelheim, "Roman Syria," 227; Kloppenborg, "Agrarian Discourse and the Sayings of Jesus: 'Measure for Measure' in Gospel Traditions," 111, 117. Heichelheim states that the usual rate of interest in Syria in Palestine for seed loans was about fifty percent. Kloppenborg writes, "From well before the common era, loans of seed grain regularly acknowledged the amount of grain loaned and contained an understanding that the borrower would repay the loan at a specified time, normally following the next harvest, using the same grain vessel that had been used to dispense the loan" ("Agrarian Discourse and the Sayings of Jesus: 'Measure for Measure' in Gospel Traditions," 111). At ibid., 111n18, he references the following sources:

"BGU III 1005.6 (III BCE); *P.Adl.* G15.14 (100 BCE); *P.Amh.* II 47.9–10 (113 BCE): με(τρω) ψ και παρείληφεν; *P.Grenf.* I 10.14 (174 BCE); *P.Grenf.* I 18.18 (131 BCE); *P.Grenf.* I 23.13.14 (118 BCE); *P.Grenf.* I 28 (108 BCE); *P.Lond.* II 218.8 (111 BCE); *P.Lond.* II 225.10–11 (118 BCE.) The same formula is attested in Demotic agreements: "And I will you your wheat as artabae of wheat . . . by your measure whereby you have measured it to me" (Field Papyrus II.9, 12–13; see N. J. Reich, "The Field Museum Papyrus [A Promissory Note of the Year of 109/8 BCE]:" *Mizraim* 2 [1936]: 35–51 + 1 plate); *P.Adl.* D 3.5 (116/15 BCE): "by the measure with which you measured it to me"; *P.Adl.* D5.11–12 (108–7 BCE): "by the measure with which you measured it to me." Compare also *P.Adl.* D6.10 (107 BCE); *P.Adl.* D11.10 (100–199 BCE)."

89. Freyne, *Galilee: From Alexander the Great to Hadrian*, 195; Kautsky, *Aristocratic Empires*, 100; Davis, *Scripture, Culture, and Agriculture*, 123. I have argued in chapter 4 that even a small increase in taxes or rents would move a sizeable portion of the peasant

The result was peasant landowners becoming tenants on their own land[90] or they were displaced from their land.[91] The point is that peasants had no voice in decisions that moved their households closer to not having access to sufficient food.[92]

The second situation that exacerbated the loss of control of the land worked by small landowners was the increasing presence of aristocracy in international trade.[93] Early scholarship cited the stigma associated with trade for aristocrats, but more recent scholarship has shown that trade and manufacturing involved people at all social levels.[94] Given the kinship nature of first-century society, the business organization functioned as an extended family.[95] Aristocrats often used their freedmen as agents.[96] An emerging

---

population to below-subsistence living (PS 7).

90. Garnsey and Saller, *The Roman Empire*, 71. Garnsey and Saller lament the inadequacy of sources concerning tenancy in the first century and the inability to perform a comparative historical development of tenancy.

91. Applebaum, "Economic Life in Palestine," 691; Josephus, *Ant.* 14.158–60. Josephus describes bandits slain in Syria. Applebaum argues that one can deduce Herod's policy of confiscation of peasant lands from the increase in bandits, particularly between 40 and 66 CE. I assert that not all bandits were landless peasants. Some might have been landed peasants who could not grow sufficient food crops.

92. Although speaking of a different aspect of entitlement relationships, Scott's observations fit this scenario: "As a formal matter, subordinate groups in these forms of domination have no political or civil rights, and their status is fixed by birth. Social mobility, in principle if not practice, is precluded. The ideologies justifying the domination of this kind include formal assumptions about inferiority and superiority which, in turn, find expression in certain rituals or etiquette regulating public contact between strata" (*Arts of Resistance*, x). Clark, in talking about the purchase value of land, notes that land is more valuable when its tenants have nowhere else to go. Consequently, the proportion of the lease to production can be higher—perhaps as high as fifty percent—than if tenants have options. Clark and Haswell, *The Economics of Subsistence Agriculture*, 159.

93. West, "Phases of Commercial Life in Egypt," 47. Syria furnished a large quantity of items to Egypt: wine, clothing, cedar-wood, and bitumen.

94. Frederiksen, "Theory, Evidence and the Ancient Economy," 167; D'Arms, *Commerce and Social Standing in Ancient Rome*, 145; Robinson, "Re-Thinking the Social Organization of Trade and Industry in First Century AD Pompeii." The essay by Robinson explores the issue thoroughly.

95. Polanyi, "The Economy as Instituted Process," 262; Sahlins, *Stone Age Economics*, 298; Pleket, "Urban Elites and Business in the Greek Part of the Roman Empire," 137, 141; Liebeschuetz, *Antioch in the Later Roman Period*, 46n43. Sahlins observes that social relations, not prices, connect buyers and sellers.

96. Garnsey, "Grain for Rome," 124; D'Arms, *Commerce and Social Standing in Ancient Rome*, 5; Pleket, "Urban Elites and Business in the Greek Part of the Roman Empire," 137, 141. Garnsey argues against this proposition specifically for grain trade for Rome, but not necessarily for trade in general.

interest in wealth accumulation[97] and profits[98] encouraged aristocrats to move agricultural production to cash crops for speculation in the grain market[99] (Matt 6:19) which meant reduced acreage devoted to local food production. The influx of cash from trade provided the means for an aristocrat to buy land.[100] Having the means, an aristocrat only needed the opportunity. If a small landowner[101] did not want to sell, an aristocrat had the political and legal power through the dominant entitlement system to force the peasant landowner to take out loans that used the excess cash of the aristocrat.[102] Peasant landowners could not afford to borrow and would default on their loans.[103]

97. Malina, "Wealth and Poverty in the New Testament and Its World," 365; Plutarch, *On Love of Wealth* 3–4. Plutarch compares being greedy to being sick, but this view did not seem to deter all aristocrats.

98. Osborne, "Pride and Prejudice, Sense and Subsistence," 140; Garnsey and Saller, *The Roman Empire*, 44. Investment in land brought steady low income and security while trade was riskier but offered more profits. Juvenal, a satirist, writes, "Good is the smell of profits, from whatever source derived, money should be sought first, virtue after cash" (*Satires* 14.204–5 [Braund, LCL]). D'Arms, *Commerce and Social Standing in Ancient Rome*, 154, argues that aristocrats, at least at a senatorial level, would have rejected such a maxim. Philostratus speaks to the greed of the Greeks, who "pretend they cannot live unless one penny begets another and unless they can force up the price of their goods by chaffering or holding them back ... What a splendid thing then it would be, if wealth were held in less honour and equality flourished a little more!" (*Apollonius* 6.2 [Jones, LCL]).

99. Hanson and Oakman, *Palestine in the Time of Jesus*, 153; Garnsey, "Grain for Rome," 118.

100. Goodman, "The First Jewish Revolt: Social Conflict and the Problem of Debt," 419; Dio Chrysostom, *Discourses* 46.45; Pliny, *Letters* 10.54. Both of these ancient authors speak to wealth as consisting of land and money out on interest.

101. I use the term *small landowner* to denote households in the PS 5 through PS 7 categories who work their own land. Landowners at the upper end of the PS 5 category would not be at risk of insufficient food to eat. They might hire neighbors, who needed to supplement their income, to work during planting and harvesting seasons. Landowners at the PS 7 level were not eking out a sufficient living. Pages 124–29 has a more in-depth analysis of the PS categories and survival mechanisms.

102. Carney, *The Economies of Antiquity*, 82; Moxnes, *The Economy of the Kingdom*, 102; Friesen, "Injustice or God's Will," 241. Hands discusses schemes that involved inviting landowners to accept low interest loans that they were not permitted to ever pay off. In a catalogued inscription, the interest funded the *alimenta* (see pages 121–23 for a discussion of this practice) to provide subsistence for some children. Freisen does not make the point exactly but he does argue that aristocrats controlled regional government and could do what they pleased. Hands catalogs an inscription from 161–69 CE in Gytheion on the Greek mainland (IG V, I, 1028 [Wilhelm, *Griechische Inscrifften*, 90ff; Laum No.9]), which reads in part: "And this money is to be lent out and those who borrow the money are to give adequate security in land." See Hands, *Charities and Social Aid in Greece and Rome*, 109, 206.

103. Hanson and Oakman, *Palestine in the Time of Jesus*, 153; Finger, *Of Widows and Meals: Communal Meals in the Book of Acts*, 103, 269; Garnsey and Scheidel, *Cities*,

The *dominium* aspect of the land would go to aristocrats (Matt 25:24–25) who then had the power to move agricultural production to cash crops and to divert acreage from food production.[104] The result would be less consumable food for peasant landowners forced into tenancy[105] and increased risk of major crop loss. Depending on the lease arrangement,[106] a tenant might still owe the full lease amount.[107] To make the payment, a tenant would need to borrow, and a debt spiral would ensue.[108]

Matthew and the Dominant Entitlement System (Matt 25:24–46)

As noted in the paragraphs above, Matthew's Gospel mentions various practices that exemplify the dominant entitlement system. Paying taxes is a given (Matt 9:9; 17:24–25; 22:19–20; 21:12), although a hidden transcript implies that taxes will not be a threat to their livelihood and putting food on their tables (Matt 17:27; 22:19–21), even when they are to be paid in coin.[109] A passage (Matt 13:24–30) about the realm of the heavens alludes to strong-arm tactics when an enemy (for example, a more politically powerful neighbor who wants the land) planted weeds in another's

---

Peasants, and Food, 98–99; Lewis and Reinhold, *Roman Civilization*, 2, 489. Garnsey and Scheidel note that conditions did not favor the survival of the free peasant. Taxes and military obligations weighed him down leading to debt and loss of land. Only veterans stood a chance because they were exempt from taxes, but they usually failed as well because they were not allotted enough land. Lewis gives an example of the tax exemption for veterans that is found in an edict of Domitian in 88–89 CE as catalogued in Wilcken, no. 463, col. 2, lines 10–20 (= Dessau, no. 9,059 = FIRA, vol. I, no. 76).

104. Hanson and Oakman, *Palestine in the Time of Jesus*, 106; Moxnes, *The Economy of the Kingdom*, 78. Moxnes argues that agricultural methods were resistant to change. The only way to increase profits from agriculture was to change the crops planted.

105. Garnsey and Saller, *The Roman Empire*, 71, 77; Hanson and Oakman, *Palestine in the Time of Jesus*, 106; Foxhall, "The Dependent Tenant: Land Leasing and Labour in Italy and Greece," 99–111. Garnsey and Saller note that peasants may retain part of their own land and work as a tenant on other land. Foxhall speaks to some advantages of being a tenant vice an independent landowner.

106. Garnsey and Saller, *The Roman Empire*, 71; Oakman, *Jesus and the Economic Questions*, 56; Grimshaw, "Luke's Market Exchange District," 38. Lease arrangements included both fixed amounts and proportions of the harvest. Grimshaw writes that planting was needed in the first century, and land was rent-free for the first five years.

107. Oakman, *Jesus and the Economic Questions*, 51, defines rent as "surpluses extracted from peasantry on the basis of asymmetrical power relations."

108. Oakman, "Jesus and Agrarian Palestine," 66, 70; Brunt, *Roman Imperial Themes*, 521. See especially Figure 1: Social Dynamics of Debt in First-Century Palestine and Figure 2: Procedures in Case of Insolvency. Both Oakman and Brunt indicate the dispossession of indebted peasants occurred.

109. Carter, *Matthew and the Margins*, 359.

plot. From a food-access perspective, the implication is that the enemy will fail at ruining the crops[110] and wresting control of the land from the peasant. Instead, at the end time, perpetrators of such actions will be condemned. A piece of wise advice is given in Matt 5:25–26 to stay out of the judicial system controlled by aristocrats in the dominant entitlement system.[111] None of these examples indicates a big reversal in the realm of the heavens as embodied by the Matthean community. However, Stephen Barton correctly writes that an overarching condemnation of the dominant entitlement system seems to be present.

> Economic matters are used in Matthew to offer the reader a stark moral-theological choice between two kinds of people, those who show their love of God and neighbor by their deployment of money and power, and others (typified by the Pharisees) who show their lack of integrity and failure in love by their idolatrous pride and self-interest. According to Matthew's apocalyptic theology these two kinds of people follow one of two ways, one leading to life, the other to destruction (cf. 7:13–14, 24–27; 25:31–46).[112]

In the Parable of the Talents (Matt 25:24–27), one finds the strongest criticism in the Gospel of abusive practices. I examine the parable from the perspective of what it implies about the character of the master and the activities in which he and the first two servants participated. The context of the parable is often described as being in the eschatological discourse where it is the third in a series of parables describing events in the end time.[113] The

---

110. Garnsey, *Famine and Food Supply*, 39. Garnsey notes that weeds, including darnel of Matt 13:26, grew naturally with wheat. Darnel was noxious, especially if in larger percentages of the bread flour. Not everyone sifted it out at harvest, especially if the harvest were poor. Both peasants and urban bakers left such contaminates in the flour. By increasing the amount of weeds in the wheat, the enemy was trying to render the wheat inedible.

111. Neyrey, *Honor and Shame in the Gospel of Matthew*, 193–95. Neyrey argues the situation is one of a series in which Jesus tells the auditors who have challenged someone's honor to make restitution, even to their own detriment. He puts honor-shame as the underlying theme of the entire Sermon on the Mount (Matt 5:1—7:29). He is especially partial to the shunning of a rebellious son (that is, one who has become a disciple of Jesus) by his own family. Yet, he does concede that other scenarios are also possible.

112. Barton, "Money Matters: Economic Relations and the Transformation of Value in Early Christianity," 45.

113. Hultgren, *The Parables of Jesus*, 274. Hultgren ties this parable to the previous two (that is, the Faithful and Wise Servant and the Ten Maidens) as wisdom teachings. He does say that this parable is weaker as wisdom, although the first two servants were wise and the third foolish.

parable has many elements that could be, and are, construed symbolically.[114] However, now being aware of abusive practices condoned by the dominant entitlement system, I argue that the parable takes on a different function in its Gospel context. Warren Carter asserts that the Gospel has co-opted the abusive values of the dominant entitlement system when describing the realm of the heavens. He writes that the rhetorical message about discipleship is so important that a critique of the bad practices of the master and the first two servants is not given. Yet, the auditors will supply the critique and know they are not to imitate the bad practices, but be good and faithful disciples. Carter draws a connection between the first servant being called *good* and the attributed trait reflects his commitment to imitate God who is good.[115] My approach diverges from that of Carter on these last two points.

Richard Rohrbaugh poses a question that points to a different interpretation. "We know the master condemned the third servant, but did Jesus?" Rohrbaugh continues that it is possible that Jesus is condemning the master in the same manner that the peasant auditors might have condemned him.[116] Rohrbaugh's question and suggestion warrant consideration since the following passage is a strong eschatological judgment scene (Matt 25:31–46). In the judgment scene, people of all nations are divided into goats and sheep depending upon whether they took actions to help people in times of food crises. Could the Parable of the Talents perhaps be a negative example of behavior by the first two servants and the master that will make them goats? I argue that the actions implied in the parable would not have helped in times of food crises, but quite the contrary, could have seriously inhibited access to food by people in the lower socio-economic segments of the population.

In the parable, the master is going away and gives sizeable amounts of money to three of his servants to conduct business for him while he is away. The first two servants made a profit, or gained more money, for their master through business pursuits. The Greek word translated *made* [a profit] can also have a negative connotation as in *reap disadvantage from a thing*.[117] The scenario does not indicate the servants were day laborers, but agents fronting for their master in some type of business. The size of the amounts

---

114. Jeremias, *Die gleichnisse Jesu*, 64–65; Davies and Allison, *The Gospel According to Matthew 1–7*, 1:402; Luz, *Matthew 21–28*, 3:506, 509; Hultgren, *The Parables of Jesus*, 278.

115. Carter, *Matthew and the Margins*, 488–90.

116. Rohrbaugh, "Social Location of Thought as A Heuristic Construct in New Testament Study,'" 38.

117. LSJ, s.v. "ἐργάζομαι." In its second usage, the word is working at, manufacturing, or trade and business; LSJ, s.v. "κερδαίνω." Word is gain, derive profit, or advantage.

would indicate big business or international trade.[118] There was more risk to those types of businesses than banking, the alternative suggested to the third servant who was risk-averse.

The master returns and wants an accounting from his agents. He praises the first two servants who have been successful in conducting business on his behalf.[119] The third servant describes his master as σκληρός, which can take on meanings such as hard, strict, harsh, cruel, and merciless.[120] The servant also describes the master as one who harvests where he did not sow and gathers where he did not scatter.[121] These descriptions construct an aristocrat enmeshed totally in the dominant entitlement system. One could excuse the descriptions as a polemic hurled at the master by a servant who has failed. Yet, the master does not disagree with his servant's description. He could be bragging that he has taken over the land of others, or that he has tenants in untenable situations. The description of the master worsens in v. 27 when he tells his servant that the servant should, at a minimum, have placed his money with the bankers and drawn interest on it. As I delineated above, one of the abusive practices of aristocrats was to use the money they had made in international trade and force loans onto peasants who could not afford them. Ironically, the master calls the third servant *evil* because the servant did not do what his master would have done.[122] Yet, Aristotle writes that making unlimited wealth (coins have no natural limit) is unnatural. Usury is the most unnatural economic action.[123] Hence, it is the master and the first two servants who are the evil ones. The reaction of a peasant audience might have been that the master and the first two slaves were greedy to their core.[124]

Some scholars downplay the description(s) of the master by saying an auditor would focus on the failure of the third servant and ignore the accuracy

---

118. France, "On Being Ready (Matthew 25:1–46)," 185; Carter, *Matthew and the Margins*, 489. Often scholars compare *talents* to *denarii* and calculate the huge number of days a day laborer would need to work. The scenario does not indicate a day laborer, but an agent fronting for his master in some type of business.

119. Gordon, *The Economic Problem in Biblical and Patristic Thought*, 57. Gordon describes the activities as "astute commercial behaviour."

120. BAGD, s.v. "σκληρός."

121. Hultgren, *The Parables of Jesus*, 276. Hultgren writes that the metaphors of reaping without sowing and gathering without broadcasting show a person who enriches himself at the expense of others.

122. Ibid.

123. Aristotle, *Politics* 1.9.13.

124. Rohrbaugh, "Social Location of Thought as A Heuristic Construct in New Testament Study," 35.

of the descriptions.[125] Indeed, the structure and the story ending could indicate that the third servant is where the emphasis should be.[126] Nonetheless, the descriptions of the master and the first two servants are in the narrative, and any interpretation must address them. The Gospel does not say that the situation reflects the realm of the heavens, but many interpretations of the parable equate the master with Jesus or God. If such a link were correct, the parable would condone the practices, even if those practices were not the main theme, since the implication is that God or Jesus would do such things.[127] On the other hand, if the third servant is the primary focus then he could be seen in a more heroic light of not going along with the exploitative practices of his master. His being condemned using words from eschatological judgments links this passage ironically to the next where eschatological judgment falls on the master and the first two slaves.

The parable imitates language from the dominant entitlement system to describe a world in which the little that one has ended up in the hands of one who had much. People in the lower socio-economic segments of the population would have wondered if the realm of the heavens was going to be like the world in which they already lived. The next scene answers with a resounding no. In the end, Jesus will judge people by their actions that helped people who are suffering from a bad year and do not have enough to eat. Giving food is an obvious response in situations of food shortages. Drink may be weak wine and not water, which might naturally come to mind. Wine provided part of the needed nutrition. Less obvious is clothing. People sold their clothes to try to purchase food and, in dire circumstances, tried to eat their clothing.[128] Illness killed many people during famines when malnutrition weakened them.[129] Often peasants could not discharge their financial obligations when crops were bad. They might be incarcerated and need friends and family to supply them with the essentials of life.[130] During food shortages when food was no longer available in the country, people would flock to cities, where they would be strangers, and hope for alms to feed them. People who tended to such needs were doing the will of God and

---

125. Osborne, *Matthew*, 927.

126. Davies and Allison, *The Gospel According to Matthew 1–7*, 1:401; France, "On Being Ready (Matthew 25:1–46)," 185–86, writes, "The message is not that God is a 'rapacious capitalist' (E.W. Beare, *Matthew*, 486), but that he is not satisfied with inaction."

127. Contra France, "On Being Ready (Matthew 25:1–46)," 186.

128. Garnsey, *Famine and Food Supply*, 24–25, 28; Petronius, 44. Petronius is a satirist and the reference may be exaggeration.

129. Garland, *The Eye of the Beholder*, 20; Stambaugh, *The Ancient Roman City*, 135–37.

130. See Paul in Phil 2:25–30; 4:10–20.

would be sheep. The master, who condemned the third slave, and his first two servants would be goats and condemned according to these criteria.

Summary of Dominant Entitlement System and Polyculture

To summarize, the primary function of all societies is to feed the population but social structures determine who gets what. In the first-century Roman East, kinship was the principal social structure and other aspects such as the political and legal systems came under kinship. I have argued that there were two entitlement systems that operated in parallel that determined who got what: the dominant system and the local systems. The aristocrats controlled the dominant entitlement system and, consequently, with impunity they could exploit the lower socio-economic segments of the population. I have given examples of how aristocrats could use dubious methods to wrest control of land and crop selection from peasants. Peasants needed to plant a variety of crops—called polyculture—to survive the vagaries of the climate. However, losing control of land and crop selection pushed them from polyculture to cash crops to pay for rents and taxes and loans. Adding to this bad situation was the push by aristocrats to participate in the lucrative international grain trade. Consequently, aristocrats forced peasants into even more cash crops which put them at greater risk for catastrophic crop failures and hunger. In the discussions, I have noted references in Matthew's Gospel to such practices. Some references just allude to the practice without commenting on it one way or another. I examined the Parable of the Talents using this life context and the parable's Gospel context. My conclusion was that the parable is a negative example (that is, how not to be disciples) and does not condone such exploitative practices. Plutarch sums up the situation as aristocracy killing and destroying people and taking from others what they themselves could not use.

> Thus as vipers, blister-beetles, and venomous spiders offend and disgust us more than bears and lions, because they kill and destroy men without using what they destroy, so too should men whose rapacity springs from meanness and illiberality disgust us more than those in whom it springs from prodigality, since the miserly take from others what they have no power or capacity to use themselves.[131]

---

131. Plutarch, *On Love of Wealth* 6 (Clement and Hoffleit, LCL).

The Two Sides of Grain Storage

As I argued in chapter 4, food shortages were endemic in the first-century Roman East, and occasional severe food shortages were catastrophic to all but the higher socio-economic segments of the population. Moreover, I argued that one of the shared survival mechanisms of the lower socio-economic segments of the population was storage of food products as a hedge against poor future years. Yet, in the Sermon on the Mount, the crowd is told simply, "Do not store up for yourselves treasures on earth, where insects and decay[132] consume and where thieves break in and steal" (Matt 6:19). Following this admonition, the Matthean Jesus tells the crowd not to worry about life or what food or drink will be available (Matt 6:25). This point is reinforced with a similar message in Matt 6:31 that connects provision of daily food with keeping focused on doing God's righteousness. One's immediate impression of these teachings might be that the Matthean Jesus is telling the people in the crowd who were of lower socio-economic status to abandon their most important survival mechanism—storage of food. Instead, they are to be content with future heavenly rewards (Matt 6:20). They are to commit themselves to the realm of the heavens being embodied and revealed by Jesus.[133] They are to pray for daily bread[134] (Matt 6:11).[135] Continuing the argument, Matthew tells them that if they but ask they will receive bread and/or fish (Matt 7:7–11). Yet, as I argued in chapter

---

132. LSJ, s.v. "σής." Often the explanation for *moth* and *rust* involve cloth and coins. However, both terms refer to threats to grain storage. Moths are insects that can attack different things, including grain; LSJ, s.v. "βρῶσις." *Rust* is best translated decay, which was a serious problem for grain storage. The cited examples are Galen 6.422 and 12.870 and Hesiodus, *Theogonia*, 797.

133. Carter, *Matthew and the Margins*, 172; Neyrey, *Honor and Shame in the Gospel of Matthew*, 176–78, offers an interesting discussion of these passages and gender differentiation in first century. Using honor-shame analysis, he concludes that there was "no family, no household, and no kinship network to catch them as they fall." Hence, not only are they giving up their primary survival mechanism, the social safety network would not function either.

134. Grimshaw, *Analysis of Matthew's Food Exchange*, 54; Carter, *Matthew and the Margins*, 166–67; Sahlins, *Stone Age Economics*, 215; Luz, *Matthew 1–7*, 1:321. A number of scholars note the obvious point that is sometimes forgotten: food requirements do not go away after a day in which a person receives food. The need for food recurs every day. Further, the word *today* is important because a large number of people in PS 6 and PS 7 cannot take for granted they will have food on any given day.

135. Luz, *Matthew 1–7*, 1:314, 319–20. Luz notes that the petitions in the Lord's Prayer are short and open, which leads to ambiguity in meaning. He states that this petition is worse—impossible to interpret with any certainty. Two facts add to the normal dilemma. First, no parallel has been found in Greco-Roman writings; LSJ, s.v. "ἐπιούσιος." Second, the word translated *daily* is quite rare and its meaning is speculative.

4, at least 25 percent of the population was not receiving daily bread consistently and another 30 percent were barely at subsistence. In the face of widespread hunger, does the petition reflect their hope that God, or God's agent on earth, can be relied on for daily needs?[136] Knowing more about the context of storing up grain leads one to a nuanced understanding of the thrust of these teachings.

Grain Speculation Caused Food Shortages

As I argued on pages 103–7, both large and small landowners routinely practiced storage of food products. Storage by small landowners was a survival mechanism for them. Large estates may have had their own *horrea*, but medium to small landowners could not afford either to build a *horrea* or to defend it. Merchants built commercial *horrea* and rented space to medium landowners. Storage was also necessary to sustain the populations of cities year round.[137] The provision of sufficient daily food for urban residents resided with aristocrats.

Wealthy merchants and large landowners controlled the bulk of the food crops—especially grain—and their intent was to make money. They stockpiled grain for speculation, which kept grain from the local food market.[138] Usually the prices would fluctuate in an acceptable range depending on how much grain remained for the local market.[139] The difficulty lay in the absence of a clearly demarcated boundary between legitimate storage for domestic consumption and stockpiling with a view to profiteering.[140] This manipulation of the grain supply occurred frequently, but the city council rarely took permanent corrective action because it was not in their best

---

136. Heinen, "Göttliche Sitometrie: Beobachtungen zur Brotbitte des Vaterunsers," 76, 73–74, 78. Heinen notes the psalmist making a similar petition (Ps 103:27 [LXX 104]). He connects this petition with the practice of *sitomatrion*, which I discuss below. Using primarily Egyptian papyri, he connects daily bread to *sitomeria*, the daily nourishment for slaves and wages for workers. He argues that God is a *sitones*. On pages 201–6, I discuss the function of *sitones* in more detail.

137. Horden and Purcell, *The Corrupting Sea*, 208.

138. Garnsey, *Famine and Food Supply*, 77.

139. Jones, *The Roman World of Dio Chrysostom*, 19. In discussing relative stability in prices, Sahlins writes that "the customary rates have moral force, understandable from their function as standards of fair conduct in an area where tenuous intergroup relations constantly menace the peace of trade" (*Stone Age Economics*, 308).

140. Garnsey, *Famine and Food Supply*, 77.

interest to do so.¹⁴¹ The members of the council were in the ranks of the manipulators.¹⁴² Petronius writes,

> Damn the magistrates, who play "Scratch my back, and I'll scratch yours" in league with the bakers. So the little people come off badly; for the jaws of the upper classes are always keeping carnival ... This town goes downhill like the calf's tail. But why do we put up with a magistrate not worth three peppercorns, who cares more about putting two pence in his purse than keeping us alive? He sits grinning at home, and pockets more money a day than other people have for a fortune.¹⁴³

If the price of grain went up too high (that is, grain became scarce), unrest would begin to foment. The lower socio-economic segments of the population directed the unrest toward the wealthy merchants whom the poor assumed were hoarding grain.¹⁴⁴

The common solution for balancing profit and unrest was for the city to appoint a market controller (*agoranomos*). One of his duties was to ensure adequate supply of provisions, including grain, at a fair price.¹⁴⁵ When shortages occurred, he might induce a merchant to offer grain at a lower price, or might actually enter the market himself undercutting the merchants.¹⁴⁶ Sometimes local landowners or merchants who owned the store of grain might come forward voluntarily when the price went out of range.¹⁴⁷ For their efforts, they received laud and honor and they maintained the social order.¹⁴⁸ An example is Manius Salarius Sabinus who provided grain within the acceptable range several times, and once when the price rose due to the Roman army passing through Lete in Macedonia in Hadrian's time.¹⁴⁹

---

141. Ibid., 74, 78.

142. Hamel, *Poverty and Charity in Roman Palestine*, 49; Garnsey, *Famine and Food Supply*, 32.

143. Petronius, 44 (Heseltine, LCL).

144. Garnsey, *Famine and Food Supply*, 77–78; Jones, *The Greek City*, 19.

145. Sperber, *The City in Roman Palestine*, 33–34. Sperber notes that graft occurred when certifying weights and measures used by the shopkeepers.

146. Jones, *The Greek City*, 216–17; Hands, *Charities and Social Aid in Greece and Rome*, 182, D112. Hands catalogues SEC, XV, 330 which speaks to a city in Greece in 42 CE that was reduced to dire straits. The *agoranomos* and others "supplied out of their own resources, as a gift, corn for the bakers and for the rest money as an interest-free loan for a year, through which we enjoy unfailing cheap supplies."

147. Sperber, "Drought, Famine and Pestilence in Amoraic Palestine," 288–89; Garnsey, *Famine and Food Supply*, 38, 74, 69; Garnsey, *Food and Society*, 43.

148. Hands, *Charities and Social Aid in Greece and Rome*, 95.

149. Garnsey, *Food and Society*, 247–48; Temin, "Market Economy," 176.

However, at other times, grain would be released in too small quantities or too slowly,[150] and the price would go higher than many urban households could pay. Since the poorer people had little recourse to change their situation politically or legally, they resorted to violence.

Lucan wrote, "The causes of hatred and mainsprings of popularity are determined by the price of food. Hunger alone makes cities free; and when men in power feed the idle mob, they buy subservience; a starving people is incapable of fear."[151] Dio Chrysostom wrote of an incident in Euboea. "This wrath of theirs was something terrible, and they at once frightened men against whom they raised their voices, so that some of them ran about begging for mercy; while others threw off their cloaks through fear. I too myself was once almost knocked over, as though a tidal wave or thunderstorm had suddenly broken over me."[152] Seneca writes, "a hungry people neither listens to reason nor is appeased by justice nor is bent by any entreaty."[153] The council and the wealthy grain merchants should have been afraid as the incidents below demonstrate.[154]

In 70–80 CE, a riotous crowd did not believe Dio Chrysostom when he insisted he had no grain. Chrysostom had recently purchased shops so he was doubly suspect when food prices rose in the city. The people assumed he had enough money and did not need to stockpile grain for speculation. They were intent on stoning him and another man after which they planned on raiding and burning down the two offenders' barns. Chrysostom's household was prepared to resist and the crowd dispersed. The following day he rebuked the crowd by saying that while the cost of grain had risen higher than was customary, they should not have become desperate. He conceded that something needed to be done but argued that their behavior was unwarranted and savage.[155] In 14–37 CE in Aspendus, Philostratus relates an incidence in which aristocrats were holding the stored grain for speculation. A crowd of all ages set upon a magistrate and lit a fire to burn him alive, despite his clinging to a statue of the emperor as refuge. Apollonius quelled

---

150. Garnsey, *Famine and Food Supply*, 271.

151. Lucan, *Pharsalia* 3.55–59 (Duff, LCL).

152. Jones, *The Roman World of Dio Chrysostom*, 21; Dio Chrysostom, *Discourses* 7.25–26, Euboean (Cohoon, LCL).

153. Seneca, *Moral Essays on the Shortness of Life* 18.5 (Basore, LCL).

154. Winter, "Responses to Corinthian Famines," 91. Winter catalogues *I. Ep.*, 215, II, 1–4. This second-century CE inscription from Ephesus notes the usual response to food shortages. "Thus it happens at times that the populace is plunged into disorder and riots".

155. Dio Chrysostom, *Discourses* 46:46, 10–13; Jones, *The Roman World of Dio Chrysostom*, 20.

the riot by threatening the grain merchants with a curse. In response to his threat, merchants supplied the city with grain.[156] Not all such incidents were resolved without the fury being satisfied. Ammianus writes of the cruelty of the emperor Gallus. In Antioch in 354 CE, a food crisis was building and the city council petitioned Gallus to intervene, as was custom, to bring in food from neighboring regions. Instead, he turned them down and blamed the situation on the governor.

> To the multitude, which was in fear of the direst necessity, he [Gallus] delivered up Theophilus, consular governor of Syria, who was standing nearby, constantly repeating the statement that no one could lack food if the governor did not wish it. These words increased the audacity of the lowest classes, and when the lack of provisions became more acute, driven by hunger and rage, they set fire to the pretentious house of a certain Eubulus, a man of distinction among his own people; then, as if the governor had been delivered into their hands by an imperial edict, they assailed him with kicks and blows, and trampling him under foot when he was half dead, with awful mutilation tore him to pieces. After his wretched death each man saw in the end of one person an image of his own peril and dreaded a fate like that which he had just witnessed.[157]

If a crisis did ensue, a Roman official, or city council,[158] might eventually intervene and require the release of grain. An example comes from a decree issued in 92 or 93 CE in Antioch in Pisidia.

> Therefore—may good fortune attend!—all who are either citizens or residents of Antioch shall declare before the *duovirs* of the colony of Antioch, within thirty days after this edict of mine is posted in public, how much grain each has and in what place, and how much he deducts for seed or for the year's supply of food for his household, and he shall make all the remaining grain available to purchasers in the colony of Antioch . . . It is most unjust for anyone to profiteer from the

---

156. Philostratus, *Apollonius* 1.15; Garnsey, *Famine and Food Supply*, 32. Garnsey references a similar situation much later in Caesarea in Cappadocia in the time of Basil.

157. Garnsey, *Famine and Food Supply*, 260; Ammianus, 14.17.15. In 14.7.2, Ammianus reports that Gallus had ordered the council to release grain at a reduced price, and they had vigorously opposed his edict.

158. Jones, *The Roman World of Dio Chrysostom*, 20; Garnsey, *Famine and Food Supply*, 69–74; Winter, "Responses to Corinthian Famines," 95. Jones asserts that other aristocrats who were eager to stop the unrest, especially at the expense of someone else, also pressured the recipient of the ire of the mob to release grain.

hunger of his fellow citizens. I forbid the price of grain to exceed one denarius per *modius*.[159]

Officials would seize all undeclared grain and would sell it at below-market prices and they would give a portion of sales revenue to the informant. In some cases, the offending aristocrat faced loss of political privileges, exile, or death.[160]

To recap, the storage of grain for speculation exacerbated situations of endemic food shortages in cities. Generally, the poorer people had no recourse, as the council would rule in favor of the grain owners, who may have been members of the council. If prices rose too steeply, the *agoranomos* would intervene in an attempt to get grain released to the markets. If pushed too far, the masses might turn to violence against those whom they perceived as being responsible for there not being enough food. On rare occasions, a Roman official might intervene and force the release of grain.

Matthew and Grain Speculation (Matt 6:19—17:12)

Now in the context of the preceding discussion, I return to the question posed above. Is the Gospel exhorting its auditors to give up a principal survival mechanism: storing up of food? The full passage contrasts storing up selfishly for oneself (Matt 6:19) with treating neighbors as you would like to be treated (Matt 7:12). In between is instruction and encouragement concerned with living in a world where actions of the aristocracy were causing hunger and physical, as well as spiritual, poverty.[161] I argue that the extended passage does not eliminate the principal survival mechanism of storage of food, especially for the lower socio-economic segments of the population. Instead, it deals with attitudes toward food accumulation that limit access to food for some and undermine the social safety network for many. I argue that the interpretation varies with the auditors—wealthier (PS 4 through PS 5)[162] or poorer (PS 6 through PS 7). I argue that the Gospel targets wealthier

---

159. Lewis and Reinhold, *Roman Civilization*, 2, 250. Lewis and Naphtali catalog this inscription from AE 1925, 162b.

160. Garnsey, *Famine and Food Supply*, 7; Jones, *The Roman World of Dio Chrysostom*, 20.

161. Allison, *Studies in Matthew: Interpretation Past and Present*, 189–96. Allison notes that pairs thematically unite the unit: treasures, eyes and masters. He also constructs structures linking topics between the first section (Matt 6:1–18) and the second (Matt 6:19—17:12).

162. Matthew 4:25 includes people in the crowds who had come from cities. Hence, one cannot eliminate from the crowds people who might have been in the specified socio-economic range. Furthermore, in these arguments, I specifically refer to the

people since their positive response would relieve the angst of the poorer people that was driving them to hoard their meager supplies. Yet, the Gospel directs its message to the poorer auditors as well. The Gospel exhorts poorer people to continue to share critical food stores despite aristocratic actions that caused those stores to dwindle. They are to live without worry (fear) despite being hungry and, thereby lessen the influence of aristocratic actions on their lives.[163] Epitetus offers similar advice concerned with not worrying about food and clothes. He connects the thought with persons lessening the power of a ruler over them.[164]

The motif of the third major block of the Sermon on the Mount (Matt 6:19—17:12) is proper living style for the emerging realm of the heavens. The block emphasizes making the right decisions and doing righteous acts, especially within the Matthean community, but not for public acclaim and honor.[165] I address the block *in toto*[166] as a series of contrasts of imperial life style based on values of the dominant entitlement system with behavior commensurate with the realm of the heavens. For the wealthier auditors, I argue using two points that the command against storing up treasures on earth (Matt 6:19) reflected the practices of storing crops in *horrea*.[167] The first point arises from an interpretation of the Greek words translated *store up treasures* and the discussions above and in chapter 3. I argue the second point in the context of the longer passage Matt 6:22–34 and its veiled message against an ostentatious life style,[168] which required large amounts of cash.

Matthean community to emphasize that the Gospel was concerned with real-life situations of flesh-and-blood people. Obviously, Matthew's Gospel was heard by many Christians. Yet, by emphasizing the original community, I hope to accentuate the crucial nature of the Gospel's pragmatic messages.

163. Riches, "The Sociology of Matthew: Some Basic Questions Concerning Its Relation to the Theology of the New Testament," 266.

164. Epictetus, *Discourses* 1.9.7–8, 1.9.12–21.

165. Goodman, *State and Society in Roman Galilee, A.D. 132–212*, 122. Goodman describes the village magistrate called a *gabbiam*. A *gabbiam* carried a bag of money collected from others to give to beggars. When distributing to the poor they would announce it in public. This practice might be behind the criticism of Matt 6:1–4.

166. Betz and Collins, *Sermon on the Mount*, 428–29; Carter, *Matthew and the Margins*, 158–15; Davies and Allison, *The Gospel According to Matthew 1–7*, 1:572–73; Luz, *Matthew 1–7*, 1:295; Osborne, *Matthew*, 217. Many scholars divide the block between vv. 18 and 19.

167. *Horrea* is the general term for a storehouse in which many different types of goods might be stored.

168. Carter, *Matthew and the Margins*, 172. Carter relates the message to the practice of accumulation of goods and a materialistic attitude.

Both the verb and the noun—translated *store up* and *treasure*, respectively—come from the same root: θησαυρ-[169] Each can take on several meanings, which renders any translation of the verses ambiguous and highly dependent on the perspective of the translator relative to the context. Perhaps Matthew was intentionally using the word so that meaning for aristocrats stood in tension with meaning for peasants. The verb, θησαυρίζω, primarily means *to store up* or *to treasure*, but it also means *to hoard*, as in laying up more θησαυρός than needed for survival. The noun θησαυρός carries three primary meanings: (1) store or treasure, (2) strong-room or magazine, and (3) receptacle for valuables. The first meaning points to *what* is put into storage, while the second and third meanings point to *where* something is stored. What was stored? Grain was obviously stored. Other items would include anything valued by the person doing the storing. Money, bullion, clothing, and jewels were stored.[170] Non-grain items were most likely stored in receptacles for valuables (that is, definition 3).[171] The example given for the second meaning is the *banks*[172] at Delphi, which were involved in international trade. M. W. Frederiksen notes that men who acted as bankers often operated *horrea* to store payments in kind.[173] None of the meanings listed for the noun are for *horrea*, but compound words derived from it do refer to *horrea*. For example, θησαυρικός refers to the charges to rent space in (use) a public granary. Θησαυθυλᾰκῠτῐκόν was the tax levied for the

169. LSJ, s.v. "θησαυρ-."

170. Josephus, *J.W.* 6.282. After the fall of Jerusalem to the Romans, Roman soldiers burned a Temple treasury (γαζοφυλάκιον) in which members of the aristocracy had not only deposited a lot of money, but also an immense number of garments.

171. Matthew uses three different words in this block that all have as one meaning, storage place. In addition to the words being addressed in the text above, Matthew 6:6 uses ταμεῖον, and Matthew 6:26 uses θησαυρίζω. Osiek, "'When You Pray, Go into Your Ταμεῖον' (Matthew 6:6): But Why?" Osiek examines the first word and, based in part on later translations into Latin, concludes that the meaning indicates a private space, not necessarily a storeroom in a house; LSJ, s.v. "ἀποθήκη." The word can mean *what* is laid by or *where* it is laid by. The *where* is defined as a magazine or storehouse, or a refuge; LSJ, s.v. "ἀποθήκιον." Used in a compound noun, the root takes on a food connotation as a larder.

172. I observed that the banks, some of whose foundations still exist at Delphi, were rather small buildings of varying sizes that line the main road going up to the top of the mound. They have thick walls, and I would estimate that the larger ones are approximately sixteen by eight feet. A bank was often associated with a particular region or city. Money, as coins, was rarely transported, but records of transactions were maintained (that is, ledgers were kept). Gold and silver hoards may have been stored. Polanyi and Pearson, *The Livelihood of Man*, 264; Garnsey and Saller, *The Roman Empire*, 55; Hanson and Oakman, *Palestine in the Time of Jesus*, 121–23. Contra Hopkins, "Taxes and Trade in the Roman Empire (200 B.C.—A.D. 400)," 106.

173. Frederiksen, "Theory, Evidence and the Ancient Economy," 167.

protection of a granary.¹⁷⁴ Given the Gospel context of food availability that follows, part of the metamessage of the verse could be an admonition against hoarding of valuable items, including grain, in granaries.

Who stored food items in granaries? Peasants stored food in various types of jars, sometimes buried for temperature control, and in lofts in their homes for grain. As discussed on pages 103–7, *horrea* were the targets of thieves. Although desperate people may steal from their poor neighbors, I assert that it is more likely that they steal from those whom they see as causing the problem.¹⁷⁵ Further, valuables, including grain, that were stored in *horrea*, would be susceptible to grain moths and decay (Matt 6:19). I conclude that auditors at any socio-economic level easily heard the message as condemning the hoarding of grain in *horrea* to generate income to support aristocratic ostentatious lifestyles. The wealthier landowners and grain merchants were the ones storing up in *horrea*, not the rural peasants and small landowners. The storage of quantities of grain generated cash for such grain speculators.

The imperial lifestyle of aristocrats created status through land, honor from public acts (Matt 6:1–18), and wealth as expressed by clothes worn and types of food consumed (Matt 6:19—17:5).¹⁷⁶ Matthew's gospel condemns the imperial lifestyle because people lived for human acclaim, and because it generated deleterious side effects. With respect to food access, the issue behind the extended passage is that the imperial lifestyle required substantial cash.¹⁷⁷ To acquire the cash, some aristocrats speculated in the lucrative international grain trade. As argued above, the result of these actions to support an ostentatious, imperial lifestyle was artificially induced food shortages negatively affecting many people in the lower socio-economic segments of the population.¹⁷⁸

What is the message to members of the Matthean community who may be landowners or merchants? In the realm of the heavens embodied by that community, they are not to store up grain (food products) excessively

---

174. LSJ, s.v. "θησαυρικός" and s.v. "θησαυθυλᾰκῠ́τῐκόν."

175. Neyrey, *Honor and Shame in the Gospel of Matthew*, 178, observes that peasants could not have treasures, "especially in this period of ruinous taxation." Contrary to my position, he suggests that the prime targets of thieves would be unprotected villages.

176. I have discussed land ownership and public acts as honor-producing. See the chapter 4 discussion on foods consumed by aristocrats contrasted with the diets of the lower socio-economic segments of the population.

177. Osborne, "Pride and Prejudice, Sense and Subsistence." Osborne's hypothesis is that aristocrats needed large sums of money to support their lifestyles, which did include civic obligations. Osborne deals with extractions from rents and not international trade.

178. Horsley and Hanson, *Bandits, Prophets, and Messiahs*, 52.

for profiteering in the international markets. If they do not worry about what clothes they will wear (Matt 6:25, 28–31) parading in the streets or what food they will eat (Matt 6:25, 31) at the banquets they host,[179] they will not need to store up treasures in *horrea* and banks. They live at income levels that do not warrant worrying about having more than sufficient food and clothes. The Gospel admonishes them not be worried (ambitious)[180] about how they would be judged by their peers, nor are they to judge each other by imperial standards (Matt 7:1–5).[181] They cannot serve both mammon and God (Matt 6:24).[182] Instead, the implication is that they are to be generous (that is, the good eye of Matt 6:22–23). Generous grain merchants release their hoards in the *horrea* at a fair price for their neighbors in Antioch. The land they want for status and the rents they want are to remain with the peasants. They are not to force peasants into increased grain production with the attendant increased risk of losing their food crops and going hungry. If the grain speculators respond appropriately to the exhortations, some of the pressures causing worry for people in the lower socio-economic segments of the population would ease. Unfortunately, the Gospel realistically indicates that wealthier grain owners often remained ensconced in the dominant entitlement system (Matt 19:24).

While it is obvious that the Gospel exhorts the wealthier people to share, I suggest that the admonitions also include anyone, including the poorer persons (that is, PS 6 and PS 7), who hold back what little food they possess from kin or a neighbor who had a bad year and needs help. The worry about what to wear would not be the same as the wealthier people. Peasants might be concerned if they were going to need to sell their clothes to buy food.[183] The

---

179. Hamel, *Poverty and Charity in Roman Palestine*, 79. Malina notes that James 5:1–7 presents a full description of what it means to be moral for the rich: "The rich trust in their perishable possessions—in garments, gold, silver, fields, amassed goods; they keep back wages of laborers who work for them and harvest their fields, defraud them, condemn the righteous, kill the righteous" ("Wealth and Poverty in the New Testament and Its World," 357).

180. Bultmann, "μεριμνάω," *TDNT* 4:589–93. The word also has a meaning of striving for something, even to the point of ambition.

181. Allison, *Studies in Matthew: Interpretation Past and Present*, 192, 195–96. Allison structurally pairs the prohibition of not storing up (Matt 6:19–21) with the prohibition of not judging (Matt 7:1–2).

182. "Wealth, the Aramaic term for which is *mamona*, would be the storage of resource values for creating, preserving, displaying, or recovering public reputation ('honor'), and for protecting the economic integrity of family and household" (Hanson and Oakman, *Palestine in the Time of Jesus*, 122).

183. Hamel, *Poverty and Charity in Roman Palestine*, 57, 71, 84, 82. Hamel offers a good discussion of clothes for both wealthier and poorer persons. People in the lower socio-economic segments of the population shared their clothing. Hamel cites m.*Nidd*

worry about what to eat would not be the same as the wealthier people. Peasants might be concerned whether they were going to be able to eat enough of a healthy diet or be reduced to *famine* foods that cannot sustain a healthy body and would eventually lead to their deaths. This passage assumes that people will be concerned about their well-being. There is a juxtaposition of the admonition not to worry (Matt 6:25–34) with a later recognition that God knows and will provide what is needed (Matt 7:7–12).[184]

However, being members of the realm of the heavens brings new understanding about what their concerns should be. First, one cannot secure one's life through worry and caring for things of this world that will lead to downfall.[185] The correct path is not suspension of care for others, but for all to have concern for each other—general reciprocity. People are to work, which the flora and fauna cannot, but as the flora and fauna show, worry is not part of the scenario.[186] They are to trust in God and their neighbors that enough food would be available through general reciprocity of the social safety network. A poorer person needs to balance judicious storing for a bad year with trust in God and community that enough food will be available in all but catastrophic food shortages. In support of this argument, Hans Dieter Betz and Adela Yarbro Collins argue that while the Sermon on the Mount is optimistic, it is also realistic in the sense that it recognizes the necessity of preparing for rough times.[187] Petronius offers the following adage. "'There's ups and there's downs,' as the country bumpkin said when he lost his spotted pig. What is not today, will be tomorrow: so we trudge through life."[188]

9.3. Yet, she says that being forced to borrow a garment, especially for a religious festival, was shaming. Outer garments for a person in the lower socio-economic segments of the population cost 12–20 *denarii*. In Pompeii, a tunic cost 15 *sesterces* to buy and one *denarius* to clean.

184. Moxnes, *The Economy of the Kingdom*, 95; Bultmann, "μέριμνάω," *TDNT* 4:589–93.

185. "By embracing scarcity, humanity burdens itself beyond the intention of the Creator" (Gordon, *The Economic Problem in Biblical and Patristic Thought*, 3, 11–14). He argues further that the approach to overcoming scarcity by observance of Torah overrode the importance of faith and trust.

186. Bultmann, "μέριμνάω," *TDNT* 4:589–93; Hengel, *Property and Riches in the Early Church*, 24. Bultmann casts his argument in eschatological terms. I lean toward the position of Oakman, who argues that this passage is not about "waiting passively for God's rule to triumph," but about "actively taking the leap of faith that issues in carefree dependence upon God's beneficence" (*Jesus and the Economic Questions*, 160). The question is, how carefree? I do not accept Hengel's more radical position of renunciation of all care and, perhaps, possessions.

187. Betz and Collins, *Sermon on the Mount*, 61.

188. Petronius, 1.9.45 (Heseltine, LCL).

Members of the Matthean community are not to hoard[189] their dwindling food supplies either, but rely on neighbors and the blessings of God who brings the rain and sun. The message indicates "the possibility for a full and ultimately satisfying experience of life at the edge of subsistence." Struggling to seek the realm of the heavens brings the enjoyment of God's blessings.[190]

The interpretative keys for all members of the Matthean community occur in two places. The first key is the final verse of the logion:[191] "For where your treasure is, there your heart will be also" (Matt 6:21). The question is whether the heart[192] of the wealthy person resides in the dominant entitlement system in which wealth accumulation to maintain an ostentatious life style is a goal and consideration is not given for the needs of the lower socio-economic segments of the population. Is the grain owner willing to be part of the social safety network that was another primary survival mechanism? The challenge—and the second interpretative key—is to store up rewards in heaven by performing acts of charity and giving alms to those in need.[193] In Judaisms of the first century, this saying reflects a belief in an actual location above (or below) earth where good and bad works of the faithful are stored in an indestructible place.[194] At judgment, these *treasures* are testimony to use in rendering a just verdict on the person's life.[195] A similar teaching to the logion is Sir 29:10–14:

---

189. Surprisingly perhaps, the word translated *store up*, or *hoard*, is also in the food semantic field where it means *preserving* or *pickling* when the object is a food product. In times of food shortages, perhaps peasants would consider food to be treasures. Preserving and pickling are two methods that peasants used prior to storing their food treasures for the coming year. See the discussion in chapter 4.

190. Vaage, *Galilean Upstarts*, 61; Pamment, "The Kingdom of Heaven According to the First Gospel," 45–46. Pamment makes similar points such as a need for low valuation in the present, satisfaction of needs comes as a by-product of seeking, and the term *seek* suggests living with uncertainty.

191. Robinson, Hoffmann, and Kloppenborg, *The Critical Edition of Q*, 332; Luz, *Matthew 1–7*, 1:331–32. This logion is not unique to Matthew but comes from Q 12:34. Luz argues against the common view that this logion is a core wisdom saying. In its strong opposition to wealth, it differs from traditional wisdom. Luz writes that the message fits Jesus' social criticism. He writes that verse 21 intensifies the warning against earthly wealth accumulation of verse 19.

192. Carter, *Matthew and the Margins*, 135, 173. In the first-century understanding of body zones, the heart is the essence of a person. With the heart, a person thinks, knows, and wills into action.

193. Luz, *Matthew 1–7*, 1:332; Carter, *Matthew and the Margins*, 173. Luz suggests that the contrast between v. 19 and v. 20 suggests almsgiving and other acts of charity. Josephus writes that the Pharisees held a similar view.

194. Josephus, *Ant.* 18.14–15. Josephus reports that Pharisees share a similar view.

195. Betz and Collins, *Sermon on the Mount*, 434.

> ¹⁰Lose your silver for the sake of a brother or a friend, and do not let it rust under a stone and be lost. ¹¹Lay up your treasure according to the commandments of the Most High, and it will profit you more than gold. ¹²Store up almsgiving in your treasury, and it will rescue you from every disaster; ¹³better than a stout shield and a sturdy spear, it will fight for you against the enemy. ¹⁴A good person will be surety for his neighbor, but the one who has lost all sense of shame will fail him."

All members of the Matthean community must be involved in actively doing good deeds[196] (that is, the narrow gate of Matt 7:13). The alternative is doing bad deeds,[197] which spans storing grain for speculation to doing nothing to help another. Matthew's Gospel exhorts the auditors to do the will of God (Matt 7:21; 12:50; 18:14). The practice of mercy (Matt 5:7)—general reciprocity of the social safety network—is one way a righteous person[198] follows God's example: "He has gained renown by his wonderful deeds; the LORD is gracious and merciful. He provides food for those who fear him; he is ever mindful of his covenant" (Ps 111:4–5).[199]

As I previously argued for abuses condoned by the dominant entitlement system, physical hunger can be the result of social injustice as well as from a fickle climate. A person, or the Matthean community, who actively hungers and thirsts for righteousness (Matt 5:6) is to act to begin the way out of injustice.[200] They are to perform good deeds such as sharing of their dwindling food stores with a neighbor whose plots did not yield enough food. In the Gospel context, the principle of the Golden Rule (Matt 7:12), which ends this block of the Sermon on the Mount, is that if one has received God's abundance relative to a neighbor, one is to share what God has provided with others so that they have their daily bread (Matt 6:11).[201] The point is one should respond if one is just blessed more than another is blessed. There is no assumption that one would need to have received abundantly or would have a large surplus. All members of the Matthean community—richer or poorer—are to live a lifestyle consonant with the

---

196. Ibid., 61.

197. Ibid., 61–62.

198. Ibid., 133.

199. A common refrain attests to the LORD as merciful, gracious, slow to anger, and abounding in steadfast love and faithfulness (Neh 9:17; Ps 86:15; 103:8; 145:8; Joel 2:13; Jonah 4:2).

200. Betz and Collins, *Sermon on the Mount*, 129; Carter, *Matthew and the Margins*, 184–85.

201. Betz and Collins, *Sermon on the Mount*, 432. I am not arguing for egalitarianism and a leveling of social structure.

local entitlement system based on general reciprocity. When people—richer or poorer—hoard their food, they are in effect participating in the imperial lifestyle. In so doing, they will not be able to enter through the narrow gate (Matt 7:13).

Stored Grain Fed People

In times of extreme food shortages, the stockpiling of grain could work for the benefit of the lower socio-economic segments of the population. In such situations, the people expected members of the aristocracy to provide grain at a reasonable price, even when the local aristocrats were not responsible for the shortage.[202] Numerous inscriptions from the Roman East honoring the benefactions of leading citizens show that this expectation was often satisfied.[203] Yet, the motives of aristocrats were rarely altruistic. Pliny, the Younger, writes, "The boast of their good deed is considered to be the motive, not the consequence."[204] Some believed such acts could ensure against possible disasters of fortune.[205] Others had thoughts of immortality by establishing permanent annuities linked to them (for example, *alimenta* to feed children) that provided food, or other materials such as oil.[206] Normally aristocrats did not direct these distribution activities at the most destitute,

202. Hamel, *Poverty and Charity in Roman Palestine*, 219; Dmitriev, *City Government in Roman Asia Minor*, 24; Garnsey, *Famine and Food Supply*, 272, 243.

203. Dmitriev, *City Government in Roman Asia Minor*, 123, 224; Garnsey, *Famine and Food Supply*, 14, 261; MacMullen, *Enemies of the Roman Order*, 249–50; Liebeschuetz, *Antioch in the Later Roman Period*, 121; Di Segni, "Dated Greek Inscriptions from Palestine"; Lehmann and Holum, *The Greek and Latin Inscriptions of Caesarea Maritima*; McLean, "Epigraphical Evidence in Caesarea Maritima." Garnsey mentions Perge, Apamia, Epidaurus, and Megalopolos. The inscriptions cited are not from the Galilee or from Antioch. One should not conclude that the lack of such inscriptions in the Galilee or Antioch meant no such actions existed. There are almost no inscriptions of any type from the first century in Galilee. Liebeschuetz notes the lack of inscriptions in Antioch and its surrounds lauding benefactions on behalf of village folk. Di Segni and Lehmann each catalogue inscriptions from the Levant, but none of the inscriptions are for persons who provided grain during shortages.

204. Pliny, *Letters* 1.8.15 (Radice, LCL).

205. Hands, *Charities and Social Aid in Greece and Rome*, 78–79, 81; Harland, *Associations, Synagogues, and Congregations*, 100.

206. Hands, *Charities and Social Aid in Greece and Rome*, 37, 25,189–92. He catalogues inscriptions to this effect on pages 189–90. From Petelia in southern Italy: 138–61 CE, Dessau, 6468 (Duncan-Jones, *Historia* 1964, 199f). From Spoletium in central Italy: date unknown, *CIL*, XI, 4789. From Sillyon, Pisidai in Asia Minor: second century CE, *IGRP*, III, 801 (*BCH* 1889, 486ff) concerns a woman who gave money whose interest was "for the maintenance of children" and varying amounts of money for everyone including freedmen and non-citizens who received three *denarii* per person.

but benefits were extended to those who might be able to show something in return.[207] This inscription from the second-century addresses most of these points.

> I have left the aforementioned money so that those who are holding magistracies from year to year, when they also relax the rest of the public burdens, may loan it out, from the year of the generalship of Aristopolis, according to the resolutions of the councillors of the city and of the people . . . And this money is to be lent out and those who borrow the money are to give adequate security in land, so that from the interest oil may be supplied forever to the citizens of Gytheion and the non-citizens, and the magistrates and councillors are to display all energy and good faith each year, so that my beneficent act [*philanthropia*] may remain eternally for the gymnasium and for the city . . . I wish also the slaves to share in the gift [*philanthropia*] of oil for six days each year, three days during the festival of the *Augusti* and three of the goddess; and no archon or gymnasiarch is to hinder them using the oil . . . And I wish my gift and favour bestowed upon the gymnasium on the stated conditions to be published on three marble pillars; of these, one should be set up . . . in the market before my house, and one should be erected in the *Gaesareum*, set close by the gates of the temple, and one in the gymnasium, so that both to the citizens of Gytheion, and to the non-citizens, my philanthropic and kindly act may be clear and well-known to all . . . And I entrust to the city and the council also my houseslaves and freedmen, all of them, both male and female; and I beseech you, by all the gods and by the Fortune of the *Augusti*, even when I live, that, whenever I suffer the common lot of men, you may take the utmost thought, both individually and collectively, for the carrying out of my wish and for the houseslaves whom I honour and have honoured . . . My idea is to achieve immortality in making such a just and kindly disposal [of my property] and, in entrusting it to the city, I shall surely not fail in my aim.[208]

Garnsey writes, "Euergetism, the public generosity of the wealthy, was an institution devised by the rich in their own interests. As the grain stocks of the community were in their barns, they could time their release to suit

207. Hamel, *Poverty and Charity in Roman Palestine*, 217–19; Garnsey, *Famine and Food Supply*, chap. 5; Whittaker, "The Poor," 294; Longenecker, *Remember the Poor*, 72.

208. Hands, *Charities and Social Aid in Greece and Rome*, 206. Hands catalogues this inscription from 161–69 CE from Gytheion on the Greek mainland. IG V, I, 1208 (Wilhelm, *Griechische Inschrissien*, 90ff; Laum No.9).

themselves; that is why the same class produced euergetists and profiteers."²⁰⁹ They made distributions under different guises: selling at a lower price than could be commanded but still making a profit, public banquets and religious festivals, and the establishment of *alimenta* systems. A typical inscription from the first century in Epidaurus on the Greek mainland reads, "In marketing corn on numerous occasions, whenever there was need, he harmed his private livelihood for the sake of the good of all."²¹⁰ The praise and laud of the person's generosity could not be as jaded as Garnsey's observation because the city might hope that others would follow the example. "The link between this urge [for honor] and civic generosity is shown by the fact that the word originally signifying 'love of honor' (*philotimia*) early developed the meaning of 'public munificence.'"²¹¹ The inscription from one city made this point explicitly when it speaks to being known as a city of generous benefactors with *philotimia*.

> [B]eing unfailing in their devotion and ambitious spirit of service (*philotimia*), and in addition supplied a ration of corn for the people and for all those dwelling in Aigiale and for the foreigners lodging in the city, and, sacrificing oxen to Apollo and Hera, they provided meat and a feast for the people on two days, Providing all that was beneficial for the sacred gathering, with no thought for expense and in a spirit of ambitious service (*philotimia*); so that our city may be seen to honour men of ambitious spirit (*philotimoi*) and honest worth.²¹²

During periods of extreme food shortages, some cities would temporarily appoint officials as grain buyers (called *sitones*),²¹³ who were in effect treasurers in charge of property for the provision of grain during the shortage.²¹⁴ Examining inscriptions in Asia Minor during the Principate, J. H. M.

209. Garnsey, *Famine and Food Supply*, 272.

210. Hands, *Charities and Social Aid in Greece and Rome*, 183. Hands catalogues IG, IV2, 6S.

211. Jones, *The Roman World of Dio Chrysostom*, 20.

212. Hands, *Charities and Social Aid in Greece and Rome*, 186. Hands catalogues this inscription from not earlier than 50 CE located in Aigiale, Amorgos (Aegean). IG, XII, 389.

213. Polanyi and Pearson, *The Livelihood of Man*, 238. Polanyi asserts that this figure appears for the first time in 328 BCE, and is actually a three-person board appointed to purchase grain during a period of famine; LSJ, s.v. "σιτωνης." Word is a buyer of corn (grain); Danylak, "Tiberius Claudius Dinippus and the Food Shortages in Corinth," 232, 238. Danylak specifies other terms for this office such as *curator annonae* (curator of the grain supply), *praefectus annonae, procurator annonae, curator frumenti or rei frumentariae, curator annonae frumentarie populique,* and *curator frumenti comparandi.*

214. This discussion relies on two principal sources: Dmitriev, *City Government*

Strubbe found seventy-one examples spread over thirty-three cities, with no more than nine attested in any one city.[215] A *sitones* contributed heavily to the effort from personal funds. Being a *sitones* was one of the more costly *leitourgai* (public services) of a city.[216] The office of *sitones* gave the person very high social prestige and inscriptions sometimes indicate repeat providers.[217] Even people of modest means would contribute to the fund.[218] Men were not the only contributors. An inscription from Oenoanda tells of Ammias, a woman, who gave ten thousand *drachmas* to the city "for the distribution."[219] Legislation was passed to prohibit the funds[220] being used by the city for purposes other than for what the funds were designated. Arthur Hands catalogues the following inscriptions that speak of *sitonia*.[221]

> Early 1st C C.E.; Oenoanda (Lycia and Pamphylia); *IGRP* III, 493: He [C. Licinius Marcius Thoantianus Fronto] was town clerk, serving his native town with his heart set on honour [*philotimos*] and he was a Roman and a citizen of Oenoanda who served as clerk of the Lycian confederacy, *gymnasiarch* and officer in charge of the corn ration providing corn at [?] denarii; and he held the office of priest of the Augusti with his most distinguished wife, Licinia Flavilla, with all reverence and magnanimity, and he was in charge of the corn ration a second time, distributing [*epididonai*] to the citizens both from the public supply and also from his own supply in a most difficult time; and he contributed to a public subscription for a distribution of money, ten denarii to each citizen, so that all who dwell in the city share this benevolence, and in every office he showed his concern for honour (*philotimeisthai*).

---

in Roman Asia Minor, 122–27, 142–48, 224–33; Garnsey, *Famine and Food Supply*, 259–68.

215. Strubbe, "The Sitonia in the Cities of Asia Minor under the Principate," 99–121.

216. Liebeschuetz, *Antioch in the Later Roman Period*, 126; Dmitriev, *City Government in Roman Asia Minor*, 123.

217. Dmitriev, *City Government in Roman Asia Minor*, 224; Winter, "Responses to Corinthian Famines," 86–87. Winter discusses inscriptions in Corinth from the first century that laud Tiberius Claudius Dinippus for his multiple benefactions during periods of food shortages.

218. Dmitriev, *City Government in Roman Asia Minor*, 142. Not only did a *sitones* contribute to the fund but other people contributed as well.

219. Garnsey, *Famine and Food Supply*, 263.

220. Ibid., 264. Some of the funds were set up to distribute every year according to what the fund had earned in interest.

221. Hands, *Charities and Social Aid in Greece and Rome*, 183, 188.

100–150 C.E.(?); Iuvavum (Salzburg); *JOAI*, XLIII (1956–58), 52ff: To Marcus Haterius Summus, son of Lucius, town-councillor of the municipality of Iuvavum, *duovir* with power of jurisdiction, the people [dedicated this] to an excellent citizen for his relief of the corn supply.

A *sitones* managed and contributed to the fund set up to buy grain (sometimes levying grain from other landowners) or to disburse money in times of need so the poor could buy grain. If local grain stores were not available, a *sitones* would try to purchase grain nearby by activating existing formal and informal agreements with other cities and with private traders functioning as intermediaries.[222] Sometimes severe food shortages affected all nearby areas simultaneously, and a *sitones* might petition the emperor to buy grain from Egypt.[223]

As an indication of the severity and apprehension concerning famines, sometimes a city might have a permanent grain fund,[224] funded by voluntary contributions or special levies.[225] To enhance their reputations, aristocrats preferred to contribute when required by shortages as opposed to making periodic payments to a fund. Cicero writes, "We may also observe that a great many people do things that seem inspired more by a spirit of ostentation than by heart-felt kindness; for such people are not really generous but are rather influenced by a sort of ambition to make a show of being open-handed."[226] Regular and obligatory contributions to a standing fund would bring the contributor no credit and might cost more.[227]

Thus far, I have argued that during periods of extreme food shortages the general population would expect one or more aristocrats to make grain available within the usual range of prices. The city council would appoint a temporary official to find grain and release it so that rioting would not ensue.

222. Garnsey, *Famine and Food Supply*, 73.

223. Jones, *The Greek City*, 218. Jones catalogues CIG 2927, 2930. The inscriptions refer to *sitones* of Tralles who bought sixty thousand bushels of corn from Egypt with the permission of Hadrian.

224. Garnsey, Gallant, and Rathbone, "Thessaly and the Grain Supply of Rome During the Second Century B.C," 35. Garnsey cites inscriptions from ancient Greece in the *chora* of Larisa that indicate the establishment of a grain-purchase fund for which the man had been named treasurer (IG IX, 2,1029, 1093).

225. Jones, *The Greek City*, 217–18; Dmitriev, *City Government in Roman Asia Minor*, 142–43; Garnsey, *Famine and Food Supply*, 15; Liebeschuetz, *Antioch in the Later Roman Period*, 131; Libanius, *Or.* 27.26, 21.205. The only documentation for such a fund in Antioch comes from the fourth century. The lack of evidence does not necessarily mean the absence of such a fund earlier.

226. Cicero, *Off.* 1.4.44 (Miller, LCL).

227. Garnsey, *Famine and Food Supply*, 272–73.

Sometimes a *sitones* would use personal resources to effect the requirement, sometimes other aristocrats would be approached to contribute, and if not enough grain was available locally, the *sitones* would activate trading agreements with other cities, or might buy from grain merchants who had stockpiled their grain for just such occasions when higher profits could be made. For their efforts, the city itself and other organizations would accord the *sitones* laud and honor, often in the form of inscriptions extolling the actions.

Matthew and the Hungry Masses (Matt 14:13–21; 15:29–38)

With this description of interventions during extreme food shortages, two passages in the Gospel depict Jesus emulating the *sitones* role of the dominant entitlement system (Matt 14:13–21; 15:29–38). I argue that the two feeding of the multitudes passages[228] depict widespread food shortage situations to which the Matthean Jesus responds as a *sitones*.[229] The Gospel setting of the two passages gives hints of a food shortage situation, particularly the second narrative. First, prior to the first feeding story is a banquet given by Herod which would remove more food than usual from circulation (Matt 14:1–12). Second, in a food shortage scenario, crowds of hungry people indicate a widespread condition. Third, prior to both narratives, Jesus has been healing the sick, which is a Matthean addition to the Markan version (Mk 6:34) of the first feeding narrative.[230] Numbers of people needing healing can be an indication of food shortages since malnutrition weakened people leaving them more susceptible to disease.[231] Prior to the second narrative, the description of the healings expands

---

228. Anderson, *Matthew's Narrative Web*, 21; Carter, *Matthew and the Margins*, 327. Anderson notes that the repetition of the feeding story would emphasize its importance. The auditors would have increased understanding that the doing of the will of God includes feeding the hungry. Carter points toward my interpretation. He relates this passage with its imperial context in the sense that the feeding contrasts with the imperial economy, which does not ensure sufficient food—much less eating until sated. The contrast with the dominant entitlement system is enhanced since the first feeding story follows the narrative describing Herod's banquet.

229. I am not arguing that there is no Exodus or Zion typology in the passage or against the eschatological images of an abundant messianic banquet. These allusions can also be present. See, for example, the following scholars: Carter, *Matthew and the Margins*, 325–26; Davies and Allison, *The Gospel According to Matthew 8–18*, 2:566–67; Smit, *Fellowship and Food in the Kingdom*, 31, 225–29; Luz, "Intertexts in the Gospel of Matthew," 133. Luz does express some reluctance to say that the early auditors of Matthew would have been familiar enough with these themes for them to be an intertext.

230. Davies and Allison, *The Gospel According to Matthew 8–18*, 2:483.

231. Garland, *The Eye of the Beholder*, 21; Garnsey, *Food and Society*, 45–60; Carter, *Matthew and the Margins*, 123–25.

greatly to include people who would have trouble finding work even when they were otherwise healthy: the lame, maimed and crippled.[232] Such people, left unhealed and unemployed, would have less access to food, and would be more liable to die in a food shortage situation. The narrator pointedly says they are healed and capable of earning food, were employment and food available: the mute could speak, the maimed were whole, the lame walking, and the blind seeing.

Fourth, both narratives take place in the wilderness. The wilderness is the *Uncultivated Land*[233] where both urban and rural people in the lower socio-economic segments of the population went to scavenge when food was scarce. The crowds come to Jesus in the wilderness. In the first narrative, they come from villages, but in the second narrative, their origins are not noted, and the crowds may include people who were already in the wilderness. In the first narrative, the people sit on edible grass,[234] but in the second narrative, the people sit on the ground with no grass mentioned, which could indicate a temporary drought.

The cumulative effect of the hints in the narratives suggests that food shortages were the Gospel context. The second narrative indicates a more severe situation than the first feeding narrative given its greater emphasis on healing and the lack of grass. Further, Matthew 15:32 says that Jesus was concerned that the people had been without food for three days, and they might faint. Whether one takes *three days* literally, or as an approximate period,[235] the point is that they had no food and were weak from hunger.

232. LSJ, s.v. "χυλλός." This Greek word for crippled appears in the New Testament only here and in Matt 18:8. The definition for the word is *bandy-legged*; Davies and Allison, *The Gospel According to Matthew 8–18*, 2:568; Garland, *The Eye of the Beholder*, 34. Such physical deformities can be the result of malnutrition, particularly vitamin C deficiency. A person crippled in such a manner would find the hard physical work of a day laborer difficult at best. In general, Garland argues that an urban person who was lame would fare better than a lame rural peasant because more jobs that are sedentary were available, such as pottery making, leather-working, and metal-working. Nonetheless, opportunities for earning food would be limited.

233. See *Uncultivated Land* in the model description on pages 63–75. Pages 101–3 expands on its description.

234. The Greek word, χόρτος, in Matt 14:19 is usually translated *grass*. The LXX uses it many ways, but the sense of a food source is frequently present. In Matt 13:26, it has this connotation because it is what was planted. In Matt 6:30, it is what God clothes. Matthew drops the Markan adjective of *light green*. In the Markan narrative, the timing would be in the spring at the beginning the pre-harvest famine period. Matthew chooses to make the timing ambiguous; Heil, "Ezekiel 34 and the Narrative Strategy of the Shepherd and Sheep Metaphor in Matthew," 703. Heil brings in the parallel to Ezek 34:14–15, where God will shepherd God's people on good grazing ground on a mountain.

235. Davies and Allison, *The Gospel According to Matthew 8–18*, 2:570; Smit, *Fellowship and Food in the Kingdom*, 226.

As described above, in times of widespread food shortages, peasants had no recourse except to hope and pray for a *sitones* with the necessary resources to feed them until a better period when crops, or grain at a reasonable price in the cities, were once again available. The narrative indicates that the social safety mechanism of sharing food is not available since the crowds have depleted food reserves. In a Matthean addition (Matt 14:16), Jesus says the crowds do not need to go away and the disciples should feed them. The disciples' approaches to feeding a mass of hungry people are not viable. In the first narrative, even if some food were available, the auditors hearing this story know that the villages and towns would not have enough food to feed such a large crowd. In the second narrative, only the wilderness sources are available. The wilderness with no edible grass, cannot yield enough food for such a large crowd.

The Matthean Jesus accepts the role of a *sitones* to provide food to the crowds who are in need, probably serious need, of food. In both narratives, the disciples are willing to contribute what they can to the food fund: a little bread and a few fish.[236] Jesus, the *sitones*, asks a blessing on the food fund by God,[237] who has been known miraculously to contribute food in wilderness situations to sate people's hunger (Exod 16:15-18), contributes more than enough.[238]

What message would auditors hear from these passages? A common interpretation is that the feeding narratives foreshadow the Eucharist in Matt 26:17-30, although having eucharistic symbolism does not preclude the possibility that the narrative could be concerned with satisfaction of actual bodily hunger.[239] I argue that these narratives have eucharistic hopes without pointing to the banquet in Matt 26:17-30. Didache 9-10

---

236. Smit, *Fellowship and Food in the Kingdom*, 68, 71-72. Smit discusses the connection between the Elisha tradition (2 Kgs 4:42-44) and the feeding narratives. He makes two points especially germane for the argument in this section. First, the setting for the Elisha tradition is a famine. Second, he argues that the feeding story circulated without fish. He suggests that the fishes were included because fish was a common side dish and because it made the meal more substantial.

237. Davies and Allison, *The Gospel According to Matthew 8-18*, 2:490-91. They give a brief overview of differing interpretations of whether Jesus blesses the food or God.

238. This final point is a substantial deviation from the Exodus manna feeding. Exodus 16:17 strongly makes the point that just enough manna to satisfy each person was collected—despite some people trying to gather more.

239. Davies and Allison, *The Gospel According to Matthew 8-18*, 2:493-94; Luz, *Matthew 8-20*, 2:312-13, 345. Luz presents overviews of the *social* and *spiritual* interpretations, as well as the *eucharist* interpretation. He is more drawn to symbolic interpretations, but criticizes spiritual interpretations as missing the mark by distracting from God's concern for concrete, physical needs.

contains prayers that encircle a real meal reserved for baptized members of the community.[240] The prayers follow the Jewish notion that food was originally God's possession and so acknowledge food as a gift from God.[241] These prayers make no mention of the body or the blood of Christ, but concentrate the symbolism on food as God's gift in the feeding of the multitudes. "Just as this broken bread was scattered upon the mountains and then was gathered together and made one" (Did. 9.4). As discussed on pages 155–59, the Matthean community in Antioch suffered through a number of severe food shortages. No data relates how well they survived or how they survived. These narratives in their gospel suggest that poorer auditors might hear that they need to pray that God will miraculously provide manna[242] or anoint someone to act as a *sitones*. An auditor who is less destitute might hear that acting as a provider of food at any level is a righteous act in times of food shortages.

Summary of Two Sides of Grain Storage

In summary, I have followed up the argument of chapter 4 that storage of food products was an essential survival mechanism by arguing that storage of grain could cause food shortages or could alleviate severe food shortages. In the former case, large landowners and merchants would hold grain out of the local market with the intent of selling it for higher prices to an area needing grain. This withholding of grain exacerbated the normal condition of endemic food shortage for urban households in the PS 7 and PS 6 categories. If the prices rose too much from this contrived shortage, or there was no grain to be bought, the hungry masses often resorted to violence since peaceful means through the dominant entitlement system rarely relieved

---

240. Holmes, *The Apostolic Fathers: Greek Texts and English Translations*, 260–63. In the argument in chapter 5 for location, I noted that some scholars make a connection between the Didache and the Matthean community. A direct connection is not necessary to make this argument, which only needs to show that eucharist connected to the feeding stories was part of early traditions.

241. Sandt, "'Do Not Give What Is Holy to the Dogs' (Did 9:5d and Matt 7:6a): The Eucharistic Food of the Didache in Its Jewish Purity Setting," 223–25. I agree with Sandt against Kereszty, who describes this passage as exemplifying "the mystery of the Kingdom since the risen Lord himself comes to us in the Eucharistic assembly" (*Wedding Feast of the Lamb: Eucharistic Theology from a Historical, Biblical and Systematic Perspective*, 93).

242. Garnsey, *Famine and Food Supply*, 38, writes, "Manna is the classic wild famine food of the Mediterranean region, or at least in hotter drier parts . . . Neither the Israelites nor anyone else in antiquity (nor the Middle Ages) knew where it came from. The fact that it was often airborne, carried by the winds, added to the confusion."

the situations. The mob directed the violence at aristocrats whom it believed were holding back grain. Sometimes, owners of the grain would release it to avoid violence. The *agoranomos* could commandeer grain, but more likely, he would release grain and undercut the merchants. Occasionally the Roman authority would direct the owners of the stored grain to release it. In the latter case, stored grain was available for release when a famine hit the local area. The majority of the people assumed that the owners would provide grain. A special liturgy would be established, and the appointed *sitones* would administer a fund to purchase grain and provide it at a reasonable price to the population. The majority of the fund would come from his own resources, but others could and did contribute to the fund. The *sitones* was a highly valued and esteemed public service.

The Gospel critiques the storage issue from both sides. The Matthean Jesus tells wealthier grain owners that they are not to strive for (worry about) amassing cash through storing up critical grain supplies for speculation in order to maintain ostentatious lifestyles. They are to remove themselves from the judging game of the dominant entitlement system. Righteous landowners and merchants in the realm of the heavens would no longer participate in practices that wrest control of land from others, put many at risk of crop failures, and lessened access to food. In the same passage, the Matthean Jesus tells people in the lower socio-economic segments of the population that, regardless of what wealthier people do or do not do, they must share with an unfortunate neighbor from whatever they had received from God. They are to live their lives not letting worry about their base necessities drive them to hoarding what little they have but showing their faith by righteous actions. For an environment in which 55 percent of the people are living below or barely above subsistence, the message to them appears harsher than to their wealthier neighbors. They are the ones who have physical, life-threatening troubles today and may have troubles tomorrow. Yet, the attitude toward storage of food crops seems to be the determining factor. "For where your treasure is, there your heart will be also" (Matt 6:21). Their treasures need to be acts of mercy and kindness in the realm of the heavens. These treasures are stored up in heaven for God to reward them in the end. The realm of the heavens is populated with people who have faith that if they share what they have now that God and neighbors will reciprocate when they are in need.

Chapter Summary

The principal survival mechanisms for peasants were polyculture, storage of food, and social safety networks. The principal survival mechanisms for urban dwellers were social safety networks and being employed in order to have money to buy food from the various food establishments. After looking at land ownership and control in the first century, I demonstrated that as aristocrats took increasing control over land and crop selection, access to sufficient food for people in the lower socio-economic segments of the population was diminished. While noting specific allusions in the Gospel to practices that permitted aristocrats to wrest control of land, I interpreted the Parable of the Talents (Matt 25:14–28) in the context of the judgment scene which follows (Matt 25:41–46) to condemn people exercising such practices.

In the next section, I explored the storage of enormous amounts of grain, which both led to artificial food shortages and provided grain in times of severe, naturally occurring food shortages. For the negative side, I demonstrated that the admonitions in Matt 6:19–34 against storing up treasures and not worrying targeted larger landowners and grain merchants, but also people in the lower socio-economic segments of the population. Auditors would hear two distinct messages. As had already been demonstrated in the first section, one of the drivers for large-scale grain storage was the generation of cash. Wealthier people were to be less concerned about what foods and fine clothes fit their ostentatious life styles that required large cash expenditures. Rid of the worry about being judged, they could ease their drive for profits that were creating diminished access to food for many. On the other hand, the admonitions exhort people in the lower socio-economic segments of the population to continue to trust in God and their neighbors to help them when food is scarce. Similarly, they are to share what limited resources they have with neighbors. For the positive side of grain storage, I looked at the aristocratic roles to provide sufficient food. In particular, I discussed the civic role of a *sitones* to provide food in times of severe shortages. I noted two passages that re-inscribe that imperial practice: the feeding stories (Matt 14:15–31; 15:32–38). I argued that the Gospel depicts Jesus as a *sitones* providing for mass feedings for hungry people.

I have addressed scenarios that Matthew's Gospel critiques that deal with aristocrats using the dominant entitlement system to the detriment of peasants having access to sufficient food, as well as aristocrat and peasant relationships that provided needed food in times of severe food shortages. What remains is to examine the Gospel's position on the key social safety network that concerned peasant-to-peasant relationships. At the end of the next chapter, I will have addressed Matthean critiques of all three primary survival mechanisms: polyculture, storage of food, and social safety networks.

7

Not Enough Food and Social Safety Networks

I HAVE ARGUED IN the previous chapter that the dominant entitlement system most often caused problems with households in the lower socio-economic segments of the population having access to sufficient food. The exception was aristocrats taking actions to provide food during more severe food shortages. The practices described in chapter 6—polyculture and grain storage—were under the control of aristocrats and condoned by the dominant entitlement system. In this chapter, I turn to practices that were under the control of people in the lower socio-economic segments of the population and condoned by the local entitlement system. As I have argued on pages 108–15, a strong social safety network was the third major survival mechanism for both urban and rural households in PS 5—PS 7. For both urban and rural settings, the practice of reciprocal sharing and helping out of persons, or households, who were experiencing a downturn in their situation was a principal component of a strong social safety network.[1] As I have argued in chapter 4, the social safety network for the urban sector also involved the provision of jobs, which allowed a person to have access to sufficient food. In this chapter, I examine possible rhetorical messages that Matt 19:1—20:14 presents concerned with upholding the social safety network based on general reciprocity with its hungering and thirsting for righteousness that exceeds that of the Pharisees.

---

1. "Friends and neighbours were perhaps more valuable than kin, providing a readily expandable and also, to a certain extent, controllable support network, but they suffered from the drawback that they shared the same economic context as the person who might require help" (Meggitt, *Paul, Poverty and Survival*, 170).

Warren Carter has argued that chapter 19 through chapter 20 is a household-discipleship discourse.[2] He shows that, in the first century, household discourses typically covered four relationships: (1) husband—wife, (2) father—children, (3) wealth accumulation, and (4) master—slave. Carter links the topics of chapter 19 with the first three relationships: (1) divorce (Matt 19:3–12), (2) blessing of the children (Matt 19:13–15), and (3) rich young man (Matt 19:16–26). Matthew breaks the pattern with the insertion of the parable of the householder and the workers and does not address the fourth topic: master—slave (servant) until later (Matt 20:17–28). In Carter's approach, rhetorically the passages inform the auditors on proper household practices in the present and future transformative realm of the heavens. The context of food shortages does not negate Carter's analysis. It narrows the focus of the three areas to critical proper behavior within the extended household known as the Matthean community in times of food shortages.

Matthew 19:1, with the phrase "When Jesus had finished saying these things," indicates that a new topic is beginning.[3] Jesus leaves Galilee and moves toward Jerusalem (Matt 21:1). Jerusalem, as the seat of Roman power and the Temple establishment,[4] hosts forces that were responsible for lessened access to food (that is, taxes and tributes). Consequently, the narrative is rhetorically moving toward a situation of lessened access to food. The sequence posited below is but one of many scenarios that could be posited. It is based on conditions that existed in the first-century Roman East. Through a lens of food access, the cluster of examples beginning in chapter 19 could reflect situations occurring during more serious food shortages. "Is it lawful for a man to divorce his wife?" (Matt 19:3–12) could include divorces that took place during food shortages when the husband had little ability to feed his spouse or children. One could construe the ensuing scene as a situation when children of households no longer have access to food (Matt 19:13–15) because they have been abandoned by their fathers. Primary sources depict such a situation when soldiers abandoned their families. This situation was one basis for the practice of *alimenta*, discussed on pages 121–23. The third scene answers the question about how the community is to provide food for the children.[5] The rich young man volunteers for a

---

2. Carter, *Households and Discipleship: A Study of Matthew 19–20*, 19–22, 146, 152–57; Talbert, *Matthew*, 231.

3. Matthew uses such a phrase to close major discourses (Matt 7:28; 11:1; 13:53).

4. Herzog, *Jesus, Justice, and the Reign of God*, 112–22, 142. Herzog has a succinct discussion of the business practices of the Temple establishment that contributed to increasing economic pressures on the peasants, including those of Galilee, and to decreasing access to food.

5. Talbert, *Matthew*, 232. Talbert argues that children are not used here symbolically,

one-time solution of *alimenta* instead of discipleship that requires a major lifestyle change (Matt 19:16–22). The Parable of the Householder and Workers (Matt 20:1–14)[6] provides a critique of an unacceptable breakdown of the social safety network for the urban population.[7] One of its messages could be that the solution to both wives and children having access to food is for the husbands and fathers to have a way in which to acquire enough food for their households.

Space does not permit a full examination of each of these passages. I briefly touch on the passage dealing with divorce. I connect the passage concerned with Jesus blessing the children to the encounter with the rich young man as a rejection of the imperial *alimenta* schemes. I go into more depth with the parable and argue that the parable reinforces the pragmatic[8] notion that a householder should provide work for unemployed day laborers so that they can have access to food. Further, the parable condemns a weakening of the social safety network expressed by one worker, who represents a group of workers, wanting access to more food at the expense of needier neighbors who would go hungry.[9] A strong social network can ease

---

but they are a group within the household needing special care.

6. Carter, *Households and Discipleship: A Study of Matthew 19–20*, 151; Davies and Allison, *The Gospel According to Matthew 8–18*, 2, 69n21; Jones, *The Matthean Parables: A Literary and Historical Commentary*, 418, 421. Usually the title of the parable emphasizes either the householder or the workers depending on whom a scholar views as the principal character. In his analysis of the parable and especially movement of characters, Carter argues for the householder being the focus of the narrative. Some more recent scholarship argues that this parable should be classified as either complex or epic. Both classifications involve multiple principal characters and multiple points to the parable (that is, both the householder and the workers are principal characters).

7. Luz, *Matthew 8–20*, 2:530. Luz argues unconvincingly for a non-urban setting based on the householder doing the hiring.

8. "Notwithstanding the enormous volume and complexity of modern parables research, any discussion of specific parables must begin with the simple observation that their purpose is essentially pragmatic. Nowhere is this clearer than in the case of parables that specifically focus on discipleship. For whether at the level of their original audience, in the context of the Gospel writers and the audiences for which they wrote, or as they apply to audiences of a subsequent age, parables are intended to provoke, to challenge, and to elicit concrete response to Jesus' invitation to discipleship" (Knowles, "'Everyone Who Hears These Words of Mine': Parables on Discipleship [Matt 7:24–27||Luke 6:47–49; Luke 14:28–33; Luke 17:7–10; Matt 20:1–16," 286]).

9. In a society based on the concept of limited good, all desirable aspects of life: health, food, land, honor, or power for example, are assumed to be limited in some quantity that cannot be increased. The companion belief is that any significant increase by a person or household in any such commodity was at the expense of someone else or some other household. "In a village, any significant improvement experienced by one individual or family was thus perceived as a threat to all others within the community" (Elliott, "Matthew 20:1–15: A Parable of Invidious Comparison and Evil Eye

pressures to divorce wives and not feed children or other weaker members of the community. The parable is unique to Matthew's Gospel and one could construe that it had an important message for the Matthean community.

Husbands Must Feed Their Wives (Matt 19:3–12)

I have previously argued that food shortages were prevalent and survival mechanisms worked better for some people than for others (see pages 124–29). When examining the question about conditions under which a man would divorce his wife, the interpretation changes when addressing a situation of a severe enough food shortage to drive a man to abandon his household.[10] That such conditions existed is confirmed by Gildas Hamel who reports on rabbinic teachings (*mTa'an.* 1.7; *tKeth.* 4.5) that permit divorce of a wife in times of food shortages.[11] Barry Danylak researched food shortages in Corinth and how they might be reflected in 1 Cor 7:26. He writes, "In addition to the explicit food references in the letter, Paul also mentions that 'in view of the present distress' (διὰ τὴν ἐνεστῶσαν ἀνάγκην), 'it is good for a person to remain as he is (i.e. in his respective marital state)'. In 1742, J. A. Bengel proposed the 'distress' expressed by the term ἀνάγκην to be the Claudian famine recorded in Acts 11:28."[12] Carter argues well that the eunuch teaching (Matt 19:10–12) is a continuation of the earlier advocacy

---

Accusation," 55). For succinct discussions of limited good, see Malina, *New Testament World*, 89–90; Esler, *The First Christians in Their Social Worlds: Social-Scientific Approaches to New Testament Interpretation*, 34–35.

10. Carter, *Households and Discipleship: A Study of Matthew 19–20*, 69–71; Fitzmyer, "Matthean Divorce Texts and Some New Palestinian Evidence"; Allison, "Divorce, Celcibacy and Joseph (Matthew 1.18–25 and 19.1–2)"; Wenham, "Matthew and Divorce: An Old Crux Revisited," 104; McGinn, "The Law of Roman Divorce in the Time of Christ." A food-shortage scenario does not influence main-line interpretations of this passage. Scholars, such as Fitzmyer, have dealt with this passage as conflicts of authority and interpretation between Jesus and the Pharisees. Others, such as Allison and Wenham, explore the issue of the stated exception to a divorce prohibition. Still another topic is Roman versus Jewish laws with respect to divorce, which is the approach of McGinn.

11. Hamel, *Poverty and Charity in Roman Palestine*, 48; Steinsaltz, *The Talmud: The Steinsaltz Edition: A Reference Guide*, 41–42. In general, in the Talmud, the Third Order: Nashim (Women) deals with laws connected with marriage and the obligations resulting from it. Third Order: Gittin (Bills of Divorce) deals with the arrangements for writing a bill of divorce, handing it over, and sending it by means of an agent (Mishnah 9; Tosefta 7; Babylonian Talmud 90; Jerusalem Talmud 54).

12. Danylak, "Tiberius Claudius Dinippus and the Food Shortages in Corinth," 233. Danylak is citing Bengel, *Gnomon of the New Testament*, 3:251, to which I do not have access.

for permanent marriage relationships based on mutual loyalty and unity of partners (Matt 19:3-9). In such a marriage relationship, a man would not intentionally put his wife, or children, in a position of not having enough food. However, apparently not all men were so committed.

Not *Alimenta* for Hungry Children (Matt 19:13-24)

This passage has no overt message about food access. Simply put, unspecified people bring little children to Jesus hoping that he will lay hands on them and pray over them. The disciples try to stop the procession; Jesus admonishes the disciples; and then lays hands on the children. Jesus does not pray for them or give them food, but he does lay hands on them, while attesting to their properly being members of the realm of the heavens. In the realm of the heavens, people are to have enough to eat and, hence, so should children. The question for the community was how to feed the children in their situation of on-going endemic food shortages with sporadic severe food shortages. Jesus has the ability to feed them miraculously (Matt 14:13-21; 15:32-39), but in the narrative he has begun his journey to Jerusalem. He will be executed there, but the realm of the heavens will need to feed hungry children. The ensuing two passages address two solutions: wealthy aristocrats providing the food (Matt 19:16-22) through *alimenta* schemes or jobs being available for anyone (Matt 20:1-16). In the latter case, maybe the husband and father would not need to divorce and abandon his family.

I have previously argued that *alimenta* schemes were one way in which aristocrats provided food for children (see pages 121-23). Such schemes were most prevalent in rural areas with large numbers of tenants who were having problems living above subsistence level.[13] The Roman emperor Nerva used *alimenta* in a campaign to revive rural life and feed children, whom the empire needed to grow to adulthood.[14] The practice of feeding children gained preeminence in the time of the emperor Trajan,[15] whose statue in the Roman Forum has him seated on a platform with two children before him.[16] What

---

13. Foxhall, "The Dependent Tenant: Land Leasing and Labour in Italy and Greece," 104; Lewis and Reinhold, *Roman Civilization*, 2:255.

14. Garnsey and Woolf, "Patronage of the Rural Poor in the Roman World," 161; Grimshaw, "Luke's Market Exchange District," 38; Clark, "SPES in the Later Imperial Cult," 318.

15. Bennett, *Trajan: Optimus Princeps: A Life and Times*, 121; Smit, *Fellowship and Food in the Kingdom*, 68; Clark, "SPES in the Later Imperial Cult," 315. Providing sufficient food to its people was a primary function of a deity or its representative: the Roman emperor.

16. Hands, *Charities and Social Aid in Greece and Rome*, 109-10, esp. 110

is most germane to the Matthean passage is the image of *alimenta* on coins. There is a strong parallel between the image Matthew depicts and the image on coins. Coin images likewise depicted a Roman emperor receiving children so he can bless them with food.[17] Harold Mattingly catalogues the following three coins depicting *alimenta* practices.

Figure 13. Coins depicting emperors and *alimenta*

The leftmost coin commemorates Trajan's concern for Italian orphans. It is a typical *alimenta* coin. Such coins refer to charity and serve to encourage the nurture of children. The middle coin is a *Libertas Restitua* coin that depicts women presenting their children to the emperor Trajan. The depiction could involve the approval of children of mixed marriages with Roman soldiers abandoned by their fathers, but Mattingly notes that the type is of *alimenta* coins of Trajan.[18] The liberty of *Libertas Restitua* involves freedom from want, including freedom from hunger.[19] The rightmost coin depicts the influence Trajan's *alimenta* practices had on others. Mattingly describes it as "A rare and beautiful *aureus* of the deified Faustina I records the granting of a charter by her husband to the 'Puella Faustinianae,' orphan girls for whom he provided in her honor."[20] Pliny extols the emperor for being the means of caring for impoverished children.[21]

> And so nothing in your generosity commands my admiration so much as the fact that these donations and allowances are paid from your own purse, so that the nation's children are not fed like wild beasts' cubs on blood and slaughter; and what is most

---

17. Ibid., 109–10.

18. Mattingly, *Roman Coins: From the Earliest Times to the Fall of the Western Empire*, 166. Mattingly writes that an alternative explanation concerns whether the Emperor would care for children left behind by their fathers.

19. Hands, *Charities and Social Aid in Greece and Rome*, 110.

20. Mattingly, *Roman Coins: From the Earliest Times to the Fall of the Western Empire*, 166, Plate XLV. The leftmost coin is XLV 9; middle, XLV 10; rightmost, XLV 14. I also found similar coin images for Galba and Nerva on internet sites dealing with ancient coins.

21. Pliny, *Panegyricus* 28.26–27 (Radice, LCL).

> welcome to the recipient is his knowledge that no one has been robbed to provide for him, that there is one alone who is the poorer for so many thus enriched—his prince. And perhaps not even he—for anyone with a share in a common wealth is as rich or as poor as the whole.
>
> Let the gods only grant you, Caesar, the long life which you deserve and preserve the spirit you owe to them, and the lists of children entered at your bidding will ever multiply! These grow increasingly day by day, not so much because parents care more for children, as because every citizen is cared for by his prince. Go on with subsidies and allowances if it is your wish; but the true reason for these births lies in yourself.

Pliny also donated one-half million sesterces to set up such a fund.[22] The motive behind the schemes was sometimes to bring immortal life to the donor in the sense of perpetual public honor for him or her.

The passage (Matt 19:13) reflects these images in that the children are brought to Jesus. The verb indicates the people bringing the children were intending for Jesus to use his power and favor on behalf of the children. The Gospel attests the authority of Jesus to determine human destiny,[23] not unlike the Roman emperor. The intent was for Jesus to lay his hands on the children (perhaps heal as in Matt 8:3, 15; 9:18, 25) and pray over them. Matthew's Gospel has Jesus himself praying when he feeds hungry people (Matt 14:18–19; 15:36), but does not have him praying over the children. Matthew's gospel does not indicate that the children received food leaving the auditors to question how their children are to eat.

Immediately, the narrative continues[24] when a wealthy, young man[25] poses the question, "What good thing must I do (make) to possess everlasting life?" (Matt 19:16). Matthew varies from the Markan (Mk 10:17) and Lukan (Lk 18:18) version of this question. First, Matthew attaches the adjective *good* to the thing to be done or made. Second, Matthew phrases the goal

---

22. Garnsey, *Famine and Food Supply*, 262.

23. Carter, *Households and Discipleship: A Study of Matthew 19–20*, 93.

24. Not all scholars keep these passages together. See, for example, Carter, *Households and Discipleship: A Study of Matthew 19–20*, 116–17. Even if the topic has now shifted to a householder's approach to wealth and away from the householder's relationship to his children, the narrative can continue the argument. Gundry, on the other hand, argues for the two passages being united based on the theme of accepting young people in the church. *Handbook for a Mixed Church*, 383–91. I disagree with his basis for uniting the two passages.

25. Clark, "SPES in the Later Imperial Cult," 315. Clark argues that Vespasian associated imperial hope of freedom from want with youth. Symbolically, the wealthy young man may also represent the Roman emperor.

in economic terms using ἔχω, which has as its principal meaning to possess property, with its object ζωή. ζωή has three meanings: (1) one's property or substance, (2) physical life, and (3) way of life.[26] Hearing the question in physical and pragmatic terms, the auditors might perceive their prayers to be answered and would respond, "Set up an *alimenta* to feed our children and we will honor your memory forever." However, this is not the answer that Jesus gives.

In response to the young man's question concerning what single deed he needs to perform to achieve everlasting life, Jesus shifts the answer away from a one-time event to what it takes to live a full, perfect life.[27] Jesus turns the dialog from a thing being good to emulating God who is good. Jesus enumerates continual participation in upholding the Decalogue and its commandments to keep the community intact. Jesus summarizes the commandments as loving one's neighbor as oneself, which hearkens back to Matt 7:12, the Golden Rule.[28] The young man claims to have followed the commandments to not murder, steal, bear false witness, and love his neighbor. But, he is so ensconced in the dominant entitlement system that he does not recognize that his actions which permitted him to amass his possessions would have led to people dying from starvation, others having their land stolen through debt,[29] taxes, courts (false witness), and strong-arm tactics.[30]

26. LSJ, s.v. "ἔχω" and "ζωή."

27. Carter, *The Roman Empire and the New Testament*, 101; Carter, *Matthew and the Margins*, 389; Davies and Allison, *The Gospel According to Matthew 19–28*, 3:48. Carter elaborates these terms as being synonyms for *eternal life*. Davies and Allison suggest that *perfect* here implies completeness of obedience. Having previously argued that the kingdom of heaven is a *place*, Pamment takes a different approach and argues that the question is "synonymous with: How shall I enter the kingdom of heaven?" ("The Kingdom of Heaven According to the First Gospel," 224).

28. In the discussion above, Matt 7:12 has been associated with attitudes toward material possessions when neighbors do not even have minimal food on which to survive.

29. Josephus, *J.W.* 2.425–29; Bennett, *Trajan: Optimus Princeps: A Life and Times*, 167, Plate 164. Josephus describes the burning of debt records during the reign of Agrippa. Bennett has a photograph of a relief showing the burning of account records in Rome.

30. See discussion above on abusive practices condoned by the dominant entitlement system. Carter, *Matthew and the Margins*, 388–91; Malina, "Wealth and Poverty in the New Testament and Its World"; Hengel, *Property and Riches in the Early Church*, 12–26. Carter writes, "In a world that understood, or at least in which the poor understood, that there were limited but adequate resources for all, one person's excess meant another's shortfall" (*Matthew and the Margins*, 388). For a broader discussion of the concept of limited goods in the first century, see Malina or Hengel. Hengel also discusses the demands of the realm of the heavens for freedom from possessions. He continues on page 24, contrary to my arguments, that also required is "the renunciation of all care,

The neighbor he loved as himself was his socio-economic peer. Further, he may have participated in schemes that forced loans on landowners and deprived them of their land and food on their tables. Why not do it again if it will give him perpetual human acclaim?

The Gospel describes the man as having many pieces of property,[31] which would place him in the higher ranks of wealthy landowners and grain merchants, some of whom set up *alimenta* schemes. Jesus suggests to the young man that he can choose to make a new level of commitment to God by selling some of his property and giving the proceeds to the poor (Matt 19:21).[32] As in the discussion above on Matt 6, if he does divest himself of wealth being his heart's desire and does give some of his possessions to the poor, he will have treasures amassed for him in heaven. Changing his ongoing approach to wealth accumulation and redistribution is more difficult than setting up an *alimenta*, no matter how beneficial it would be for feeding the children of the previous scene (Matt 19:13–24). The better solution is for him to quit participating in practices that force children to need food from outside sources. Giving possessions to the poor could involve not only redistribution of wealth, but also a move away from oppressive aristocratic practices. For example, as an alternative to taking away more land to set up an *alimenta*, or raising rents, he could return the land to the tenant. Instead, he leaves highly vexed[33] that Jesus does not honor his high social status. Jesus rejects the young man's offer of euergetism, despite people who need their children to be fed by someone. Jesus will offer a different solution for ensuring children are fed (Matt 20:1–16).

The pervasiveness of the dominant entitlement system blinded the young man to his responsibilities in the greater social safety network and his role in the breakdown of the crucial social safety network needed by the

---

complete trust in the goodness and providence of the heavenly Father (Matt. 6.25–34 = Luke 12.22–32). Service of God and service of mammon are mutually exclusive."

31. LSJ, s.v. "κτῆμα." The Greek word can mean *anything gotten* or *possessions*, but also means *pieces of property*. It is used in the latter sense in Acts 2:45 and 5:1. The only other place it is used in the New Testament is in the Markan parallel (Mk 10:22).

32. Carter, *Matthew and the Margins*, 389; Talbert, *Matthew*, 243. Carter sees this as an act of repentance, of restitution, and a re-redistribution where grain is returned to peasants who produced it originally and lost it to aristocrats in the dominant entitlement system. Talbert argues against the notion that the man was to sell all of his possessions.

33. Translating the participle as *vexed* is a better match than *grieving*, which has a strong connotation of sadness. In many of its uses in Matthew's Gospel, the word *vex* would fit the situations: Herod on killing John the Baptist (Matt 14:9); slaves over the behavior of the evil servant (Matt 18:31); the disciples both when Jesus tells them of his not being a Davidic Messiah (Matt 17:23); and the reaction of the disciples when they are quick to say that they are not traitors (Matt 26:22).

lower socio-economic segments of the population. Consequently, he will fail the criterion of Matt 25:31–46 (that is, providing food and drink) for entering the realm of the heavens. This passage is connected to the discussion above on Matt 6:19 when it mentions having treasures in heaven at the expense of treasures on earth. The heart of the young man is not in the realm of the heavens; he fails the Golden Rule (Matt 7:12); and he wants to stay on the path to which he is accustomed and which goes through the wide gate (Matt 7:13–14). The disciples are astonished that he, a wealthy man, will not enter the realm of the heavens. Their astonishment is a reminder that it is easy for members of the poorer socio-economic segments of the population to be taken in by the dominant entitlement system,[34] especially when it offers bandaids for serious problems that it creates and maintains.

Jobs and Sharing Provide Food for Everyone (Matt 20:1–16)

Scholars have interpreted and analyzed the Parable of the Householder and Workers (Matt 20:1–16) from many perspectives, as the approaches to parable interpretation have evolved and shifted and expanded. There is no consensus on the meaning of the parable.[35] I suggested above that the interpretation of this parable should be set in the Gospel context of a food

---

34. Carter, *Matthew and the Margins*, 388–91. The disciples would seem to follow the strand of Hebrew Scripture that equates wealth with divine favor (for example, Deut 28:1–48; Ps 1). Both of these passages exhort the idea of the two paths. It is interesting to note that in Deuteronomy the curse passage is substantially longer than the blessing passage. The curse for failing to do the will of God ends with God promising to bring in a foreign power who shall consume all food and drink leading finally to cannibalism within a household (Deut 28:49–57). The strand within the Hebrew Scripture that equates wealth to divine favor is strong but has counters such as the book of Job.

35. Luz, *Matthew 8–20*, 2:526–20, 534; Gowler, *What Are They Saying About the Parables?*, 1; Davies and Allison, *The Gospel According to Matthew 8–18*, 2:67–68, 71. Gowler's book is a well-written survey of the trends and issues related to interpretation of parables, as well as how parable interpretation coincided with Kingdom of God/Heaven interpretation. Luz, as well as Davies and Allison, presents succinct overviews of the various interpretative frameworks.

shortage scenario,[36] which is indicated by the abundance of workers, dearth of jobs, and the accusation of Evil Eye[37] at the end.

The dialogue with Peter sets up the parable. It concerns the rewards of discipleship exemplified by behavior similar to that which was suggested to the rich young man (Matt 19:16–22). At this point in the narrative, Peter exaggerates[38] that the disciples have left everything for Jesus (Matt 4:18–22) and questions what their reward will be. His question implies that he thinks that they, the *first*, should receive more than later disciples should. More wealth is apparently not the answer to how the first shall be rewarded. In the passage concerned with the rich young man, wealth as a sign of God's blessing[39] was not affirmed. Yet, Jesus replies to Peter ambiguously that in the end time, the twelve will receive great honor and all members of their households will experience abundance and eternal life (Matt 19:16, 25). Matthew inserts a free-standing logion that "many who are first will be last, and the last will be first."[40] Matthew ends the next parable with the reprise "so the last will be first, and the first will be last."[41] One would expect that

36. Dodd, *The Parables of the Kingdom*, 13–27, chap. 14. Dodd was an early strong proponent of using the first-century context and argued against allegorical interpretations. Although he advocated that the parables needed to be understood as Jesus told them in their original life setting, he accepted the idea that conditions experienced between the death of Jesus and the completion of the Gospels would have affected the original teaching. Snodgrass summarizes, with examples, approaches that include context in parable interpretation. He might label my pragmatic approach as a "Reduction to Banality" since he views most social-science approaches as reduction to simple interpretations and separating a parable from its gospel context. Yet, he writes, "The parables derive their meaning from Jesus who told them, and they cannot legitimately be understood apart from the context of his ministry." See Snodgrass, "From Allegorizing to Allegorizing: A History of the Interpretation of the Parables of Jesus," 16–28, esp. 28. As I have argued frequently, the context of Jesus' ministry was widespread food shortages.

37. "The situations in which suspicion of an Evil Eye occurs can variously include that of famine and the begrudging of food to the starving (Deut 28:53–57) and the sharing/non-sharing of food in general (Prov 23:1–8; Sir 31:12–31), lust after wealth (Prov 28:22), the miserly unwillingness to share with those in need (Deut 15:7–11; Sir 14:3–10, 18:18; Tob 4:1–21)" (Elliott, "Matthew 20:1–15: A Parable of Invidious Comparison and Evil Eye Accusation," 55).

38. "Both Jesus and Peter, for instance, have houses (8:14; 9:10, 28; 13:1, 36)" (Carter and Heil, *Matthew's Parables: Audience-Oriented Perspectives*, 126).

39. Malina, "Wealth and Poverty in the New Testament and Its World," 356. Malina writes that since the wealthy have access to earthly powers (for example, Joseph of Arimathea in Matt 27:57), people in the lower socio-economic segments of the population assumed aristocrats had ready access to God as well (Mk 10:23–24 || Matt 19:23–24 || Lk 18:23–25).

40. Hultgren, *The Parables of Jesus*, 35.

41. Knowles, "'Everyone Who Hears These Words of Mine': Parables on Discipleship (Matt 7:24–27||Luke 6:47–49; Luke 14:28–33; Luke 17:7–10; Matt 20:1–16," 302;

the intervening parable should shed light on the rhetorical message of the logion in its position in the Gospel. The parable of The Householder and Workers more fully explains what an equitable sharing of wealth looks like in practice in the realm of the heavens[42] where first and last (that is, prestige) should not be important.[43] What messages does the parable convey with respect to proper behavior and attitudes within one's social safety network while waiting for the end time?

I argue that the Parable of the Householder and Workers, when viewed through the lens of access to food, makes three points. First, wealthy householders should hire people who want to work, but for whom no jobs are available. Second, the wage should be at least the daily minimum wage so that they and their households have food. Third, all members of the community should participate in mutual reciprocity of sharing and not holding back resources from those who have none or little. These practices further the vision of sufficient food for everyone in the realm of the heavens and its embodiment in the Matthean community before the end time.

The basic narrative tells of a wealthy householder who employs day laborers[44] in his vineyard for varying durations of the day (Matt 20:1–7).[45] At the end of the day, the householder has his bailiff pay all the day laborers the same wage, and this decision causes serious dissension within the

---

Carter, *Households and Discipleship: A Study of Matthew 19–20*, 147; Carter, *Matthew and the Margins*, 394. The reversal in order of first-last and the double use have generated questions about who the *first* represent and who the *last* represent (for example, Jews—Gentiles or Pharisees and scribes—sinners and social outcasts. Carter notes the reversal motif at judgment if workers like the first continue to misunderstand the householder's actions. Carter attests to the parable being about relationships among disciples that has been shaped by imperial context.

42. Davies and Allison, *The Gospel According to Matthew 8–18*, 2:67–71. They present an overview of several interpretations.

43. Contra Carter, *Matthew and the Margins*, 397. I am not proposing equality. The householder remains wealthier than his workers do. All workers should be at least at subsistence level, but some may be better or worse off than others are.

44. Blue, "The House Church at Corinth and the Lord's Supper: Famine, Food Supply, and the Present Distress," 233–34. Day laborers were at risk of not having enough to eat in a good year (PS 7 and PS 6). In a situation of food shortages, they were at greater risk. A crop failure would cause landowners not to hire them since fewer crops needed to be worked. The day laborers would be without financial means to purchase food at its usual prices, and the price of food would rise. Furthermore, they probably lived in the city away from their families and did not have them for help..

45. Hultgren, *The Parables of Jesus*, 37; Davies and Allison, *The Gospel According to Matthew 8–18*, 2:73. Hultgren discusses various scholars' positions on the multiple hirings and concludes that it made a good story and set up the second half of the parable. Davies and Allison further note that explanations are just guesses and do not contribute to an understanding of the parable.

workers. The householder emphatically dismisses the dissenting worker(s) from the group (Matt 20:8–15).[46] Each part of the parable ends with a dialogue between the householder and workers. The key to interpretation of the parable are the two dialogues[47] and, in particular, the connotations of words used in the dialogues.

Toward the end of the day in the first part of the narrative, day laborers are still without work. One could surmise that those still waiting to be hired are those who are physically weaker or crippled.[48] Bailiffs and landowners would have passed them over and chosen workers that were more able-bodied. Consequently, they—and possibly household members—would go hungry, get weaker, and be susceptible to disease due to malnutrition. The minimum daily wage of one *denarius* would provide critical money for access to food for several days.[49] When the householder asks the remaining unemployed[50] workers why they have been there all day, they reply simply, "Because no one hired[51] us." (Matt 20:7) The narrative does not say that the

---

46. Harnisch, "Metaphorical Process in Matthew 20:1–15," 239. Harnisch is an example of scholars who divide the parable into three sections. He splits the second section between paying the workers and defense of the householder. I see the dialogue (that is, defense of the householder for Harnisch) as an integral part of the payment scene.

47. Luz, *Matthew 8–20*, 2:525, suggests that the length of the second dialogue in particular indicates that it "carries significant weight" in the narrative.

48. Ibid., 2:531. Luz surmises similar conditions. Yet, he notes that the narrator gives us no specifics, but wants the auditors to pay attention to these *last*.

49. I have argued on pp. 90–96 that scholars estimate 200–250 *denarii* per year to support a rural household of four and the need for more income to support a urban household.

50. The Greek word often translated *idle* is ἀργός. Given the context in the parable, a better translation would be *unemployed*. Other scholars concur with this position. Hultgren, *The Parables of Jesus*, 38; Davies and Allison, *The Gospel According to Matthew 8–18*, 2:73, agree, but write, "the only point is the men's availability." I disagree. Another major point is that the laborers had not worked and would go hungry.

51. LSJ, s.v. "μισθόω" and BAGD, s.v. "μισθόω." The Greek word is *hired*. Many words from the same root are agriculturally oriented and relate to leasing of land and tenancy. I take the position that μισθόω has a pragmatic sense in the parable; Davies and Allison, *The Gospel According to Matthew 8–18*, 2:71; Luz, *Matthew 8–20*, 2:531. Not all scholars share my position. For example, Davies and Allison lean toward an eschatological sense given the vineyard setting reminiscent of Isa 5. Luz argues against an eschatological interpretation.

day laborers came late[52] or that they were lazy,[53] but that no householder had hired them. So, the householder hires them (Matt 20:8), which leads to the first point. One trait of the realm of the heavens is that all who need work will get to work.[54] In the realized reign, householders of the Matthean community bring about this trait. They are personally to ensure the hiring of all willing workers.

The narrative specifies a wage only at the beginning. An undefined *just* (δίκαιον) amount is promised the second group, but by the last group, the size of the wage is a mystery. This progression related to remuneration heightens the drama and rhetorically pulls the auditor into the narrative.[55]

The second half of the narrative sets up the situation that causes the *first* to cast an Evil Eye on the *last*. John Elliott treats this situation in his excellent essay.[56] I summarize his arguments and context information here. A belief in Evil Eye was pervasive in the first-century Roman East (52). A person possessing an Evil Eye could through a look damage or destroy life, health, livelihood, honor, or well-being (53). The presence of Evil Eye tears at the underpinnings of the crucial social safety network (60). The Gospel raised the specter of Evil Eye previously in the Sermon on the Mount (Matt 6:22–23), where the Gospel indicates that the condition of the eye reflected the inner goodness or evilness of the person (Matt 6:22) (55). Immediately before this allusion to Evil Eye, there is the teaching that one stores up treasure (wealth) where one's heart is. The Gospel brings out the same connection in this parable when the *first* want to build up their treasures on earth, at the expense of others.

Envy was one of the malevolent emotions associated with Evil Eye. Envy was associated with resentment of another's sudden good fortune (for

---

52. Contra Harnisch, "Metaphorical Process in Matthew 20:1–15," 240. The parable does have details in conflict since the implication of v. 4 is that all who were standing there were hired. Yet, groups appear for the sixth, ninth, and eleventh hours. One might argue that the workers had been working their land and came later, but that scenario is unlikely if they needed supplemental income. Further, verse 6 says the workers had been there all day. Given the later dropping out of all but the first and last groups, the intra-inconsistency may not be important; Osborne, *Matthew*, 729; Kolendo, "The Peasant," 200.

53. Contra Jeremias, *Die Gleichnisse Jesu*, 33. Yet, Jeremias posits that the motivation for the full day's pay is pity for the worker's children who will go hungry.

54. Contra Derrett, who writes, "If charity had been his principal object he need not have gone so frequently" ("Workers in the Vineyard," 70). From my perspective, the hiring of laborers wanting work is not the same as charity.

55. Harnisch, "Metaphorical Process in Matthew 20:1–15," 240.

56. Elliott, "Matthew 20:1–15: A Parable of Invidious Comparison and Evil Eye Accusation."

example, a full day's wage for one hour of work) and an unwillingness to share with those in more dire straits (53).[57] In summarizing the writings of early Christian Fathers, Elliott writes,

> [E]nvy is displeasure caused by neighbor's prosperity, those equal in role and rank. It is aroused by a comparison of our lot with that of those close to us and sees their sudden gain as a diminishment of our status. It is resentment at not having that to which we believe ourselves entitled. Our envy begrudges both the good fortune of beneficiaries and generosity of benefactors although in actuality these in no way diminish our own condition.[58]

To avoid the appearance of possessing Evil Eye, a person needed to be unreservedly generous to those in need[59] (54). A situation that heightened fear of Evil Eye was extreme food shortage (55), which could be, as I noted above, the Matthean context.

Elliott argues that Matt 20:8–10 is the pivot point of the parable (60). By reversing the order of payment, the narrative creates the situation out of which evil-eye envy would arise[60] (60). The *last* and *first* are paid the same amount. The response of the *first* is one that many might *naturally* have in such a situation.[61] They believe that justice would require the householder positively to differentiate them from the late comers.[62] The response parallels that of Peter (Matt 19:27). Elliott argues that when the *first* focus on their perceived loss of status, they do not see the goodness of the householder (60) and experience evil-eye envy. The householder challenges the

---

57. Polanyi and Pearson, *The Livelihood of Man*, 61. Within a society that believes in limited good, the *first* wanting more pay would mean that unspecified others would get less. Solidarity of the community would be at jeopardy.

58. Elliott, "Matthew 20:1–15: A Parable of Invidious Comparison and Evil Eye Accusation," 59.

59. Cf. Sirach 14:8–13 "The miser is an evil person; he turns away and disregards people. The eye of the greedy person is not satisfied with his share; greedy injustice withers the soul. A miser begrudges bread, and it is lacking at his table . . . Do good to friends before you die, and reach out and give to them as much as you can."

60. Hultgren, *The Parables of Jesus*, 39. Hultgren argues that the contrast between the generosity of the householder and the evil eye of the *first* is coherent with the narrative.

61. Knowles, "'Everyone Who Hears These Words of Mine': Parables on Discipleship (Matt 7:24–27||Luke 6:47–49; Luke 14:28–33; Luke 17:7–10; Matt 20:1–16," 300.

62. Carter, *Households and Discipleship: A Study of Matthew 19–20*, 156; Carter and Heil, *Matthew's Parables: Audience-Oriented Perspectives*, 141. Carter explains the distress of the *first* in terms of their not accepting the householder's actions as reflecting justice in terms of equality and solidarity of the workers. According to Carter, they saw justice in terms of achievement. While his argument has merit, I find Elliott's explanation for the distress of the first workers to be stronger from a cultural perspective.

first to see that they are not on the receiving end of injustice[63] by asking a rhetorical question that expects an affirmative answer.[64] The accused householder becomes the accuser.[65] He addresses the first-hired workers with the term *friend* in a way that implies he is exposing an insolent and deceitful person.[66] He then hurls an evil-eye accusation at them. Its intent is to shame and discredit them publically.[67] In such a state, they would be pariahs to the community and unable to live within the community. The accusation is a powerful condemnation of Evil Eye. The second dialogue rhetorically causes auditors to question their own attitude toward what is just in their relationships with less blessed neighbors.[68] The expulsion of the *first* rhetorically avows that such behavior and attitude are not tolerated within the Matthean community. (61)

The second point of the parable is that all day laborers are to be paid more than *daily bread* (Matt 6:11).[69] They are to earn a full day's wages, which will provide food for them and their households for several days. Such actions on the part of Matthean householders should not be considered extraordinary and do not render them *more righteous* (Matt 5:20) than the official religious establishment.[70] They are no better than religious

63. Hultgren, *The Parables of Jesus*, 39; Davies and Allison, *The Gospel According to Matthew 8–18*, 2:74–75; Harnisch, "Metaphorical Process in Matthew 20:1–15," 241; Herzog, *Parables as Subversive Speech*. Davies and Allison note that the householder's argument supports both a legal defense and a moral defense. Harnisch adds that both arguments acquit the householder of brutal arbitrariness.

64. Carter and Heil, *Matthew's Parables: Audience-Oriented Perspectives*, 142.

65. Harnisch, "Metaphorical Process in Matthew 20:1–15," 241.

66. Hultgren, *The Parables of Jesus*, 39; Herzog, *Parables as Subversive Speech*, 92. Hultgren's interpretation contradicts that of Herzog who sees the term as feigning courtesy and as condescending.

67. Contra Herzog, "Why Peasants Responded to Jesus," 63–65. Herzog asserts that the workers believe their work has been shamed. Further, he argues that if the first workers did not grumble then daily wages would fall and plunge them more into debt. He argues that the owner's generosity is a figment of his imagination and he is a typical evil landowner.

68. Harnisch, "Metaphorical Process in Matthew 20:1–15," 245; Carter and Heil, *Matthew's Parables: Audience-Oriented Perspectives*, 143; Luz, *Matthew 8–20*, 2:526. Luz argues that by Jesus only speaking to one of the first group, the impression is the speech is to the auditors, especially the final question of v. 15.

69. Oakman, *Jesus and the Peasants*, 4. Oakman has an excellent discussion of the term in his chapter on the Lord's Prayer.

70. Derrett, "Workers in the Vineyard," 75–77. Derrett presents an interesting argument concerning the Jewish concept of unemployment pay. The gist of the argument is that if a laborer is employed "without a stipulated wage and the work takes no more than half a day to perform he is entitled, if he cannot easily obtain other employment, to a wage for the remainder of the day which is not less than the pay of *po'el batel*, i.e.

officials were in the near past. At the time of Agrippa II when the Jerusalem Temple construction was completed, Josephus writes that eighteen thousand workers lost work. While food was available, a famine ensued because people had no money with which to buy food. The Temple officials created public-works jobs and even paid a person who only worked one hour.[71]

The situation depicted in the Parable of the Householder and Workers is like the realm of the heavens. The situation exhorts householders and workers to sustain a strong social safety network with each participating in generous reciprocity as each is able. Such practices and attitudes are to be maintained in the realm of the heavens embodied by the Matthean community. Implicit in the teaching is that all can eat if everyone trusts in God's provision and shares God's gifts with others (Matt 5:42). In the broader context of the Gospel message, the parable relates to the sections above, which also speak of a combination of trust in God and of the obligation of one's neighbors to assist through periods of food shortages with tangible expressions of help. In its particular Matthean context, the parable warns against competition for favor and status—the dominant entitlement system perspective—especially in times of food shortages, which often had as their genesis actions of aristocracy condoned by the dominant entitlement system.

The Matthean Jesus further illustrates the point that the dominant entitlement system emphasizing status as material possession is not the answer by telling the twelve that he will be mocked, flogged and crucified in Jerusalem, but, on the third day, he will be raised as a validation of the vision of the realm of the heavens (Matt 20:17–20). Another teaching is required to reinforce further the first-last reversal of the dominant entitlement system in terms of political power (Matt 20:20–28), followed by the inclusion of another disenfranchised group that the community will care for on behalf of God:[72] maimed beggars who were blind (Matt 20:29–34). They would be among the first to die in times of food shortages.

To recap, the Matthean context indicates that the realm of the heavens depicted in chapters 19 is to have the household (community) intact with all members receiving food, food available for children, and food for the poor when food is scarce for all but the wealthy. Chapter 19 ends with promises of eschatological rewards for sharing one's resources instead of accumulating wealth or hoarding one's scarce resources..

---

he must not be deprived of a notional minimum remuneration." This minimum wage balanced "the social and moral rights of the employer and employee" (ibid., 76).

71. Josephus, *Ant.* 20.218–20.

72. Davies and Allison, *The Gospel According to Matthew 8–18*, 2:110; Carter, *Matthew and the Margins*, 407.

Chapter Summary

I have discussed three consecutive passages from the perspective of food provision and access in times of shortages for people who were weaker members of society: wives (Matt 19: 3–12), children (Matt 19:13–22), and barely employable day laborers (Matt 20:1–15). In each case, the scenes highlight the need for a strong social safety network. Husbands protect their wives, even if starvation is looming. Wealthy aristocrats do not take the easy path with grand one-time gestures that reap human admiration. Instead, they ease the tensions of too little food by providing it and by disengaging from the more oppressive practices contributing to food shortages. Finally, householders hire as many as they can so that the marginally employable and their households can have access to food. Members of the community who put themselves first—have an evil eye—are to be cast out of the community. Their attitude would destroy the social safety network.

At this point, I have contributed to an understanding of the complex web of pressures and practices that impinged on access to sufficient food by the majority of the people in the first-century Roman East. In particular, by showing that Matthew's gospel condemns practices undermining the principal survival mechanisms, I have shown that the Gospel is concerned with people having access to sufficient food. Moreover, understanding the two entitlement systems provides a mechanism both to interpret the power structures that were causing food shortages and to provide a better understanding of the two visions in the Gospel, namely: the Roman-Temple system and the realm of the heavens. Chapters 6 and 7 do not exhaust the passages that identify practices that helped and hindered access to food by the lower socio-economic segments of the population. With the hermeneutic demonstrated in these chapters, other Matthean passages would yield similar interpretations that deal with the pragmatics of food access.

8

It Is Important That No One Goes Hungry

I HAVE ARGUED IN chapter 4 that, despite the effect of poor climate on food production in the first-century Roman East, survival mechanisms enabled about half of the people to have access to sufficient food. There was a serious problem for about 30 percent of the population and a potential problem for another 25 percent of the population. In chapters 6 and 7, I have demonstrated that the Gospel portrays actions and attitudes that were undermining the survival mechanisms critical to the 25 percent on the verge of falling below subsistence level. The Gospel's critiques of these particular practices assert that God desires a more righteous and just realm than the dominant entitlement system. The question remains as to how pervasive the concern about people getting enough to eat is in the Gospel of Matthew. Table 2 in chapter 1 highlights the references to various food-access processes over the course of the entire Gospel. In discussing the table, I have noted that references to food-access passages comprise 30 percent of the Matthean passages. In this chapter I will demonstrate that not only are the references frequent, but that Matthew uses them in the narrative flow of the Gospel to exemplify the difference between the realm of the heavens and the dominant entitlement system. As I examine the narrative of Matthew's gospel, I will surface the references as they occur, which permits them to be seen in their narrative context.

In chapters 6 and 7, I have provided exegeses of a few of these references. It is beyond the scope of this study to provide an exegesis of each reference. On the other hand, connecting the references to the narrative flow enables one to begin to see how Matthew used the concept of access to sufficient food as one marker to distinguish the realm of the heavens from the dominant entitlement system.

First, I briefly link the Savior-Immanuel commission in Matthew's gospel (Matt 1:21, 23) to three questions that I propose the Gospel rhetoric will answer through the course of its narrative. Second, the majority of this chapter examines both the teachings and actions related to everyone having sufficient food that are portrayed in the Gospel. I examine the narrative and the role passages addressing food-access issues play in the context of the narrative rhetoric and the realm of the heavens. Lastly, I summarize the topic of food access in the narrative blocks.

Jesus, As Savior-Immanuel, Brings Access to Food

I have argued that the Gospel of Matthew fits comfortably into the genre of ancient biography, of which there were variations depending on the function.[1] I further argued that, like some ancient deliberative biographies, the Gospel portrays Jesus as the Greek ideal man. Jesus is the incarnation of the spirit and divine purpose of God's Law. I have argued that the Gospel is a rhetorical document *in toto*. The Gospel is not merely a chronicle of the life of Jesus but rhetorically conveys what the Matthean community viewed as the significance of Jesus as Savior-Immanuel (Matt 1:21–23). The rhetorical arguments are conveyed through the actions and teachings of the Matthean Jesus. I argue that one way in which the saving presence of God through Jesus is manifest concerns the issue of access to sufficient food for everyone in the realm of the heavens.

The Gospel of Matthew depicts Jesus as Savior-Immanuel, who shows mercy and compassion in the face of great suffering, including hunger. In Matt 9:36, Jesus describes the condition of the people in the lower socio-economic segments of the population as "harassed and helpless." They are victims of oppressive practices leading to poverty, malnutrition, sickness, and death. Jesus sends his disciples to tell the oppressed people, and by extension the auditors, an end is in sight for their suffering.[2] On the other hand, the auditors are also culpable. In the course of the narrative, the Gospel reveals *their sins* that need to be confessed and repented of. As I argued in chapters 6 and 7, their sins often include not helping neighbors get enough to eat, and non-actions can keep the auditors out of the realm of the heavens.

---

1. Talbert, *What Is a Gospel?*, 92–109, 124–27; Kupp, *Matthew's Emmanuel*, 56. As I discussed on pages 29–38 and 135–41, Matthew's gospel is principally a deliberative βίος. The intent of such a βίος was to provide a hermeneutical key for the teacher's doctrine. The Gospel also has a sense of judicial biography, which uses the true tradition of the founder as a pattern to copy. Kupp notes that the auditor never encounters God as a directly accessible character in the plot, and Jesus exemplifies Immanuel.

2. Carter, *Matthew Storyteller*, 125.

it is important that no one goes hungry 231

In this chapter, I argue that Matthew's gospel unveils, through the development of its plot, answers to three questions concerned with how Jesus as Savior-Immanuel is manifest for them. What will the realm of the heavens be like? What response is expected? What resources will be available for those making a positive response to assist them in living in the realm of the heavens until the return of Jesus? Adequate answers require the full story of the Matthean Jesus.

Analysis of Matthew's Gospel

In the remainder of this chapter, I examine Matthew's biographical narrative of Jesus as the ideal king of the realm of the heavens who is a model for anyone living in the realm of the heavens. I restrict the discussion to teachings and actions related to the theme of everyone having sufficient food. I use narrative analysis,[3] which scholars have applied previously to the Gospel.[4] This study has close parallels to Warren Carter's work in analyzing the Gospel as ancient narrative.[5] He organizes the plot of the Gospel into six narrative blocks and identifies a kernel for each block, which I use in my analysis.[6] Unlike Carter, I am overtly assuming an authorial

---

3. Combrink, "The Structure of the Gospel of Matthew as Narrative," 61-66; Kingsbury, *Matthew: Structure, Christology, Kingdom*, xiii-xx, 1-9; Carter, "Structure of Matthew's Gospel," 463, 465; Smit, *Fellowship and Food in the Kingdom*, 201. Numerous scholars have surveyed the work on the diversity of structures proposed for understanding the Gospel of Matthew and noted that no consensus exists. Further, looking at narrative flow is a better match for the analysis of this study. Using narrative flow permits one to overcome Smit's problem when he observes that the obscure structure of the Gospel prevents him from making general statements about the use Matthew makes of meal scenes across the whole Gospel. Rhetorical narrative analysis does permit one to make generalized statements.

4. Chatman, *Story and Discourse*, 20, 45, 53; Matera, "The Plot of Matthew's Gospel," 237; Kingsbury, *Matthew as Story*, Ch 1; Carter, "Structure of Matthew's Gospel," 463-66. A brief summary of the fuller discussion of chapter 2 will be of benefit. Chatman observes that *plot* is how an auditor becomes aware of what is happening. A *kernel* is a major event that advances the plot as well as raising and satisfying questions. Causality occurs between kernels. A kernel cannot be deleted without destroying the logic of the narrative. *Satellites* are events that fill in details. Finally, the plot organizes kernels and satellites into *narrative blocks*.

5. Matera, "The Plot of Matthew's Gospel," 242-52; Carter, "Structure of Matthew's Gospel," 467. Matera proposed a different specification of kernels and narrative blocks, but Carter's arrangement fits better the task of looking at the plot development vis-à-vis food access in the realm of the heavens compared to the dominant entitlement system.

6. Talbert, *Matthew*, 7. In discussing various structures for Matthew, Talbert observes that no one has used Carter's structure. My evaluation of the various structures

audience that has suffered through periods of mild to extreme hunger (see pages 155–59).[7] In this scenario, God's point of view is strongly oriented toward Jesus as Savior-Immanuel.[8] Carter emphasizes the imperial context of the Gospel, and I narrow the focus to food-access issues. The result is that we differ when positing possible questions generated in the minds of the auditors that the plot is answering. I am not suggesting only one set of questions is possible, but only that one can analyze the Gospel from different plausible perspectives. Below I delineate the narrative blocks developed by Carter. The left column presents his description of the narrative blocks with an imperial lens,[9] and the right column presents my description of the narrative blocks from the perspective of Jesus as Savior-Immanuel and the realm of the heavens in which people have access to sufficient food.

Narrative block one: 1:1—4:16

"God initiates the story of Jesus" who will "manifest God's salvation from Roman imperial control."	Immanuel provided food in the past and is now present again as Jesus, who meets strong resistance from the dominant entitlement system.

Narrative block two: 4:17—11:1

"Jesus manifests God's saving presence in his public ministry of preaching and healing" and "bringing into existence and by shaping a community of followers (Matt 4:18–22; ch. 10)."	Jesus' teaching and actions reveal the realm of the heavens as distinctly different from the realm of the dominant entitlement system. The basis of the realm of the heavens is mercy and trust in God.

---

indicated the Carter approach to be best for analyzing food access issues in the Gospel.

7. Chatman, *Story and Discourse*, 153. Point of view is the perspective(s) from which a narrative is presented. Chatman notes that different roles (for example, narrator, specific characters, implied reader) can have different points of view. Kupp writes, "Within any story, at the level of deep compositional structure we find a view of the world by which the implied author has shaped the composition. This may mean a single dominating point of view or multiple evaluative views. The implied author, the narrator and each of the characters are possible vehicles of an ideological point of view" (*Matthew's Emmanuel*, 46).

8. Carter, *Matthew Storyteller*, 106–15. Carter includes the Immanuel theme in relation to Jesus, justice, and the Roman empire. I accentuate the concept of Immanuel's justice having strong ties to people getting enough to eat. Carter discusses how Matthew established God's point of view in the opening narrative block. I make similar arguments in the analysis of the first narrative block.

9. Carter, "Structure of Matthew's Gospel," 473; Carter, *Matthew and the Margins*, 555–56. The quotes in the left column come from *Matthew and the Margins*.

Narrative block three: 11:2—16:20

"Jesus' actions reveal his identity as God's commissioned agent, necessitating a response from human beings, raising the question of whether Israel will recognize God's Messiah."

Jesus is Isaiah's Suffering Servant, who has the authority to ease the burdens on people who choose his realm and to condemn those who remain in the dominant entitlement system

The realm of the heavens is a place where people, acting in accord with God's will, are in reciprocal relationships, which ensures access to sufficient food for everyone.

Narrative block four: 16:21—20:34

"Jesus teaches his disciples (those who do believe and understand) that God's purposes for him involve his death and resurrection, an event that also shapes discipleship."

Jesus journeys to Jerusalem, the seat of Roman law and Temple practices condemned by the prophets, where the dominant entitlement system will try to destroy him. The path for members of the reign of the heavens is likewise dangerous needing increased faith and trust to withstand the forces of *status quo*.

The realm of the heavens is not like Jerusalem where economic practices and attitudes enable the strong to take advantage of the weak, who then no longer have access to sufficient food.

Narrative block five: 21:1—27:66

"In Jerusalem, Jesus conflicts with and is rejected by the Jewish leaders, and dies at their hands."

Jesus invades Jerusalem, as Immanuel who frees God's people from enemy forces, to retake Jerusalem for God and God's people. Jesus calls for the condemnation of all dominant entitlement systems that do not feed and care for all people. Jerusalem's dominant entitlement system now succeeds in killing Jesus and shaking the faith of his disciples.

Yet, the realm of the heavens in Jerusalem will again have a Temple where people receive food when hungry and are not robbed of food by forced homage to the Temple establishment.

Narrative block six: 28:1–20

"God's saving purposes are not thwarted; the resurrected Jesus commissions his disciples to worldwide mission." "His death (26:28), like his return (24:27–31), is part of God's purposes to save people from the sins punished by Rome in the fall of Jerusalem in 70 C.E."

Jesus, as Immanuel, will be with them until the end of the age.

Jesus turns stewardship of the realm of the heavens over to disciples whom he has taught through word and actions.

Having provided a synopsis of the narrative blocks above, I concentrate on the role access to food has in the context of the narrative. I only surface the references and do not attempt detailed exegesis. I spend more space on the early narrative blocks to demonstrate the overt and covert manner in which the Gospel entwines food access with the narrative flow. For later narrative blocks, I delineate the passages, but do not go into such detail.

For each section, I briefly review the plot development of the block. I present a list of satellites with a special notation (→) indicating which satellites involve access to food. As I demonstrated in chapters 3, 6, and 7, access to food involves more practices than feeding, and the noted passages might concern practices that indirectly impinge on access to food (for example, debt issues). I then briefly connect food-access issues to the narrative block, and where appropriate use a table to highlight how food-access issues provide contrasts between the realm of the heavens and the dominant entitlement system.

Narrative Block One (1:1—4:16)

The first narrative block initiates the plot, sub-plots, and themes that appear repeatedly in the remainder of Matthew's gospel. After establishing that God has been with God's people (that is, Immanuel) from the first covenant with Abraham, the stage is set for the beginning of the story. The plot begins with God orchestrating a new in-breaking through Jesus. God commissions Jesus to be savior and to manifest Immanuel (Matt 1:21, 23). With the commissions naturally come questions. What does Immanuel mean for the auditors? Repentance from what sins would encourage Jesus to save them from the oppressive conditions in which they find themselves?[10] Before

---

10. IDB, s.v. "Sin, sinners." De Vries elucidates seventeen Hebrew words for sin and says that his list is not exhaustive. Alienation from God is the dominant concept for sin. Further, most words have association with the penalty for sin. The leading term for sin in the Hebrew scripture, *hamat*, is the least theologically profound. It does include its penalty. Typically in Hebrew thought, suffering becomes the penalty side of sin. Relief from sin comes by confessing and by casting oneself on the mercy of God in an act of

providing any answers, the Gospel moves to responses. The first responses to Jesus are positive by Gentile magi, but negative by the dominant entitlement system. The narrative depicts God as being stronger than the enemies in Jerusalem (Matt 2:1–12) and Jesus stronger than the Devil (Matt 4:1–11). The narrative block closes (Matt 4:12–16) with an allusion to Isa 9. Isaiah 9 prophesizes that a child has been born to rule with justice and righteousness and to break the hold of the current oppressive realm. Exactly how this vision will become reality remains to be experienced.

S1.1	1:1–17	↠ Immanuel in the past[1]

K1[2]	1:18–25	• commission of Jesus
		  • savior
		  • Immanuel in the present

S1.2	2:1–12	• vs. Rome and Temple establishment[3] • foreign acknowledgment of child as ruler (see S1.6)
S1.3	2:13–23	• Rome as threat ↠ exodus to Egypt and return
S1.4	3:1–17	↠ Jesus feeds God's people ↠ Jesus as judge against those who do not feed hungry • God's acknowledgment

S1.5	4:1–11	• will Jesus be a proper Immanuel?[4]
		  • (vs. Rome)
		  • (vs. Temple)

S1.6	4:12–16	• Rome as threat (John the Baptist arrested)
		• Isa 9:1–7 coming of a righteous ruler (savior)
		  • oppression of Rome has come to an end
		  ↠ child born to rule with justice and righteousness, and there will be peace

1. ↠ indicates a satellite involving access to food.
2. Carter, "Matthew and the Gentiles: Individual Conversion and/or Systemic Transformation?," 140–41; Carter, "Structure of Matthew's Gospel," 473; Matera, "The Plot of Matthew's Gospel," 244. Carter argues convincingly that the kernel for narrative block 1 is not Matt 2:1a (birth of Jesus) as proposed by Matera.
3. Kupp, *Matthew's Emmanuel*, 61. Herod and the Temple establishment are the antithesis of leaders God intends for the reign of the heavens.
4. Carter, *Matthew and the Margins*, 106. Carter sees the question being whether Jesus will be loyal to God.

Food access is not overtly visible in the first narrative block, but is present in the Hebrew scripture references, as the following discussion elaborates.

trust (Ps 130:3–4; Matt 9:27–30).

[S1.1] The genealogy provides an interpretative framework[11] for the entire Gospel and prepares the auditors for the Matthean rhetoric.[12] While auditors might not hear food access, or the realm of the heavens, in the genealogy, both reside in the images evoked by the names in the genealogy. Not all of the people listed have any known tradition related to food access, but a sizeable number do.

Food shortages play a role in some of the matriarchal-patriarchal stories. When a famine occurred, Abram (Matt 1:2) abandoned the land to which Yahweh had led him. He went to Egypt (Gen 12:10–20) and made a series of decisions and took actions displaying a lack of trust in Yahweh's presence. Despite Abram's lack of trust, Yahweh's presence preserved his marriage and increased his possessions. On the other hand, Isaac (Matt 1:2) is faithful to God's guidance when a famine occurs (Gen 26:1–23). He remains in the land. Yahweh's presence rewards Isaac's trust and causes his harvest to yield a hundred-fold (cf. Matt 19:29). Jacob (Matt 1:2) presents a mixed picture. Instead of alleviating another's hunger, Jacob used it to take the birthright from Esau (Gen 25:29–34). Yet later, the narrative indicates that Jacob's success was due to the presence of Yahweh (Gen 30:25–43).[13]

In the book of Ruth, Boaz (Matt 1:5) is an early positive example of the crucial social safety network, with kin providing food for kin. Following this strong positive example comes a block of names that evoke images of times when access to food was compromised due to unjust rulers. Solomon (Matt 1:6) was the first of a series of rulers who behaved as a potentate,[14] much like the Roman rulers and governors, with oppressive practices that would

---

11. "Literary theorists have shown that authors 'educate' their readers to read their narrative correctly" (Howell, *Matthew's Inclusive Story*, 115). Consequently, this first narrative block is of critical importance in the subsequent interpretation by auditors of the Gospel. Green, "Introduction: Messiah in Judaism: Rethinking the Question," 4–5, notes that giving Jesus an "Israelite pedigree" and using a promise-fulfillment scheme casts Jesus as a "foreseen figure."

12. Carter, "Structure of Matthew's Gospel," 473; Carter, *Matthew and the Margins*, 55; Talbert, *What Is a Gospel?*, 106. In the conflict depicted between Jesus and the Temple establishment concerning who has the true interpretation of the Law and the will of God, the genealogy also functioned as a succession list to show that the Matthean community was the current, true child of God.

13. Westermann, *The Promises to the Fathers: Studies on the Patriarchal Narratives*, 129. Under the umbrella of Immanuel traditions, the promise of presence as aid is only found in the Jacob/Esau cycle.

14. Miller and Hayes, *A History of Ancient Israel and Judah*, 204–16; Carter, "Solomon in All His Glory: Intertextuality and Mt. 6.29," 3–25, esp. 10–13. Miller and Hayes provide a concise, thorough description of Solomon from a historical perspective, using archeological and scriptural sources. Carter also notes the negative image of Solomon and most of the kings in this part of the genealogy.

have taken food off the table of their subjects, God's people.[15] First Kings (4:4, 21-23; 5:13) describes thirty thousand people forced into *corveé* labor and out of agricultural pursuits needed to feed their households. Ironically, the writer of 1 Kgs 4:29-31 says God gave Solomon exceeding wisdom. Rehoboam (Matt 1:7) ruled more oppressively than his father Solomon (1 Kgs 12:1-14; 2 Chr 10:1-15; Sir 47:23), which would imply more seriously negative consequences on food supply. Ahaz (Matt 1:9) ruled during times of the prophets Hosea and Micah (2 Kgs 16:2-3; 2 Chr 28:1-3). The prophets condemn practices similar to those discussed in chapters 6 and 7 above that were taking food away from people (Hos 2:5, 8; 4:1; 6:6-7; Mic 2:1-2, 4; 3:1-3;[16] 6:10-13; 7:3-4). The next person is Hezekiah (Matt 1:9-10) whom Sir 28:21-23 describes as good, and 2 Chr 32:26-29 describes him as humbling the pride of his heart (Matt 5:8; 6:21; 13:15; 22:37). Hezekiah is also an immensely wealthy king who stored costly objects in treasuries, and stored grain, wine and oil in storehouses (2 Kgs 20:13). According to the chronicler, Hezekiah uses his own wealth for burnt offerings and commands his people to bring their tithes, which they did abundantly (2 Chr 31:3-21). God gives Hezekiah very great possessions because "every work that he undertook in the service of the house of God, and in accordance with the law and the commandments, to seek his God, he did with all his heart; and he prospered" (2 Chr 31:21; cf. Matt 6:19-21). On the other hand, Manasseh (Matt 1:10) is evil (2 Kgs 21:2; 2 Chr 33:2; Jer 15:4-11). Jeremiah 15:7 uses the winnowing image for judgment that John the Baptist proclaims Jesus will use against the Temple establishment leaders of his day (Matt 4:12). The third block of names (Matt 1:12-16) begins with a list of men who were associated with the Temple. Zadok (Matt 1:14) was an overseer of the Temple storehouses. His job was to ensure the proper distribution of the tithes of grain, oil, and wine (Neh 13:10-13). His sons became a Temple dynasty

---

15. Birch, *What Does the Lord Require? The Old Testament Call to Social Witness*, 68-74. Birch discusses royal ideal versus royal reality. He traces passages dealing with the ideal king, who is part of the Davidic messiah image. For example, Ps 72:4 says "may he defend the cause of the poor of the people, give deliverance to the needy, and crush the oppressor." Deut 17:14-20 permits a covenant-based king who is not to be exploitative (vv. 16-17), but after David this type of ruler does not happen. Birch writes, "Solomon brings into full view a royal reality which in practice produces kings who subvert the covenant for their own purposes of power and wealth" (Ibid., 70).

16. Brown, "Techniques of Imperial Control: The Background of the Gospel Event," 373; Carter, "Matthew and the Gentiles: Individual Conversion and/or Systemic Transformation?," 270. The passage describes the flaying of the weak. Brown mentions the actual flaying of enemies, though this passage is more metaphorical. In discussing Matt 9:36, Carter writes that flaying is a graphic metaphor for violent plundering. Plundering takes food off the table of peasants.

(Ezek 43:19; Sir 51:12). By the time of Jesus, the Temple was taking more food crops than it was distributing tithes.[17]

To recap, the genealogy hints that God was Immanuel for the ancestors when food was short and faith was weak. God was present through periods when people and rulers were acting in positive ways with respect to people having access to food, as well as when others were not acting positively. Given the inconsistency on the issue in the genealogical references, the Gospel leaves open the question of the stance that God will take on people having access to food.

Matthew 2 has no passages dealing directly with food access, but the underlying Hebrew scripture passages are replete with food images. [S1.2] References to Bethlehem (Matt 2:2, 8), which means "house of bread," evoke Micah 5:2, with the addition of a line from 2 Sam 5:2, with its shepherd theme[18] found in Matthew's gospel (Matt 2:6; 9:36; 18:12; 25:32; 26:31).[19] Matthew changed Mic 5:2 to say *rulers* instead of *clans*,[20] which links the reference more closely to the situation of the Matthean community, and places Jesus in conflict with Roman rule. The context of Mic 5:2 is important. Micah 4 portrays an image of Yahweh gathering God's people (cf. Matt 11:5; 15:10, 31; 21:14 where Jesus heals God's people in the Temple) in peace to their own lands. The restored people will thresh their oppressors (Mic 4:12–13; Matt 3:12) and the coming leader from Bethlehem will feed the people through the strength of Yahweh. [S1.3] Lastly, the description of the escape from danger in the Promised Land to Egypt (Matt 2:13–15) and then return (Matt 2:19–23) evokes images of the patriarchs and matriarchs who made similar trips to avoid famines (Gen 12:10—13:7; 42:1—46:34).[21]

---

17. Herzog, *Jesus, Justice, and the Reign of God*, 112–22, 142. Herzog has a succinct discussion of the business practices of the Temple establishment that contributed to increasing economic pressures on the peasants and to decreasing access to food.

18. The Temple rulers are often portrayed as the shepherds of God's people. In the Matthean context, Ezek 34:2-4 is a powerful passage that condemns the Temple establishment for feeding and clothing themselves while not feeding nor helping the weaker people under their care (see Matt 9:36). Yahweh accuses them of ruling harshly with force (like the Gentile rulers of Matt 20:25).

19. Davies and Allison, *The Gospel According to Matthew 1–7*, 1:241–44, 243. Davies and Allison suggest that adding the reference from 2 Sam more strongly links the shepherd image to David and away from Moses. The emphasis on David would fit the counter Rome context in this Matthean passage.

20. Ibid., 1:242. Davies and Allison note that the reference matches neither the MT nor the LXX. They suggest that perhaps it is not a quote but an interpretation. They do not make my inference to a possible reason for the change.

21. Jesus and his parents returning from Egypt might be an implicit reminder of the Exodus, during which God provided food for the Hebrews in the wilderness. This pivotal point in Israelite history and tradition is conspicuously absent in the geneology.

The implication of Matt 2 is that God will stand against the contemporary conditions of food shortages brought about by Romans and by the leaders of the Temple establishment. As in the past, God will be a steadfast (*hesed*)[22] resource to them in their trying times that include food shortages for many.

Matthew 3 and 4 indirectly address food shortages in two places. [S1.4] First, Matthew describes John the Baptist as the one spoken of in Isa 40:3. In its greater context, Isa 40 was to bring comfort to God's people who had been oppressed and put off their ancestral lands, much like many peasants from the first-century Roman East. Isaiah 40:10–11 says that God will come with might and will feed his flock like a shepherd. [S1.5] Second, the temptation scene begins with the observation that Jesus is hungry (Matt 4:2). He had voluntarily fasted,[23] which implies that the first temptation has to do with more than Jesus' hunger. The issue is the fact of scarcity of food and who supplies it and how.[24] Jesus quotes Deut 8:3 in response to the suggestion to turn the stones to bread. Ironically, given the pervasiveness of endemic food shortages, the context of Deut 8:3 is a warning not to forget God and God's commandments in the coming **prosperity**. Then there will be no scarcity of bread and the stones are iron (that is, not fitting for consumption but for agricultural tools). Moses tells the Hebrews that Yahweh led them for forty years in the wilderness, tested them by letting them be hungry, and then provided manna. Not only did they not have to worry about food, they did not need to worry about the clothes on their backs (Deut 8:4). Matthew later portrays Jesus exemplifying the "do not worry" teaching (Matt 6:25–35) and not acting for his own benefit as aristocrats do.[25] The use of Deut 8:3 hints at a new Promised Land where there will be no scarcity of food, if people will be humble (Deut 8:17) and keep God's commandments (Deut 11:13–17).[26]

---

22. Sakenfeld, *Faithfulness in Action*; Birch, *Let Justice Roll Down*, 151–53. Yahweh's steadfast loyalty, loving-kindness, goodness, and compassion combine as a strong Hebrew scripture theme (referenced over 175 times). Birch gives a succinct synopsis of Sakenfeld's extensive discussion of this difficult concept.

23. Davies and Allison, *The Gospel According to Matthew 1–7*, 1:356–59; Carter, *Matthew and the Margins*, 108–9. See these references for discussions of various positions taken on fasting and forty days.

24. Gordon, *The Economic Problem in Biblical and Patristic Thought*, 43; Hasitschka, "Die Verwendung Der Schrift in Mt 4,1–11," 488, 490. Hasitschka writes that the temptations throw light on God's relationship with God's people in the past when those in need called upon God in life threatening situations.

25. Carter, *Matthew and the Margins*, 109. Carter notes that the temptation is not about miracle working since there is no crowd to be impressed. Rather, the temptation is whether Jesus will act like a godless aristocrat and act in response to Satan's command.

26. Claassens, *The God Who Provides*, 16–17.

To recap, in this first narrative block, Matthew has indirectly indicated that God had provided food in the past through various means and had promised to feed God's people if they were obedient to God's will (Matt 1:1–5, 9–10).[27] God, through Jesus inaugurated a new realm of the heavens (confirmed in S1.6). Some people, particularly those aligned with the dominant entitlement system—Rome and the Jerusalem Temple—will oppose the in-breaking of God through his beloved Son, and God will condemn them (Matt 3:1–17).[28] Others will repent of practices and attitudes that do not trust that God can provide. God was and would continue to be a powerful source for the Matthean community to survive the oppressive situation in which they lived (Matt 4:12–16). The three important questions suggested above have been raised but remain only partially answered. (1) What will the realm of the heavens be like? Will people have access to sufficient food? (2) What expectations and demands will Jesus place on people who want to enter the realm of the heavens? (3) The third question has a preliminary answer. The mighty God of the past is still available to God's people today.

Narrative Block Two (4:17—11:1)

Matthew 4:17–25, with its emphases on Jesus' teaching, preaching, and healing activity, marks the beginning of answers to the questions posed by the first narrative block.[29] The second narrative block opens with a proclamation that the realm of the heavens is at hand coupled with a call to repentance and discipleship (Matt 4:17). The call does not specify from what the auditors are to repent. Yet, the reaction of the first-called disciples suggests an unquestioning and trusting response is required[30] for people who desire to live in the realm of the heavens. The disciples left the security of family fishing businesses,[31] that

---

27. "Obedience to the declared will of God is probably the strongest model for ethical obligation in most books of the Hebrew Scriptures" (Barton, *Understanding Old Testament Ethics*, 47.) See ibid., 47–54, for a full discussion.

28. Kingsbury, "The Developing Conflict between Jesus and the Jewish Leaders in Matthew's Gospel," 57; Kingsbury, *Matthew: Structure, Christology, Kingdom*, x. Kingsbury is an example of scholars who see the conflict with the Temple establishment as essence of the plot. He argues his position beginning with the observation that the Jewish leaders play a more significant role than the disciples play. For him the first kernel is the baptismal passage (Matt 3:13).

29. Carter, "Structure of Matthew's Gospel," 474.

30. "In 4:18–22, the call to repentance means leaving the claims and priorities of the economic and social worlds to 'follow Jesus' (4:19) as an acknowledgment of God's rule as the constitutive basis of existence" (Carter, "Structure of Matthew's Gospel," 475); Kingsbury, "Verb Akolouthein ("to Follow")," 58–60. Kingsbury uses two markers—Jesus offers and there is a cost—to ascertain if the verb, ἀκολουθέω, indicates discipleship.

31. Hanson, "The Galilean Fishing Economy," 100, 105–8. Hanson describes the

fed them (Matt 4:18–22) and their employees, for a more precarious life (Matt 19:27). The remainder of this narrative block provides more details both in the form of descriptions and actions of what the realm of the heavens looks like, and what responses are appropriate.

K2	4:17–24	• *Repent, for the realm of the heavens is at hand*[1] • calls disciples • preaching and healing is part of the realm • vs. Rome (demoniacs[2])
summary	4:25	• what does following Jesus involve?
Chaps 5 through 7 emphasis on things said[3]		
S2.1	5:1—7:27 Sermon on the Mount	↠ how does the realm of the heavens compare to the dominant entitlement system? ↠ discipleship requires taking positive actions that are anxiety producing[4]
summary	7:28–29	• people are astonished, but astonishment is not enough • Jesus has authority
Chaps 8 through 9 emphasis on actions taken		

S2.2	8:1–16	• heals leper with touch
		  • co-opt Roman military and heals by command
		  • eschatological banquet with foreigners
		• heals Peter's mother-in-law with touch
		• vs. Rome (demoniacs)

1. Powell, *God with Us*, 9. The announcement constitutes an essential shift in power. Satan and his dominions are unequivocally the enemy. The end game has begun and only moves to a different plane in the death and resurrection of Jesus.
2. Filson, *A Commentary on the Gospel According to St. Matthew*, 37; Hollenbach, "Jesus, Demoniacs, and Public Authorities: A Socio-Historical Study," 572–80; Malina and Rohrbaugh, *Social Science Commentary on the Synoptic Gospels*, 351; Hagner, "Matthew's Eschatology," 165; Carter, *Matthew and the Margins*, 211; Carter, *The Roman Empire and the New Testament*, 117; Sim, "Theories, Methods, Models," 94. Following the lead of these scholars, I arbitrarily declare any exorcism as being against the imperial rule of Rome. Authors discuss this topic in terms of behaviors of demon-possessed persons being a way to cope with oppression or to refuse to accept the demands of the dominant entitlement system. In *Matthew and the Margins*, Carter summarizes the claim when he writes, "To cast out demons is to defeat the devil's agents and to represent the defeat and rejection of Rome, the devil's ally and agent (4:8–9)" (211).
3. Davies and Allison, *The Gospel According to Matthew 8–18*, 2:36. Davies and Allison suggest the distinction between Matthean chapters 5–7 and chapters 8–9.
4. Kupp, *Matthew's Emmanuel*, 148. Jesus is personally present to release anxieties. Kupp references Deut 20:1; 31:23; 1 Chron 28:20; 2 Chron 20:17; 32:8; Isa 41:10; 43:5; Jer 42:11; 46:28; Hag 2:4–5.

---

web of political and domestic relations through which the Romans controlled the fishing business.

summary	8:17	• Isa 53: Jesus will not come through unscathed
S2.3	8:18–27	• not everyone who volunteers can be a disciple[5] • discipleship can be very dangerous • Jesus, not the emperor, rules the chaos of the sea[6]

S2.4	8:28—29:8	• healings
		  • vs. Rome and dominant entitlement system
		  • vs. Temple

S2.5	9:9–25	• co-opt dominant entitlement system (taxes) • new realm dawning based on mercy • Jesus has power to raise the dead
summary	9:26	• news of Jesus' power spreads everywhere
S2.6	9:27–34	• healing of two blind men who have faith • healing of mute demoniac (vs. Rome) • two responses: positive (people) and negative (Pharisees / Temple establishment)
summary	9:35	• Jesus in villages and cities—teaching, proclaiming the good news of the reign of the heavens, healing all diseases and all people who are weak (perhaps from malnutrition)

S2.7	9:36—10:42[7]	• Jesus commissions new leadership (disciples)
		• new leadership to heal and raise the dead
		• responses to new leadership will be mixed
		  • inhospitality
		  • danger—in the midst of wolves and own household
		  • do not fear any human (cf. Matt 6:26)
		  • must persevere in mission
		  • hospitality

summary	11:1	• (disciples go out?)[8] • Jesus teaches and preaches in cities

    5. Kingsbury, "Verb Akolouthein ("to Follow")," 58–60. Jesus extends an offer of discipleship to second person but not the scribe, and there is a cost associated with following in the second case.

    6. Carter, *Matthew and the Margins*, 211.

    7. Barta, "Mission in Matthew; the Second Discourse as Narrative," 530. An example of many factors contributing to the definition of kernels is Barta who conceives of Matt 10:5–42 itself to be composed of three kernels: 10:5–6 in which Jesus sends out the twelve; 10:23–25 as the turning point with new persecutions; and 10:40–42 as open-ended promises.

    8. Patte, *The Gospel According to Matthew*, 138. Patte argues unconvincingly that Matt 10:5–42 could not be part of a narrative because the disciples do not go on the mission trip and report to Jesus upon return. He argues that the section is pedagogical instruction to teach the disciples what to expect.

[S2.1] The vision of the new realm of the heavens begins with Jesus going up a mountain[32] to describe the new realm of the heavens in contrast to the dominant entitlement system. After the description of the way in which Jesus has come and the trust it must engender in respondents, a summary statement at Matt 7:28-29 has the crowd astonished, but unconvinced. The positive responses to Jesus by the crowds at the beginning of the narrative block are short-lived (Matt 4:22, 25; 7:28-29)[33] with a hint of more dangerous responses in Matt 8:17. This summary statement of pending danger is unexpected since the previous summary statements indicated the crowd moving toward acceptance. While the summary has to do with the response of people associated with the Temple establishment, a general response to anyone performing actions consonant with the realm of the heavens will be dangerous. Yet, the disciples are to rely on God and persevere in their mission. [S2.5] This dangerous situation occurs despite the basis of the new realm being a return to God's mercy, and reports of Jesus' incredible power to raise people from the dead spreading near and far. [S2.6] The healing of the blind men demonstrates the proper response to mercy is faith (see S2.1). Despite the doom and gloom portrayed in Matt 10:16-39, the Matthean Jesus concludes the narrative block on a positive note. Some will respond positively to those who carry on the mission, and the slightest response of compassion—demonstrated in the sharing of water—will bring eternal reward to those who receive the missionaries (Matt 10:40-42).[34] Jesus wants to show mercy and forgiveness. The realm of the heavens is to model Jesus' practices and be a place where acts of mercy help people obtain enough food to sustain their lives.

The table below shows the competing visions in this narrative block between the realm of the heavens and the dominant entitlement system when it comes to food access.

---

32. Levenson, *Sinai and Zion*, 111–12. Levenson writes about Immanuel and Zion, which is given characteristics of a cosmic mountain. He delineates four points. First, the mountain is where the gods come together. Second, it is "the battleground of natural forces" (ibid., 111). Most significantly, it is the meeting place between gods and humans and, hence, is the place where laws are issued. Fourth, it is where life-giving waters emanate. Describing the mountain this way, and not just simply from a Moses typology, emphasizes the notion of Immanuel with them in the wilderness. Describing the mountain this way also puts the scene in opposition to the Temple establishment, which claimed the Temple as the cosmic mountain.

33. Carter, "Structure of Matthew's Gospel," 476.

34. Barta, "Mission in Matthew; the Second Discourse as Narrative," 533. Barta writes that these sayings are precursors of final judgment scene.

Table 8. Food access in visions for two realms found in narrative block two

Passage	Realm of the Heavens	Dominant Entitlement	Food Access
[K2] 4:23	curing diseases and sicknesses		perhaps, sick from malnutrition[1]
[K2] 4:24	curing diseases, pains, demoniacs, epileptics, paralytics		perhaps, sick and in pain from malnutrition
[S2.1] 5:5	inherit the earth	dispossess people from their lands[2]	get back control of land and crop selection
[S2.1] 5:10–11	righteousness	persecution	righteousness and sufficient food are related[3]
[S2.1] 5:17–20	following covenant as expressed in Law and prophets		prophets: helping and sharing of food and essentials
[S2.1] 5:21–48	covenant goal is to aspire to greater righteousness (be perfect)[4]	debt imprisonment, false witness, strong-arm techniques, impress labor	social safety network: not participating in practices that took away land, access to food
[S2.1] 6:1–8	alms, praying		alms
[S2.1] 6:9–15 (Lord's Prayer)	access to sufficient food daily; no debt	temptation of dominant entitlement system; evil one from whom need rescuing	social safety network: access to sufficient food daily; no debt

1. Sen, *Poverty and Famines*, 14; Stambaugh, *The Ancient Roman City*, 135–37; Whittaker, "The Poor," 286; Garland, *The Eye of the Beholder*, 20; Garnsey, *Food and Society*.

2. Contra Pamment, "The Kingdom of Heaven According to the First Gospel," 216. Pamment claims that the Sermon on the Mount was given to individuals and would have no political message; Davies and Allison, *The Gospel According to Matthew 1–7*, 1:542, claim it is "impossible to empty the passage altogether of political meaning."

3. Smit, *Fellowship and Food in the Kingdom*, 210, 207. Smit references Jer 22:15 and points to the series of petitions in Matt 6:10–11 as an example of divine rule implying sufficient food. Hence, in Matt 5:6 with its desire for righteousness, the promised satiation would not be abstract but real.

4. "The thought that Matthew intends to express the demands placed upon the community members and the actions expected of them through his use of *dikaiosyne* has not been universally accepted by scholars. Some have sought to see the term righteousness as referring to a gift from God and not necessarily the behavior and response expected of a disciple . . . Matthew stresses the behavior and actions (praxis) expected of his community throughout his Gospel" (Overman, *Matthew's Gospel and Formative Judaism*, 92 (quote), 112); Pamment, "The Kingdom of Heaven According to the First Gospel," 214.

Passage	Realm of the Heavens	Dominant Entitlement	Food Access
[S2.1] 6:16–17		fasting for public acclaim	proper fasting concerns justice and feeding the hungry[5]
[S2.1] 6:19—17:14	no worry about food or clothing—Golden Rule	endemic shortages of food and other essentials	see pages 193–201
[S2.2] 8:5–13	all people are invited to a table fellowship where there is sufficient food[6]	impress, tributes of money and crops	see pages 156–58
[S2.5] 9:9–13	honest tax collectors	dominant entitlement system	see pages 168–87
[S2.5] 9:13, 27–30	merciful acts	Temple establishment oppressing people through tithes and offerings[7]	no debt leading to loss of control of land and crop selection (see pages 189–93)
[S2.7] 10:10	principle: worker should be fed	debts, rents, and taxes in-kind at threshing floor	residual after obligations may not provide enough food

5. "Look, you serve your own interest on your fast day, and oppress all your workers. Look, you fast only to quarrel and to fight and to strike with a wicked fist. Such fasting as you do today will not make your voice heard on high. Is such the fast that I choose, a day to humble oneself? Is it to bow down the head like a bulrush, and to lie in sackcloth and ashes? Will you call this a fast, a day acceptable to the LORD? Is not this the fast that I choose: to loose the bonds of injustice, to undo the thongs of the yoke, to let the oppressed go free, and to break every yoke? Is it not to share your bread with the hungry, and bring the homeless poor into your house; when you see the naked, to cover them, and not to hide yourself from your own kin?" (Isa 58:3b–7)

6. Carter, *Matthew and the Margins*, 203. See Carter for a discussion of other views limiting those who are invited to the table.

7. Herzog, *Jesus, Justice, and the Reign of God*, 112–23, 142–43; Anderson, *Matthew's Narrative Web*, 109. By using Hos 6:6, Jesus is accusing the Pharisees of being unmerciful followers of the Law which they do not understand at its core.

To summarize the table above, Jesus in the realm of the heavens is very active in healing illnesses and pain (Matt 4:23–24; 8:1–17 [3x]; 8:28–32; 9:18–35 [5x]), which could be related to food shortages.[35] Particularly important for enabling access to sufficient food is that people will get their land back (Matt 5:5). Social safety networks, renewed under the covenant as expressed in the Law and the prophets (Matt 5:17–48), will mean general reciprocity of the social safety network is once again working well, especially when one has temporarily fallen on hard times. Relief will be in the form of alms, debt forgiveness, and a minimum daily ration of food (Matt 6:1–8,

35. I have argued this point on pp. 87–90.

11). The realm will encompass acts of mercy to help, and not continue the heavy yoke of the dominant entitlement system,[36] which did not help the needy, but only enhanced the wealth of the ruling aristocracy. The Matthean Jesus has described a return to the trust in God and to a life in covenant with God and neighbors.

Central to the Mosaic Law is justice (Deut 10:12–21, especially 17–19), and covenant sharing with the needy is a key part of justice in the Hebrew scripture (Deut 15:7–11). Generically, justice is "the standard by which the benefits and penalties of living in society are distributed."[37] The Hebrew scripture strongly connects justice to the ability of every person—widow, orphan, physically impaired, foreigner—to be able to live (that is, to have access to sufficient food to sustain life). Bruce Birch writes

> Justice is a chief attribute of God's activity in the world. "The LORD of hosts is exalted by justice" (Isa. 5:16). Obviously, God is not acting out of some abstract legal norm to be administered. God is the source of care for the right of every person, and the giver of the law which seeks to embody that right in structures of faithful community. Thus, the context for apprehending the activity of God as justice is the wider covenant community.[38]

Jeremiah connects food and drink to justice and righteousness (Jer 22:15–17). The prophets connect God's punishment to the failures of justice. Amos (2:6–8; 5:11–12) refers to taking levies of grain among the sins. Micah 2:1–4 refers to seizing fields among the sins.

The lens of food access sometimes surfaces references that might otherwise go unnoticed. While not going into detailed exegesis, I will summarily address The Lord's Prayer, which I argue deals with access to sufficient food.

[S2.1] Poor, hungry auditors might hear the Lord's Prayer as speaking about their situation.[39] Their first—hence, important—expectation for God is that God's realm come and God's will be done on earth as it is in heaven. This

---

36. Carter, *Matthew and Empire*, chap. 7.
37. Mott, "Justice," 557.
38. Birch, *Let Justice Roll Down*, 155–56.

39. Ringe, *Jesus, Liberation, and the Biblical Jubilee: Images for Ethics and Christology*, 81–87, xiv. This interpretation is through a different lens than the massive amount of scholarly work on this important passage. I am not presenting a detailed exegesis, but illustrating again how the food-access lens can affect one's response. Supporting the view here is Ringe's work. She argues that the Lord's Prayer brings together Jubilee images of release, forgiveness, and good news to the poor. Earlier she notes that Jubilee included, among other items, cancellation of debt, restoration of land, healing, and food for the hungry. Each of these aspects contributes to better access to food.

coming will bring sufficient daily food (Matt 6:11).[40] Next, the auditors hear the Matthean Jesus suggesting the elimination of debt (Matt 6:12), which was a major cause of loss control of land and, hence, less access to food for many of them.[41] The temptation they want to avoid—and probably want their neighbors to avoid—is the lure of the dominant entitlement system (Matt 13:22). In particular, everyone is to avoid the temptation to hoard his or her meager supplies.[42] As with the psalmist, they want to be delivered from the evil one who is oppressing them and taking their land and food. "Rescue me, O my God, from the hand of the wicked, from the grasp of the unjust and cruel" (Ps 71:4). The wealthy were considered wicked and evil,[43] and the greedy, sick.[44] The auditors are sure that Jesus has the authority and the power (to be confirmed in Matt 8:23–34; 9:25–26, 28) to bring about these petitions. In the realm of the heavens brought about by Jesus, the auditors pray that food sufficient for the day can be available (Matt 6:11), if enough people do the will of God and the righteousness of those people exceeds that of the Pharisees.

To recap, the second narrative block depicts the Matthean Jesus performing physical healing as a sign of his power to reverse the consequences of the dominant entitlement system for some, namely too little food to eat (Matt 4:23–24; 8:1–17; 8:28–32; 9:18–35). The auditors get a partial answer to the question concerning what the realm of the heavens will be like. Jesus describes the realm of the heavens as a place where health for those in the community can be maintained when disciples re-enter the Mosaic covenant with God and neighbor (Matt 5:1—7:27). Jesus and his realm are about mercy from God and merciful acts by neighbors (Matt 6:1–8, 11; 7:12), which might help alleviate food shortages for neighbors. The responses are

40. Oakman, *Jesus and the Peasants*, 4, 199–242; Carter, *Matthew and the Margins*, 166–67; Grimshaw, *Analysis of Matthew's Food Exchange*, 54; Sahlins, *Stone Age Economics*, 215; Luz, *Matthew 1–7*, 1:321. A number of scholars note the obvious point that is sometimes forgotten: food requirements do not go away after a day in which a person receives food. The need for food recurs every day. Further, the word *today* is important because a large number of people in PS 6 and PS 7 cannot take for granted they will have food on any given day.

41. Oakman, *Jesus and the Economic Questions*, 72–75; Horsley, "Jesus Movements and the Renewal of Israel," 35; Hanson and Oakman, *Palestine in the Time of Jesus*, 153; Finger, *Of Widows and Meals: Communal Meals in the Book of Acts*, 104.

42. See pages 193–201 for a fuller discussion of the passage on storing up treasures and the detrimental effects on community.

43. Aristotle, *Politics* 1.8.12–11.13. Malina, "Wealth and Poverty in the New Testament and Its World," 361, 363–66, argues that "the rich might be presumed to be wicked on the basis of a series of commonly held, stereotypical assessments"(364). Malina discusses the concept of *limited good*. "The pursuit, acquisition, and maintenance of such wealth is inherently demented, vicious, and evil" (366).

44. Plutarch, *"On Love of Wealth"* 3–4 (524B-525A).

mixed. The first response of the disciples is the proper response of trust (Matt 4:18–22). The response of the auditors becomes less enthusiastic as the risks increase (Matt 4:22, 25; 7:28–29). Aristocrats who benefit from the dominant entitlement system will resist the move to a more just realm (Matt 10:16–20, 28–31). Both Jesus and his disciples may be subject to persecution (Matt 8:17–27; 9:14–39), and the conflict that began in the first narrative block continues (Matt 2:1–22). Nonetheless, disciples are to persevere and remain faithful to the covenant renewal. Resources are available to them now in the form of Jesus whose power includes raising a girl from the dead (Matt 9:23–25), and symbolically taking away the ultimate threat of starvation.[45] He grants such power to his disciples (Matt 10:8).

Narrative Block Three (11:2—16:20)

Jesus has taught well (Matt 5—7, 10). He has provided stopgap measures to disease and illness caused by insufficient food by continual healing, and has brought a girl back to life (Matt 9:23–25). His teachings have indicated that people should have enough to eat (Matt 6:19—17:14). Yet, his own actions have not provided any food. Actions are important to the auditors, who would not find teaching without actions to be reliable.[46] Jesus has established new leadership who were to heal and raise the dead (Matt 10:8). Yet, they have not done anything about relieving food shortages either. How much trust can one put into a new realm with no one making much of a difference in the *status quo*? Is he a teacher or Immanuel, who actually can and will provide food for them as Immanuel did in the past? Despite such confusion about who Jesus is, the central issue of this narrative block is the demand to make a response[47] and the consequences of one's response.

The kernel (Matt 11:2–6) opens the discussion when John the Baptist asks, "Are you the one who is to come, or are we to wait for another?" (Matt 11:3). The immediate answer enumerates God working through Jesus to give sight to the blind, hearing to the deaf, and healing to the lepers,[48] but not food to the hungry. The Matthean Jesus then challenges his auditors: accept what he is doing at the pace he is doing it and be blessed, or reject

---

45. Sometimes death was preferable to starvation. In Rome in 441–40 BCE, numerous people who were starving chose suicide over starvation (Livy, 4.12.11).

46. See the discussion of ancient biographies similar to Matthew on pp. 29–38 and 135–41.

47. Carter, *Matthew Storyteller*, 207.

48. Carter, *Matthew and the Margins*, 250. Passive verbs often indicate divine intervention.

him and sin.[49] As in the first narrative block, a negative and violent response is highlighted first (Matt 11:12–15). The rest of the narrative block depicts more strongly Jesus as the ideal king in the face of persistent negative responses by the Temple establishment (Matt 12:1–8, 9–14, 24–32, 38–39; 15:1–9; 16:11–12). Auditors must make a definite decision concerning the realm in which they will live (Matt 12:22–33). The narrative uses the actions of Jesus, as well as parables, to demonstrate that the realm of the heavens comprises people who are doing the will of God. The narrative answers in the affirmative the outstanding question: is Jesus just a teacher who talks about people needing food, or Immanuel who can feed them? He feeds them twice (Matt 14:13–23; 15:29–39). The reprise to the question of John the Baptist occurs in Matt 16:13–20 when Jesus poses a similar question about himself. Peter's answer is Messiah, God's anointed one, which covers both Savior and Immanuel of the commissions (Matt 1:21–23). The narrative block addresses, but does not fully answer, the question concerning discipleship by demonstrating the inconsistent responses of the disciples. They have made their decision. Their responses stand in contrast to the dominant entitlement system. Yet, their hearts need strengthening and they still have much to learn.[50]

K3	11:2–6	• Are you the one who is to come? (Are you Immanuel?) • Jesus blesses those who are not offended by him
S3.1	11:7–15	• earlier realm of the heavens taken by the violent
S3.2	11:16–24	• today's generation is no better than violent ones in the past • Jesus' realm of the heavens rejected again • Jesus condemns Bethsaida and Capernaum[1]
S3.3	11:25–30	• Jesus is the ideal ruler who embodies God's law • Jesus has all authority • Jesus can ease the burdens of the dominant entitlement system on people
S3.4	12:1–5	⇀ alleviating hunger more righteous than Pharisaic interpretation of Law
summary	12:6–13	• Jesus is more than Temple establishment • Jesus desires mercy not ritual that helps no one ⇀ example of mercy: heals (starving) man with withered hand
summary	12:14–16	• plot to kill Jesus • crowds follow Jesus for healing

1. Barta, "Mission in Matthew; the Second Discourse as Narrative," 530. Barta argues that the woes against unrepentant cities indicate a failed mission effort to cities by Jesus and, perhaps, his disciples.

---

49. Ibid., 251; Carter, *Matthew Storyteller*, 145.
50. Carter, *Matthew Storyteller*, 219.

S3:5	12:17–21	→ Jesus is Isaiah's Suffering Servant, for Gentiles as well
S3.6	12:22–33	• pick a side: the dominant entitlement system or the realm of the heavens[2]
S3.7	12:34–45	• condemns Pharisees and crowds
S3.8	12:46–50	→ new community (realm of the heavens) composed of people who do will of God
S3.9	13:1–50	→ parables demonstrating what it means to live in the realm of the heavens
summary	13:51–53	• disciples claim to understand and claim to be capable of taking on the role of scribes (leaders) in the realm of the heavens (contra 15:16)
S3.10	13:54–58	• Jesus returns to his hometown and they take offense at him (see 11:6 in particular, as well as 15:12)
S3.11	14:1–12	• Herod is afraid John the Baptist has come back as Jesus • retrospect on death of John at Herod's banquet
S3.12	14:13–23	→ Jesus feeds multitude
S3.13	14:24–33	• Jesus walks on water; Peter cannot follow Jesus due to doubt and little faith; chaos is calmed • disciples in boat worship Jesus as Son of God
summary	14:34–36	• more crowds come for healing • power of Jesus to heal is accentuated
S3.14	15:1–20	• Jesus argues with Pharisees over importance of being ritually clean • Pharisees take offense (see K3) • God will destroy false teachers (for example, Pharisees) • sin in the heart defiles, not what is eaten by the mouth
S3.15	15:21–28	→ altercation with Canaanite woman over feeding children
S3.16	15:29–39	→ Jesus tends to the needs of people in more severe food shortage situation—healing and feeding
S3.17	16:1–4a	• altercation with Pharisees and Sadducees
S3.18	16:4b–12	• hungry disciples confusion resolved
S3.19	16:13–20	• Reprise of kernel • Who do you say that I am after everything I have taught and done since John the Baptist asked?

2. Mowery, "The Matthean References to the Kingdom: Different Terms for Different Audiences," 402–3. The referenced passage says "kingdom of God" and not "realm of the heavens." Mowery argues that the Gospel uses the former phrase when the Matthean Jesus is speaking to Temple establishment people (for example, Pharisees in this passage).

[S3.3] Jesus claims God has given him all power so that he can take actions to relieve all people who are heavy laden (Sir 40:1), and who do not

it is important that no one goes hungry 251

take offense at him (K3). Jesus extends an invitation to all to be blessed by throwing off the yokes of their lives under the dominant entitlement system and putting on his good yoke[51] in the realm of the heavens. [S3.4] Contrasts between the yokes is made and connected to provision of food: eating food left in the fields for hungry people and healing a (possibly starving[52]) man so he can work for food. Because these life-giving events took place on a Sabbath, the Pharisees are offended by Jesus and plot to condemn him.

[S3.5] In response, God affirms Jesus as a servant who is representing God very well and that Jesus is willing to give his life in service to create a just realm of the heavens for all nations.

[S3.6] For a potential disciple, being amazed is no longer enough (Matt 8:27; 9:33; 12:23); a decision is required. [S3.7] After a powerful polemic, attention shifts to those who choose the realm of the heavens, which will be in conflict with the dominant entitlement system (Matt 10). More teaching ensues about the realm in which the disciples will live. [S3.9] The first parable (Matt 13:3–9) uses agricultural images on two levels to demonstrate the mixed response to Jesus described in the preceding two chapters in the gospel[53] and to indicate pragmatically what the benefit is to responding positively. Matthew 13:9 tells the auditors that this message is important and they need to understand a heart is not easy to keep focused on the realm of the heavens. At the summary of the appeal (Matt 13:51–53), the disciples claim to understand how the realm works, to have the heart to participate in it, as well as to disciple others. Subsequent narrative will suggest some had not counted the consequences of persecution from people ensconced in the dominant entitlement system and forces who want to keep the *status quo*.

The violence anticipated in S3.2 emerges in S3.11 during a banquet that Herod is hosting when he executes John the Baptist (Matt 14:1–12). The auditors would know that for people in the lower socio-economic segments of the population, *violence* also came about because banquets hosted by rulers consumed enormous supplies from surrounding areas.[54] Temporary food shortages could occur, but Jesus can overcome them. As I

---

51. Carter, *Matthew and the Margins*, 261; Carter, *Matthew and Empire*, chap. 7. Carter argues that *easy* is not a proper translation, especially given that later in the Gospel the disciples may be persecuted and die. In the latter reference, Carter argues convincingly that the yoke was more than "religious duties" and encompassed burdens placed on people in the lower socio-economic segments of the population by the entire dominant entitlement system.

52. Hesiod, *Work and Days* 493, 503. Hesiod describes a person who is starving as having swollen feet and withered hands.

53. Hagner, "Matthew's Parables of the Kingdom (Matthew 13:1–52)," 104.

54. Dando, *Geography of Famine*, 75.

argued on pages 206–9, Jesus responds as a *sitones* to provide food during shortages—not once but twice (Matt 14:13-23; 15:29-39).

Table 9. Food access in visions for two realms found in narrative block three

Passage	Realm of the Heavens	Dominant Entitlement	Food Access
[S3.3] 11:28-30	burden is good (light)	taxes and tributes heavy; forced labor	see pp. 168–87
[S3.4] 12:1-7	merciful[1]		people not greedy and willing to share food
[S3.5] 12:9-13	justice	dominant entitlement system subverts justice	justice concerned with people having sufficient food (see pp. 241–49)
[S3.8] 12:35	(general reciprocity—see pages 193–206 and its discussion of heart and treasure)		social safety network
[S3.10] 13:1-8	crop yields high for peasants who accept and follow the example of Jesus (that is, are not offended)	aristocrats take their share regardless of yield[2]	Isaac trusted Immanuel during a famine and was rewarded with such high yields (Gen 26:1-23)
[S3.10] 13:21		people hoard what little they have	negative impact on the social safety network
[S3.10] 13:22		wealth enhancing status	see pp. 168–87 re shift to profit motives negatively affect food supply

1. "The merciful lend to their neighbors; by holding out a helping hand they keep the commandments" (Sir 29:1).

2. Herzog, *Jesus, Justice, and the Reign of God*, 195, sees the Parable of the Sower/Seeds as a possible hidden transcript dealing with the issue of scarcity in a land that produces abundantly. Oakman argues against metaphorical interpretations as the only interpretation for this parable. He writes, "Certainly Jesus is speaking metaphorically. Yet were the original meanings of the parables radically disjoined from the agrarian realities depicted or the material interests of their original audience?" (*Jesus and the Economic Questions*, 4).

Passage	Realm of the Heavens	Dominant Entitlement	Food Access
[S3.10] 13:24–30³		dominant entitlement condones any methods the powerful use against less powerful to wrest away land	see pp. 168–87 re planting weed by enemies and loss of control of land leading to lessened access to food
[S3.10] 13:32–34	baker with abundant resources		abundant food⁴
[S3.13] 14:15–23	Jesus provides *manna* (daily bread)	Herod hosts a banquet and kills John the Baptist	see pp. 206–9 describing Jesus as a *sitones*
[S3.15] 15:4–9	parents taken care of by their children per Mosaic covenant	find ways not to fulfill household obligations	perhaps about parents not able to acquire food
[S3.17] 15:29–39	Jesus provides *manna* (daily bread)		see pp. 206–9 on Jesus as a *sitones*

3. Oakman, *Jesus and the Economic Questions*, 117–23; Hultgren, *The Parables of Jesus*, 295–302. Oakman has a detailed discussion of the agricultural implications of this parable. Yet, he interprets it allegorically. Hultgren argues that this is a parable whose interpretation has very different outcomes depending on whether the focus is on the parable or the parable in interpretation, including Matthew's interpretation.

4. Hultgren, *The Parables of Jesus*, 406–7; Ringe, *Jesus, Liberation, and the Biblical Jubilee*, 4–5. The quantity of three measures is immense since each measure is approximately one and one-half pecks or 144 cups. That amount would weigh some forty pounds and would make forty to eighty loaves of bread. The usual interpretation is allegorical (that is, the realm though small when inaugurated will transform all of creation through the power of God). Ringe offers a succinct and interesting analysis of the parable from several perspectives.

In the table above, the basic parables (that is, not their symbolic interpretations) related to food access are primarily concerned with threats to the vital social safety network. The maintenance of this survival mechanism is within the grasp of people who have hearts to trust God (Matt 6:25–34) and to share their dwindling supplies. It is not easy to trust and share as the first three situations in the Parable of the Seeds (Matt 13:3–9) show. Practices, like enemies planting weeds (Matt 13:24–30) to cause a crop to be useless (Matt 13:31–32), put enormous pressures on peasants to move (stay) away from the covenant of the social safety network. On the other hand, for those who are faithful, Jesus suggests that they could be rewarded with abundant yields that might break them out of a debt cycle, for example. The woman preparing bread will have more leavened flour than she needs for her own household. There will be plenty of bread to share. Jesus' realm is immensely valuable (Matt 13:44–50) to those willing to live in covenant with God and neighbors. Jesus' yoke is good (Matt 11:28–30) because worry will be unnecessary since sufficient food will be available (Matt 6:25–34; 7:7–13). Eventually Immanuel will deal with the evil ones.

The Parable of the Householder (Matt 13:51–52) sits at a structurally significant point in this narrative block.[55] It introduces a new set of questions. Will the disciples be capable of making disciples? Can they have the wisdom of their carpenter leader and know which old teaching and practice to throw out while being open to the new? Can they replace false teachers (for example, the Pharisees [Matt 15:13–14])?

To recap, the third narrative block depicts Jesus continuing to heal, but now Jesus is the ideal king who embodies the spirit of God's law, and to whom God has given all authority (Matt 11:25–30). The Gospel expands the vision of the realm of the heavens. For example, Jesus eases unnecessary burdens placed on people by the dominant entitlement system, including the Temple establishment (Matt 11:25–30). Proper worshipping of God moves to actions of mercy that ease physical burdens (Matt 12:1–13), such as hunger, for those needing relief. In the face of increasingly hostile responses by the dominant entitlement system, Matthew identifies Jesus as Isaiah's Suffering Servant for Gentiles, as well as Jews (Matt 12:14–21). In the middle of the narrative block comes a critical decision point for would-be disciples when the question of what constitutes a proper response is sharpened (Matt 12:22–33). They must pick a realm: the *status quo* of the dominant entitlement system or Jesus' realm of the heavens. The consequences of the decision are severe: choosing the first brings condemnation; choosing Jesus' realm brings mortal danger from the dominant entitlement system. Yet, many peasants in the PS 6 and PS 7 categories were already in mortal danger from the dominant entitlement system (that is, in danger of starving [see pages 4–11 and 90–96]). Jesus demonstrates the power to provide food (Matt 14:13–23; 15:29–39). Thus far, the narrative indicates that the realm of the heavens demands trust, and the disciples are still struggling to have a consistent response. The block ends with the question, "Now that you have experienced Immanuel first-hand, who do you say that I am?" (Matt 16:13–20) The resources that Jesus provides to them include miraculous provision of food when shortages are past the ability of the community to provide for one another. Not understanding and having little faith will

---

55. Jones, *The Matthean Parables: A Literary and Historical Commentary*, 121; Phillips, "Casting out the Treasure: A New Reading of Matthew 13.52," 22, 26. Using semantic analysis, Phillips translates the verb ἐκβάλλω as *expel*, not *bring out*. The verb is used elsewhere of exorcisms. The image is of a scribe who empties his treasury (heart in Matt 6:19–21) to make ready for new demands and new learning.

not be enough to sustain them through the events ahead in Jerusalem. Is it possible for the disciples to be ready in time for Jerusalem?

Narrative Block Four (16:21—20:34)

The fourth narrative block depicts Jesus going toward Jerusalem, the seat of enemies of the realm of the heavens and location of the first attempt on his life. The kernel (Matt 16:21-28) intensifies the persecution motif of earlier blocks to suffering leading to death. Jesus will die and the disciples must decide whether to continue bringing about the realm of the heavens since that work could cause their deaths as well. Jesus' promise of his resurrection on the third day would be confusing. If Jesus was going to be raised from the dead and thus conquer their enemies, then why might they be persecuted and die? Their role and the nature of the realm of the heavens are still unclear. The narrative block will make clear that the death of Jesus is the model for how they are to live in community until his return,[56] even if their oppression worsens.

The narrative immediately clarifies the answer by Peter in the previous narrative block with respect to what Messiah means in the current situation. Jesus is a suffering servant who will go to Jerusalem and be executed by leaders of the dominant entitlement system. He will be raised from the dead on the third day. As a representative of the disciples, Peter shows that they still do not understand what Jesus is trying to do, or what is expected of them (Matt 16:21-27). The Transfiguration (Matt 17:1-9) glorifies Jesus and reinforces that Jesus, as God's beloved son, speaks and acts as God. God commands the disciples to understand (cf. Matt 13:51-52) and to heed the critical things Jesus will teach them. The last two passion predictions (Matt 17:22-23; 20:17-19) each precede teachings about community in the realm of the heavens. The teachings advocate for the return to covenant with neighbor because God, and God's attendant support and mercy, assures the viability of the covenant by the death and resurrection of Jesus.[57] The fourth block is quite clear that Jesus will die and be resurrected. *Why* is becoming clearer as the contrasts sharpen between the realm of the heavens and the dominant entitlement system.

The answer to the question concerning whether the disciples will be wise enough as scribes to disciple others is rapidly moving toward a negative response. The last two passion predictions elicit thoughts of greatness by the disciples (Matt 18:1; 20:20). Jesus replies more strenuously the second

56. Carter, *Matthew Storyteller*, 148.

57. Forgiveness of sins is assured, which ensures a merciful relationship with Jesus, as Savior-Immanuel, for those having trust in God's power to provide in the realm of the heavens.

time. The greatest in the realm of the heavens is not like autocratic rulers in Jerusalem (Matt 20:20–28). The greatest will be a Suffering Servant like Jesus. The narrative block closes with the auditors still expecting failure of the disciples in the future. Two blind men may have a better chance of seeing the vision of the realm of the heavens (Matt 20:30–34) than the disciples who have been experiencing the vision in the life of Jesus.

K4	16:21–28	• first passion prediction
		• journey back to Jerusalem, the seat of powers that had attempted the death of Jesus
		   • Jesus through God's power will be ultimately victorious
		   • demands of discipleship require great faith

S4.1	17:1–13	• transfiguration
		   • confirmation that Jesus is the ideal king (see pages 36–37)
		   ↠ continuation of Law and prophets
		• the prophecies are being fulfilled for the Messiah

S4.2	17:14–20	• the disciples' faith is not strong enough to stand against the dominant entitlement system (exorcism) • crowd following but staying with *status quo*
S4.3	17:22–23	• second passion prediction
S4.4	17:24–27	↠ tax is provided[1]
S4.5	18:1–20	↠ community of care (social safety network)
S4.6	18:21–35	↠ forgiveness of debts essential to community[2]
summary	19:1–2	• moving toward Jerusalem • great crowds following but not as disciples • healing
S4.7	19:3—20:16	↠ community practices during food shortages (see chapter 7)
S4.8	20:17–19	• third passion prediction
S4.9	20:20–28	• community politics not like dominant entitlement system
summary	20:29	• great crowds following on way to Jerusalem
S4.10	20:30–34	• heals two blind men (see Matt 9:27–31) • crowds, not disciples, rebuke • blind men follow (as disciples?)

1. Carter, "Paying the Tax to Rome as Subversive Praxis: Matthew 17.24–27," 3–31; Carter, *Matthew and Empire*, chap. 8. This is often referred to as the Temple tax, although the Greek, δίδραχμον, only specifies a small silver coin. Carter argues against the *didrachma* referring to the Temple tax since after 70 CE there was no Jerusalem Temple.

2. Hultgren, *The Parables of Jesus*, 21–35; Pamment, "The Kingdom of Heaven According to the First Gospel," 216. Hultgren notes the parable is unique to Matthew. As such, Pamment's point, that neglect of forgiveness and mercy have dire consequences here and other places in the Gospel, indicates that forgiveness and mercy, like God's forgiveness as an act of mercy, are to be foundations of the realm of the heavens.

The presence of Moses at the Transfiguration reinforces the images of God with them as liberator of the Exodus and with them in the Law to show a just way of life. The presence of Elijah reinforces the image of prophets who had led God's people in an earlier battle against embracing the values and practices (sins) of the dominant entitlement system. This scene is a repeat of previous meta-messages from the Sermon on the Mount (Matt 5:1—7:12) concerning food being available if the realm of the heavens functions as a continuation of the Mosaic covenant tradition of the Hebrew scriptures.

The principal sections dealing overtly with food access in the fourth narrative block occur in Matt 18:1—20:16,[58] although the message must sometimes be recovered from between the lines. Matthew 18 begins with the question, "Who is the greatest in the realm of the heavens?" In response, the Gospel depicts Jesus as one concerned about people needing help, but who is not tolerant of people who reject his mission of mercy. Jesus had already been depicted as Isaiah's Suffering Servant (Matt 12:14-21), not a role of greatness. The answer to a similar question Jesus posed about himself (Matt 16:13-20) elicits the title Messiah. Jesus immediately clarifies the significance of Messiah as not worldly greatness but suffering and death (Matt 16:21-23). Further, any disciple should be willing to suffer the same fate (Matt 16:24-26). Apparently moving away from the power of the dominant entitlement system is extremely hard (Matt 13:1-9; 18-23).

The realm of the heavens will not have some of the traits of the dominant entitlement system: greatness does not oppress but takes care of the weak (Matt 18:1-14; 19:3—20:16); power struggles are prohibited (Matt 18:15-20); and using economics to further one's agenda is not permitted (Matt 18:21-35). Each of these topics deals with a community that exhibits a strong social safety network so important for access to sufficient food for the more unfortunate people. With Jerusalem down the road, the disciples desire worldly greatness that the Matthean Jesus contrasts with greatness in the realm of the heavens (Matt 20:25-28). [S4.5] Worldly status and its permission to exploit the weak are unacceptable, despite the temptation to want to behave like the wealthy aristocrats. Instead of exploitation, a great person in the realm of the heavens will try to keep the weakest member from dying (Matt 18:12-14).[59] Instead of using debt to gain unfair advantage over neighbors and take food

---

58. Carter, "Structure of Matthew's Gospel," 477-78. Carter writes that the satellites maintain the focus on Jesus' death and resurrection, and draw out the implications of being a disciple of the crucified Jesus. Community relationships are to the fore in Matt 18, while chapters 19-20 collect together instruction on marriage and family relationships (19:3-15), wealth and possessions (19:16-30), rank and power (20:1-28). As noted in chapter 7, I focus the discipleship more narrowly to implications of limited food access.

59. Perhaps the reference includes preventing starvation.

off their tables (see pages 168–87), relationships shall be based on general reciprocity (see pages 110–13) where the needs of another are provided for because strengthening them strengthens the community. [S4.6] Even the greatest in the dominant entitlement system performs *merciful* acts, which can involve forgiveness of monetary debts (Matt 18:23–27).[60] An unmerciful heart does not lead to greatest through wealth-enhanced status, but to condemnation (Matt 18:32–35).[61]

[S4.7] As I argued in chapter 6, Matthew 19:3—20:16 describes the proper relationships and functions within a household, or within the extended household of the Matthean community. The proper relationships ensure, amongst other things, that all members of the household community receive sufficient food. A person with an evil heart that is exposed through an evil eye is to be cast out of the community (Matt 20:14–15). Such attitudes undermine the covenant relationships of general reciprocity that are critical to a strong social safety network.

To recap, the fourth narrative block emphasizes that time is growing short for the earthly ministry of Jesus, which God re-affirmed in the Transfiguration. In that scene, Jesus, as Savior-Immanuel, continues the emphasis on the Law and the prophets concerned with people having enough to eat. The vision of the realm of the heavens places more responsibility on peasants and people in the lower socio-economic segments of the population with its renewed emphasis on re-building the social safety network (Matt 18—19). The emerging vision may be one contributor to the rising conflict with the dominant entitlement system that eventually leads to Jesus' execution. For example, a society in which debt cannot be used to forcibly enable the goals of the aristocracy is not acceptable to the powers represented by Jerusalem. A society that does not support an unquestioned hierarchy of power is not acceptable to those who hold the power with little regard for their people who are starving (Matt 20:25–28). The proper response is to reject the dominant entitlement system, but the vision of the new realm of the heavens is difficult for all, including the disciples to see, understand, and accept. With respect to what resources would be available to help them, the Transfiguration scene narratively conveys the messages that God, through Jesus, is available to help them.

---

60. MacMullen, *Roman Social Relations*, 34–35. MacMullen describes situations in which a ruler wipes the debt slate clean in a ceremony depicted on coins and bas-reliefs. Such an action normally followed repeated years in which debt could not be repaid.

61. Jones, *The Matthean Parables: A Literary and Historical Commentary*, 119. Jones writes that the parable closes the discussion of who is the greatest. It explores in narrative form the standards of behavior and attitude that the preceding context presents.

Narrative Block Five (21:1—27:66)

This narrative block begins with the entry of Jesus into Jerusalem, the seat of both Roman power and the Temple establishment (Matt 21:1-13). Both of these entities were responsible for people going hungry (see pages 168-87).[62] The kernel describes the entry and sets up escalated conflict with both the Roman government and the Temple establishment. In the fourth narrative block, Jesus had predicted he would suffer at the hands of the leaders (Matt 16:21; 17:10-12; 20:18), but had not directly supplied details about why his death would come about. This narrative block answers more fully the question of how and why Jesus will meet his death.[63] The Matthean Jesus strongly denounces the failures of the Temple establishment to fulfill its duty on behalf of God's concern for God's people (Matt 21:14-16).[64] For example, the Hebrew scriptures view the Temple as a place of refuge from the harsh realities of common life. God shares food with God's worshippers, which the scripture sometimes depicts as participating in a common meal (for example, Ps 36:8-10). Another important provision was the *second tithe* (Deut 14:22) that was to be given to the poor.[65] Unfortunately, no scholarly consensus exists with respect to how often it occurred, or was supposed to occur.[66] The Gospel describes the learned of the Temple establishment (Pharisees, Herodians, Sadducees) as not understanding the Mosaic Law (Matt 22:29, 32-34; 23:13-28) with its central tenet of love God (Deut 6:5; 11:1) or the covenant with the patriarchs to bless all peoples (Gen 12:2-3). Because of the failures of the Temple establishment, Immanuel will vacate Jerusalem again (Matt 23:29-39), and chaos will ensue until the end of the age. How those who live in the meantime are to understand God's will and cultivate the heart to act accordingly is the question. Three parables tell how to live in the meantime. With Jesus' pending death predicted, the question

---

62. Hanson and Oakman, *Palestine in the Time of Jesus*, 154. Hanson and Oakman offer a succinct discussion of Temple economic practices that were oppressive, and which would lead to people having access to less food.

63. Carter, "Structure of Matthew's Gospel," 478; Carter, *Matthew and the Margins*, 413.

64. Applebaum, "Economic Life in Palestine," 691.

65. Levenson, *Sinai and Zion*, 132.

66. Each of these scholars writes about different effects of the tithe and the response of peasants to it. Bruce, "Render to Caesar," 254; Büchler, *The Political and the Social Leaders of the Jewish Community of Sepphoris in the Second and Third Centuries*, 36; Garnsey, "Grain for Rome," 120, 126; Hamel, *Poverty and Charity in Roman Palestine*, 217; Hanson and Oakman, *Palestine in the Time of Jesus*, 153; Malina and Rohrbaugh, *Social Science Commentary on the Synoptic Gospels*, 420.

arises concerning who will be the victor in the conflict. Will Jesus' plan for a new realm of the kingdom of the heavens come to an end?[67]

K5	21:1–27	• entry into Jerusalem[1]
		  • vs. Rome
		  • vs. Temple establishment
		• question authority of Jesus

S5.1	21:28–46	• parables against the Temple establishment
		  • Two Sons
		  ↠ Absent Owner and Workers in Vineyard

S5.2	22:1–14	↠ parable of the Wedding Feast against other religious groups[2]

S5.3	22:15–45	• specific examples of why other religious groups are being replaced
		• Pharisees and Herodians misinterpret taxation
		• Sadducees do not understand the Law
		↠ greatest commandments (summarizes Decalogue)
		  • love God
		  • love God's people
		• Pharisees cannot interpret the Scripture (see Matt 23:34–45)

summary	22:46	• other religious groups shamed showing Jesus as superior
S5.5	23:1–35	• Jesus presses attack on other religious groups
S5.6	23:36—24:12	• Immanuel will vacate Zion until the end of the age • chaos will rule
summary	24:13–14a	• the ones who endure to the end will be saved and proclaim the good news to the nations of the judgment (of those who do not feed, give drink, clothe, and visit those in need)
S5.7	24:14b–28	• description of the worsening chaos
S5.8	24:29–31	• Jesus, Immanuel, will return in heavenly triumph and gather the faithful ones (of the realm of the heavens)
S5.9	24:32–44	• when? live in readiness

1. Kupp, *Matthew's Emmanuel*, 148. Kupp references Immanuel as liberator from Exod 3:12; Deut 20:1; Jer 1:8, 17, 19; 15:20; 20:11.
2. Hultgren, *The Parables of Jesus*, 340. Hultgren makes an interesting argument when he writes that "the element of refusal is the means by which to make the main point of the parable come to light. The parable centers in the good news of God, who seeks to embrace those who have nothing to offer, who must in fact be urged to come to the banquet, the feast of eschatological salvation." His observation points to a re-inscribing of the public banquet to include people from the lower socio-economic segments of the population whose inclusion on the guest list would not increase the honor rating of the host.

---

67. Carter, "Structure of Matthew's Gospel," 479.

S5.10	24:45—25:30	• examples of how to live in meantime ↣ Parable of the Faithful and Unfaithful Servants • Parable of the Ten Maidens ↣ Parable of the Talents
S5.11	25:31–46	↣ Jesus, Savior-Immanuel, will judge the nations by how they lived in community during the chaos of the meantime
S5.12	26:1—27:66	• passion narrative

As the previous narrative block began to suggest, part of the reason *why* Jesus will be executed involves returning to a realm in which the practices that take food off the tables of peasants are no longer acceptable. [S5.3] When asked which commandment is the greatest, Jesus replies that one is to love God and love neighbor. He further says that this is the basis for all of the Law and the prophets (Matt 22:34–39). All of the dimensions of life were to be lived in relation to God's will (that is, to love God with all one's heart, one's soul, and one's mind).[68] The Hebrews, as a people of God, were to be righteous like their God.[69] The Matthean community is also to be a community of righteousness (Matt 5:20). The Matthean will of God is likewise exemplified as servant leadership (Matt 20:25–28), expressed by good works (for example, good fruit in Matt 3:8, 10; 7:17–19; 12:33; 13:23), at the heart of the realm of the heavens (Matt 7:16, 20; 13:19; 21:43).[70] The service of disciples to God is actually their service to others (Matt 5:42; 7:12; 10:40; 18:5; 20:25–28; 22:34–40; 25:35–40, 42–45).[71] Jesus would seem to be referring to the strong justice theme in the Law and the prophets and the consequences of not living justly (Matt 23:29–39). In Exod 33:19–23, God's presence depends on the actions of God's people.[72] For example, God preserving the Hebrews' possession of the Promised Land is connected to their keeping a covenant that requires righteous living and just acts towards people who are weak and needy (Deut 10:12–20; 11:8–17; and Josh 24:20 is a threat that says God will annihilate Israel if they behave otherwise). The LORD their God "executes justice for the orphan and the widow," and "loves the strangers, providing them food and

---

68. Powell, *God with Us*, 12–13. Powell notes the similar ethical dimension of the Gospel seen in "the crisis of decision imposed on people who encounter Jesus" (Matt 10:34–39; 11:3–6; 12:41; 13:9, 43)

69. Birch, *Let Justice Roll Down*, 165, writes that the function of the laws were more than moral actions to take: "Their function is not just in shaping of community conduct, but in the formation and maintenance of a particular community character."

70. Powell, *God with Us*, 16, 21, 92–93.

71. Ibid., 13, 21, 102–3.

72. Brueggemann, "The Crisis and Promise of Presence in Israel," 56.

clothing" (Deut 10:18). One important aspect of the execution of justice provides food for those who do not have enough.

[S5.10] Three parables tell how to live expectantly in the meantime (that is, until Jesus comes in his glory [Matt 19:28; 24:30; 25:31]). The first and the last parables condemn oppressive practices that compromised people having enough to eat due to the greed of those operating under the values of the dominant entitlement system. [S5.11] To make it clear what the realm of the heavens is principally about, the key to interpretation is succinctly put in the ensuing final judgment scene: "When I was hungry you fed me . . ." (Matt 25:35). To ensure that the auditors do not miss the message, it is repeated three more times (Matt 25:37, 42, 44).

The Gospel exhorts people to seek God's righteousness (Matt 5:6, 20) with their whole hearts (Matt 5:8; 12:34–35; 22:37). In the Sermon on the Mount, what lies in the heart is what counts the most. Yet, the outward life is a manifestation of the inner spirit and heart (Matt 7:15–27). The final judgment scene points to specific actions that demonstrate a heart doing God's will and seeking God's righteousness.[73]

> Then the king will say to those at his right hand, "Come, you that are blessed by my Father, inherit the kingdom prepared for you from the foundation of the world;
> for I was hungry and you gave me food, I was thirsty and you gave me something to drink, I was a stranger and you welcomed me, I was naked and you gave me clothing, I was sick and you took care of me, I was in prison and you visited me."
> Then the righteous will answer him,
> "Lord, when was it that we saw you hungry and gave you food, or thirsty and gave you something to drink? And when was it that we saw you a stranger and welcomed you, or naked and gave you clothing? And when was it that we saw you sick or in prison and visited you?"
> And the king will answer them, "Truly I tell you, just as you did it to one of the least of these who are members of my family, you did it to me." (Matt 25:34–40)

The seven actions alleviate the distress of people experiencing a food shortage. Truly righteous people doing the will of God take such actions in community to alleviate the suffering of neighbors and kinsfolk. The first

---

73. Gray, *The Least of My Brothers*, 8. This text has exerted great influence on all aspects of Christianity—preaching, practice, literature, art—over the full history of Christianity. See Gray for a history of interpretation, by scholars through the seventeenth century, and by groups—with individuals cited—for the more recent periods.

two, giving food and giving drink, are the most basic acts of mercy.[74] For an urban-based community, seeing strangers who flock to the city during times of food shortages would be common. Welcoming them in the sense of sharing the few resources available might be another issue.[75] During periods of food shortages people sometimes sold their clothes for food and giving them clothing would help to restore their honor.[76] Illnesses were rampant when people were under-nourished and weak (see pages 87–90). People were imprisoned for debts they could not meet when crops failed to produce sufficiently.[77] Members of the Matthean community were to minister to others in need without regard to the person's social status and without demanding anything in return.

Concern for people getting enough to eat comes to a dramatic head in this narrative block for two reasons. First, providing for the physical needs of people, including feeding the hungry, is the ultimate criteria in the final judgment scene. Second, the judgment scene immediately precedes the passion narrative. As such, it effectively becomes Jesus' last words before his execution. Ivor Jones writes that this passage joins with the ethical concerns of Matt 7:24–27, the morality and understanding of Jesus' revelation in Matt 13:52, and the emphasis on compassion in Matt 18:21–35. He goes on to argue that its position in the narrative makes it the concluding teaching for all of the Matthean discourse. It is a call for responsibility and it says actions of righteousness, justice, mercy and compassion count more than knowledge.[78] Ensuring food for all is one such action.

The answers to the three questions posed when I began this analysis have become quite visible. What will the realm of the heavens be like? What response is expected? What resources will be available for those making a positive response to assist them in living in the realm of the heavens until the return of Jesus? The judgment scene makes it clear that acts of mercy will be carried out by members of the realm of the heavens. These acts ensure

---

74. Hultgren, *The Parables of Jesus*, 314. Hultgren notes several texts concerned with feeding people: Isa 58:7; Job 22:7; Prov 25:21; Ezek 18:7, 16; Tob 1:17; 4:16; *T. Iss.* 7:5; *T. Jos.* 1:5; and *Sifre* 118. Texts concerned with providing drink are Job 22:7; Prov 25:21; and *T. Jac.* 2:23.

75. Ibid., 315. Hultgren notes several texts concerned with bringing the homeless poor into one's home: Job 31:32; Isa 58:7; *T. Jac.* 2:23; *Vision of Ezra* 31; and *b. Sabb.* 127a.

76. Ibid., 315–16. Hultgren notes several texts concerned with clothing the naked: Ezek 18:7; Tob 1:17; 4:16; 2 Esdr 2:20; *T. Zeb.* 7:1; *T. Jac.* 2:23; *Vision of Ezra* 7; and *b.Sot.* 14a.

77. Hanson and Oakman, *Palestine in the Time of Jesus*, 152; Oakman, *Jesus and the Economic Questions*, 73–75, 155; Frederiksen, "Caesar, Cicero, and the Problem of Debt," 128, 134–35.

78. Jones, *The Matthean Parables*, 119.

that people have the basics, including sufficient food. People will respond accordingly or will be condemned. Jesus will ultimately have all power and, in his final word to them says he will be with them always (Matt 28:20).

Narrative Block Six (28:1–20)

The plot proceeds to an open-ended future of hope, when the death of Jesus, in the fifth narrative block, had taken away hope for the future.[79] This narrative block brings together the three strands from the first narrative block. The kernel proclaims that Jesus is indeed the Son of God, who is no longer dead (Matt 28:1–10). People ensconced in the dominant entitlement system still oppose him (Matt 28:11–15). Some people still had little faith (Matt 6:30; 8:26; 14:31; 16:8; 17:20; 28:17). The expectation for the disciples is to make more disciples (Matt 28:19–20). All disciples, new and old, are to live like the ideal king (Matt 28:20a) who is Jesus who ruled, and continues to rule, over the realm of the heavens. Jesus has complete authority in the realm of the heavens (Matt 28:18). The disciples, new and old, can participate in the new realm of the heavens because Jesus, Savior-Immanuel, will be with them until he comes in his glory and inaugurates the fullness of the realm of the heavens (Matt 28:20).

K6	28:1–10	• resurrection of Jesus • commission of women as disciples
S6.1	28:11–15	• Temple establishment's alternate lie • bribe of soldiers
S6.2	28:16–20a	➔ risen Jesus commissions disciples to make disciples • Jesus has all authority
summary	28:20b	• Immanuel until the end of the age

While there are no direct references to food access in the final narrative block, the life and teachings of the Matthean Jesus reflected repeatedly his concern that people have enough to eat. The final narrative block gives Jesus all authority (Matt 28:18) and the final judgment scene (Matt 25:31–46) in the previous narrative block says he will judge all, not just disciples, on whether they helped hungry people get enough to eat. In the meantime, Jesus will be with them as they attempt to live as members of the realm of the heavens (Matt 28:20).

---

79. Carter, "Structure of Matthew's Gospel," 479.

it is important that no one goes hungry 265

Chapter Summary

The question for the final chapter of this study is whether the concern about people getting enough to eat was restricted to a few anecdotal passages to illustrate a point or whether the topic is enmeshed in the narrative rhetoric of the Gospel. I argued that each of the narrative blocks associates Jesus and the realm of the heavens with people having food to eat. I demonstrated that access to food was an on-going vision of the realm of the heavens revealed throughout the narrative. This on-going vision of the realm of the heavens with people having enough to eat, through the trusting and faithful actions of neighbors, becomes the criteria in the climatic final judgment scene (Matt 25:31–46).

Connected with the commissions of Savior and Immanuel (Matt 1:21–23) in the first narrative block is the genealogy that ties the Matthean community to Savior-Immanuel in the past. Immanuel's relationships with many of the people in the genealogy involved providing food, or desiring God's people to have access to sufficient food (Matt 1:1–17). The severe opening conflict with Herod and the Temple establishment is not openly about access to food (Matt 2:1–23). Yet, the first disagreement of Jesus with the devil, who controls all the empires of the earth, is over provision of food (Matt 4:8–11).

In the second narrative block, exploration of the differences between the realm of the heavens and the dominant entitlement system began, and food access has a role in defining the differences. This narrative block indicates that a major worry for people is whether they will have food. The healing ministry of Jesus may confirm insufficient food (Matt 4:23–24; 8:1–17 [3x]; 8:28–32; 9:18–35 [5x]). In his Sermon on the Mount, Jesus teaches that people are not to worry (Matt 6:25–34; 7:7–11). Jesus' realm of the heavens will include the intention of the Law to take care of the needy (Matt 5:17–20; 7:12). Earlier the prophets had reminded the Israelites of this intention when their society was no longer taking care of the needy. The people were not worshipping their God (Matt 7:15–23) with hearts like God's heart that produced merciful acts (Matt 6:1–8; 9:13, 27–30). People to whom Jesus is speaking will need to repent of living more in the dominant entitlement system than living as God intended for them to live in the abundance of the Promised Land (that is, the new realm of the heavens) (Matt 5:48; 7:24–27). When abundance is missing, they are to repent of not trusting God's mercy (Matt 6:25–34).

The third narrative block depicts Jesus as Isaiah's Suffering Servant (Matt 12:17–21). The teaching becomes stronger relative to acts of mercy to ease physical burdens. The conflict increases with the Pharisees over the issue that relieving hunger is more important than human-made laws (Matt 12:1–13). The contrast between the two realms is especially clear with the first feeding following Herod's banquet. Auditors would know the negative effect on food supplies that such a banquet would cause. Jesus, on the other hand, takes action to alleviate the adverse effects of the dominant entitlement system on the people's tenuous food supply (Matt 11:25–30). Jesus actually feeds the multitudes twice (Matt 14:13–23; 15:29–39). Jesus also teaches using examples of practices of the dominant entitlement system that destroyed crops and took land away from peasants (Matt 13:24–33). The resistance becomes stronger as the contrasts become stronger, and food access is a prominent part of the contrast. People must choose between the dominant entitlement system and the realm of the heavens (Matt 12:22–33). Jesus suggests that Immanuel may reward well people who choose the increasingly dangerous realm of the heavens (Matt 13:1–8, 32–34, 44–50).

Narrative block four more explicitly criticizes the value system fortifying the dominant entitlement system. Greatness and abuse of power do not belong in the realm of the heavens (Matt 18:1–14; 19:3—20:28). In particular, monetary debts that were decimating peasants' ability to have enough food are not to be part of the new realm (Matt 18:21–27). To make the point clear, Jesus condemns people who use debts against people (Matt 18:32–35). However, Jesus also condemns peasants who would begrudge needy neighbors minimum food for their tables (Matt 20:14). In fact, this narrative block emphasizes the need for a functioning social safety network, which is under the control of people in the lower socio-economic segments of the population. Jesus has increased the stakes for would-be disciples. They must have a heart for God's will or be out, regardless of what pain the dominant entitlement system visits on them. Their good hearts will find expression in merciful acts that help people get enough to eat.

In narrative block five, the importance of people getting enough to eat is paramount in the realm of the heavens. Aristocratic practices to generate profits at the expense of people having enough to eat are condemned (Matt 25:14–30). Feeding hungry people is part of the criteria by which all peoples will be judged when Jesus returns in glory at the end time (Matt 25:31–46).

In narrative block six, Jesus entrusts his vision of the realm of the heavens to his disciples to pass on to future disciples (Matt 28:19–20). A key piece of that vision is the provision of daily food to all. The vision is to be lived until Jesus returns in his glory. The disciples had already been given authority and power to perform acts of mercy like Jesus (Matt 10:7–8). Jesus will be with them in the meantime to help them live in an imperfect realm of the heavens (Matt 28:20).

As I argued on pp. 124–29, people who hungered in the first-century Roman East were people in the lower socio-economic segments of the population who were mostly powerless against the practices of the dominant entitlement system. The sins of this system were principal causes of their lack of access to sufficient food. Yet, the focus of the Gospel is also on the sins of ordinary people who could make a difference, but do not do so primarily because of lack of faith in God's power to provide. Ideological conformity has only one standard of judgment: full conformity and obedience to the will of God as defined by alignment with (ἀκολουθέω) Jesus. The alignment includes doing the will of the Father and thinking the things of God (Matt 3:8; 4:10; 5:17–20, 48; 6:24, 33; 7:21; 12:50; 15:3–9; 16:23; 26:39–44; 28:20).[80] Jesus reveals that God desires people to live in covenant with God and with neighbors. Covenant demands people living in the realm of the heavens have the heart mercifully to help neighbors in need and to ensure that they have sufficient food to sustain full life.

---

80. Kupp, *Matthew's Emmanuel*, 46; Kingsbury, *Matthew as Story*, 34.

9

Concluding Remarks

THE MAJOR CONCLUSION OF this study is that, in the face of endemic food shortages, the Gospel of Matthew advocates for a society, described as the realm of the heavens, in which all people have access to sufficient food. The Gospel of Matthew critiques first-century practices of both aristocrats and peasants that helped or hindered that goal. The critique comes in the form of an ancient biographical narrative depicting Jesus teaching and performing positive practices that provided the Matthean community with a model to emulate living in the new realm of the heavens. The provision of adequate food is one embodiment of the realm of the heavens. In the remainder of this chapter, I highlight the findings of this study that support this major conclusion.

The first finding is that a complex web of relationships determined how people of varying socio-economic segments of the population gained access to food (pp. 4–11, 63–75, and 76–80). This web was influenced by two different entitlement systems: a dominant entitlement system and local (peasant) entitlement systems (pp. 128 and 168–210). The most influential power resided in the dominant system controlled by the aristocracy. They controlled the political infrastructure, including the court system. Control of the legal system granted them almost *carte blanc* permission to engage in practices that wrested from peasants control of land the aristocrats coveted for status, but which was crucial to the survival of peasants living and working it (pp. 166–93). With control of the land came the concomitant authority for crop selection. For example, aristocrats could force more land to be planted in lucrative grain crops, which they used to generate cash to support their ostentatious lifestyle. In addition to such actions increasing the risk of widespread crop failures, such actions undermined the local entitlement concluding remarks 269

system that operated on the tenets of general reciprocity. Under the local system, neighbors and kinsfolk responded to each other in compassion and with willingness to help another even if it meant denying themselves (pp. 124–29). Peasants knew that if the situation reversed, the person they were helping would help them. They not only shared tangible items such as food and utensils, but they shared their time to help a neighbor. Such a social organization was a key survival factor to peasants whose livelihood could easily be damaged by natural calamities or by actions of people controlling the dominant entitlement system. Reciprocal relations ensured two things: distribution of goods would be equitable, and help would be available. Pressures from the dominant system were undermining the solidarity of the village, or urban enclaves, because peasants could no longer trust that they, or neighbors, might have a good year. They began to hoard what little they had at the expense of needier neighbors or kinsfolk (pp. 215–16).

The second finding is that peasants were correct in their perceptions about their precarious situation. According to recent studies of ancient Roman economics (pp. 4–11 and 123–24), 25 percent of the population lived below subsistence level (that is, they consistently had access to less food than they needed to sustain their lives over the long term). Another 30 percent of the population lived on the cusp of subsistence level (for example, a small increase in extraction from rent or taxes would leave them without enough food). People in the lower socio-economic segments of the population in the first-century Roman East used survival mechanisms to keep from slipping below subsistence level. If already below subsistence level, they needed help to stave off starvation by relying on the cooperation of neighbors and strangers. The primary survival mechanisms were (1) diversity of plant and animal food sources, including those found in the wild; (2) for urban residents, eating establishments with reasonable food prices; (3) storage of food items to spread across the current year and against a bad future year; (4) patronage; (5) receipt of doles; and (6) the very important social safety network (chapter 4, pp. 188–210). The availability of these survival mechanisms was not uniform across PS levels, but when available could be the difference between eking out a living or not (pages 129–33).

The third finding is that the Matthean community developed its identity and solidified its Gospel in the latter first century or early second century. The location of the Matthean community may well have been Antioch in Syria (pp. 128–55), which was quite susceptible to natural calamities (pp. 155–59) that would exacerbate the generally poor conditions found in the first-century Roman East, as noted in finding two above. In addition to natural calamities of flood, earthquakes, and fires, the on-going presence of the Roman military would have taken needed food resources from general circulation. The situation worsened just before the Jewish War of 66–70 CE when Roman troops massed in Antioch prior to marching on Jerusalem (pp. 76–80). These food shortages probably traumatized the citizens of Antioch, including the Matthean community. Such traumas would have affected the way the Matthean community *remembered* and shaped the teaching and actions of Jesus relative to food shortages, which it recorded in the Gospel of Matthew (pp. 159–62).

The fourth finding is that the Gospel alludes to food-access practices throughout its narrative (chapter 8). Further, one notices that the Gospel rhetoric is working at a very pragmatic level to exhort its auditors to have a heart for doing God's will that emulates Jesus taking actions that positively helped their neighbors have enough to eat. Some of the rhetoric negatively portrays values and practices of the dominant entitlement system that undermined consistent access to food by people in the lower socio-economic segments of the population (chapter 5). This rhetoric is part of the impetus for the resistance of members of the dominant entitlement system, and helps to contribute to the execution of Jesus. Yet, the Gospel claims that by trusting God to be more powerful than the dominant entitlement system, they could live in covenant with God and neighbor. They could resist the temptation to live by the values and practices of the dominant entitlement system. The social safety network of the local entitlement system pragmatically would help them survive as a community until the realm of the heavens comes into its fullness (chapter 6).

In conclusion, the Gospel does portray the Matthean Jesus as being concerned that every person have sufficient food. The Gospel of Matthew depicts Jesus as Immanuel who is overtly present in human history again to establish a new just realm of the heavens where people with a heart for doing God's will perform merciful acts. Throughout the Gospel a major part of doing God's will is merciful care for neighbors who need help, especially by providing food for the hungry. In his final days, the Matthean Jesus declares that the greatest commandments are based on the Mosaic covenant (Matt 22:37–39). One is to love God. Another is to love neighbor. The importance of these commandments and their application to the situation of endemic food shortages is found in the final judgment scene (Matt 25:31–46). Love of one's neighbor must include ensuring every hungry person receives sufficient daily bread. Jesus will entrust the reign of the heavens to his disciples until his return. As enlightened scribes for the new realm (Matt 13:51–52), they are to disciple others to live just, righteous lives until the end of time. As they are able, they are to live in a community patterned after Jesus' realm of the heavens. One strong characteristic of the realm of the heavens is the provision of sufficient daily food for everyone.

Further questions concerning this topic remain for investigation. For example, what kind of relationship exists between the Matthean portrayal of Immanuel and the passages concerned with food access? How closely tied are food-access passages to the strong, often eschatological, threats and admonitions of the Gospel relative to discipleship? Is there any correlation between the tenor or frequency of passages related to people getting enough to eat and the conflict with the dominant entitlement system as it escalates in the narrative? Further questions such as these, and exegesis of all the references, are beyond the scope of this study.

Bibliography of Sources Cited

Primary Sources

Ammianus, Marcellinus. *Ammianus Marcellinus*. Translated by John Carew Rolfe. LCL. Cambridge, MA: Harvard University Press, 1950.

Apuleius. *Metamorphoses: Books 1–4*. Translated by J. Arthur Hanson. Vol. 1 LCL. Cambridge, MA: Harvard University Press, 1989.

Aristotle. *Aristotle's Politics*. Translated by Benjamin Jowett. LCL. Oxford: Claredon, 1926.

Cassius, Dio. *Roman History Books 61–70*. Translated by Earnest Cary. Vol. 8. LCL. Cambridge, MA: Harvard University Press, 2005.

Cato, Marcus Porcius. *On Agriculture*. Translated by William Davis Hooper and Harrison Boyd Ash. LCL. Cambridge, MA: Harvard University Press, 1967.

Cato, Marcus Porcius, and Marcus Terentius Varro. *Marcus Porcius Cato, On Agriculture; Marcus Terentius Varro, On Agriculture*. Translated by William Davis Hooper and Harrison Boyd Ash. LCL. Cambridge, MA: Harvard University Press, 1967.

Chrysostom, Dio. *Discourses*. Translated by J. W. Cohoon. 5 vols. LCL. New York: Putnam's Sons, 1932–1939.

Cicero, Marcus Tullius. *Cicero De Officiis*. Translated by Walter Miller. LCL. New York: Macmillan, 1913.

———. *Cicero the Speeches*. Translated by N. H. Watts. LCL. New York: Putnam's Sons, 1923.

———. *The Verrine Orations*. Translated by L. H. G. Greenwood. Vol. 2. LCL. Cambridge, MA: Harvard University Press, 1966.

Columella, Lucius Junius Moderatus. *On Agriculture: Books 1–9*. Translated by Harrison Boyd Ash. Vol. 1. LCL. 1941. Reprint, Cambridge, MA: Harvard University Press, 1960.

———. *On Agriculture: Books 10–12*. Translated by E. S. Forester and Edward H. Heffner. Vol. 3. LCL. 1955. Reprint, Cambridge, MA: Harvard University Press, 1968.

Epictetus. *Books*. Translated by W. A. Oldfather. 2 vols. LCL. Cambridge, MA: Harvard University Press, 2000.

Fronto, Marcus Cornelius. *The Correspondence of Marcus Cornelius Fronto with Marcus Aurelius Antoninus, Lucius Veres, Antoninus Pius, and Various Friends*. Translated by C. R. Haines. Vol. 1. LCL. Cambridge, MA: Harvard University Press, 1962.
Hesiod. *Hesiod: Theogony, Works and Days, Testimonia*. Translated by Glenn W. Most. LCL. Cambridge, MA: Harvard University Press, 2006.
Josephus. *Jewish Antiquities Books XII-XIV*. Translated by Ralph Marcus. Vol. 7. LCL. London: Heinemann, 1926.
———. *Jewish Antiquities Books XIV-XV*. Translated by Ralph Marcus and Allen Wikgren. Vol. 10. LCL. Cambridge, MA: Harvard University Press, 1998.
———. *Jewish Antiquities Books XVIII-XX*. Translated by Louis H. Feldman. Vol. 9. LCL. Cambridge, MA: Harvard University Press, 1965.
———. *The Jewish War Books I-III*. Translated by H. St. J. Thackery. Vol. 2. LCL. Cambridge, MA: Harvard University Press, 1967.
———. *The Jewish War Books IV-VII*. Translated by H. St. J. Thackery. Vol. 3. LCL. 10. Cambridge, MA: Harvard University Press, 1990.
———. *The Life; against Apion*. Translated by H. St. J. Thackeray. Vol. 1. LCL. Cambridge, MA: Harvard University Press, 2004.
Joshua. *The Chronicle of Joshua the Stylite*. Translated by William Wright. 1882. Reprint, Amsterdam: Philo, 1968.
Julianus Apostata. *The Works of the Emperor Julian*. Translated by Wilmer Cave Wright. Vol. 3. LCL. Cambridge, MA: Harvard University Press, 1953.
Juvenal and Persius. *Juvenal and Persius*. Translated by Susanna Morton Braund. LCL. Cambridge, MA: Harvard University Press, 2004.
Libanius. *Selected Works*. Translated by A. F. Norman. 2 vols. LCL. Cambridge, MA: Harvard University Press, 1969.
Livy. *Livy II Books 3 and 4*. Translated by B.O. Foster. Vol. 2. LCL. Cambridge, MA: Harvard University Press, 1953.
———. *Livy VIII Books 27–30*. Translated by Frank Gardner Moore. Vol. 8. LCL. Cambridge, MA: Harvard University Press, 1962.
Lucan. *Lucan*. Translated by J. D. Duff. LCL. New York: Putnam's Sons, 1928.
Martial. *Epigrams*. Translated by D. R. Shackleton Bailey. 3 vols. LCL. Cambridge, MA: Harvard University Press, 1993.
Petronius, Arbiter. *Petronius*. Translated by Michael Heseltine. LCL. Cambridge, MA: Harvard University Press, 1930.
Philo. *Philo*. Translated by F. H. Colson. Vol. 7. LCL. Cambridge, MA: Harvard University Press, 1937.
Philostratus. *Apollonius of Tyrana, Books I-IV*. Translated by Christopher P. Jones. Vol. 1. LCL. Cambridge, MA: Harvard University Press, 2005.
———. *Apollonius of Tyrana, Books V-VIII*. Translated by Christopher P. Jones. Vol. 2. LCL. Cambridge, MA: Harvard University Press, 2005.
Pliny. *Letters and Panegyricus*. Translated by Betty Radice. 2 vols. LCL. Cambridge, MA: Harvard University Press, 1969.
Plutarch. *Plutarch's Moralia*. Translated by Phillip H. De Lacy and Benedict Einarson. Vol. 7. LCL. Cambridge, MA: Harvard University Press, 1959.
———. *Plutarch's Moralia*. Translated by Paul A Clement and Herbert B. Hoffleit. Vol. 8. LCL. Cambridge, MA: Harvard University Press, 1969.
Seneca, Lucius Annaeus. *Moral Essays*. Translated by John W. Basore. 3 vols. LCL. Cambridge, MA: Harvard University Press, 1964.

Seneca, The Elder. *Declamations*. Translated by M. Winterbottom. Vol. 1. LCL. Cambridge, MA: Harvard University Press, 1974.
Tacitus, Cornelius. *Dialogus, Agricola, Germania*. Translated by William Peterson. LCL. New York: Putnam's Sons, 1925.
———. *The Histories, Books 1-3*. Translated by Clifford H. Moore. Vol. 2. LCL. Cambridge, MA: Harvard University Press, 2006.
Theophrastus. *Enquiry into Plants*. Translated by Arthur Hort. 2 vols. LCL. Cambridge, MA: Harvard University Press, 1916.
Varro. *On Agriculture*. Translated by William Davis Hooper and Harrison Boyd Ash. LCL. Cambridge, MA: Harvard University Press, 1967.

Secondary Sources

Abrams, Philip. "Introduction." In *Towns in Societies: Essays in Economic History and Historical Sociology*, edited by Philip Abrams and E. A. Wrigley, 1-7. Cambridge: Cambridge University Press, 1978.
Aguliar, Mario. "The Archaeology of Memory and the Issue of Colonialism: Mimesis and the Controversial Tribute to Caesar in Mark 12:13-17." *BTB* 35 (2005) 60-66.
Alcock, Joan P. *Food in the Ancient World*. Westport, CT: Greenwood, 2006.
Alexander, Jeffrey C. "Social Construction of Moral Universes." In *Cultural Trauma and Collective Identity*, edited by Jeffrey C. Alexander, Ron Eyerman, Bernhard Giesen, Neil J. Smelser, and Piotr Sztompka, 196-263. Berkeley: University of California Press, 2004.
———. "Toward a Theory of Cultural Trauma." In *Cultural Trauma and Collective Identity*, edited by Jeffrey C. Alexander, Ron Eyerman, Bernhard Giesen, Neil J. Smelser, and Piotr Sztompka, 1-30. Berkeley: University of California Press, 2004.
Alexander, Loveday. "Ancient Book Production and the Circulation of the Gospels." In *The Gospels for All Christians: Rethinking the Gospel Audiences*, edited by Richard Bauckham, 71-112. Grand Rapids: Eerdmans, 1998.
Allison, Dale C. "Divorce, Celcibacy and Joseph (Matthew 1.18-25 and 19.1-12)." *JSNT* 49 (1993) 3-10.
———. *Studies in Matthew: Interpretation Past and Present*. Grand Rapids: Baker Academic, 2005.
Amador, J. David Hester. *Academic Constraints in Rhetorical Criticism of the New Testament: An Introduction to a Rhetoric of Power*. JSNTSup 174. Sheffield: Sheffield Academic, 1999.
Andersen, Oivind. "Oral Tradition." In *Jesus and the Oral Gospel Tradition*, edited by Henry Wansbrough. JSNTSup 64. Sheffield: JSOT Press, 1991.
Anderson, Janice Capel. "Matthew: Sermon and Story." In *SBL 1988 Seminar Papers*, edited by David J. Lull, 496-507. Atlanta: Scholars, 1988.
———. *Matthew's Narrative Web: Over, and Over, and Over Again*. JSNTSup 91. Sheffield: JSOT Press, 1994.
Applebaum, Shimon. "Economic Life in Palestine." In *The Jewish People in the First Century: Historical Geography, Political History, Social, Cultural and Religious Life and Institutions*, edited by Shemuel Safrai and M. Stern, 631-700. Compendia Rerum Iudaicarum Ad Novum Testamentum, Section 1. Assen, Netherlands: van Gorcum, 1976.

———. "Judaea as a Roman Province: The Countryside as a Political and Economic Factor." In *Aufstieg und Niedergang der Römischen Welt*, edited by Hildegard Temporini and Wolfgang Haase, 355-96. Principat 8. Berlin: de Gruyter, 1977.

Arav, Rami. "Bethsaida Excavations: Preliminary Report, 1994-1996." In *Bethsaida: A City by the North Shore of the Sea of Galilee*, edited by Rami Arav and Richard A. Freund, 3-114. Kirksville, MO: Truman State University Press, 1991.

Ascough, Richard S. *Paul's Macedonian Associations: The Social Context of Philippians and 1 Thessalonians*. Tübingen: Mohr/Siebeck, 2003.

Ausband, Stephen C. *Myth and Meaning, Myth and Order*. Macon, GA: Mercer University Press, 1983.

Badian, E. *Publicans and Sinners: Private Enterprise in the Service of the Roman Republic, with a Critical Bibliography*. Ithaca, NY: Cornell University Press, 1983.

Bailey, Kenneth E. "Informal Controlled Oral Tradition." *AJT* 5 (1991) 34-54.

Balch, David L. "Two Apologetic Encomia: Dionysius on Rome and Josephus on the Jews." *Journal for the Study of Judaism* 13 (1982) 102-22.

Baloglou, Christos P. "Hellenistic Economic Thought." In *Ancient and Medieval Economic Ideas and Concepts of Social Justice*, edited by S. Todd Lowry and Barry Gordon, 105-45. New York: Brill, 1998.

Barclay, John M. G. *Jews in the Mediterranean Diaspora: From Alexander to Trajan (323 BCE–117 CE)*. Edinburgh: T. & T. Clark, 1996.

———. "Poverty in Pauline Studies: A Response to Steven Friesen." *JSNT* 26, no. 3 (2004) 363-66.

Barta, Karen A. "Mission in Matthew; the Second Discourse as Narrative." In *SBL 1988 Seminar Papers*, edited by David J. Lull, 527-35. Atlanta: Scholars, 1988.

Barth, Gerhard. "Matthew's Understanding of the Law." In *Tradition & Interpretation in Matthew*, edited by Gunther Bornkamm, Gerhard Barth, and Heinz Joachim Held, 58-164. London: SCM, 1982.

Barton, John. *Understanding Old Testament Ethics: Approaches and Explorations*. 1st ed. Louisville: Westminster John Knox, 2003.

Barton, Stephen C. "Can We Identify the Gospel Audiences?" In *The Gospels for All Christians: Rethinking the Gospel Audiences*, edited by Richard Bauckham, 173-94. Grand Rapids: Eerdmans, 1998.

———. "Money Matters: Economic Relations and the Transformation of Value in Early Christianity." In *Engaging Economics: New Testament Scenarios and Early Christian Reception*, edited by Bruce W. Longenecker and Kelly D. Liebengood, 37-57. Grand Rapids: Eerdmans, 2009.

Batten, Alicia. "The Degraded Poor and the Greedy Rich: Exploring the Language of Poverty and Wealth in James." In *The Social Sciences and Biblical Translation*, edited by Dietmar Neufeld, 65-77. SBL Symposium Series. Atlanta: SBL, 2008.

Bauckham, Richard. "For Whom Were Gospels Written?" In *The Gospels for All Christians: Rethinking the Gospel Audiences*, edited by Richard Bauckham, 9-48. Grand Rapids: Eerdmans, 1998.

———. *The Gospels for All Christians: Rethinking the Gospel Audiences*. Edited by Richard Bauckham. Grand Rapids: Eerdmans, 1998.

Bauer, Walter, William Arndt, F. Wilbur Gingrich and Frederick W. Danker. *A Greek-English Lexicon of the New Testament and Other Early Christian Literature : A Translation and Adaptation of the Fourth Revised and Augmented Edition of Walter Bauer's Griechisch-Deutsches Wörterbuch zu Den Schriften des Neuen Testaments und der übrigen urchristlichen Literatur*. 2nd ed. Chicago: University of Chicago Press, 1979.

Beardslee, William A. "Saving One's Life by Losing It." *JAAR* 47, no. 1 (1979) 57–72.

Bednarz, Terri. "Humor-Neutics: Analyzing Humor and Humor Functions in the Synoptic Gospels." PhD diss., Texas Christian University, 2009.

Bengel, Johann Albrecht. *Gnomon of the New Testament*. Translated by Andrew R. Fausset. Vol. 3. Edinburgh: T. & T. Clark, 1877.

Bennett, Justin. *Trajan: Optimus Princeps: A Life and Times*. Florence, KY: Routledge, 2000. Online: http://site.ebrary.com/lib/tculibrary/Doc?id=10097437&ppg=167.

Betz, Hans Dieter, and Adela Yarbro Collins. *The Sermon on the Mount: A Commentary on the Sermon on the Mount, Including the Sermon on the Plain (Matthew 5:3—7:27 and Luke 6:20–49)*. Hermeneia. Minneapolis: Fortress, 1995.

Birch, Bruce C. *Let Justice Roll Down: The Old Testament, Ethics, and Christian Life*. 1st ed. Louisville: Westminster John Knox, 1991.

———. *What Does the Lord Require? The Old Testament Call to Social Witness*. Philadelphia: Westminster, 1985.

Bloomquist, Gregory. "A Possible Direction for Providing Programmatic Correlation of Textures in Socio-Rhetorical Analysis." In *Rhetorical Criticism and the Bible*, edited by Stanley E. Porter, Dennis L. Stamps, and Thomas H. Olbricht, 61–96. JSNTSup 195. New York: Sheffield Academic, 2002.

Blue, Bradley B. "The House Church at Corinth and the Lord's Supper: Famine, Food Supply, and the Present Distress." *CTR* 5 (1991) 221–39.

Bockmuehl, Markus N. A. *Jewish Law in Gentile Churches: Halakhah and the Beginning of Christian Public Ethics*. 1st paperback. ed. Grand Rapids: Baker Academic, 2003.

Bormann, Ernest G. "Symbolic Convergence: Organizational Communication and Culture." In *Communication and Organizations: An Interpretive Approach*, edited by Linda A. Putnam and Michael E. Pacanowsky. 99–122. Beverly Hills: SAGE, 1983.

Borowski, O. "Eat, Drink and Be Merry: The Mediterranean Diet." *Near Eastern Archaeology* 67, no. 2 (2004) 96–107.

Braidwood, Robert J., and Linda S. Braidwood. *Excavations in the Plain of Antioch*. Oriental Institute Publications. Chicago: University of Chicago Press, 1960.

Branden, Robert Charles. *Satanic Conflict and the Plot of Matthew*. SBL. New York: Lang, 2006.

Brandon, S. G. F. *The Fall of Jerusalem and the Christian Church: A Study of the Effects of the Jewish Overthrow of A.D. 70 on Christianity*. 2nd ed. 1957. Reprint, London: SPCK, 1968.

Braund, David. *Augustus to Nero: A Sourcebook on Roman History, 31 BC–AD 68*. Totowa, NJ: Barnes & Noble, 1985.

———. "Function and Dysfunction: Personal Patronage in Roman Imperialism." Chap. 6 In *Patronage in Ancient Society*, edited by Andrew Wallace-Hadrill. 137–52. New York: Routledge, 1989.

Brockriede, Wayne and Douglas Ehninger. "Toulmin on Argument: An Interpretation and Application." *Quarterly Journal of Speech* 46, no. 1 (1960) 44.

Brooks, O. S. "The Function of the Double Love Command in Matthew 22:34–40." *AUSS* 36, no. 1 (1998) 7–22.

Brown, J. P. "Techniques of Imperial Control: The Background of the Gospel Event." In *The Bible and Liberation: Political and Social Hermeneutics*, edited by Norman

K. Gottwald and Richard A. Horsley, 357–77. The Bible & Liberation Series. Maryknoll, NY: Orbis, 1993.

Brown, Raymond Edward, and John P. Meier. *Antioch and Rome: New Testament Cradles of Catholic Christianity*. Ramsey, NJ: Paulist, 1983.

Bruce, F. F. "Render to Caesar." In *Jesus and the Politics of His Day*, edited by Ernst Bammel and C. F. D. Moule, 249–63. New York: Cambridge University Press, 1984.

Brueggemann, Walter. "The Crisis and Promise of Presence in Israel." *HBT* 1 (1979) 47–86.

Brunt, P. A. *Roman Imperial Themes*. Oxford: Clarendon, 1990.

Büchler, Adolf. *The Political and the Social Leaders of the Jewish Community of Sepphoris in the Second and Third Centuries*. Oxford: H. Hart at the University Press, 1909.

Buckley, Walter Frederick. *Sociology and Modern Systems Theory*. Englewood Cliffs, NJ: Prentice-Hall, 1967.

Bultmann, R. "μέριμνάω." In *Theological Dictionary of the New Testament*, edited by Gerhard Kittel and Gerhard Friedrich, translated by Geoffrey William Bromiley, 4:589–93. Grand Rapids: Eerdmans, 1964.

Burke, Kenneth. "Colloquy." *Quarterly Journal of Speech* 62 (1976) 62–77.

Burke, Peter. "History as Social Memory." In *Memory: History, Culture, and the Mind*, edited by Thomas Butler, 97–113. Wolfson College Lectures. Oxford: Blackwell, 1989.

Burridge, Richard A. "About People, by People, for People: Gospel Genre and Audiences." In *The Gospels for All Christians: Rethinking the Gospel Audiences*, edited by Richard Bauckham, 113–46. Grand Rapids: Eerdmans, 1998.

———. *What Are the Gospels? A Comparison with Graeco-Roman Biographies*. Cambridge: Cambridge University Press, 1992.

Butler, Thomas. *Memory: History, Culture, and the Mind*. Wolfson College Lectures. New York: Blackwell, 1989.

Carcopino, Jerome. *Daily Life in Ancient Rome: The People and the City at the Height of the Empire*. Translated by E. O. Lorimer. New Haven: Yale University Press, 2003.

Carmichael, D. B. "David Daube on the Eucharist and the Passover Seder." *JSNT* 42 (1991) 45–67.

Carney, Thomas F. *The Economies of Antiquity: Controls, Gifts, and Trade*. Lawrence, KS: Coronado, 1973.

———. *The Shape of the Past: Models and Antiquity*. Lawrence, KS: Coronado, 1975.

Carpenter, Ronald H. *History as Rhetoric: Style, Narrative, and Persuasion*. Studies in Rhetoric/Communication. Columbia: University of South Carolina Press, 1995.

Carter, Warren. "Challenging by Confirming, Renewing by Repeating: The Parables of 'the Reign of the Heavens' in Matthew 13 as Embedded Narratives." In *Society of Biblical Literature 1995 Seminar Papers*, edited by Eugene H. Lovering Jr., 399–424. SBLSP. Atlanta: Scholars, 1995.

———. "Community Definition and Matthew's Gospel." In *Society of Biblical Literature 1997 Seminar Papers*, 637–63. SBLSP. Atlanta: Scholars, 1997.

———. "Contested Claims: Roman Imperial Theology and Matthew's Gospel." *BTB* 29 (1999) 56–67.

———. *Households and Discipleship: A Study of Matthew 19–20*. JSNTSup 103. Sheffield: JSOT Press, 1994.

———. "How Would Jesus Eat? The Gospel of Matthew, the Empire, and Jesus' Food Practices." In *How Would Jesus Eat? Food as a Gospel Resource for the Church*, edited by Shannon Jung. Minneapolis: Fortress, forthcoming.

———. "Kernels and Narrative Blocks: The Structure of Matthew's Gospel." *CBQ* 54, no. 3 (1992) 463–81.

———. *Matthew and Empire: Initial Explorations*. Harrisburg, PA: Trinity, 2001.

———. "Matthew and the Gentiles: Individual Conversion and/or Systemic Transformation?". *JSNT* 26, no. 3 (2004) 259–82.

———. *Matthew and the Margins: A Sociopolitical and Religious Reading*. The Bible & Liberation Series. Maryknoll, NY: Orbis, 2000.

———. "Matthew: Empire, Synagogues, and Horizontal Violence." In *Mark and Matthew I: Comparative Readings: Understanding the Earliest Gospels in the First-Century Settings*, edited by Eve-Marie Becker and Anders Runesson, 285–308, Tübingen: Mohr/Siebeck, 2011.

———. *Matthew: Storyteller, Interpreter, Evangelist*. Rev. ed. Peabody, MA: Hendrickson, 2004.

———. "Matthew's Gospel: An Anti-Imperial/Imperial Reading." *CurTM* 34, no. 6 (2007) 424–33.

———. "Matthew's People." In *Christian Origins: People's History of Christianity*, edited by Richard A. Horsley, 138–60. Minneapolis: Fortress, 2005.

———. "Paying the Tax to Rome as Subversive Praxis: Matthew 17.24–27." *JSNT* 76 (1999) 3–31.

———. "Resisting and Imitating the Empire: Imperial Paradigms in Two Matthean Parables." *Int* 56, no. 3 (2002) 260–72.

———. *The Roman Empire and the New Testament: An Essential Guide*. Nashville: Abingdon, 2006.

———. "Solomon in All His Glory: Intertextuality and Mt. 6.29." *JSNT* 65 (1997) 3–25.

Carter, Warren, and John Paul Heil. *Matthew's Parables: Audience-Oriented Perspectives*. Catholic Biblical Quarterly Monograph. Washington, DC: Catholic Biblical Association of America, 1998.

Chancey, Mark A. *Greco-Roman Culture and the Galilee of Jesus*. Society for Biblical Studies Monograph. Cambridge: Cambridge University Press, 2005.

Chatman, Seymour Benjamin. *Story and Discourse: Narrative Structure in Fiction and Film*. Ithaca, NY: Cornell University Press, 1978.

Claassens, L. Juliana M. *The God Who Provides: Biblical Images of Divine Nourishment*. Nashville: Abingdon, 2004.

Clark, Colin, and Margaret Rosary Haswell. *The Economics of Subsistence Agriculture*. 4th ed. New York: Macmillan, 1970.

Clark, Mark Edward. "SPES in the Later Imperial Cult." In *Society of Biblical Literature 1983 Seminar Papers*, edited by Kent Harold Richards, 315–19. Chico, CA: Scholars, 1983.

Clarke, Andrew D. *Serve the Community of the Church: Christians as Leaders and Ministers*. Grand Rapids: Eerdmans, 2000.

Cohen, Anthony P. *The Symbolic Construction of Community*. Key Ideas. New York: Routledge, 1989.

Combrink, H. J. Bernard. "The Structure of the Gospel of Matthew as Narrative." *TynBul* (1983) 61–90.

Cooley, Alison E., and M. G. L. Cooley. *Pompeii: A Sourcebook*. New York: Routledge, 2004.

Corbier, M. "City, Territory, and Taxation." Chap. 9 In *City and Country in the Ancient World*, edited by John Rich and Andrew Wallace-Hadrill, 211–39. Leicester-Nottingham Studies in Ancient Society. New York: Routledge, 1991.

Cotter, Wendy J. "Cornelius, the Roman Army and Religion." In *Religious Rivalries and the Struggle for Success in Caesarea Maritima*, 279–301. Waterloo, ON: Wilfrid Laurier University Press, 2000.

———. "Greco-Roman Apotheosis Traditions and the Resurrection Appearances in Matthew." In *Gospel of Matthew in Current Study*, 127–53. Grand Rapids: Eerdmans, 2001.

Crook, Z. A. "Structure Versus Agency in Studies of the Biblical Social World: Engaging with Louise Lawrence." *JSNT* 29, no. 3 (2007) 251–75.

Crosby, Michael. *House of Disciples: Church, Economics, and Justice in Matthew*. Maryknoll, NY: Orbis, 1988.

Crossley, James G. *Why Christianity Happened: A Sociohistorical Account of Christian Origins (26–50 CE)*. Louisville: Westminster John Knox, 2006.

D'Arms, John H. *Commerce and Social Standing in Ancient Rome*. Cambridge, MA: Harvard University Press, 1981.

Dalby, Andrew. *Food in the Ancient World from A to Z*. The Ancient World from A to Z. New York: Routledge, 2003.

Dando, William A. *The Geography of Famine*. Scripta Series in Geography. Silver Spring, MD: Winston, 1980.

Danker, Frederick W. *Benefactor: Epigraphic Study of a Graeco-Roman and New Testament Semantic Field*. St. Louis: Clayton, 1982.

Danylak, Barry N. "Tiberius Claudius Dinippus and the Food Shortages in Corinth." *TynBul* 59, no. 2 (2008) 231–70.

Davies, John. "Linear and Non-Linear Flow Models for Ancient Economies." In *The Ancient Economy: Evidence and Models*, edited by Joseph Gilbert Manning and Ian Morris, 127–56. Social Science History. Stanford, CA: Stanford University Press, 2005.

Davies, W. D. "A Different Approach to Jamnia: The Jewish Sources of Matthew's Messianism." In *The Conversation Continues: Studies in Paul & John in Honor of J. Louis Martyn*, edited by J. Louis Martyn, Robert Tomson Fortna, and Beverly Roberts Gaventa, 378–95. Nashville: Abingdon, 1990.

Davies, W. D., and Dale C. Allison. *The Gospel According to Matthew*. 3 vols. The International Critical Commentary on the Holy Scriptures of the Old and New Testaments. New York: T. & T. Clark, 1997–2004.

Davis, Ellen F. *Scripture, Culture, and Agriculture: An Agrarian Reading of the Bible*. New York: Cambridge University Press, 2009.

De Vries, S. J. "Sin, Sinners." In *The Interpreter's Dictionary of the Bible*, edited by George Arthur Buttrick, 4:361–62. Nashville: Abingdon, 1962.

Derrenbacker, R. A. *Ancient Compositional Practices and the Synoptic Problem*. Bibliotheca Ephemeridum Theologicarum Lovaniensium. Dudley, MA: University Press, 2005.

Derrett, J. Duncan M. *Jesus's Audience: The Social and Psychological Environment in Which He Worked; Prolegomena to a Restatement of the Teaching of Jesus*. New York: Seabury, 1974.

———. "Workers in the Vineyard: A Parable of Jesus." *JJS* 25, no. 1 (1974) 64–91.
DeSilva, David Arthur. *Honor, Patronage, Kinship & Purity: Unlocking New Testament Culture*. Downers Grove, IL: InterVarsity, 2000.
Di Segni, Leah. "Dated Greek Inscriptions from Palestine from the Roman and Byzantine Periods." PhD diss., Hebrew University of Jerusalem, 1997.
Dmitriev, Sviatoslav. *City Government in Hellenistic and Roman Asia Minor*. New York: Oxford University Press, 2005.
Dodd, C. H. *The Parables of the Kingdom*. New York: Scribner's Sons, 1936.
Donaldson, T. L. "The Law That Hangs (Matthew 22:40) Rabbinic Formulation and Matthean Social World." *CBQ* 57, no. 4 (1995) 689–709.
Douglas, Mary. "Deciphering a Meal." In *Myth, Symbol, and Culture*, edited by Clifford Geertz, 61–81. New York: Norton, 1974.
Downey, Glanville. *Ancient Antioch*. Princeton: Princeton University Press, 1963.
———. *A History of Antioch in Syria: From Seleucus to the Arab Conquest*. Princeton: Princeton University Press, 1961.
Duling, Dennis C. "Empire: Theories, Methods, Models." In *The Gospel of Matthew in Its Roman Imperial Context*, edited by John Kenneth Riches and David C. Sim, 49–74. New York: T. & T. Clark, 2005.
———. *A Marginal Scribe: Studies of the Gospel of Matthew in Social-Scientific Perspective*. Eugene, OR: Cascade, 2011.
———. "The Matthean Brotherhood and Marginal Scribal Leadership." In *Modelling Early Christianity: Social-Scientific Studies of the New Testament in Its Context*, edited by Philip Francis Esler, 159–82. New York: Routledge, 1995.
Duncan-Jones, Richard. *Structure and Scale in the Roman Economy*. Cambridge: Cambridge University Press, 1990.
Dunn, James D. G. "Jesus in Oral Memory: The Initial Stages of the Jesus Tradition." In *Society of Biblical Literature 2000 Seminar Papers*, edited by SBL, 287–326. Atlanta: SBL, 2000.
Edwards, Douglas. "The Socio-Economic and Cultural Ethos of the Lower Galilee in the First-Century: Implications for the Nascent Jesus Movement." In *The Galilee in Late Antiquity*, edited by Lee I. Levine, 53–74. Cambridge, MA: Harvard University Press, 1992.
Edwards, J. R. "The Gospel of the Ebionites and the Gospel of Luke." *NTS* 48, no. 4 (2002) 568–86.
Elliott, John Hall. "Matthew 20:1–15: A Parable of Invidious Comparison and Evil Eye Accusation." *BTB* 22 (1992) 52–65.
———. "Patronage and Clientage." In *The Social Sciences and New Testament Interpretation*, edited by Richard L. Rohrbaugh, 144–56. Peabody, MA: Hendrickson, 1996.
———. *What Is Social-Scientific Criticism?* Minneapolis: Fortress, 1993.
Esler, Philip Francis. *The First Christians in Their Social Worlds: Social-Scientific Approaches to New Testament Interpretation*. New York: Routledge, 1994.
Evans, Jane DeRose. *The Coins and the Hellenistic, Roman, and Byzantine Economy of Palestine*. Boston: American Schools of Oriental Research, 2006.
Fernandez, James W. *Persuasions and Performances: The Play of Tropes in Culture*. Bloomington: Indiana Univ Press, 1986.

Fiensy, David A. "Ancient Economy and the New Testament." In *Understanding the Social World of the New Testament*, edited by Dietmar Neufeld and Richard E. DeMaris, 194–206. New York: Routledge, 2010.

———. *The Social History of Palestine in the Herodian Period: The Land Is Mine*. Studies in the Bible and Early Christianity. Lewiston, NY: Mellen, 1991.

Filson, Floyd Vivian. *A Commentary on the Gospel According to St. Matthew*. Black's New Testament Commentaries. London: A. & C. Black, 1960.

Finger, Reta Halteman. *Of Widows and Meals: Communal Meals in the Book of Acts*. Grand Rapids: Eerdmans, 2007.

Firth, Raymond. *Primitive Polynesian Economy*. London: Routledge & Sons, 1939.

Fitzmyer, Joseph A. "Matthean Divorce Texts and Some New Palestinian Evidence." *Theological Studies* 37, no. 2 (1976) 197–226.

Flint-Hamilton, K. B. "Legumes in Ancient Greece and Rome: Food, Medicine, or Poison?" *Hesperia* 68, no. 3 (1999) 371–85.

Foxhall, Lin. "The Dependent Tenant: Land Leasing and Labour in Italy and Greece." *JRS* 80 (1990) 97–114.

France, R. T. *The Gospel of Matthew*. Grand Rapids: Eerdmans, 2007.

———. "On Being Ready (Matthew 25:1–46)." In *The Challenge of Jesus' Parables*, edited by Richard N. Longenecker, 177–95. McMaster New Testament Studies. Grand Rapids: Eerdmans, 2000.

Frayn, Joan M. "Wild and Cultivated Plants: A Note on the Peasant Economy of Roman Italy." *JRS* 65 (1975) 32–39.

Frederiksen, M. W. "Caesar, Cicero, and the Problem of Debt." *JRS* 56, no. 1–2 (1956) 128–41.

———. "Theory, Evidence and the Ancient Economy." Review of *The Ancient Economy*, by M. I. Finley. *JRS* 65 (1975) 164–71.

Freyne, Sean. "Galilee and Judaea in the First Century." In *Origins to Constantine*, edited by Margaret Mary Mitchell, Frances M. Young, and K. Scott Bowie, 37–51. Cambridge History of Christianity. New York: Cambridge University Press, 2006.

———. *Galilee: From Alexander the Great to Hadrian, 323 B.C.E. to 135 C.E.: A Study of the Second Temple Judaism*. Edinburgh: T. & T. Clark, 1998.

———. "Herodian Economics in Galilee: Searching for a Suitable Model." In *Modelling Early Christianity: Social-Scientific Studies of the New Testament in Its Context*, edited by Philip Francis Esler, 23–46. London: Routledge, 1995.

———. "Urban-Rural Relations in First-Century Galilee." In *The Galilee in Late Antiquity*, edited by Lee I. Levine, 95–102. Cambridge, MA: Harvard University Press, 1992.

Friesen, Steven J. "Injustice or God's Will: Explanations of Poverty in Proto-Christian Texts." In *Christian Origins: People's History of Christianity*, edited by Richard A. Horsley, 240–60. Minneapolis: Fortress, 2005.

———. "Poverty in Pauline Studies: Beyond the So-Called New Consensus." *JSNT* 26, no. 3 (2004) 323–61.

Fuglseth, Kåre. *Johannine Sectarianism in Perspective: A Sociological, Historical, and Comparative Analysis of Temple and Social Relationships in the Gospel of John, Philo, and Qumran*. Boston: Brill, 2005.

Fusfeld, Daniel B. "Economic Theory Misplaced: Livelihood in Primitive Society." In *Trade and Market in the Early Empires; Economies in History and Theory*, edited by Karl Polanyi, 342–56. Glencoe, IL: Free, 1957.

Gale, Aaron M. "Tradition in Transition, or Antioch Versus Sepphoris: Rethinking the Matthean Community's Location." In *Society of Biblical Literature 2003 Seminar Papers*, edited by SBL, 141–56. Atlanta: SBL, 2003.

Gamble, Harry Y. *Books and Readers in the Early Church: A History of Early Christian Texts*. New Haven: Yale University Press, 1995.

Gapp, Kenneth Sperber. "The Universal Famine under Claudius." *HTR* 28, no. 4 (1935) 258–65.

Gardner, Jane F., and Thomas Wiedemann. *The Roman Household: A Sourcebook*. New York: Routledge, 1991.

Garland, Robert. *The Eye of the Beholder: Deformity and Disability in the Graeco-Roman World*. Ithaca, NY: Cornell University Press, 1995.

Garnsey, Peter. *Famine and Food Supply in the Graeco-Roman World: Responses to Risk and Crisis*. Cambridge: Cambridge University Press, 1988.

———. *Food and Society in Classical Antiquity*. Key Themes in Ancient History. Cambridge: Cambridge University Press, 1999.

———. "Grain for Rome." In *Imperialism in the Ancient World: The Cambridge University Research Seminar in Ancient History*, edited by Peter Garnsey and C. R. Whittaker, 118–30. Cambridge Classical Studies. New York: Cambridge University Press, 1978.

Garnsey, Peter, Tom Gallant, and Dominic Rathbone. "Thessaly and the Grain Supply of Rome During the Second Century B.C." *JRS* 74 (1984) 30–44.

Garnsey, Peter, and Richard P. Saller. *The Roman Empire: Economy, Society, and Culture*. Berkeley: University of California Press, 1987.

Garnsey, Peter, and Walter Scheidel. *Cities, Peasants, and Food in Classical Antiquity: Essays in Social and Economic History*. Cambridge: Cambridge University Press, 1998.

Garnsey, Peter, and Gregory Woolf. "Patronage of the Rural Poor in the Roman World." In *Patronage in Ancient Society*, edited by Andrew Wallace-Hadrill, 153–70. New York: Routledge, 1989.

Geertz, Clifford. *The Interpretation of Cultures: Selected Essays*. New York: Basic, 1973.

Gerhardsson, Birger. *The Reliability of the Gospel Tradition*. Peabody, MA: Hendrickson, 2001.

Geyer, Patrick Scott. "Evidence of Flax Cultivation from the Temple-Granary Complex Et-Tell (Bethsaida/Julias)." *IEJ* 51, no. 2 (2001) 231–34.

Giardina, Andrea. "The Merchant." In *The Romans*, edited by Andrea Giardina, 245–71. Chicago: University of Chicago Press, 1993.

Gillis, John R. *Commemorations: The Politics of National Identity*. Princeton: Princeton University Press, 1994.

Goodman, Martin. "The First Jewish Revolt: Social Conflict and the Problem of Debt." *JJS* 33, no. 1–2 (1982) 417–27.

———. *State and Society in Roman Galilee, A.D. 132–212*. Edited by Oxford Centre for Postgraduate Hebrew Studies. Totowa, NJ: Rowman & Allanheld, 1983.

Goody, Jack. *Cooking, Cuisine, and Class: A Study in Comparative Sociology*. Themes in the Social Sciences. Cambridge: Cambridge University Press, 1982.

Gordon, Barry. *The Economic Problem in Biblical and Patristic Thought*. Supplements to Vigiliae Christianae. New York: Brill, 1989.

Goulder, M. D. *Midrash and Lection in Matthew: The Speaker's Lectures in Biblical Studies 1969–1971*. London: SPCK, 1974.

Gowler, David B. "The Chreia." In *The Historical Jesus in Context*, edited by Amy-Jill Levine, Dale C. Allison, and John Dominic Crossan, 132–48. Princeton Readings in Religions. Princeton: Princeton University Press, 2006.

———. *What Are They Saying About the Parables?* New York: Paulist, 2000.

Gray, Sherman W. *The Least of My Brothers: Matthew 25: 31–46: A History of Interpretation*. SBLDS. Atlanta: Scholars, 1989.

Green, William Scott. "Introduction: Messiah in Judaism: Rethinking the Question." In *Judaisms and Their Messiahs at the Turn of the Christian Era*, edited by Jacob Neusner, William Scott Green, and Ernest S. Frerichs, 1–11. Cambridge: Cambridge University Press, 1987.

Grimshaw, James P. "Luke's Market Exchange District: Decentering Luke's Rich Urban Center." *Semeia* 86 (1999) 33–51.

———. *The Matthean Community and the World: An Analysis of Matthew's Food Exchange*. New York: Lang, 2008.

Gundry, Robert H. *Matthew: A Commentary on His Handbook for a Mixed Church under Persecution*. 2nd ed. Grand Rapids: Eerdmans, 1994.

———. *Matthew: A Commentary on His Literary and Theological Art*. Grand Rapids: Eerdmans, 1982.

Hagner, Donald A. "The Gospel of Matthew." In *The New Testament Today*, edited by Mark Allan Powell, 31–44. Louisville: Westminster John Knox, 1999.

———. "Matthew's Eschatology." In *Society of Biblical Literature 1996 Seminar Papers*. SBLSP, 163–81. Atlanta: Scholars, 1996.

———. "Matthew's Parables of the Kingdom (Matthew 13:1–52)." In *The Challenge of Jesus' Parables*, edited by Richard N. Longenecker, 102–24. McMaster New Testament Studies. Grand Rapids: Eerdmans, 2000.

Halbwachs, Maurice. *On Collective Memory*. Translated by Lewis A. Coser. Chicago: University of Chicago Press, 1992.

Hamel, Gildas H. *Poverty and Charity in Roman Palestine, First Three Centuries C.E.* Berkeley: University of California Press, 1990.

Hands, Arthur Robinson. *Charities and Social Aid in Greece and Rome*. Aspects of Greek and Roman Life. Ithaca, NY: Cornell University Press, 1968.

Hanson, K. C. "The Galilean Fishing Economy and the Jesus Tradition." *BTB* 27, no. 3 (1997) 100–108.

Hanson, K. C., and Douglas E. Oakman. *Palestine in the Time of Jesus: Social Structures and Social Conflicts*. Minneapolis: Fortress, 1998.

Hariman, Robert. "The Forum: Norms of Rhetorical Criticism." *Quarterly Journal of Speech* 80, no. 3 (1994) 329–32.

Harland, Philip. *Associations, Synagogues, and Congregations: Claiming a Place in Ancient Mediterranean Society*. Minneapolis: Fortress, 2003.

Harnisch, Wolfgang. "Metaphorical Process in Matthew 20:1–15." In *Society of Biblical Literature 1977 Seminar Papers*, edited by Paul J. Achtemeier, 231–50. Missoula, MT: Scholars, 1977.

Hasitschka. "Die Verwendung der Schrift in Mt 4,1–11." In *The Scriptures in the Gospels*, edited by C. M. Tuckett, 487–90. Bibliotheca Ephemeridum Theologicarum Lovaniensium. Leuven: Leuven University Press, 1997.

Heichelheim, F. "Roman Syria." In *An Economic Survey of Ancient Rome*, edited by Tenney Frank, 121–257. New York: Octagon, 1975.

Heil, John Paul. "Ezekiel 34 and the Narrative Strategy of the Shepherd and Sheep Metaphor in Matthew." *CBQ* 55 (1993) 698–708.
Heinen, Heinz. "Göttliche Sitometrie: Beobachtungen zur Brotbitte des Vaterunsers." *Trierer Theologische Zeitschrift* 99, no. 1 (1990) 72–79.
Hengel, Martin. *Property and Riches in the Early Church: Aspects of a Social History of Early Christianity*. Mifflintown, PA: Sigler, 1997.
Herzog, William R. *Jesus, Justice, and the Reign of God: A Ministry of Liberation*. Louisville: Westminster John Knox, 2000.
———. *Parables as Subversive Speech: Jesus as Pedagogue of the Oppressed*. Louisville: Westminster John Knox, 1994.
———. "Why Peasants Responded to Jesus." In *Christian Origins: People's History of Christianity*, edited by Richard A. Horsley, 47–69. Minneapolis: Fortress, 2005.
Hitchcock, D. "Good Reasoning on the Toulmin Model." *Argumentation* 19, no. 3 (2005) 373–91.
Hodgkin, Katharine, and Susannah Radstone. "Introduction: Contested Pasts." In *Contested Pasts: The Politics of Memory*, edited by Katharine Hodgkin and Susannah Radstone, 1–21. New York: Routledge, 2003.
Hollenbach, Paul W. "Jesus, Demoniacs, and Public Authorities: A Socio-Historical Study." *JAAR* 49, no. 4 (1981) 567–88.
Holmes, Michael William. *The Apostolic Fathers: Greek Texts and English Translations*. Updated ed. Grand Rapids: Baker, 1999.
Hopkins, David C. "Agriculture." In *Near Eastern Archaeology*, 124–30. Winona Lake, IN: Eisenbrauns, 2003.
Hopkins, Keith. "Economic Growth and Towns in Classical Antiquity." In *Towns in Societies: Essays in Economic History and Historical Sociology*, edited by Philip Abrams and E. A. Wrigley, 35–77. Cambridge: Cambridge University Press, 1978.
———. "Taxes and Trade in the Roman Empire (200 B.C.–A.D. 400)." *JRS* 70 (1980) 101–25.
Hopkins, W. J. "The City Region in Roman Palestine." *PEQ* 112 (1980) 19–31.
Hopwood, Keith. "Bandits, Elites and Rural Order." In *Patronage in Ancient Society*, edited by Andrew Wallace-Hadrill, 171–87. New York: Routledge, 1989.
Horden, Peregrine, and Nicholas Purcell. *The Corrupting Sea: A Study of Mediterranean History*. Malden, MA: Blackwell, 2000.
Horsley, G. H. R. *New Documents Illustrating Early Christianity: A Review of Greek Inscriptions and Papyri*. 5 vols. North Ryde, New South Wales: Ancient History Documentary Research Centre, Macquarie University, 1981–1989.
Horsley, Richard A. *Galilee: History, Politics, People*. Valley Forge, PA: Trinity, 1995.
———. *Jesus and Empire: The Kingdom of God and the New World Disorder*. Minneapolis: Fortress, 2003.
———. "Jesus Movements and the Renewal of Israel." In *Christian Origins: People's History of Christianity*, edited by Richard A. Horsley, 23–46. Minneapolis: Fortress, 2005.
———. "Moral Economy, Little Tradition, and Hidden Transcript: Applying the Work of James C. Scott to Q." In *Society of Biblical Literature 2001 Seminar Papers*, 240–59. SBLSP. Atlanta: SBL, 2001.
———. *Scribes, Visionaries, and the Politics of Second Temple Judea*. Louisville: Westminster John Knox, 2007.

Horsley, Richard A., and John S. Hanson. *Bandits, Prophets, and Messiahs: Popular Movements in the Time of Jesus.* 1st Harper & Row paperback ed. New Voices in Biblical Studies. San Francisco: Harper & Row, 1988.
Howell, David B. *Matthew's Inclusive Story: A Study in the Narrative Rhetoric of the First Gospel.* JSNTSup. Sheffield UK: JSOT Press, 1990.
Hultgren, Arland J. *The Parables of Jesus: A Commentary.* The Bible in Its World. Grand Rapids: Eerdmans, 2000.
Incigneri, Brian J. *The Gospel to the Romans: The Setting and Rhetoric of Mark's Gospel.* Biblical Interpretation Series. Boston: Brill, 2003.
Isaac, Benjamin H. *The Limits of Empire: The Roman Army in the East.* Rev. ed. New York: Oxford University Press, 1992.
Isaac, Benjamin H., and I. Roll. "A Milestone of A.D. 69 from Judaea: The Elder Trajan and Vespasian." *JRS* 66 (1976) 15–19.
Jefford, Clayton N. "Did Ignatius of Antioch Know the Didache?" In *The Didache in Context: Essays on Its Text, History and Transmission,* edited by Clayton N. Jefford, 330–51. New York: Brill, 1995.
Jeremias, Joachim. *Die Gleichnisse Jesu.* 6th ed. Göttingen: Vandenhoeck & Ruprecht, 1965.
Johnston, David. "Munificence and Municipia: Bequests to Towns in Classical Roman Law." *JRS* 75 (1985) 105–25.
Jones, Arnold Hugh Martin. *The Greek City from Alexander to Justinian.* Oxford: Clarendon, 1940.
Jones, C. P. *The Roman World of Dio Chrysostom.* Loeb Classical Monographs. Cambridge, MA: Harvard University Press, 1978.
Jones, Ivor H. *The Matthean Parables: A Literary and Historical Commentary.* Supplements to Novum Testamentum. New York: Brill, 1995.
Jones, James L. "The Roman Army." In *The Catacombs and the Colosseum: The Roman Empire as the Setting of Primitive Christianity,* edited by Stephen Benko and John J. O'Rourke, 187–217. Valley Forge, PA: Judson, 1971.
Kautsky, John H. *The Politics of Aristocratic Empires.* New Brunswick, NJ: Transaction, 1997.
Kealy, Sean P. *Matthew's Gospel and the History of Biblical Interpretation.* Mellen Biblical Press Series 55a. Lewiston, NY: Mellen Biblical, 1997.
Kelber, Werner H. "The Generative Force of Memory: Early Christian Traditions as Processes of Remembering." *BTB* 36, no. 1 (2006) 15–32.
———. *The Oral and the Written Gospel.* Philadelphia: Fortress, 1983.
Kennedy, George Alexander. *Classical Rhetoric & Its Christian & Secular Tradition from Ancient to Modern Times.* 2nd ed. Chapel Hill: University of North Carolina Press, 1999.
———. *New Testament Interpretation through Rhetorical Criticism.* Chapel Hill: University of North Carolina Press, 1984.
Kereszty, Roch A. *Wedding Feast of the Lamb: Eucharistic Theology from a Historical, Biblical and Systematic Perspective.* Mundelein, IL: Hillenbrand, 2004.
Kilpatrick, G. D. *The Origins of the Gospel of St. Matthew.* Oxford: Clarendon, 1946.
Kingsbury, Jack Dean. "The Developing Conflict between Jesus and the Jewish Leaders in Matthew's Gospel: A Literary-Critical Study." *CBQ* 49, no. 1 (1987) 57–73.
———. *Matthew as Story.* 2nd ed. Philadelphia: Fortress, 1988.

———. *Matthew: Structure, Christology, Kingdom*. Paperback ed. Minneapolis: Fortress, 1989.

———. "Verb Akolouthein ('to Follow') as an Index of Matthew's View of His Community." *JBL* 97, no. 1 (1978) 56–73.

Klauck, Hans-Josef. "The Roman Empire." In *Origins to Constantine*, edited by Margaret Mary Mitchell, Frances M. Young, and K. Scott Bowie, 69–83. Cambridge History of Christianity. Cambridge: Cambridge University Press, 2006.

Kloppenborg, John S. "Agrarian Discourse and the Sayings of Jesus: 'Measure for Measure' in Gospel Traditions." In *Engaging Economics: New Testament Scenarios and Early Christian Reception*, edited by Bruce W. Longenecker and Kelly D. Liebengood, 104–28. Grand Rapids: Eerdmans, 2009.

———. "Collegia and *Thiasoi*: Issues in Function, Taxonomy and Membership." In *Voluntary Associations in the Graeco-Roman World*, edited by John S. Kloppenborg and S. G. Wilson, 16–30. New York: Routledge, 1996.

———. "Halakhic Evidence of Didache 8 and Matthew 6 and the Didache Community's Relationship to Judaism." In *Matthew and the Didache: Two Documents from the Same Jewish-Christian Milieu?*, edited by Hubertus Waltherus Maria van de Sandt, 105–30. Minneapolis: Fortress, 2005.

———. *Q, the Earliest Gospel: An Introduction to the Original Stories and Sayings of Jesus*. Louisville: Westminster John Knox, 2008.

———. *The Tenants in the Vineyard: Ideology, Economics, and Agrarian Conflict in Jewish Palestine*. Wissenschaftliche Untersuchungen zum Neuen Testament. Tübingen: Mohr/Siebeck, 2006.

Kloppenborg, John S., and S. G. Wilson. *Voluntary Associations in the Graeco-Roman World*. New York: Routledge, 1996.

Knowles, Michael P. ""Everyone Who Hears These Words of Mine": Parables on Discipleship (Matt 7:24–27||Luke 6:47–49; Luke 14:28–33; Luke 17:7–10; Matt 20:1–16." In *The Challenge of Jesus' Parables*, edited by Richard N. Longenecker, 286–305. McMaster New Testament Studies. Grand Rapids: Eerdmans, 2000.

Köhler, Wolf-Dietrich. *Die Rezeption des Matthèausevangeliums in der Zeit vor Irenèaus*. Tübingen: Mohr/Siebeck, 1987.

Kolendo, Jerzy. "The Peasant." In *The Romans*, edited by Andrea Giardina, 199–213. Chicago: University of Chicago Press, 1993.

Kraeling, Carl Hermann. "The Jewish Community at Antioch." *JBL* 51, no. 2 (1932) 130–60.

Kupp, David D. *Matthew's Emmanuel: Divine Presence and God's People in the First Gospel*. Monograph Series Society for New Testament Studies. Cambridge: Cambridge University Press, 1996.

LaBianca, Oystein S. "Subsistence Pastoralism." In *Near Eastern Archaeology*, 116–23. Winona Lake, IN: Eisenbrauns, 2003.

Langellier, Kristin M., and Eric E. Peterson. "Family Storytelling as a Strategy of Social Control." In *Narrative and Social Control: Critical Perspectives*, edited by Dennis K. Mumby, 49–76. Newbury Park, CA: Sage, 1993.

Lassus, J. "Antioch on the Orontes." In *The Princeton Encyclopedia of Classical Sites*, edited by Richard Stillwell, William Lloyd MacDonald, and Marian Holland McAllister, 61–63. Princeton: Princeton University Press, 1976.

Lazer, Estelle. *Resurrecting Pompeii*. New York: Routledge, 2009.

Lehmann, Clayton Miles, and Kenneth G. Holum. *The Greek and Latin Inscriptions of Caesarea Maritima*. Boston: American Schools of Oriental Research, 2000.

Lendon, J. E. *Empire of Honour: The Art of Government in the Roman World*. Oxford: Oxford University Press, 1997.

Lenski, Gerhard Emmanuel. *Power and Privilege: A Theory of Social Stratification*. New York: McGraw-Hill, 1966.

Levenson, Jéon Douglas. *Sinai and Zion: An Entry into the Jewish Bible*. New Voices in Biblical Studies. Minneapolis: Winston, 1985.

Lewis, Naphtali, and Meyer Reinhold. *Roman Civilization: Selected Readings*. Records of Civilization, Sources and Studies 2. New York: Columbia University Press, 1951.

Liddell, Henry George, Robert Scott, Henry Stuart Jones, and Roderick McKenzie. *A Greek-English Lexicon*. Oxford: Clarendon, 1996.

Liebeschuetz, J. H. W. G. *Antioch: City and Imperial Administration in the Later Roman Empire*. Oxford: Clarendon, 1972.

Ling, Timothy J. M. "Virtuoso Religion and the Judean Social World." In *Anthropology and Biblical Studies: Avenues of Approach*, edited by Louise J. Lawrence and Mario I. Aguilar, 227–58. Leiden: Deo, 2004.

Llewelyn, S. R., and Macquarie University Ancient History Documentary Research Centre. *New Documents Illustrating Early Christianity: A Review of Greek Inscriptions and Papyri Published in 1986–87*. Vol. 9. North Ryde, New South Wales: Ancient History Documentary Research Centre, Macquarie University, 2002.

Longacre, Robert E. "A Top-Down, Template-Driven Narrative Analysis, Illustrated by Application to Mark's Gospel." In *Discourse Analysis and the New Testament*, edited by Stanley E. Porter, 140–68. JSNTSup. Sheffield: Sheffield Academic, 1999.

Longenecker, Bruce W. *Remember the Poor: Paul, Poverty, and the Greco-Roman World*. Grand Rapids: Eerdmans, 2010.

Love, Stuart L. *Jesus and Marginal Women: The Gospel of Matthew in Social-Scientific Perspective*. Matrix: The Bible in Mediterranean Context. Eugene, OR: Cascade, 2009.

Luz, Ulrich. "Intertexts in the Gospel of Matthew." *HTR* 97, no. 2 (2004) 119–37.

———. *Matthew*. Translated by James E. Crouch. 3 vols. Hermeneia. Minneapolis: Fortress, 1989–2007.

MacMullen, Ramsay. *Enemies of the Roman Order: Treason, Unrest, and Alienation in the Empire*. New York: Routledge, 1992.

———. "A Note on Roman Strikes." *CJ* 58, no. 6 (1963) 269–71.

———. *Roman Social Relations, 50 B.C. To A.D. 284*. New Haven: Yale University Press, 1974.

Malina, Bruce J. *Christian Origins and Cultural Anthropology: Practical Models for Biblical Interpretation*. Atlanta: Knox, 1986.

———. *The New Testament World: Insights from Cultural Anthropology*. 3rd ed. Louisville: Westminster John Knox, 2001.

———. "Social Scientific Approaches and the Gospel of Matthew." In *Methods for Matthew*, edited by Mark Allan Powell, 154–93. Methods in Biblical Interpretation. New York: Cambridge University Press, 2009.

———. "Wealth and Poverty in the New Testament and Its World." *Int* 41, no. 4 (1987) 354–67.

Malina, Bruce J., and Richard L. Rohrbaugh. *Social Science Commentary on the Synoptic Gospels*. Minneapolis: Fortress, 1992.
Mann, Michael. *The Sources of Social Power*. Cambridge: Cambridge University Press, 1986.
Marcus, Joel. *Mark 1–8: A New Translation with Introduction and Commentary*. Vol. 1. Anchor Bible 27. New York: Doubleday, 2000.
Martin Nagy, Rebecca. *Sepphoris in Galilee: Crosscurrents of Culture*. Winona Lake, IN: Eisenbrauns, 1996.
Marxsen, Willi. *Mark the Evangelist; Studies on the Redaction History of the Gospel*. Nashville: Abingdon, 1969.
Matera, F. J. "The Plot of Matthew's Gospel." *CBQ* 49 (1987) 233–53.
Mattingly, Harold. *Roman Coins: From the Earliest Times to the Fall of the Western Empire*. 2nd ed. Chicago: Quadrangle, 1962.
McArthur, Harvey K. *Understanding the Sermon on the Mount*. New York: Harper & Brothers, 1960.
McFeat, Tom. *Small-Group Cultures*. New York: Pergamon, 1974.
McGinn, Thomas A. J. "The Law of Roman Divorce in the Time of Christ." In *The Historical Jesus in Context*, edited by Amy-Jill Levine, Dale C. Allison, and John Dominic Crossan, 309–22. Princeton Readings in Religions. Princeton: Princeton University Press, 2006.
McGowan, Andrew Brian. *Ascetic Eucharists: Food and Drink in Early Christian Ritual Meals*. New York: Oxford University Press, 1999.
McLean, Bradley H. "Epigraphical Evidence in Caesarea Maritima." In *Religious Rivalries and the Struggle for Success in Caesarea Maritima*, edited by Terence L. Donaldson, 57–64. Waterloo, ON: Wilfrid Laurier University Press, 2000.
Mealand, David L. *Poverty and Expectation in the Gospels*. London: SPCK, 1980.
Meeks, Wayne A. *The First Urban Christians: The Social World of the Apostle Paul*. New Haven: Yale University Press, 1983.
Meeks, Wayne A., Robert Louis Wilken, Libanius, and John Chrysostom. *Jews and Christians in Antioch in the First Four Centuries of the Common Era*. Sources for Biblical Study. Missoula, MT: Scholars, 1978.
Meggitt, Justin J. *Paul, Poverty and Survival*. Studies of the New Testament and Its World. Edinburgh: T. & T. Clark, 1998.
Meier, John P. *Law and History in Matthew's Gospel: A Redactional Study of Mt. 5:17–48*. Analecta Biblica Investigationes Scientificae in Res Biblicas 71. Rome: Biblical Institute Press, 1976.
———. "Matthew and Ignatius: A Response to William R. Schoedel." In *Social History of the Matthean Community: Cross-Disciplinary Approaches*, edited by David L. Balch, 178–86. Minneapolis: Fortress, 1991.
Meyers, Carol L. *Discovering Eve: Ancient Israelite Women in Context*. New York: Oxford University Press, 1988.
Meyers, Eric M. *Galilee through the Centuries: Confluence of Cultures*. Duke Judaic Studies. Winona Lake, IN: Eisenbrauns, 1999.
Meynet, Roland. *Rhetorical Analysis: An Introduction to Biblical Rhetoric*. Sheffield: Sheffield Academic, 1998.
Milavec, A. "Synoptic Tradition in the Didache Revisited." *JECS* 11, no. 4 (2003) 443–80.

Millar, Fergus. *The Roman Near East, 31 B.C.-A.D. 337*. Cambridge, MA: Harvard University Press, 1993.
Miller, James Maxwell, and John Haralson Hayes. *A History of Ancient Israel and Judah*. 2nd ed. Louisville: Westminster John Knox, 2006.
Miller, Stuart S. *Studies in the History and Traditions of Sepphoris*. Studies in Judaism in Late Antiquity. Leiden: Brill, 1984.
Mitchell, Stephen. "Requisitioned Transport in the Roman Empire: A New Inscription from Pisidia." *JRS* 66 (1976) 106–31.
Morel, Jean-Paul. "The Craftsman." Chap. 8 In *The Romans*, edited by Andrea Giardina, 214–43. Chicago: University of Chicago Press, 1993.
Morley, Neville. "The Poor in the City of Rome." In *Poverty in the Roman World*, edited by E. M. Atkins and Robin Osborne, 21–39. Cambridge: Cambridge University Press, 2006.
———. *Theories, Models and Concepts in Ancient History*. Approaching the Ancient World. New York: Routledge, 2004.
Mosala, Itumeleng J. "Social Scientific Approaches to the Bible: One Step Forward, Two Steps Back?" *Biblical Hermeneutics and Black Theology in South Africa*, edited by Itumeleng J. Mosala, 43–66. Grand Rapids: Eerdmans, 1989.
Mott, Stephen C. "Justice." In *Harper Collins Bible Dictionary*, edited by Paul J. Achtemeier and Society of Biblical Literature. 557–58. San Francisco, CA: HarperSanFrancisco, 1996.
Mournet, Terence C. *Oral Tradition and Literary Dependence: Variability and Stability in the Synoptic Tradition and Q*. Wissenschaftliche Untersuchungen zum Neuen Testament 195. Tübingen: Mohr/Siebeck, 2005.
Mowery, Robert L. "The Matthean References to the Kingdom: Different Terms for Different Audiences." *ETL* 70, no. 4 (1994) 398–405.
Moxnes, Halvor. *The Economy of the Kingdom: Social Conflict and Economic Relations in Luke's Gospel*. Overtures to Biblical Theology. Philadelphia: Fortress, 1988.
Mussies, G. "Greek in Palestine and the Diaspora." In *The Jewish People in the First Century. Historical Geography, Political History, Social, Cultural and Religious Life and Institutions*, edited by Shemuel Safrai and M. Stern, 1040–1064. Compendia Rerum Iudaicarum Ad Novum Testamentum, Section 1. Assen, Netherlands: van Gorcum, 1976.
Negev, A. "Sepphoris Later Diocarsarea." In *The Princeton Encyclopedia of Classical Sites*, edited by Richard Stillwell, William Lloyd MacDonald, and Marian Holland McAllister, 827–28. Princeton: Princeton University Press, 1976.
Neyrey, Jerome H. *Honor and Shame in the Gospel of Matthew*. Louisville: Westminster John Knox, 1998.
Nijf, Onno van. *The Civic World of Professional Associations in the Roman East*. Dutch Monographs on Ancient History and Archaeology. Amsterdam: Gieben, 1997.
Oakes, Peter. "Constructing Poverty Scales for Graeco-Roman Society: A Response to Steven Friesen's 'Poverty in Pauline Studies.'" *JSNT* 26, no. 3 (2004) 367–71.
———. "Urban Structures and Patronage: Christ Followers in Corinth." In *Understanding the Social World of the New Testament*, edited by Dietmar Neufeld and Richard E. DeMaris, 178–93. New York: Routledge, 2010.
Oakman, Douglas E. "The Ancient Economy in the Bible." *BTB* 21 (2001) 34–39.

———. "Jesus and Agrarian Palestine: The Factor of Debt." In *Society of Biblical Literature 1985 Seminar Papers*, edited by Kent Harold Richards, 57–73. Atlanta: Scholars, 1985.

———. *Jesus and the Economic Questions of His Day*. Studies in the Bible and Early Christianity. Lewiston, NY: Mellen, 1986.

———. *Jesus and the Peasants*. Matrix: The Bible in Mediterranean Context 4. Eugene, OR: Cascade, 2008.

Ohrenstein, Roman A. "Talmud and Talmudic Tradition: A Socio-Economic Perspective." In *Ancient and Medieval Economic Ideas and Concepts of Social Justice*, edited by S. Todd Lowry and Barry Gordon, 209–68. New York: Brill, 1998.

Olick, Jeffrey K. Review of *Frames of Remembrance: The Dynamics of Collective Memory*, by Iwona Irwin-Zarecka. *Social Forces* 74, no. 2 (1995) 748–49.

Olick, Jeffrey K., and Joyce Robbins. "Individual and Society—Social Memory Studies: From 'Collective Memory' to the Historical Sociology of Mnemonic Practices." *Annual Review of Sociology* 24 (1998) 105–40.

Olufowote, James. "Rousing and Redirecting a Sleeping Giant." *Management Communication Quarterly* 19, no. 3 (2006) 451–92.

Osborne, Grant R. *Matthew*. Zondervan Exegetical Commentary Series, New Testament. Grand Rapids: Zondervan, 2010.

Osborne, Robin. "Introduction: Roman Poverty in Context." In *Poverty in the Roman World*, edited by E. M. Atkins and Robin Osborne, 1–20. Cambridge: Cambridge University Press, 2006.

———. "Pride and Prejudice, Sense and Subsistence: Exchange and Society in the Greek City." In *City and Country in the Ancient World*, edited by John Rich and Andrew Wallace-Hadrill, 119–45. Leicester-Nottingham Studies in Ancient Society. New York: Routledge, 1991.

Osiek, Carolyn. "'When You Pray, Go into Your Ταμεῖον' (Matthew 6:6): But Why?" *CBQ* 71 (2009) 723–40.

Overman, J. Andrew. *Church and Community in Crisis: The Gospel According to Matthew*. The New Testament in Context. Valley Forge, PA: Trinity, 1996.

———. *Matthew's Gospel and Formative Judaism: The Social World of the Matthean Community*. Minneapolis: Fortress, 1990.

———. "Matthew's Parables and Roman Politics: The Imperial Setting of Matthew's Narrative with Special Reference to His Parables." In *Society of Biblical Literature 1995 Seminar Papers*, 425–39. SBLSP. Atlanta: Scholars, 1995.

Pamment, Margaret. "The Kingdom of Heaven According to the First Gospel." *NTS* 27, no. 2 (1981) 211–32.

Parkin, Anneliese. "'You Do Him No Service': An Exploration of Pagan Almsgiving." Chap. 4 In *Poverty in the Roman World*, edited by E. M. Atkins and Robin Osborne, 60–82. Cambridge, MA: Cambridge University Press, 2006.

Pastor, Jack. *Land and Economy in Ancient Palestine*. New York: Routledge, 1997.

Patte, Daniel. *The Gospel According to Matthew: A Structural Commentary on Matthew's Faith*. Philadelphia: Fortress, 1987.

Pennington, Jonathan T. *Heaven and Earth in the Gospel of Matthew*. Supplements to Novum Testamentum 126. Boston: Brill, 2007.

———. "The Kingdom of Heaven in the Gospel of Matthew." *Southern Baptist Journal of Theology* 12, no. 1 (2008) 44–51.

Petersen, Lauren Hackworth. "The Baker, His Tomb, His Wife, and Her Breadbasket: The Monument of Eurysaces in Rome." *Art Bulletin* 85, no. 2 (2003) 230–57.

Petrov, Krinka Vidakovic. "Memory and Oral Tradition." In *Memory: History, Culture, and the Mind*, edited by Thomas Butler, 77–96. Wolfson College Lectures. Oxford: Blackwell, 1989.

Phillips, Gary A. "History and Text: The Reader in Context in Matthew's Parables Discourse." In *Society of Biblical Literature 1983 Seminar Papers*, edited by Kent Harold Richards, 415–37. Chico, CA: Scholars, 1983.

Phillips, P. "Casting out the Treasure: A New Reading of Matthew 13.52." *JSNT* 31, no. 1 (2008) 3–24.

Pleket, Henri W. "Urban Elites and Business in the Greek Part of the Roman Empire." In *Trade in the Ancient Economy*, edited by Peter Garnsey, Keith Hopkins, and C. R. Whittaker, 131–44. Berkeley: University of California Press, 1983.

Polanyi, Karl. "Aristotle Discovers the Economy." In *Trade and Market in the Early Empires; Economies in History and Theory*, edited by Karl Polanyi, 64–91. Glencoe, IL: Free, 1957.

———. "The Economy as Instituted Process." In *Trade and Market in the Early Empires; Economies in History and Theory*, edited by Karl Polanyi, 243–70. Glencoe, IL: Free, 1957.

———. *The Great Transformation: The Political & Economic Origin of Our Time*. Boston: Beacon, 1957. Online: http://hdl.handle.net.ezproxy.tcu.edu/2027/heb.03171.0001.001.

Polanyi, Karl, and Harry W. Pearson. *The Livelihood of Man*. Studies in Social Discontinuity. New York: Academic, 1977.

Powell, Mark Allan. *God with Us: A Pastoral Theology of Matthew's Gospel*. Minneapolis: Fortress, 1995.

Reed, Chris, and Glenn Rowe. "Translating Toulmin Diagrams: Theory Neutrality in Argument Representation." *Argumentation* 19, no. 3 (2005) 267–86.

Reed, Jeffrey T. "The Cohesiveness of Discourse: Towards a Model of Linguistic Criteria for Analyzing New Testament Discourse." In *Discourse Analysis and the New Testament*, edited by Stanley E. Porter, 28–46. JSNTSup. Sheffield: Sheffield Academic, 1999.

Reed, Jonathan L. *Archaeology and the Galilean Jesus: A Re-Examination of the Evidence*. Harrisburg, PA: Trinity, 2000.

———. "The Social Map of Q." In *Conflict and Invention: Literary, Rhetorical, and Social Studies on the Sayings Gospel Q*, edited by John S. Kloppenborg, 17–36. Valley Forge, PA: Trinity, 1995.

Reinhartz, Adele. "Reflections on Table Fellowship and Community Identity." *Semeia* 86 (1999) 227–33.

Reynolds, Joyce, Mary Beard, and Charlotte Roueche. "Roman Inscriptions 1981–85." *JRS* 76 (1986) 124–46.

Rhoads, David. "The Political Jesus: Can There Be Any Other?" Paper presented at the Context Group, Philadelphia, PA, March 2007.

Richards, Audrey I. *Land, Labour and Diet in Northern Rhodesia: An Economic Study of the Bemba Tribe*. New York: Oxford University Press, 1939.

Riches, John K. "The Sociology of Matthew: Some Basic Questions Concerning Its Relation to the Theology of the New Testament." In *Society of Biblical Literature*

1983 Seminar Papers, edited by Kent Harold Richards, 259–71. Chico, CA: Scholars, 1983.
Riches, John K., and David C. Sim. *The Gospel of Matthew in Its Roman Imperial Context*. New York: T. & T. Clark, 2005.
Rickman, Geoffrey. *Roman Granaries and Store Buildings*. Cambridge: University Press, 1971.
Ringe, Sharon H. *Jesus, Liberation, and the Biblical Jubilee: Images for Ethics and Christology*. Overtures to Biblical Theology. Philadelphia: Fortress, 1985.
Robbins, Vernon K. *Exploring the Texture of Texts: A Guide to Socio-Rhetorical Interpretation*. Valley Forge, PA: Trinity, 1996.
———. *The Invention of Christian Discourse*. Vol. 1. Rhetoric of Religious Antiquity Series. Dorset, UK: Deo, 2009.
———. "Narrative in Ancient Rhetoric and Rhetoric in Ancient Narrative." In *Society of Biblical Literature 1996 Seminar Papers*, 368–84. SBLSP. Atlanta: Scholars, 1996.
———. "The Rhetorical Full-Turn in Biblical Interpretation: Reconfiguring Rhetorical-Political Analysis." In *Rhetorical Criticism and the Bible*, edited by Stanley E. Porter, Dennis L. Stamps, and Thomas H. Olbricht, 48–59. JSNTSup. New York: Sheffield Academic, 2002.
Robinson, Damian. "Re-Thinking the Social Organization of Trade and Industry in First Century AD Pompeii." In *Roman Working Lives and Urban Living*, edited by Ardle MacMahon, and J. Price, 88–105. Oakville, CT: Oxbow, 2005.
Robinson, James M., Paul Hoffmann, and John S. Kloppenborg. *The Critical Edition of Q*. Hermeneia. Minneapolis: Fortress, 2000.
Robinson, James M., and Helmut Koester. *Trajectories through Early Christianity*. Philadelphia: Fortress, 1971.
Robinson, John A. T. *Redating the New Testament*. Philadelphia: Westminster, 1976.
Rodd, Cyril S. "On Applying a Sociological Theory to Biblical Studies." *JSOT* 19 (1981) 95–106.
Rohrbaugh, Richard L. "The Preindustrial City." In *The Social Sciences and New Testament Interpretation*, edited by Richard L. Rohrbaugh, 108–15. Peabody, MA: Hendrickson, 1996.
———. "Social Location of Thought as A Heuristic Construct in New Testament Study." *JSNT* 30 (1987) 103–19.
Romeny, Bas ter Haar. "Hypothesis on the Development of Judaism and Christianity in Syria in the Period after 70 C.E." In *Matthew and the Didache: Two Documents from the Same Jewish-Christian Milieu?*, edited by Hubertus Waltherus Maria van de Sandt, 13–33. Minneapolis: Fortress, 2005.
Safrai, Zeev. *The Economy of Roman Palestine*. New York: Routledge, 1994.
Sahlins, Marshall David. *Stone Age Economics*. New York: Routledge, 2004.
Sakenfeld, Katharine Doob. *Faithfulness in Action: Loyalty in Biblical Perspective*. Overtures to Biblical Theology. Philadelphia: Fortress, 1985.
Saldarini, Anthony J. "The Gospel of Matthew and Jewish-Christian Conflict." In *Galilee in Late Antiquity*, edited by Lee I. Levine, 23–68. Cambridge, MA: Harvard University Press, 1992.
———. *Pharisees, Scribes, and Sadducees in Palestinian Society: A Sociological Approach*. Grand Rapids: Eerdmans, 2001.
Saller, Richard P. *Personal Patronage under the Early Empire*. Cambridge: Cambridge University Press, 1982.

Sandt, Hubertus Waltherus Maria van de. "'Do Not Give What Is Holy to the Dogs' (Did 9:5d and Matt 7:6a): The Eucharistic Food of the Didache in Its Jewish Purity Setting." *VC* 56, no. 3 (2002) 223–46

———. *Matthew and the Didache: Two Documents from the Same Jewish-Christian Milieu?* Minneapolis: Fortress, 2005.

Scheidel, Walter, and Steven J. Friesen. "The Size of the Economy and the Distribution of Income in the Roman Empire." *JRS* 99 (2009) 61–91.

Schneider, David Murray. *A Critique of the Study of Kinship*. Ann Arbor: University of Michigan Press, 1984.

Schoedel, William R. "Ignatius and the Reception of the Gospel of Matthew in Antioch." In *Social History of the Matthean Community: Cross-Disciplinary Approaches*, edited by David L. Balch, 129–77. Minneapolis: Fortress, 1991.

Schudson, Michael. "Dynamics of Distortion in Collective Memory." In *Commemorations: The Politics of National Identity*, edited by John R. Gillis, 346–64. Princeton: Princeton University Press, 1994.

Schwartz, Barry. "The Social Context of Commemoration: A Study in Collective Memory." *Social Forces* 61, no. 2 (1982) 374–401.

Scott, James C. *Domination and the Arts of Resistance: Hidden Transcripts*. New Haven: Yale University Press, 1990.

———. *Weapons of the Weak: Everyday Forms of Peasant Resistance*. New Haven: Yale University Press, 1985.

Sen, Amartya Kumar. *Poverty and Famines: An Essay on Entitlement and Deprivation*. New York: Clarendon, 1981.

Senior, Donald. "Directions in Matthean Studies." In *The Gospel of Matthew in Current Study: Studies in Memory of William G. Thompson, S.J*, edited by David Edward Aune, 5–21. Grand Rapids: Eerdmans, 2001.

———. *What Are They Saying About Matthew?* Rev. exp. ed. New York: Paulist, 1996.

Sim, David C. "The Gospels for All Christians? A Response to Richard Bauckham." *JSNT* 84 (2001) 3–27.

———. "Rome in Matthew's Eschatology." In *The Gospel of Matthew in Its Roman Imperial Context*, edited by John Kenneth Riches and David C. Sim, 91–106. New York: T. & T. Clark, 2005.

Slee, Michelle. *The Church in Antioch in the First Century CE: Communion and Conflict*. JSNTSup. New York: Sheffield Academic, 2003.

Slingerland, H. Dixon. "The Transjordanian Origin of St. Matthew's Gospel." *JSNT* 3 (1979) 18–28.

Smit, Peter-Ben. *Fellowship and Food in the Kingdom: Eschatological Meals and Scenes of Utopian Abundance in the New Testament*. Wissenschaftliche Untersuchungen zum Neuen Testament. Tübingen: Mohr/Siebeck, 2008.

Smith, Dennis E. *From Symposium to Eucharist: The Banquet in the Early Christian World*. Minneapolis: Fortress, 2003.

———. "The Historical Jesus at Table." In *Society of Biblical Literature 1989 Seminar Papers*, edited by David J. Lull, 466–86. Atlanta: Scholars, 1989.

Snodgrass, Klyne R. "From Allegorizing to Allegorizing: A History of the Interpretation of the Parables of Jesus." In *The Challenge of Jesus' Parables*, edited by Richard N. Longenecker, 3–29. McMaster New Testament Studies. Grand Rapids: Eerdmans, 2000.

Sperber, Daniel. *The City in Roman Palestine*. New York: Oxford University Press, 1998.

———. "Drought, Famine and Pestilence in Amoraic Palestine." *JESHO* 17, no. 3 (1974) 272–98.
Stambaugh, John E. *The Ancient Roman City*. Baltimore: Johns Hopkins University Press, 1988.
Stambaugh, John E., and David L. Balch. *The New Testament in Its Social Environment*. Philadelphia: Westminster, 1986.
Stark, Rodney. "Antioch as the Social Situation for Matthew's Gospel." In *Social History of the Matthean Community: Cross-Disciplinary Approaches*, edited by David L. Balch, 189–210. Minneapolis: Fortress, 1991.
———. "Urban Chaos and Crisis." In *The Rise of Christianity: A Sociologist Reconsiders History*. Princeton: Princeton University Press, 1996.
Stegemann, Ekkehard, and Wolfgang Stegemann. *The Jesus Movement: A Social History of Its First Century*. 1st English-language ed. Minneapolis: Fortress, 1999.
Steinsaltz, Adin. *The Talmud: The Steinsaltz Edition: A Reference Guide*. New York: Random House, 1989.
Stendahl, Krister. *The School of St. Matthew, and Its Use of the Old Testament*. 1st American ed. Philadelphia: Fortress, 1968.
Stewart, Eric C. "Social Stratification and Patronage in Ancient Mediterranean Societies." In *Understanding the Social World of the New Testament*, edited by Dietmar Neufeld and Richard E. DeMaris, 156–66. New York: Routledge, 2010.
Stone, Elizabeth. *Black Sheep and Kissing Cousins: How Our Family Stories Shape Us*. New York: Penguin, 1989.
Strange, James F. *Six Campaigns at Sepphoris: The University of South Florida Excavations, 1983–1989*. Galilee in Late Antiquity. Cambridge, MA: Harvard University Press, 1992.
Streeter, Burnett Hillman. *The Four Gospels: A Study of Origins*. 4th ed. London: Macmillan, 1930.
Strickert, Fred. "The Coins of Philip." In *The Bethsaida Excavations Project Reports*, edited by Rami Arav and Richard A. Freund, 165–89. Kirksville, MO: Thomas Jefferson University Press, 1995.
Stringer, Martin. *Rethinking the Origins of the Eucharist*. London: SCM, 2011.
Strubbe, Johan H. M. "The Sitonia in the Cities of Asia Minor under the Principate." *Epigraphica Anatolica* 10 (1987) 45–82.
Talbert, Charles H. *What Is a Gospel? The Genre of the Canonical Gospels*. Philadelphia: Fortress, 1977.
Temin, Peter. "A Market Economy in the Early Roman Empire." *JRS* 91 (2001) 169–81.
Theissen, Gerd. *Sociology of Early Palestinian Christianity*. 1st American ed. Philadelphia: Fortress, 1978.
Thompson, Michael B. "The Holy Internet: Communication between Churches in the First Christian Generation." In *The Gospels for All Christians: Rethinking the Gospel Audiences*, edited by Richard Bauckham, 49–70. Grand Rapids: Eerdmans, 1998.
Tilborg, Sjef van. *The Jewish Leaders in Matthew*. Leiden: Brill, 1972.
Tolbert, Mary Ann. "Social, Sociological, and Anthropological Methods." In *Searching the Scriptures*, edited by Elisabeth Schèussler Fiorenza and Shelly Matthews, 255–71. New York: Crossroad, 1993.
Toulmin, Stephen Edelston. *The Uses of Argument*. Cambridge: Cambridge University Press, 1969.

Tuckett, C. M. "The Didache and the Synoptics Once More: A Response to Aaron Milavec." *JECS* 13, no. 4 (2005) 509-18.
Vaage, Leif E. *Galilean Upstarts: Jesus' First Followers According to Q*. Valley Forge, PA: Trinity, 1994.
Varner, W. C. "The Didache 'Apocalypse' and Matthew 24." *BSac* 165, no. 659 (2008) 309-22.
Vermès, Géza. *The Religion of Jesus the Jew*. Minneapolis: Fortress, 1993.
Veyne, Paul, and Oswyn Murray. *Bread and Circuses: Historical Sociology and Political Pluralism*. London: Penguin, 1992.
Wallace-Hadrill, Andrew. "Elites and Trade in the Roman Town." In *City and Country in the Ancient World*, edited by John Rich and Andrew Wallace-Hadrill, 241-72. Leicester-Nottingham Studies in Ancient Society. New York: Routledge, 1991.
Warmington, E. H. *Remains of Old Latin*. Vol. 4. LCL. Cambridge, MA: Harvard University Press, 1935.
Watson, Duane Frederick. "Why We Need Socio-Rhetorical Commentary and What It Might Look Like." In *Rhetorical Criticism and the Bible*, edited by Stanley E. Porter, Dennis L. Stamps, and Thomas H. Olbricht, 129-57. JSNTSup. New York: Sheffield Academic, 2002.
Weber, Kathleen. "Plot and Matthew." In *Society of Biblical Literature 1996 Seminar Papers*. 400-427. Atlanta: Scholars, 1996.
Weiner, Annette B. "Reciprocity." In *Encyclopedia of Cultural Anthropology*, edited by David Levinson and Melvin Ember, 1060-1068. New York: Holt, 1996.
Wenham, Gordon J. "Matthew and Divorce: An Old Crux Revisited." *JSNT*, no. 22 (1984) 95-107.
Weren, Wim. "The History and Social Setting of the Matthean Community." In *Matthew and the Didache: Two Documents from the Same Jewish-Christian Milieu?*, edited by Hubertus Waltherus Maria van de Sandt, 51-62. Minneapolis: Fortress, 2005.
West, Louis C. "Phases of Commercial Life in Egypt." *JRS* 7 (1917) 45-58.
Westermann, Claus. *The Promises to the Fathers: Studies on the Patriarchal Narratives*. Philadelphia: Fortress, 1980.
White, L. Michael. "Crisis Management and Boundary Maintenance: The Social Location of the Matthean Community." In *Social History of the Matthean Community: Cross-Disciplinary Approaches*, edited by David L. Balch, 211-47. Minneapolis: Fortress, 1991.
White, William J. "Finances." In *The Catacombs and the Colosseum: The Roman Empire as the Setting of Primitive Christianity*, edited by Stephen Benko and John J. O'Rourke, 218-36. Valley Forge, PA: Fortress, 1971.
Whittaker, C. R. "The Poor." In *The Romans*, edited by Andrea Giardina, 272-99. Chicago: University of Chicago Press, 1993.
Wiedemann, Thomas. "The Patron as Banker." In *"Bread and Circuses": Euergetism and Municipal Patronage in Roman Italy*, edited by Kathryn Lomas and Tim Cornell, 12-27. New York: Routledge, 2003.
Wilkins, John M., and Shaun Hill. *Food in the Ancient World*. Ancient Cultures. Malden, MA: Blackwell, 2006.
Williams, Ritva H. "Social Memory and the Didache." *BTB* 36 (2006) 35-39.
Winter, Bruce W. "Secular and Christian Responses to Corinthian Famines." *TynBul* 40, no. 1 (1989) 86-106.

Wire, Antoinette Clark. "Gender Roles in a Scribal Community." In *Social History of the Matthean Community: Cross-Disciplinary Approaches*, edited by David L. Balch, 87–121. Minneapolis: Fortress, 1991.

Wrede, William. *The Messianic Secret*. Translated by J. C. G. Greig. Cambridge: Clarke, 1971.

Wrigley, E. A. "Parasite or Stimulus: The Town in a Pre-Industrial Economy." In *Towns in Societies: Essays in Economic History and Historical Sociology*, edited by Philip Abrams and E. A. Wrigley, 295–309. Cambridge: Cambridge University Press, 1978.

Wuellner, Wilhelm. "Where Is Rhetorical Criticism Taking Us?" *CBQ* 49 (1987) 448–63.

Zerubavel, Eviatar. *Social Mindscapes: An Invitation to Cognitive Sociology*. Cambridge, MA: Harvard University Press, 1997.

www.ingramcontent.com/pod-product-compliance
Lightning Source LLC
Chambersburg PA
CBHW061430300426
44114CB00014B/1620